C# 2008 For Dummies®

D1449930

Cheat Sheet

Operators

Precedence	Operators	Cardinality	Associativity
High	`() [] . new typeof`	Unary	Left to right
	`! ~ + - ++ -- (cast)`	Unary	Left to right
	`* / %`	Binary	Left to right
	`+ -`	Binary	Left to right
	`< <= > >= is as`	Binary	Left to right
	`== !=`	Binary	Left to right
	`&`	Binary	Left to right
	`^`	Binary	Left to right
	`|`	Binary	Left to right
	`&&`	Binary	Left to right
	`||`	Binary	Left to right
	`? :`	Ternary	Right to left
Low	`= *= /= %= += -= &= ^= |= <<= >>=`	Binary	Right to left

Integer Variable Types

Type	Size (bytes)	Range	In Use
sbyte	1	−128 to 127	`sbyte sb = -12;`
byte	1	0 to 255	`byte b = 12;`
short	2	−32,768 to 32,767	`short sn = -123;`
ushort	2	0 to 65,535	`ushort usn = 123;`
int	4	−2,147,483,648 to 2,147,483,647	`int n = 123;`
uint	4	0 to 4,294,967,295	`uint un = 123U;`
long	8	−9,223,372,036,854,775,808 to 9,223,372,036,854,775,807 — "a whole lot"	`long l = 123L;`
ulong	8	0 to 18,446,744,073,709,551,615	`long ul = 123UL;`

Floating Point Variable Types

Type	Size (bytes)	Range	Accuracy	In Use
float	8	$1.5 * 10^{-45}$ to $3.4 * 10^{38}$	6–7 digits	`float f = 1.2F;`
double	16	$5.0 * 10^{-324}$ to $1.7 * 10^{308}$	15–16 digits	`double d = 1.2;`

C# 2008 For Dummies®

Other Variable Types

Type	Range	In Use
decimal	Up to 28 digits	`decimal d = 123M;`
BigInteger	NA	Too humongous to list.
char	0 to 65,535 (codes in the Unicode character set)	`char x = 'c';`
		`char y = '\x123';`
		`char newline = '\n';`
string	From Empty ("") to a very large number of characters in the Unicode character set	`string s = "my name";`
		`string empty = "";`
bool	True and false	`bool b = true;`

Controlling Program Flow

```csharp
if (i < 10)
{
    // go here if i is less than 10
}
else
{
    // go here otherwise
}

while(i < 10)
{
    // keep looping through here as long as i is less than 10
}

for(int i = 0; i < 10; i++)
{
    // loop 10 times
}

foreach(MyClass mc in myCollection)
{
    // ... execute once for each mc object in myCollection
}
```

Wiley, the Wiley Publishing logo, For Dummies, the Dummies Man logo, the For Dummies Bestselling Book Series logo and all related trade dress are trademarks or registered trademarks of John Wiley & Sons, Inc. and/or its affiliates. All other trademarks are property of their respective owners. Copyright © 2008 Wiley Publishing, Inc. All rights reserved. Item 9109-5. For more information about Wiley Publishing, call 1-800-762-2974.

C# 2008
FOR
DUMMIES®

C# 2008

FOR

DUMMIES®

by Chuck Sphar and Stephen Randy Davis

WILEY

Wiley Publishing, Inc.

C# 2008 For Dummies®

Published by
Wiley Publishing, Inc.
111 River Street
Hoboken, NJ 07030-5774

www.wiley.com

Copyright © 2008 by Wiley Publishing, Inc., Indianapolis, Indiana

Published by Wiley Publishing, Inc., Indianapolis, Indiana

Published simultaneously in Canada

For general information on our other products and services, please contact our Customer Care Department within the U.S. at 800-762-2974, outside the U.S. at 317-572-3993, or fax 317-572-4002.

For technical support, please visit www.wiley.com/techsupport.

Wiley also publishes its books in a variety of electronic formats. Some content that appears in print may not be available in electronic books.

Library of Congress Control Number: 2008920770

ISBN: 978-0-470-19109-5

Manufactured in the United States of America

10 9 8 7 6 5 4 3 2 1

WILEY

About the Authors

Stephen R. Davis, who goes by the name of Randy, lives with his wife and son near Dallas, Texas. He and his family have written numerous books, including *C++ For Dummies* and *C++ Weekend Crash Course*. Stephen works for L-3 Communications.

Chuck Sphar escaped Microsoft's C++ documentation camps in 1997, after six years' hard labor as a senior technical writer. He's perpetrated three previous tomes, one on object-oriented programming for the Mac, one on Microsoft's MFC class library, and *C# 2005 For Dummies*, a revision of Randy's original edition. He's currently finishing a novel about ancient Rome (against rome.com) and gobbling great mouthfuls of .NET programming. Chuck can be reached for praise and minor nits at chuck@csharp102.info.

Dedications

For a remarkable woman and great friend, Helen Tross — and, of course, as always, my Pam — Chuck Sphar

Authors' Acknowledgments

As always, thanks to my agent, Claudette Moore, who brought the book to me in 2005. I also want to thank Randy Davis for being willing to hand over his baby to a guy he didn't know. I'd have found that very hard, and I hope I've done justice in two revisions of his original edition.

Many thanks are due as well to the fine folks at Wiley, starting with Acquisitions Editor Katie Feltman and Project Editor Pat O'Brien. I'd also like to thank Barry Childs-Helton for much of the book's consistency, and the art, media, technical, and other production folks who turn my files into a real book.

The most heartfelt thanks are due to Pam for constant encouragement and much enabling. She's my partner in all things. — Chuck Sphar

Publisher's Acknowledgments

We're proud of this book; please send us your comments through our online registration form located at www.dummies.com/register/.

Some of the people who helped bring this book to market include the following:

Acquisitions, Editorial, and Media Development

Project Editor: Pat O'Brien

Acquisitions Editor: Katie Feltman

Senior Copy Editor: Barry Childs-Helton

Technical Editor: Roy El-Rayes

Editorial Manager: Kevin Kirschner

Media Development Manager: Laura VanWinkle

Editorial Assistant: Amanda Foxworth

Sr. Editorial Assistant: Cherie Case

Cartoons: Rich Tennant (www.the5thwave.com)

Composition Services

Project Coordinator: Kristie Rees

Layout and Graphics: Stacie Brooks, Carl Byers, Reuben W. Davis, Shane Johnson, Christine Williams

Proofreader: Christine Sabooni

Indexer: Potomac Indexing, LLC

Publishing and Editorial for Technology Dummies

    Richard Swadley, Vice President and Executive Group Publisher

    Andy Cummings, Vice President and Publisher

    Mary Bednarek, Executive Acquisitions Director

    Mary C. Corder, Editorial Director

Publishing for Consumer Dummies

    Diane Graves Steele, Vice President and Publisher

    Joyce Pepple, Acquisitions Director

Composition Services

    Gerry Fahey, Vice President of Production Services

    Debbie Stailey, Director of Composition Services

Contents at a Glance

Table of Contents

Introduction

*T*his edition of *C# 2008 for Dummies* represents a pretty thorough overhaul. It adds tons of new material, an improved organization, and many new example programs. So even if you've seen the book before, it's worth another look.

The C# programming language is a powerful and, at some six years old, relatively mature descendant of the earlier C, C++, and Java languages. Programming with it is a lot of fun, as you're about to find out in this book.

Microsoft created C# as a major part of its .NET initiative. Microsoft turned the specifications for the C# language over to the ECMA (pronounced *ek-ma*) international standards committee in the summer of 2000, so that, in theory, any company can come up with its own version of C# written to run on any operating system, on any machine larger than a calculator.

When the first edition of this book came out, Microsoft's C# compiler was the only game in town, and its Visual Studio .NET suite of tools were the only way to program C# (other than at the Windows command line). Since then, however, Visual Studio has gone through three major revisions — the latest is Visual Studio 2008. And at least two other players have entered the C# game.

It's now possible to write and compile C# programs on Windows and a variety of Unix-based machines using implementations of .NET and C# such as Mono (www. mono-project.com). Mono is an open-source software project sponsored by Novell Corporation. Version 1.2 came out in November 2006. While Mono lags Microsoft's .NET by half a version or so, it appears to be moving fast, having implemented basically all of .NET 1.1 and much of .NET 2.0, along with those versions of C#.

Both Mono and a less-well-developed competitor, Portable .NET (www.dotgnu.org/pnet.htm), claim to run C# programs on Windows and a variety of Unix flavors, including Linux and Apple's Macintosh operating system. At this writing, Portable .NET reaches the greater number of flavors, while Mono boasts a more complete .NET implementation. So choosing between them can be complicated, depending on your project, your platform, and your goals. (Books about programming for these platforms are becoming available already. Check online booksellers.)

Open-source software is written by collaborating groups of volunteer programmers and is usually free to the world.

Making C# and other .NET languages portable to other operating systems is far beyond the scope of this book. But you can expect that within a few years, the C# Windows programs you discover how to write in this book will run on all sorts of hardware under all sorts of operating systems — matching the claim of Sun Microsystems' Java language to run on any machine. That's undoubtedly a good thing, even for Microsoft. The road to that point is still under construction, so it's no doubt riddled with potholes and obstacles to true universal portability for C#. But it's no longer just Microsoft's road.

For the moment, however, Microsoft's Visual Studio has the most mature versions of C# and .NET and the most feature-filled toolset for programming with them.

Note: Two authors wrote this book, but it seemed more economical to say "I" instead of "we," so that's what we (I?) do throughout.

What's New in C# 3.0

While most of C# 3.0 is still virtually the same as the previous version, C# 3.0 does add some exciting new features. The big new additions that this book covers include the following:

 ✔ **Language Integrated Query (LINQ):** LINQ lets you perform operations on data using a C# syntax much like the Standard Query Language (SQL) that generations of programmers have used to work with databases. Not only does LINQ simplify database code, you can use it to write queries on Extended Markup Language (XML) files too. Chapter 17 is a gentle introduction to LINQ, covering my favorite part: using the new query syntax to work with any collection of data, including C# arrays and collections.

 ✔ **Extension Methods, Anonymous Types, and More:** Tons of cool language features that enrich C# while serving as a base to make LINQ work. I cover these features throughout the book.

 ✔ **HashSet.** A versatile new `HashSet` collection class, covered in Chapter 5.

Leaving aside a few of the more esoteric and advanced additions, I'll mention a few smaller items here and there as appropriate. (Don't worry if parts of this Introduction are Geek to you. You'll get there.)

In addition to the brand new paint-still-wet features of C# 3.0, the book adds coverage of some older features that I just hadn't managed to cover yet — in particular, delegates, events, and enumerations. And you'll find beefed-up coverage of C# collection classes and much more on strings, interfaces, and exceptions, plus a host of tweaks, notes, and tips.

About This Book

The goal of this book is to explain C# to you, but to write actual programs, you need a specific coding environment. I'm betting that most readers will be using Microsoft Visual Studio, although I do suggest alternatives. In basing the book on Visual Studio, I've tried to keep the Visual Studio portions to a reasonable minimum. You'll find a good tour of Visual Studio and its debugger in Bonus Chapter 6 on the Web site that accompanies this book.

I realize that many, if not most, readers will want to use C# to write graphical Windows and Web applications. C# is a powerful tool for that purpose, but that's only one area for using C#, and this book must focus on C# *as a language*. To get a start in graphical Windows programs, visit my Web site at csharp102.info. I recommend you get a good grasp of C# before seeking to understand Windows programming in full. I also realize that some power users will be using C# to build Web-ready, distributed applications and database applications; however, publishing limitations require me to draw the line somewhere. *C# 2008 For Dummies* does not tackle the challenges of distributed programming, database programming, or some of the other new technologies such as Windows Presentation Foundation, Windows Communication Foundation, or Windows Workflow Foundation. The book does explain quite a bit of .NET, though, for the simple reason that much of C#'s power comes from the .NET Framework class libraries that it uses.

What You Need to Use the Book

At a minimum, you need the .NET Common Language Runtime (CLR) before you can even execute the programs generated by C#. Visual Studio 2008 copies the CLR onto your machine as part of the installation procedure. Alternatively, you can download the entire .NET package, including the C# compiler and many other nice tools, from Microsoft's Web site at msdn. microsoft.com. Look for the .NET Software Development Kit (SDK). My Web site explains how to get these items.

If all you need is C#, you can download a free version of Visual Studio called Visual C# 2008 Express from msdn.microsoft.com/vstudio/express. The Express versions include C# 3.0's new features. Alternatively, see SharpDevelop (www.icsharpcode.net), a pretty good free Visual Studio workalike, which I've provided on the Web site for this book. (At this writing, SharpDevelop has yet to release a version compatible with the new C# 3.0/.NET 3.5 features, but work is well under way.)

You can still create most of the programs in this book with earlier versions of Visual Studio — such as Visual Studio 2005 — if you need to. The exceptions are the programs that cover the new features available only with C# 3.0, listed above in the section "What's New in C# 3.0"

How to Use This Book

We've made this book as easy to use as possible. Figuring out a new language is hard enough. Why make it any more complicated than it needs to be? The book is divided into six parts. Part I introduces you to C# programming with Visual Studio. This part guides you step by step in the creation of simple C# programs. We strongly encourage you to start here and read Chapter 1 before branching out into the other parts of the book. Even if you've programmed before, the basic program framework created in Part I is reused throughout the book.

The chapters in Parts II through V stand alone but have plenty of cross-references to other chapters. I've written these chapters so that you can open the book to any one of them and start reading. If you're new to programming, or new to C-family languages, however, you will have to read Part II before you can jump ahead. But, except where noted, when you return to refresh your memory on some particular topic, you should have no trouble flipping to a section without the need to restart 20 pages back.

Of course, the Part of Tens finishes out the lineup, and there's more on the Web site that accompanies the book — plus a little extra on my Web site at csharp102.info.

How This Book Is Organized

Here's a brief rundown on what you'll find in each part of the book.

Part I: Getting Started with C#

This part shows you, step by step, how to write basic nongraphical C# programs by developing a simple framework that's used in the other parts of this book. You can find information about graphical programming on my site.

Part II: Basic C# Programming

At the most basic level, Shakespeare's plays are just a series of words all strung together. By the same token, 90 percent of any C# program you ever write consists of creating variables, performing arithmetic operations, and controlling the execution path through a program. This part concentrates on these core operations and includes a new chapter explaining C#'s collection classes in detail, including the new `HashSet` class.

Part III: Using Objects

It's one thing to declare variables here or there and to add and subtract them. It's quite another thing to write real programs for real people. Part III focuses on how to organize your data to make it easier to use in creating a program.

Part IV: Object-Oriented Programming

You can organize the parts of an airplane all you want, but until you make it do something, it's nothing more than a collection of parts. It's not until you fire up the engines and start the wings flapping that it's going anywhere.

In like fashion, Part IV explains the fundamentals of object-oriented programming (OOP). If you're completely new to OOP, Part IV should provide a smooth transition. And a much-improved chapter on interfaces takes you beyond the usual OOP fundamentals.

Part V: Now Showing in C# 3.0

After the airplane gets off the ground, it has to go somewhere. In this book, you'll be flying fearlessly into the new C# 3.0 features. In particular, you can upgrade your C# skills to command-pilot level with the new Language Integrated Query (LINQ) now built right into C#. The objects and collections of objects that you've been exploring in previous parts of the book set new cross-country flight records when you start writing LINQ queries. To help you get up to speed, I've added a new chapter on delegates and events.

Part VI: The Part of Tens

C# is great at finding errors in your programs — at times, it seems a little too good at pointing out my shortcomings. However, believe it or not, C# is trying to do you a favor. Every problem it finds is another problem that you would otherwise have to find on your own.

Unfortunately, the error messages can be confusing. This part presents the ten most common C# build error messages, what they mean, and how the heck to get rid of them.

Many readers are coming to C# from another programming language. You can find a few helpful comments on the transition you're making on my Web site.

About the Web site

The Web site contains a host of goodies. First, you find an expanded collection of all the source code from this book. A set of utilities is also included. I've used the SharpDevelop utility enough to know that it's up to the task of writing almost any of the example programs in this book (with the possible exception, for now, of the new LINQ features). The Reflector tool lets you peek under the covers to see what the compiler has turned your lovely C# source code into. The NUnit testing tool, wildly popular among C# programmers, makes testing your code easy, whether from Visual Studio or SharpDevelop. Finally, the Web site contains a bunch of bonus chapters covering features and techniques that wouldn't fit into the book, including a tour of Visual Studio.

Don't forget the ReadMe file, which has all the most up-to-date information.

Icons Used in This Book

Throughout the pages of this book, I use the following icons to highlight important information.

This icon flags technical stuff that you can skip on the first reading.

The Tip icon highlights a point that can save you a lot of time and effort.

Remember this. It's important.

Remember this, too. This one can sneak up on you when you least expect it and generate one of those really hard-to-find bugs — or it may lead you down the garden path into La-La Land.

This icon identifies code that you can find on the Web site with this book. This feature is designed to save you some typing when your fingers start to cramp, but don't abuse it. You'll gain a better understanding of C# by entering the programs yourself, then using them as test beds for your explorations and experiments in C#.

Conventions Used in This Book

Throughout this book, I use several conventions to help you out. Terms that are not "real words," such as the name of some program variable, appear in this font to minimize the confusion factor. Program listings are offset from text as follows:

```
use System;
namespace MyNameSpace
{
  public class MyClass
  {
  }
}
```

Each listing is followed by a clever, insightful explanation. Complete programs are included on the Web site for your viewing pleasure. Small code segments are not.

Finally, you'll see command arrows, as in the phrase, "Choose File➪Open With➪ Notepad." That means choose the File menu option. Then, from the pull-down menu that appears, choose Open With. Finally, from the resulting submenu, choose Notepad.

Where's the Code? And the Bonus Goodies?

In a departure from previous editions of this book, this time we chose to provide all of the code examples, along with several bonus chapters, on the Web. Thus you won't find a CD-ROM tucked into the back cover. You can obtain the code and bonus chapters on two different Web sites:

✔ www.dummies.com

Here, along with the code and bonus chapters, you can track down For Dummies titles mentioned in the book — and many related titles as well.

✔ `csharp102.info`, my Web site.

Here you'll find all of that same bonus material. But you'll also find lots of articles that extend topics in the book or introduce new topics that I'd have liked to put in the book — only of course it's impossible to include everything. The site also points you to a number of programming tools and other C# resources.

Don't forget the `ReadMe` file — also available on both Web sites — which has all the most up-to-date information.

Where to Go from Here

Obviously, the first step is to figure out the C# language, ideally using *C# 2008 For Dummies,* of course. You may want to give yourself a few months of writing simple C# programs before taking on the next step of discovering how to create graphical Windows applications. Give yourself many months of Windows application experience before you branch out into writing programs intended to be distributed over the Internet.

In the meantime, you can keep up with C# goings and comings in several locations. First, check out the official source: `msdn.microsoft.com/msdn`. In addition, various programmer Web sites have extensive material on C#, including lively discussions all the way from how to save a source file to the relative merits of deterministic versus nondeterministic garbage collection. Around my house, garbage collection is very deterministic: It's every Wednesday morning. Here are a few large C# sites:

✔ `msdn.microsoft.com/vcsharp`, the C# home page, which gets you to all sorts of C# and .NET resources

✔ `blogs.msdn.com/csharpfaq`, a C# Frequently Asked Questions blog

✔ `msdn.microsoft.com/vcsharp/team/blogs`, which is comprised of personal blogs of C# team members

✔ `www.c-sharpcorner.com` and `www.codeproject.com`, two major C# sites with articles, blogs, code, job information, and other C# resources

I maintain a Web site, `csharp102.info`, containing a set of Frequently Asked Questions (FAQs). If you encounter something that you can't figure out, try going there — maybe the FAQs have already answered your question. In addition, the site includes a list of any mistakes that may have crept into the book, the book's example code, several bonus chapters, and tons of other material on C# and programming that you may find useful. Finally, you can find a link to my e-mail address, in case you can't find the answer to your question on the site.

Part I
Getting Started with C#

"We should cast a circle, invoke the elements, and direct the energy. If that doesn't work, we'll read the manual."

In this part . . .

Y ou have a long way to go before you've mastered C#, so have a little fun just to get off the ground. Part I takes you through the steps for creating the most basic Windows console application possible, using Visual Studio 2008. The result gives you the basic C# framework for the example programs that appear throughout this book.

Chapter 1

Creating Your First C# Console Application

*I*n this chapter, I explain a little bit about computers, computer languages, C#, and Visual Studio 2008. Then I take you through the steps for creating a very simple program written in C#.

Getting a Handle on Computer Languages, C#, and .NET

A computer is an amazingly fast, but incredibly stupid servant. Computers will do anything you ask them to (within reason), they do it extremely fast — and they're getting faster all the time.

Unfortunately, computers don't understand anything that resembles a human language. Oh, you may come back at me and say something like, "Hey, my telephone lets me dial my friend by just speaking his name. I know that a tiny computer runs my telephone. So that computer speaks English." But that's a computer *program* that understands English, not the computer itself.

The language that computers really understand is often called *machine language*. It is possible, but extremely difficult and error-prone, for humans to write machine language.

Humans and computers have decided to meet somewhere in the middle. Programmers create programs in a language that is not nearly as free as human speech but a lot more flexible and easy to use than machine language. The languages occupying this middle ground — C#, for example — are called *high-level* computer languages. (*High* is a relative term here.)

What's a program?

What is a program? In a practical sense, a Windows program is an executable file that you can run by double-clicking its icon. For example, the version of Microsoft Word that I'm using to write this book is a program. You call that an *executable program,* or *executable* for short. The names of executable program files generally end with the extension .EXE. Word, for example, is called Winword.exe.

But a program is something else, as well. An executable program consists of one or more *source files.* A C# program file is a text file that contains a sequence of C# commands, which fit together according to the laws of C# grammar. This file is known as a *source file,* probably because it's a source of frustration and anxiety.

Uh, grammar? There's going to be grammar? Just the C# kind, which is much easier than the kind most of us struggled with in junior high school.

What's C#?

The C# programming language is one of those intermediate languages that programmers use to create executable programs. C# combines the range of the powerful-but-complicated C++ with the ease of use of the friendly but more verbose Visual Basic. (Visual Basic's newer .NET incarnation is almost on par with C# in most respects. As the flagship language of .NET, C# tends to introduce most new features first.) A C# program file carries the extension .CS.

Some wags have pointed out that C-sharp and D-flat are the same note, but you should not refer to this new language as "D-flat" within earshot of Redmond, Washington.

C# is

- ✓ **Flexible:** C# programs can execute on the current machine, or they can be transmitted over the Web and executed on some distant computer.
- ✓ **Powerful:** C# has essentially the same command set as C++, but with the rough edges filed smooth.

- ✔ **Easier to use:** C# error-proofs the commands responsible for most C++ errors so you spend far less time chasing down those errors.

- ✔ **Visually oriented:** The .NET code library that C# uses for many of its capabilities provides the help needed to readily create complicated display frames with drop-down lists, tabbed windows, grouped buttons, scroll bars, and background images, to name just a few.

- ✔ **Internet-friendly:** C# plays a pivotal role in the .NET Framework, Microsoft's current approach to programming for Windows, the Internet, and beyond.

  .NET is pronounced *dot net.*

- ✔ **Secure:** Any language intended for use on the Internet must include serious security to protect against malevolent hackers.

Finally, C# is an integral part of .NET.

Because this book focuses on the C# language, it's not a Web-programming book, a database book, or a Windows graphical programming book.

What's .NET?

.NET began a few years ago as Microsoft's strategy to open up the Web to mere mortals like you and me. Today it's bigger than that, encompassing everything Microsoft does. In particular, it's the new way to program for Windows. It also gives a C-based language, C#, the simple, visual tools that made Visual Basic so popular. A little background will help you see the roots of C# and .NET.

Internet programming was traditionally very difficult in older languages such as C and C++. Sun Microsystems responded to that problem by creating the Java programming language. To create Java, Sun took the grammar of C++, made it a lot more user-friendly, and centered it around distributed development.

When programmers say "*distributed*," they're describing geographically dispersed computers running programs that talk to each other — in many cases, via the Internet.

When Microsoft licensed Java some years ago, it ran into legal difficulties with Sun over changes it wanted to make to the language. As a result, Microsoft more or less gave up on Java and started looking for ways to compete with it.

Being forced out of Java was just as well because Java has a serious problem: Although Java is a capable language, you pretty much have to write your entire program *in* Java to get the full benefit. Microsoft had too many developers and too many millions of lines of existing source code, so Microsoft had to come up with some way to support multiple languages. Enter .NET.

.NET is a framework, in many ways similar to Java's libraries — and the C# language is highly similar to the Java language. Just as *Java* is both the language itself and its extensive code library, *C#* is really much more than just the keywords and syntax of the C# language. It's those things empowered by a thoroughly object-oriented library containing thousands of code elements that simplify doing about any kind of programming you can imagine, from Web-based databases to cryptography to the humble Windows dialog box.

Microsoft would claim that .NET is much superior to Sun's suite of Web tools based on Java, but that's not the point. Unlike Java, .NET does not require you to rewrite existing programs. A Visual Basic programmer can add just a few lines to make an existing program "Web-knowledgeable" (meaning that it knows how to get data off the Internet). .NET supports all the common Microsoft languages — and more than 40 other languages written by third-party vendors (see `dotnetpowered.com/languages.aspx` for the latest list). However, C# is the flagship language of the .NET fleet. C# is always the first language to access every new feature of .NET.

What is Visual Studio 2008? What about Visual C#?

(You sure ask lots of questions.) The first "Visual" language from Microsoft was Visual Basic. The first popular C-based language from Microsoft was Visual C++. Like Visual Basic, it was called "Visual" because it had a built-in graphical user interface (GUI — pronounced *gooey*). This GUI included everything you needed to develop nifty-giffy C++ programs.

Eventually, Microsoft rolled all its languages into a single environment — Visual Studio. As Visual Studio 6.0 started getting a little long in the tooth, developers anxiously awaited Version 7. Shortly before its release, however, Microsoft decided to rename it Visual Studio .NET to highlight this new environment's relationship to .NET.

That sounded like a marketing ploy to me — until I started delving into it. Visual Studio .NET differed quite a bit from its predecessors — enough to warrant a new name. Visual Studio 2008 is the third-generation successor to the original Visual Studio .NET. (See Bonus Chapter 6 on the Web site for a tour of some of Visual Studio's more potent features.)

Microsoft calls its implementation of the language Visual C#. In reality, Visual C# is nothing more than the C# component of Visual Studio. C# is C#, with or without the Visual Studio.

Okay, that's it. No more questions. (For now, anyway.)

Creating Your First Console Application

Visual Studio 2008 includes an Application Wizard that builds template programs and saves you a lot of the dirty work you'd have to do if you did everything from scratch. (I don't recommend the from-scratch approach.)

Typically, starter programs don't actually do anything — at least, not anything useful (sounds like most of my programs). However, they do get you beyond that initial hurdle of getting started. Some starter programs are reasonably sophisticated. In fact, you'll be amazed at how much capability the App Wizard can build on its own, especially for graphical programs.

The following instructions are for Visual Studio. If you use anything other than Visual Studio, you have to refer to the documentation that came with your environment. Alternatively, you can just type the source code directly into your C# environment. See the introduction to this book for some alternatives to Visual Studio.

Creating the source program

To start Visual Studio, choose Start➪All Programs➪Microsoft Visual Studio 2008➪Microsoft Visual Studio 2008.

Complete these steps to create your C# console app:

1. **Choose File➪New➪Project to create a new project, as shown in Figure 1-1.**

   Visual Studio presents you with lots of icons representing the different types of applications you can create, as shown in Figure 1-2.

2. **From this New Project window, click the Console Application icon.**

   Make sure that you select Visual C# — and under it, Windows — in the Project Types pane; otherwise Visual Studio may create something awful like a Visual Basic or Visual C++ application. Then click the Console Application icon in the Templates pane.

Figure 1-1:
Creating a new project starts you down the road to a better Windows application.

Visual Studio requires you to create a project before you can start to enter your C# program. A *project* is like a bucket in which you throw all the files that go into making your program. When you tell your compiler to build (*compile*) the program, it sorts through the project to find the files it needs in order to re-create the executable program.

The default name for your first application is `ConsoleApplication1`, but change it this time to `Program1`.

Figure 1-2:
The Visual Studio App Wizard is eager to create a new program for you.

The default place to store this file is somewhere deep in your `Documents` directory. Maybe because I'm difficult (or maybe because I'm writing a book), I like to put my programs where I want them to go, not necessarily where Visual Studio wants them. 'To simplify working with this book, you can change the default program location. Follow these steps to make that happen:

a. *Choose Tools⇨Options⇨Projects and Solutions⇨General.*

b. *Select the new location (I recommend* `C:\C#Programs` *for this book) in the Visual Studio Projects Location box, and click OK.*

You can create the new directory in the Project Location dialog box at the same time. Click the folder icon with a small sunburst at the top of the dialog box. (The directory may already exist if you've installed the example programs from the Web site.)

Leave the other boxes in the project settings alone.

3. **Click the OK button.**

After a bit of disk whirring and chattering, Visual Studio generates a file called `Program.cs`. (If you look in the window labeled Solution Explorer, you see some other files; ignore them for now. If Solution Explorer isn't visible, choose View⇨Solution Explorer.) C# source files carry the extension `.CS`. The name `Program` is the default name assigned for the program file.

The contents of your first console app appear as follows:

```
using ...

namespace Program1
{
  class Program
  {
    static void Main(string[] args)
    {

    }
  }
}
```

Along the left edge of the code window, you see several small plus (+) and minus (–) signs in boxes. Click the + sign next to `using. . . .` This expands a *code region,* a handy Visual Studio feature that keeps down the clutter. Here are the directives when you expand the region in the default console app:

```
using System;
using System.Collections.Generic;
using System.Linq;
using System.Text;
```

Regions help you focus on the code you're working on by hiding code that you aren't. Certain blocks of code — such as the `namespace` block, `class` block, methods, and other code items — get a +/- automatically without a `#region` directive. You can add your own collapsible regions, if you like, by typing **#region** above a code section and **#endregion** after it. It helps to supply a name for the region, such as `Public methods`.' Here's what this code section looks like:

```
#region Public methods
... your code
#endregion Public methods
```

This name can include spaces. Also, you can nest one region inside another, but regions can't overlap.

For now, `using System;` is the only `using` *directive* you really need. You can delete the others; the compiler lets you know whether you're missing one.

Taking it out for a test drive

To convert your C# program into an executable program, choose Build⇨Build Program1. Visual Studio responds with the following message:

```
- Build started: Project: Program1, Configuration: Debug Any CPU -

Csc.exe /noconfig /nowarn ... (and much more)

Compile complete -- 0 errors, 0 warnings
Program1 -> C:\C#Programs\ ... (and more)==Build: 1 succeeded or up-to-date, 0
                failed, 0 skipped==
```

The key point here is the `1 succeeded` part on the last line.

As a general rule of programming, "`succeeded`" is good; "`failed`" is bad.

To execute the program, choose Debug⇨Start. The program brings up a black console window and terminates immediately. The program has seemingly done nothing. In fact, this is the case. The template is nothing but an empty shell.

An alternative command, Debug⇨Start Without Debugging, behaves a bit better at this point. Try it out.

Making Your Console App Do Something

Edit the `Program.cs` template file until it appears as follows:

```csharp
using System;

namespace Program1
{
  public class Program
  {
    // This is where your program starts.
    static void Main(string[] args)
    {
      // Prompt user to enter a name.
      Console.WriteLine("Enter your name, please:");

      // Now read the name entered.
      string name = Console.ReadLine();

      // Greet the user with the name that was entered.
      Console.WriteLine("Hello, " + name);

      // Wait for user to acknowledge the results.
      Console.WriteLine("Press Enter to terminate...");
      Console.Read();
    }
  }
}
```

Don't sweat the stuff following the double or triple slashes (`//` or `///`), and don't worry about whether to enter one or two spaces or one or two new lines. However, do pay attention to capitalization.

Choose Build⇨Build `Program1` to convert this new version of `Program.cs` into the `Program1.exe` program.

From within Visual Studio 2008, choose Debug⇨Start Without Debugging. The black console window appears and prompts you for your name. (You may need to activate the console window by clicking it.) Then the window shows `Hello,` followed by the name entered, and displays `Press Enter to terminate . . . .` Pressing Enter closes the window.

You can also execute the program from the DOS command line. To do so, open a Command Prompt window and enter the following:

```
CD \C#Programs\Program1\bin\Debug
```

Now enter **Program1** to execute the program. The output should be identical to what you saw earlier. You can also navigate to the `\C#Programs\Program1\bin\Debug` folder in Windows Explorer and then double-click the `Program1.exe` file.

To open a Command Prompt window, try choosing Tools⇨Command Prompt. If that command isn't available on your Visual Studio Tools menu, choose Start⇨All Programs⇨Microsoft Visual Studio 2008⇨Visual Studio Tools⇨Visual Studio 2008 Command Prompt.

Reviewing Your Console Application

In the following sections, you take this first C# console app apart one section at a time to understand how it works.

The program framework

The basic framework for all console applications starts as the following:

```
using System;
using System.Collections.Generic;
using System.Linq;
using System.Text;

namespace Program1
{
  public class Program
  {
    // This is where your program starts.
    public static void Main(string[] args)
    {
        // Your code goes here.
    }
  }
}
```

The program starts executing right after the statement containing `Main()` and ends at the closed curly brace following `Main()`. (I explain the meaning of these statements in due course. More than that I cannot say for now.)

The list of `using` directives can come immediately before or immediately after the phrase `namespace Program1 {`. The order doesn't matter. You can apply `using` to lots of things in .NET. The whole business of namespaces and `using` is explained in Bonus Chapter 1 on the Web site.

Comments

The template already has lots of lines, and I've added several other lines, such as the following (in boldface):

```
// This is where your program starts.
public static void Main(string[] args)
```

C# ignores the first line in this example. This line is known as a *comment*.

Any line that begins with `//` or `///` is free text and is ignored by C#. Consider `//` and `///` to be equivalent for now.

Why include lines if the computer ignores them? Because comments explain your C# statements. A program, even in C#, isn't easy to understand. Remember that a programming language is a compromise between what computers understand and what humans understand. These comments are useful while you write the code, and they're especially helpful to the poor sap — possibly you — who tries to re-create your logic a year later. Comments make the job much easier.

Comment early and often.

The meat of the program

The real core of this program is embedded within the block of code marked with `Main()`, as follows:

```
// Prompt user to enter a name.
Console.WriteLine("Enter name, please:");

// Now read the name entered.
string name = Console.ReadLine();

// Greet the user with the name that was entered.
Console.WriteLine("Hello, " + name);
```

Save a ton of routine typing with the new C# Code Snippets feature. Snippets are great for common statements like `Console.WriteLine`. Press Ctrl+K and then Ctrl+X to see a pop-up menu of snippets. (You may need to press Tab once or twice to open up the Visual C# folder or other folders on that menu.) Scroll down the menu to `cw` and press Enter. Visual Studio inserts the body of a `Console.WriteLine()` statement with the insertion point between the parentheses, ready to go. When you have a few of the shortcuts like `cw`, `for`, and `if` memorized, use the even quicker technique: Type **cw** and press Tab twice. (Also try selecting some lines of code, pressing Ctrl+K, and then pressing Ctrl+S. Choose something like `if`. An `if` statement *surrounds* the selected code lines.) The program begins executing with the first C# statement: `Console.WriteLine`. This command writes the character string `Enter your name, please:` to the console.

The next statement reads in the user's answer and stores it in a *variable* (a kind of "workbox") called `name`. (See Chapter 2 for more on these storage locations.) The last line combines the string `Hello,` with the user's name and outputs the result to the console.

The final three lines cause the computer to wait for the user to press Enter before proceeding. These lines ensure that the user has time to read the output before the program continues, as follows:

```
// Wait for user to acknowledge the results.
Console.WriteLine("Press Enter to terminate...");
Console.Read();
```

This step can be important depending on how you execute the program and depending on the environment. In particular, running your console app inside Visual Studio, or from Windows Explorer, makes the lines above necessary — otherwise, the console window closes so fast you can't read the output. If you open a console window and run the program from there, the window stays open regardless.

Introducing the Toolbox Trick

Actually, the key part of the program you've created in the preceding section is the final two lines of code:

```
// Wait for user to acknowledge the results.
Console.WriteLine("Press Enter to terminate...");
Console.Read();
```

The easiest way to recreate those key lines in each future console application that you write is as follows.

Saving code in the Toolbox

The first step is to save those lines in a handy location for future use in a handy place: the Toolbox window. 'With your `Program1` console application open in Visual Studio, follow these steps:

1. **In the** `Main()` **method of class** `Program`**, select the lines you want to save — in this case, the lines above.**

2. **Make sure the Toolbox window is open. (If it isn't, open it by choosing View⇨Toolbox.)**

3. **Drag the selected lines into the General tab of the Toolbox window and drop them. (Or copy the lines and paste them into the Toolbox.)**

   The Toolbox stores the lines there for you in perpetuity. Figure 1-3 shows the lines placed in the Toolbox.

Reusing code from the Toolbox

Now that you have your template text stored in the Toolbox, you can reuse it in all of the console applications you write henceforth. Here's how to use it:

1. In Visual Studio, create a new console application as described earlier in this chapter.

2. Click in the editor at the spot where you'd like to insert some Toolbox text.

3. With the `Program.cs` file open for editing, make sure the Toolbox window is open. (If it isn't, see the procedure above.)

4. In the General tab of the Toolbox window (other tabs could be showing), find the saved text you want to use and double-click it.

   The selected item is inserted at the insertion point in the editor window.

With that boilerplate text in place, you can write the rest of your application above those lines. That's it. You now have a finished console app. Try it out for oh, say, 30 seconds. Then head for Chapter 2.

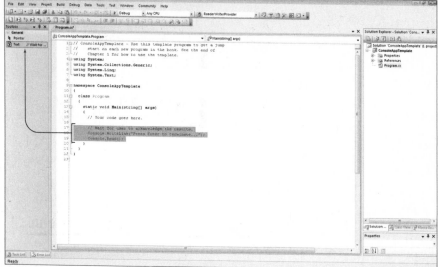

Figure 1-3:
Setting up
the Toolbox
with some
handy
saved text
for future
use.

Part II
Basic C#
Programming

"Yes, I know how to query information from the program, but what if I just want to leak it instead?"

In this part . . .

The newest e-commerce, B2B, dot-com, whiz-bang program uses the same basic building blocks as the simplest temperature-conversion program. This part presents the basics of creating variables, performing arithmetic operations, and controlling the execution path through a program. This fundamental C# is essential ground school before you can soar, especially if you're new to programming.

Chapter 2

Living with Variability — Declaring Value-Type Variables

The most fundamental of all concepts in programming is that of the variable. A C# variable is like a small box in which you can store things, particularly numbers, for later use. (The term *variable* is borrowed from the world of mathematics.)

Unfortunately for programmers, C# places several limitations on variables — limitations that mathematicians don't have to consider. This chapter takes you through the steps for declaring, initializing, and using variables. It also introduces several of the most basic *data types* in C#.

Declaring a Variable

When the mathematician says, "*n* is equal to 1," that means the term *n* is equivalent to 1 in some ethereal way. The mathematician is free to introduce variables in a willy-nilly fashion. For example, the mathematician may say the following:

```
x = y² + 2y + y
if k = y + 1 then
x = k²
```

Programmers must define variables in a particular way that's more demanding than the mathematician's looser style. For example, a C# programmer may write the following code:

```
int n;
n = 1;
```

The first line means, "Carve off a small amount of storage in the computer's memory and assign it the name *n*." This step is analogous to reserving one of those storage lockers at the train station and slapping the label *n* on the side. The second line says, "Store the value 1 in the variable *n*, thereby replacing whatever that storage location already contains." The train-locker equivalent is, "Open the train locker, rip out whatever happens to be there, and shove in a 1 in its place."

The equals symbol (=) is called the *assignment operator.*

The mathematician says, "*n* equals 1." The C# programmer says in a more precise way, "Store the value 1 in the variable n." (Think about the train locker, and you see why that's preferable.) C# operators tell the computer what you want to do. In other words, operators are verbs and not descriptors. The assignment operator takes the value on its right and stores it in the variable on the left. I'll say a lot more about operators in Chapter 3.

What's an int?

In C#, each variable has a fixed type. When you allocate one of those train lockers, you have to pick the size you need. If you picked an "integer locker," you couldn't turn around and hope to stuff the entire state of Texas in it — maybe Rhode Island, but not Texas.

For the example in the preceding section of this chapter, you select a locker that's designed to handle an integer — C# calls it an `int`. Integers are the counting numbers 1, 2, 3, and so on, plus 0 and the negative numbers –1, –2, –3, and so on.

Before you can use a variable, you must *declare* it. After you declare a variable as `int`, it can hold and regurgitate integer values, as the following example demonstrates:

```
// Declare a variable named n - an empty train locker.
int n;
// Declare an int variable m and initialize it with the value 2.
int m = 2;
// Assign the value stored in m to the variable n.
n = m;
```

The first line after the comment is a *declaration* that creates a little storage area, n, designed to hold an integer value. The initial value of n is not specified until it is *assigned* a value. The second declaration not only declares an int variable m but also *initializes* it with a value of 2, all in one shot.

The term *initialize* means to assign an initial value. To initialize a variable is to assign it a value for the first time. You don't know for sure what the value of a variable is until it has been initialized. Nobody knows.

The final statement in the program assigns the value stored in m, which is 2, to the variable n. The variable n continues to contain the value 2 until it is assigned a new value. (The variable n doesn't lose its value when you assign its value to m. It's like cloning n.)

Rules for declaring variables

You can initialize a variable as part of the declaration, as follows:

```
// Declare another int variable and give it the initial value of 1.
int p = 1;
```

This is equivalent to sticking a 1 into that int storage locker when you first rent it, rather than opening the locker and stuffing in the value later.

Initialize a variable when you declare it. In most (but not all) cases, C# initializes the variable for you — but don't rely on it to do that.

You may declare variables anywhere (well, almost anywhere) within a program.

However, you may not use a variable until you declare it and set it to some value. Thus the last two assignments shown here are *not* legal:

```
// The following is illegal because m is not assigned
// a value before it is used.
int m;
n = m;
// The following is illegal because p has not been
// declared before it is used.
p = 2;
int p;
```

Finally, you cannot declare the same variable twice.

Variations on a theme — Different types of int

Most simple numeric variables are of type int. However, C# provides a number of twists to the int variable type for special occasions.

All integer variable types are limited to whole numbers. The int type suffers from other limitations as well. For example, an int variable can only store values in the range from roughly –2 billion to 2 billion.

A distance of 2 billion inches is greater than the circumference of the Earth. In case 2 billion isn't quite large enough for you, C# provides an integer type called long (short for long int) that can represent numbers almost as large as you can imagine. The only problem with a long is that it takes a larger train locker: A long consumes 8 bytes (64 bits) — twice as much as a garden-variety 4-byte (32-bit) int. C# provides several other integer variable types, as shown in Table 2-1.

Table 2-1		The Size and Range of C# Integer Types	
Type	*Size (bytes)*	*Range of Values*	*In Use*
sbyte	1	–128 to 127	sbyte sb = 12;
byte	1	0 to 255	byte b = 12;
short	2	–32,768 to 32,767	short sh = 12345;
ushort	2	0 to 65,535	ushort ush = 62345;
int	4	–2 billion to 2 billion	int n = 1234567890;
uint	4	0 to 4 billion (exact values in the Cheat Sheet inside the front cover of this book)	uint un = 3234567890U
long	8	-10^{20} to 10^{20} — "a whole lot"	long l = 123456789012L
Ulong	8	0 to 2×10^{20}	long ul = 123456789012UL

As I explain in the section "Declaring Numeric Constants," later in this chapter, fixed values such as 1 also have a type. By default, a simple constant such as 1 is assumed to be an `int`. Constants other than an `int` must be marked with their variable type. For example, 123U is an unsigned integer, `uint`.

Most integer variables are called *signed,* which means they can represent negative values. Unsigned integers can only represent positive values, but you get twice the range in return. As you can see from Table 2-1, the names of most unsigned integer types start with a `u`, while the signed types generally don't have a prefix.

You won't need any of the unsigned integer versions in this book.

New feature — The BigInteger type

As if the types in the preceding section aren't enough, there's now a new kid on the block. In case ten to the twentieth power (the approximate size of a `long` variable) still isn't big enough, C# 3.0 introduces the new Godzilla of integers, called `BigInteger`. It's pretty humongous. In fact, your computer almost certainly doesn't have nearly enough memory to store the biggest `BigInteger` possible. I got tired after a few dozen digits here:

```
BigInteger bigOne = 306057512216440636035370461297268629388588804173576
    999416776741259476533176716867465515291422477573.........;
```

To illustrate, the *factorial* of a number is the number multiplied by each smaller number. So 3 factorial is 3 times 2 times 1, or 6. And 9 factorial (written **9!**) is 9 times 8 times 7 . . . , which comes to 362,880. To handle 300!, you'd really need the `BigInteger` because `long` integer (previously shown in Table 2-1) is far too small to hold the result, which I won't even try to give here. You may not have much use for `BigInteger`, but somebody sure will, probably a cryptographer at some spook agency.

Representing Fractions

Integers are great for most calculations. I made it into the sixth grade before I ever found out that anything else existed. I still haven't forgiven my sixth-grade teacher for starting me down the slippery slope of fractions.

Many calculations involve fractions, which simple integers can't accurately represent. The common equation for converting from Fahrenheit to Celsius temperatures demonstrates the problem, as follows:

```
// Convert the temperature 41 degrees Fahrenheit.
int fahr = 41;
int celsius = (fahr - 32) * (5 / 9)
```

This equation works just fine for some values. For example, 41 degrees Fahrenheit is 5 degrees Celsius. "Correct, Mr. Davis," says my sixth-grade teacher.

Okay, try a different value: 100 degrees Fahrenheit. Working through the equation, 100 – 32 is 68; 68 times ⅝ is 37. "No," she says, "The answer is 37.78." Even that's wrong, because it's really 37.777 . . . with the 7s repeating forever, but I'm not going to push the point.

An int can only represent integer numbers. The integer equivalent of 37.78 is 37. This lopping off of the fractional part of a number to get it to fit into an integer variable is called integer *truncation.*

Truncation is not the same thing as *rounding.* Truncation lops off the fractional part. Goodbye, Charlie. Rounding picks the closest integer value. Thus, truncating 1.9 results in 1. Rounding 1.9 results in 2.

For temperatures, 37 may be good enough. It's not like you wear short-sleeve shirts at 37.7 degrees but pull on a sweater at 37 degrees. But integer truncation is unacceptable for many, if not most, applications.

Actually, the problem is much worse than that. An int can't handle the ratio ⅝ either; it always yields the value 0. Consequently, the equation as written in this example calculates celsius as 0 for all values of fahr. Even I admit that's unacceptable.

This book's Web site includes an int-based temperature-conversion program contained in the ConvertTemperatureWithRoundOff directory. At this point, you may not understand all the details, but you can see the conversion equations and execute the program ConvertTemperatureWithRoundOff.exe to see the results. (Review Chapter 1 if you need a hand running it.)

Handling Floating-Point Variables

The limitations of an int variable are unacceptable for some applications. The range generally isn't a problem — the double-zillion range of a 64-bit-long integer should be enough for almost anyone. However, the fact that an int is limited to whole numbers is a bit harder to swallow.

In some cases, you need numbers that can have a nonzero fractional part. Mathematicians call these *real numbers.* (Somehow that always seemed like a ridiculous name for a number. Are integer numbers somehow unreal?)

Notice that I said a real number *can* have a nonzero fractional part — that is, 1.5 is a real number, but so is 1.0. For example, 1.0 + 0.1 is 1.1. Just keep that point in mind as you read the rest of this chapter.

Fortunately, C# understands real numbers. Real numbers come in two flavors: floating-point and decimal. Floating-point is the most common type. I describe the decimal type a little later in this chapter.

Declaring a floating-point variable

A floating-point variable carries the designation float, and you declare one as shown in the following example:

```
float f = 1.0;
```

After you declare it as float, the variable f is a float for the rest of its natural instructions.

Table 2-2 describes the two kinds of floating-point types. All floating-point variables are signed (there's no such thing as a floating-point variable that can't represent a negative value).

Table 2-2   The Size and Range of the Floating-Point Variable Types

Type	Size (bytes)	Range of Values	Accuracy (no. of digits)	In Use
float	8	$1.5 * 10^{-45}$ to $3.4 * 10^{38}$	6–7	float f = 1.2F;
double	16	$5.0 * 10^{-324}$ to $1.7 * 10^{308}$	15–16	double d = 1.2;

You might think float is the default floating-point variable type, but actually the double is the default in C#. If you don't specify the type for, say, 12.3, C# calls it a double.

The Accuracy column in Table 2-2 refers to the number of significant digits that such a variable type can represent. For example, ⅝ is actually 0.555 . . . with an unending sequence of 5s. However, a float variable is said to have six significant digits of accuracy — which means numbers after the sixth digit are ignored. Thus ⅝ may appear as follows when expressed as a float:

```
0.5555551457382
```

Here you know that all the digits after the sixth 5 are untrustworthy.

The same number — ⅚ — may appear as follows when expressed as a `double`:

```
0.55555555555555557823
```

The `double` packs a whopping 15 to 16 significant digits.

Use `double` variable types unless you have a specific reason to do otherwise.

Converting some more temperatures

Here's the formula for converting from Fahrenheit to Celsius temperatures using floating-point variables:

```
double celsius = (fahr - 32.0) * (5.0 / 9.0)
```

The Web site contains a floating-point version of the temperature-conversion program called `ConvertTemperatureWithFloat`.

The following example shows the result of executing the `double`-based `ConvertTemperatureWithFloat` program:

```
Enter temp in degrees Fahrenheit:100
Temperature in degrees Celsius = 37.7777777777778
Press Enter to terminate...
```

Examining some limitations of floating-point variables

You may be tempted to use floating-point variables all the time because they solve the truncation problem so nicely. Sure they use up a bit more memory, but memory is cheap these days, so why not? But floating-point variables also have limitations.

Counting

You can't use floating-point variables as counting numbers. Some C# structures need to count (as in 1, 2, 3, and so on). You and I know that 1.0, 2.0, and 3.0 are counting numbers just as well as 1, 2, and 3, but C# doesn't know that. For example, given the accuracy limitations of floating-points, how does C# know that you aren't *actually* saying 1.000001?

Whether or not you find that argument convincing, you can't use a floating-point variable when counting things.

Comparing numbers

You have to be careful when comparing floating-point numbers. For example, 12.5 may be represented as 12.500001. Most people don't care about that little extra bit on the end. However, the computer takes things extremely literally. To C#, 12.500000 and 12.500001 are not the same numbers.

So, if you add 1.1 to 1.1, you can't tell whether the result is 2.2 or 2.200001. And if you ask, "Is doubleVariable equal to 2.2?" you may not get the results you expect. Generally, you have to resort to some bogus comparison like this: "Is the absolute value of the difference between doubleVariable and 2.2 less than .000001?" In other words, "within an acceptable margin of error."

The Pentium processor plays a trick to make this problem less troublesome than it otherwise may be: It performs floating-point arithmetic in an especially long double format — that is, rather than using 64 bits, it uses a whopping 80 bits. When rounding off an 80-bit float into a 64-bit float, you (almost) always get the expected result, even if the 80-bit number was off a bit or two.

Calculation speed

Processors such as the *x*86 varieties used in older Windows-based PCs could perform integer arithmetic much faster than arithmetic of the floating-point persuasion. In those days, programmers would go out of their way to limit a program to integer arithmetic.

The ratio in additional speed on a Pentium III processor for a simple (perhaps too simple) test of about 300,000,000 additions and subtractions was about 3 to 1. That is, for every double add, you could have done three int adds. (Computations involving multiplication and division may show different results.)

Not-so-limited range

In the past, a floating-point variable could represent a considerably larger range of numbers than an integer type. It still can, but the range of the long is large enough to render the point moot.

Even though a simple float can represent a very large number, the number of significant digits is limited to about six. For example, 123,456,789F is the same as 123,456,000F. (For an explanation of the F notation at the end of these numbers, see "Declaring Numeric Constants" later in this chapter.)

Using the Decimal Type — Is It an Integer or a Float?

As I explain in previous sections of this chapter, both the integer and floating-point types have their problems. Floating-point variables have rounding problems associated with limits to their accuracy, while int variables just lop off the fractional part of a variable. In some cases, you need a variable type that offers the best of two worlds, as follows:

- ✔ Like a floating-point variable, it can store fractions.

- ✔ Like an integer, numbers of this type offer exact values for use in computations — for example, 12.5 is really 12.5 and not 12.500001.

Fortunately, C# provides such a variable type, called decimal. A decimal variable can represent a number between 10^{-28} and 10^{28} — that's a lot of zeros! And it does so without rounding problems. Not as big as the new BigIntegers, but huge.

Declaring a decimal

Decimal variables are declared and used like any variable type, as follows:

```
decimal m1 = 100;    // Good.
decimal m2 = 100M;   // Better.
```

The second declaration shown here creates a variable m1 and initializes it to a value of 100. What isn't obvious is that 100 is actually of type int. Thus, C# must convert the int into a decimal type before performing the initialization. Fortunately, C# understands what you mean — and performs the conversion for you.

The declaration of m2 is the best. This clever declaration initializes m2 with the decimal constant 100M. The letter *M* at the end of the number specifies that the constant is of type decimal. No conversion is required. (See the section "Declaring Numeric Constants," later in this chapter.)

Comparing decimals, integers, and floating-point types

The decimal variable type seems to have all the advantages and none of the disadvantages of int or double types. Variables of this type have a very large range, they don't suffer from rounding problems, and 25.0 is 25.0 and not 25.00001.

The decimal variable type has two significant limitations, however. First, a decimal is not considered a counting number because it may contain a fractional value. Consequently, you can't use them in flow-control loops, which I explain in Chapter 4.

The second problem with `decimal` variables is equally as serious or even more so. Computations involving `decimal` values are significantly slower than those involving either simple integer or floating-point values — and I do mean *significant*. On a crude benchmark test of 300,000,000 adds and subtracts, the operations involving `decimal` variables were approximately 50 times slower than those involving simple `int` variables. The relative computational speed gets even worse for more complex operations. Besides that, most computational functions, such as calculating sines or exponents, are not available for the `decimal` number type.

Clearly, the `decimal` variable type is most appropriate for applications such as banking, in which accuracy is extremely important but the number of calculations is relatively small.

Examining the bool Type — Is It Logical?

Finally, a logical variable type. Except in this case, I really mean a type "logical." The Boolean type `bool` can have two values: `true` or `false`. I kid thee not — a whole variable type for just two values. Not even a "maybe."

Former C and C++ programmers are accustomed to using the `int` value 0 (zero) to mean `false` and nonzero to mean `true`. That doesn't work in C#.

You declare a `bool` variable as follows:

```
bool thisIsABool = true;
```

No conversion path exists between `bool` variables and any other types. In other words, you can't convert a `bool` directly into something else. (Even if you could, you shouldn't because it doesn't make any sense.) In particular, you can't convert a `bool` into an `int` (such as `false` becoming 0) or a `string` (such as `false` becoming the word "false").

Checking Out Character Types

A program that can do nothing more than spit out numbers may be fine for mathematicians, accountants, insurance agents with their mortality figures, and folks calculating cannon-shell trajectories. (Don't laugh. The original computers were built to generate tables of cannon-shell trajectories to help artillery gunners.) However, for most applications, programs must deal with letters as well as numbers.

C# treats letters in two distinctly different ways: individual characters of type char (usually pronounced "char," as in singe or burn) and strings of characters — a type called, cleverly enough, string.

The char variable type

The char variable is a box capable of holding a single character. Character constants appear as a character surrounded by a pair of single quotation marks, as in this example:

```
char c = 'a';
```

You can store any single character from the Roman, Hebrew, Arabic, Cyrillic, and most other alphabets. You can also store Japanese katakana and hiragana characters, as well as many Japanese and Chinese kanjis.

In addition, char is considered a counting type. That means you can use a char type to control the looping structures that I describe in Chapter 4. Character variables do not suffer from rounding problems.

The character variable includes no font information. So you may store in a char variable what you think is a perfectly good kanji (and it may well be) — but when you view the character, it can look like garbage if you're not looking at it through the eyes of the proper font.

Special chars

Some characters within a given font are not printable, in the sense that you don't see anything when you look at them on the computer screen or printer. The most obvious example of this is the space, which is represented by the character ' ' (single quote, space, single quote). Other characters have no letter equivalent — for example, the tab character. C# uses the backslash to flag these characters, as shown in Table 2-3.

Table 2-3	Special Characters
Character Constant	*Value*
'\n'	New line
'\t'	Tab
'\0'	Null character
'\r'	Carriage return
'\\'	Backslash

The string type

Another extremely common variable type is the `string`. The following examples show how you declare and initialize `string` variables:

```
// Declare now, initialize later.
string someString1;
someString1 = "this is a string";
// Or initialize when declared - preferable.
string someString2 = "this is a string";
```

A `string` constant, often called a `string` *literal*, is a set of characters surrounded by double quotes. The characters in a `string` can include the special characters shown in Table 2-3. A `string` cannot be written across a line in the C# source file, but it can contain the new-line character, as the following examples show (see boldface):

```
// The following is not legal.
string someString = "This is a line
and so is this";
// However, the following is legal.
string someString = "This is a line\nand so is this";
```

When written out with `Console.WriteLine`, the last line in this example places the two phrases on separate lines, as follows:

```
This is a line
and so is this
```

A `string` is not a counting type. A `string` is also not a value-type — no "string" exists that's intrinsic (built in) to the processor. Only one of the common operators works on `string` objects: The + operator concatenates two strings into one. For example:

```
string s = "this is a phrase"
         + " and so is this";
```

This code sets the `string` variable s equal to the following character string:

```
"this is a phrase and so is this"
```

One other thing: The `string` with no characters, written `""` (two double quotes in a row), is a valid `string`, called an empty `string` (or sometimes a null `string`). A null `string` (`""`) is different from a null `char` (`'\0'`) and from a `string` containing any amount of space, even one (`" "`).

I like to initialize strings using the `String.Empty` value, which means the same thing as `""` and is less prone to misinterpretation:

```
string mySecretName = String.Empty;  // A property of the String type.
```

By the way, all the other data types in this chapter are *value-types*. The `string` type, however, is not a value-type, as I explain in the following section. Chapter 6 goes into much more detail about the `string` type.

What's a Value-Type?

The variable types that I describe in this chapter are of fixed length — again with the exception of `string`. A fixed-length variable type always occupies the same amount of memory. So if you assign a = b, C# can transfer the value of b into a without taking extra measures designed to handle variable-length types. This characteristic is why these types of variables are called *value-types*.

The types `int`, `double`, and `bool`, and their close derivatives (like unsigned `int`) are intrinsic variable types built right into the processor. The intrinsic variable types plus `decimal` are also known as value-types because variables store the actual data. The `string` type is neither — because the variable actually stores a sort of "pointer" to the string's data, called a *reference*. The data in the string is actually off in another location.

The programmer-defined types that I explain in Chapter 7, known as reference-types, are neither value-types nor intrinsic. The `string` type is a reference-type, although the C# compiler does accord it some special treatment because `string`s are so widely used.

Comparing string and char

Although strings deal with characters, the `string` type is amazingly different from the `char`. Of course, certain trivial differences exist. You enclose a character with single quotes, as in the following example:

```
'a'
```

On the other hand, you put double quotes around a string:

```
"this is a string"
"a"    // So is this - see the double quotes?
```

The rules concerning strings are not the same as those concerning characters. For one thing, you know right up front that a `char` is a single character, and that's it. For example, the following code makes no sense, either as addition or as concatenation:

```
char c1 = 'a';
char c2 = 'b';
char c3 = c1 + c2
```

Actually, this code almost compiles — but with a completely different meaning from what was intended. These statements convert c1 into an int consisting of the numeric value of c1. C# also converts c2 into an int and then adds the two integers. The error occurs when trying to store the results back into c3 — numeric data may be lost storing an int into the smaller char. In any case, the operation makes no sense.

A string, on the other hand, can be any length. So concatenating two strings, as follows, *does* make sense:

```
string s1 = "a";
string s2 = "b";
string s3 = s1 + s2;   // Result is "ab".
```

As part of its library, C# defines an entire suite of string operations. I describe them in Chapter 6.

Is This a Leap Year? — DateTime

What if you had to write a program that calculates whether this year is a leap year?

The algorithm looks like this:

```
It's a leap year if
   year is evenly divisible by 4
   and, if it happens to be evenly divisible by 100,
      it's also evenly divisible by 400
```

You don't have enough tools yet to tackle that in C#. But you could just ask the DateTime type (which is a value-type, like int):

```
DateTime thisYear = new DateTime(2007, 1, 1);
bool isLeapYear = DateTime.IsLeapYear(thisYear.Year);
```

The result for 2007 is false, but for 2008 it's true. (For now, don't worry about that first line of code, which uses some things you haven't gotten to yet.)

Naming conventions

Programming is hard enough without programmers making it harder. To make your C# source code easier to wade through, adopt a naming convention and stick to it. As much as possible, your naming convention should follow that adopted by other C# programmers:

- **The names of things other than variables start with a capital letter, and variables start with a lowercase letter.** Make these names as descriptive as possible — which often means that a name consists of multiple words. These words should be capitalized but butted up against each other with no underscore between them — for example, `ThisIsALongName`. Names that start with a capital are *Pascal-cased*, from the way a 1970s-era language called Pascal named things. (My first book was about Pascal.)

- **The names of variables start with a lowercase letter.** A typical variable name looks like this: `thisIsALongVariableName`. This variable naming style is called *camel-casing* because it has humps in the middle.

Prior to the .NET era, it was common among Windows programmers to use a convention in which the first letter of the variable name indicated the type of the variable. Most of these letters were straightforward: f for `float`, d for `double`, s for `string`, and so on. The only one that was even the slightest bit different was n for `int`. One exception to this rule existed: For reasons that stretch way back into the Fortran programming language of the '60s, the single letters i, j, and k were also used as common names for an `int`, and they still are in C#. This style of naming variables was called Hungarian notation, after Charles Simonyi, a famous Microsoftie who recently went to the International Space Station as a space tourist. (Martha Stewart packed his sack lunch.)

Hungarian notation has fallen out of favor, at least in .NET programming circles. With recent Visual Studio versions, you can simply rest the cursor on a variable in the debugger to have its data type revealed in a tooltip box. That makes the Hungarian prefix a bit less useful, though a few folks still hold out for Hungarian.

With the `DateTime` data type, you can do something like 80 different operations, such as pull out just the month; get the day of the week; add days, hours, minutes, seconds, milliseconds, months, or years to a given date; get the number of days in a given month; subtract two dates.

The following example lines use a convenient property of `DateTime` called `Now` to capture the present date and time, and one of the numerous `DateTime` methods that let you convert one time into another:

```
DateTime thisMoment = DateTime.Now;
DateTime anHourFromNow = thisMoment.AddHours(1);
```

You can also extract specific parts of a `DateTime`:

```
int year = DateTime.Now.Year;                  // e.g. 2007.
DayOfWeek dayOfWeek = DateTime.Now.DayOfWeek;  // e.g. Sunday.
```

If you print out that `DayOfWeek` object, it prints something like "Sunday." And you can do other handy manipulations of `DateTimes`:

```
DateTime date = DateTime.Today;              // Get just the date part.
TimeSpan time = thisMoment.TimeOfDay;        // Get just the time part.
TimeSpan duration = new TimeSpan(3, 0, 0, 0); // Specify a duration in days.
DateTime threeDaysFromNow = thisMoment.Add(duration);
```

The first two lines just extract portions of the information in a `DateTime`. The next two lines add a *duration* to a `DateTime`. A duration, or amount of time, differs from a moment in time; you specify durations with the `TimeSpan` class, and moments with `DateTime`. So the third line sets up a `TimeSpan` of three days, zero hours, zero minutes, and zero seconds. The fourth line adds the three-day duration to the `DateTime` representing right now, resulting in a new `DateTime` whose day component is three greater than the day component for `thisMoment`.

Subtracting a `DateTime` from another `DateTime` (or a `TimeSpan` from a `DateTime`) returns a `DateTime`:

```
TimeSpan duration1 = new TimeSpan(1, 0, 0);  // One hour later.
// Since Today gives 12:00:00 AM (midnight), the following gives 1:00:00 AM:
DateTime anHourAfterMidnight = DateTime.Today.Add(duration1);
Console.WriteLine("An hour from midnight will be {0}", anHourAfterMidnight);
DateTime midnight = anHourAfterMidnight.Subtract(duration1);
Console.WriteLine("An hour before 1 AM is {0}", midnight);
```

The first line of the preceding code creates a `TimeSpan` of one hour. The next line gets the date (actually midnight this morning) and adds the one-hour span to it, resulting in a `DateTime` representing 1:00 a.m. today. The next-to-last line subtracts a one-hour duration from 1:00 a.m. to get 12:00 a.m. (midnight).

For more information, see "DateTime structure" in Help, and take a look at the `DateTimeExample` program on the Web site.

Declaring Numeric Constants

There are very few absolutes in life; however, I'm about to give you a C# absolute: Every expression has a value and a type. In a declaration such as `int n`, you can easily see that the variable n is an `int`. Further, you can reasonably assume that the type of a calculation `n + 1` is an `int`. However, what type is the constant 1?

The type of a constant depends on two things: its value and the presence of an optional descriptor letter at the end of the constant. Any integer type less than 2 billion is assumed to be an `int`. Numbers larger than 2 billion are assumed to be `long`. Any floating-point number is assumed to be a `double`.

Table 2-4 demonstrates constants that have been declared to be of a particular type. The case of these descriptors is not important; 1U and 1u are equivalent.

Table 2-4	Common Constants Declared along with Their Type
Constant	*Type*
1	int
1U	unsigned int
1L	long int (avoid lowercase *l*; it's too much like the digit 1)
1.0	double
1.0F	float
1M	decimal
true	bool
false	bool
'a'	char
'\n'	char (the character newline)
'\x123'	char (the character whose numeric value is hex 123)[1]
"a string"	string
""	string (an empty string); same as String.Empty

[1]"hex" is short for hexadecimal (numbers in base 16 rather than base 10).

Changing Types — The Cast

Humans don't treat different types of counting numbers differently. For example, a normal person (as distinguished from a C# programmer) doesn't think about the number 1 as being signed, unsigned, short, or long. Although C# considers these types to be different, even C# realizes that a relationship exists between them. For example, the following code converts an int into a long:

```
int intValue = 10;
long longValue;
longValue = intValue;  // This is OK.
```

An `int` variable can be converted into a `long` because any possible value of an `int` can be stored in a `long` and because they are both counting numbers. C# makes the conversion for you automatically without comment. This is called an *implicit* type conversion.

A conversion in the opposite direction can cause problems, however. For example, the following is illegal:

```
long longValue = 10;
int intValue;
intValue = longValue;   // This is illegal.
```

Some values that you can store in a `long` don't fit in an `int` (4 billion, for example). If you try to shoehorn such a value into an `int`, C# generates an error because data may be lost during the conversion process. This type of bug is difficult to catch.

But what if you know that the conversion is okay? For example, even though `longValue` is a `long`, maybe you know that its value can't exceed 100 in this particular program. In that case, converting the `long` variable `longValue` into the `int` variable `intValue` would be okay.

You can tell C# that you know what you're doing by means of a *cast:*

```
long longValue = 10;
int intValue;
intValue = (int)longValue;   // This is now OK.
```

In a cast, you place the name of the type you want in parentheses and put it immediately in front of the value you want to convert. This cast says, "Go ahead and convert the `long` named `longValue` into an `int` — I know what I'm doing." In retrospect, the assertion that you know what you're doing may seem overly confident, but it's often valid.

A counting number can be converted into a floating-point number automatically, but converting a floating-point into a counting number requires a cast, as follows:

```
double doubleValue = 10.0;
long longValue = (long)doubleValue;
```

All conversions to and from a `decimal` require a cast. In fact, all numeric types can be converted into all other numeric types through the application of a cast. Neither `bool` nor `string` can be converted directly into any other type.

Built-in C# methods can convert a number, character, or boolean into its string "equivalent." For example, you can convert the `bool` value `true` into the string "true"; however, you cannot consider this change a direct conversion. The `bool` true and the `string` "true" are completely different things.

New Feature: Letting the C# Compiler Infer Data Types

So far in this book — well, so far in this chapter — when you declared a variable, you *always* specified its exact data type, like this:

```
int i = 5;
string s = "Hello C#";
double d = 1.0;
```

In C# 3.0, you're allowed to offload some of that work onto the C# compiler, using the new `var` keyword:

```
var i = 5;
var s = "Hello C# 3.0";
var d = 1.0;
```

Now the compiler *infers* the data type for you—it looks at the stuff on the right side of the assignment to see what type the left side is.

For what it's worth, Chapter 3 shows how to calculate the type of an expression like the ones on the right side of the assignments above. Not that you'll need to do that — the compiler mostly does it for you. Suppose, for example, you have an initializing expression like this:

```
var x = 3.0 + 2 - 1.5;
```

The compiler can figure out that x is a `double` value. It looks at `3.0` and `1.5` and sees that they're of type `double`. Then it notices that `2` is an `int`, which the compiler can convert *implicitly* to a `double` for the calculation. All of the addition terms in x's initialization expression end up as `doubles`. So the *inferred type* of x is `double`.

But now you can simply utter the magic word `var` and supply an initialization expression, and the compiler does the rest:

```
var aVariable = <initialization expression here>;
```

If you've worked with a scripting language such as JavaScript or VBScript, you may have gotten used to all-purpose-in-one data types. VBScript calls them `Variant` data types — a `Variant` can be anything at all. But does `var` in C# signify a `Variant` type? Not at all. The object you declare with `var` definitely has a C# data type, such as `int`, `string`, or `double`. You just don't have to declare what it is.

The `UsingVarForImplicitTypeInference` example on the Web site demonstrates `var` with several examples. Here's a taste.

What's really lurking in the variables declared in this example with `var`? Take a look at this:

```
var aString = "Hello C# 3.0";
Console.WriteLine(aString.GetType().ToString());
```

The mumbo jumbo in that `WriteLine` statement calls the `String.GetType()` method on `aString` to get its C# type. Then it calls the resulting object's `ToString()` method to display the object's type. (Yadda yadda.) Here's what you see in the console window:

```
System.String
```

which proves that the compiler correctly inferred the type of `aString`.

So what's the var keyword good for, besides letting you be lazy? The examples given here don't really gain you a lot, but other new C# 3.0 features, such as *anonymous types* and *query expressions* (discussed much later, in Chapter 17), make `var` a real necessity.

Most of the time, I recommend that you don't use `var`. Save it for when it's necessary. Being explicit about the type of a variable is clearer to anyone reading your code than using `var`. However, common usage in the C# world may change so much that everybody uses `var` all the time, in spite of my good advice. In that case, you can go along with the crowd.

You'll see examples later in which `var` is definitely called for, and I'll use it part of the time throughout the book, even sometimes where it's not strictly necessary. You need to see it used, and use it yourself, to internalize it. I'm still getting used to it myself. (I can't help it if I'm a slow learner.)

You can see `var` used in other ways: with arrays and collections of data, in Chapter 5, and with "anonymous types," in Chapter 17. Anonymous? Bet you can't wait.

You're going to meet lots of additional data types in this book. In fact, the concept of "type" is pretty crucial in C#.

Chapter 3

Smooth Operators

In This Chapter

▶ Performing a little arithmetic

▶ Doing some logical arithmetic

▶ Complicating matters with compound logical operators

Mathematicians create variables and manipulate them in various ways, adding them, multiplying them, and — here's a toughie — even integrating them. Chapter 2 describes how to declare and define variables. However, it says very little about how to use variables to get anything done after you've declared them. This chapter looks at the operations you can perform on variables to actually do some work. Operations require *operators*, such as +, −, =, <, and &. I cover arithmetic, logical, and other operators in this chapter.

Writing programs that get things done is good. You'll never make it as a C# programmer if your programs don't actually *do* something — unless, of course, you're a consultant.

Performing Arithmetic

The set of arithmetic operators breaks down into several groups: the simple arithmetic operators, the assignment operators, and a set of special operators unique to programming. After you've digested these, you also need to digest a separate set of logical operators. *Bon appétit!*

Simple operators

You learned most of the simple operators in elementary school. Table 3-1 lists them. ***Note:*** Computers use an asterisk (*) for multiplication, not the multiplication sign (×).

Table 3-1	The Simple Operators
Operator	*What It Means*
– (unary)	Take the negative of
*	Multiply
/	Divide
+	Add
– (binary)	Subtract
%	Modulo

Most of these operators are called *binary operators* because they operate on two values: one on the left side of the operator and one on the right side. The one exception is the unary negative. However, this one is just as straightforward as the others, as I show in the following example:

```
int n1 = 5;
int n2 = -n1;  // n2 now has the value -5.
```

The value of –n is the negative of the value of n.

The modulo operator may not be quite as familiar to you. Modulo is similar to the remainder after division. Thus, 5 % 3 is 2 (5 / 3 = 1, remainder 2), and 25 % 3 is 1 (25 / 3 = 8, remainder 1). Read it "five modulo three" or simply "five mod three." Even numbers mod 2 are 0: 6 % 2 = 0 (6/2 = 3, remainder 0).

The arithmetic operators other than modulo are defined for all the numeric types. The modulo operator is not defined for floating-point numbers because you have no remainder after division of floating-point values.

Operating orders

The value of some expressions may not be clear. Consider, for example, the following expression:

```
int n = 5 * 3 + 2;
```

Does the programmer mean "multiply 5 times 3 and then add 2," which is 17, or does this line mean "multiply 5 times the sum of 3 and 2," which gives you 25?

C# generally executes common operators from left to right. So, the preceding example assigns the value 17 to the variable n.

C# determines the value of n in the following example by first dividing 24 by 6 and then dividing the result of that operation by 2 (as opposed to dividing 24 by the ratio 6 over 2). The result is 2:

```
int n = 24 / 6 / 2
```

However, the various operators have a hierarchy, or order of precedence. C# scans an expression and performs the operations of higher precedence before those of lower precedence. For example, multiplication has higher precedence than addition. Many books take great pains to explain the order of precedence, but frankly, that's a complete waste of time (and brain cells).

Don't rely on yourself or someone else knowing the precedence order. Make your meaning (to human readers of the code as well as to the compiler) explicit with parentheses. (You can find the precedences in the Cheat Sheet inside the front cover if you really need to do some language-lawyering.)

The value of the following expression is clear, regardless of the operators' order of precedence:

```
int n = (7 % 3) * (4 + (6 / 3));
```

Parentheses can override the order of precedence by stating exactly how the compiler is to interpret the expression. To find the first expression to evaluate, C# looks for the innermost parentheses, dividing 6 by 3 to yield 2. The result follows:

```
int n = (7 % 3) * (4 + 2);    // 6 / 3 = 2.
```

Then C# works its way outward, evaluating each set of parentheses in turn, innermost to outermost, as follows:

```
int n = 1 * 6;    // (4 + 2) = 6.
```

So the final result, and the value of n, is 6.

The assignment operator

C# has inherited an interesting concept from C and C++: Assignment is itself a binary operator. The assignment operator has the value of the argument to the right. The assignment has the same type as both arguments, which must match.

This view of the assignment operator has no effect on the expressions you've seen so far:

```
n = 5 * 3;
```

In this example, 5 * 3 is 15 and an `int`. The assignment operator stores the `int` on the right into the `int` on the left and returns the value 15. However, this view of the assignment operator allows the following:

```
m = n = 5 * 3;
```

Assignments are evaluated in series from right to left. The right-hand assignment stores the value 15 into n and returns 15. The left-hand assignment stores 15 into m and returns 15, which is then dropped on the floor, leaving the value of each variable as 15.

This strange definition for assignment makes the following rather bizarre expressions legal:

```
int n;
int m;
n = m = 2;
```

I avoid chaining assignments because it's less clear to human readers. Anything that can confuse people reading your code (including you) is worth avoiding because confusion breeds errors.

The increment operator

Of all the additions that you may perform in programming, adding 1 to a variable is the most common, as follows:

```
n = n + 1;  // increment n by 1
```

C# extends the simple operators with a set of operators constructed from other binary operators. For example, n += 1; is equivalent to n = n + 1;.

An assignment operator exists for just about every binary operator: +=, -=, *=, /=, %=, &=, |=, ^=. Look up "C# language, operators" in Help for full details on them.

Yet even n += 1 is not good enough. C# provides this even shorter version:

```
++n;        // Increment n by 1.
```

All these forms of incrementing a number are equivalent — they all increment n by 1.

The increment operator is strange enough, but believe it or not, C# has two increment operators: ++n and n++. The first one, ++n, is called the *preincrement operator,* while n++ is the *postincrement operator.* The difference is subtle but important.

Remember that every expression has a type and a value. In the following code, both ++n and n++ are of type int:

```
int n;
n = 1;
int p = ++n;
n = 1;
int m = n++;
```

But what are the resulting values of m and p? (Hint: The choices are 1 or 2.) The value of p is 2, and the value of m is 1. That is, the value of the expression ++n is the value of n *after* being incremented, while the value of the expression n++ is the value of n *before* it is incremented. Either way, the resulting value of n itself is 2.

C# has equivalent decrement operators — n-- and --n. These work in exactly the same way as the increment operators.

Performing Logical Comparisons — Is That Logical?

C# also provides a set of logical comparison operators, as shown in Table 3-2. These operators are called *logical comparisons* because they return either a true or a false of type bool.

Table 3-2	The Logical Comparison Operators
Operator	*Operator Is True If . . .*
a == b	a has the same value as b
a > b	a is greater than b
a >= b	a is greater than or equal to b
a < b	a is less than b
a <= b	a is less than or equal to b
a != b	a is not equal to b

Here's an example that involves a logical comparison:

```
int m = 5;
int n = 6;
bool b = m > n;
```

This example assigns the value `false` to the variable b because 5 is *not* greater than 6.

The logical comparisons are defined for all numeric types, including `float`, `double`, `decimal`, and `char`. All the following statements are legal:

```
bool b;
b = 3 > 2;      // true
b = 3.0 > 2.0;  // true
b = 'a' > 'b';  // false - Alphabetically later = greater.
b = 'A' < 'a';  // true  - Upper A is less than lower a.
b = 'A' < 'b';  // true  - All upper are less than all lower.
b = 10M > 12M;  // false
```

The comparison operators always produce results of type `bool`. The comparison operators other than `==` are not valid for variables of type `string`. (Not to worry; C# offers other ways to compare `strings`.)

Comparing floating-point numbers: Is your float bigger than mine?

Comparing two floating-point values can get dicey, and you need to be careful with these comparisons. Consider the following comparison:

```
float f1;
float f2;
f1 = 10;
f2 = f1 / 3;
bool b1 = (3 * f2) == f1;  // b1 is true if (3 * f2) equals f1.
f1 = 9;
f2 = f1 / 3;
bool b2 = (3 * f2) == f1;
```

Notice that the fifth and eighth lines in the preceding example each contain first an assignment operator (=) and then a logical comparison (==). These are different animals, so don't type = when you mean ==. C# does the logical comparison and then assigns the result to the variable on the left.

The only difference between the calculations of b1 and b2 is the original value of f1. So, what are the values of b1 and b2? The value of b2 is clearly `true`: 9 / 3 is 3; 3 * 3 is 9; and 9 equals 9. Voilà!

The value of b1 is not so obvious: 10 / 3 is 3.333 . . . and 3.333 . . . * 3 is 9.999 . . . . Is 9.999 . . . equal to 10? That depends on how clever your processor and compiler are. On a Pentium or later processor, C# is not smart enough to realize that b1 should be true if the calculations are moved away from the comparison.

You can use the system absolute value method to compare f1 and f2 as follows:

```
Math.Abs(f1 - 3.0 * f2) < .00001; // Use whatever level of accuracy.
```

This calculation returns true for both cases. You can use the constant Double.Epsilon instead of .00001 to get the maximum level of accuracy. Epsilon is the smallest possible difference between two nonequal double variables.

For a self-guided tour of the System.Math class, where Abs and many other useful mathematical functions live, look for "Math" in Help.

Compounding the confusion with compound logical operations

The bool variables have another set of operators defined just for them, as shown in Table 3-3.

Table 3-3	The Compound Logical Operators
Operator	*Operator Is True If . . .*
!a	a is false (also known as the "not" operator).
a & b	a and b are true (also known as the "and" operator).
a | b	Either a or b or else both are true (also known as a **and/or** b).
a ^ b	a is true or b is true but not both (also known as **a xor b**).
a && b	a is true and b is true with short-circuit evaluation.
a || b	a is true or b is true with short-circuit evaluation. (I discuss short-circuit evaluation in the nearby text.)

The ! operator (NOT) is the logical equivalent of the minus sign. For example, !a (read "not a") is true if a is false and false if a is true. Can that be true?

The next two operators are straightforward enough. First, a & b is only true if both a and b are true. And a | b is true if either a or b is true (or both). The ^ (also known as *exclusive or — xor*) operator is sort of an odd beast. An *exclusive or* is true if either a or b is true but not if both a and b are true.

All three operators produce a logical bool value as their result.

The &, |, and ^ operators also have a *bitwise operator* version. When applied to int variables, these operators perform their magic on a bit-by-bit basis. Thus 6 & 3 is 2 (0110_2 & 0011_2 is 0010_2), 6 | 3 is 7 (0110_2 | 0011_2 is 0111_2), and 6 ^ 3 is 5 (0110_2 ^ 0011_2 is 0101_2). Binary arithmetic is really cool but beyond the scope of this book. You can Google it.

The remaining two logical operators are similar to, but subtly different from, the first three. Consider the following example:

```
bool b = (boolExpression1) & (boolExpression2);
```

In this case, C# evaluates boolExpression1 and boolExpression2. It then looks to see whether they are both true before deciding the value of b. However, this may be a wasted effort. If one expression is false, there's no reason to perform the other. Regardless of the value of the second expression, the result will be false. Nevertheless, & goes on to evaluate both expressions.

The && operator avoids evaluating both expressions unnecessarily, as shown in the following example:

```
bool b = (boolExpression1) && (boolExpression2);
```

In this case, C# evaluates boolExpression1. If it's false, then b is set to false and the program continues on its merry way. On the other hand, if boolExpression1 is true, then C# evaluates boolExpression2 and stores the result in b. The && operator uses this *short-circuit evaluation* because it short-circuits around the second Boolean expression, if necessary.

Most programmers use the doubled forms most of the time.

The || operator works the same way, as shown in the following expression:

```
bool b = (boolExpression1) || (boolExpression2);
```

If boolExpression1 is true, there's no point in evaluating boolExpression2 because the result is always true.

You can read these operators as "short-circuit and" and "short-circuit or."

Matching Expression Types at TrackDownAMate.com

In calculations, an expression's type is just as important as its value. Consider the following expression:

```
int n;
n = (5 * 5) + 7;
```

My calculator says the resulting value of n is 32. However, that expression also has an overall type based on the types of its parts.

Written in "type language," the preceding expression becomes the following:

```
int [=] (int * int) + int;
```

To evaluate the type of an expression, follow the same pattern you use to evaluate the expression's value. Multiplication takes precedence over addition. An int times an int is an int. Addition comes next. An int plus an int is an int. In this way, you can reduce the preceding expression as follows:

```
(int * int) + int
int + int
int
```

Calculating the type of an operation

Most operators come in various flavors. For example, the multiplication operator comes in the following forms (the arrow means "produces"):

```
int     * int     ⇨ int
uint    * uint    ⇨ uint
long    * long    ⇨ long
float   * float   ⇨ float
decimal * decimal ⇨ decimal
double  * double  ⇨ double
```

Thus, 2 * 3 uses the int * int version of the * operator to produce the int 6.

Implicit type conversion

Okay, that's great for multiplying two ints or two floats. But what happens when the left- and right-hand arguments are not of the same type? For example, what happens in the following case?

```
int anInt = 10;
double aDouble = 5.0;
double result = anInt * aDouble;
```

First, C# doesn't have an `int * double` operation. C# could just generate an error message and leave it at that; however, it tries to make sense out of what the programmer intended. C# does have `int * int` and `double * double` versions of multiplication. C# could convert `aDouble` into its `int` equivalent, but that would involve losing any fractional part of the number (digits to the right of the decimal point). Instead, C# converts the `int` `anInt` into a `double` and uses the `double * double` operator. This is known as an *implicit promotion*.

An implicit promotion is *implicit* because C# does it automatically, and it's a *promotion* because it involves some natural concept of uphill and downhill. The list of multiplication operators is in promotion order from `int` to `double` or from `int` to `decimal` — *from narrower type to wider type*. No implicit conversion exists between the floating-point types and `decimal`. Converting from the more capable type, such as `double`, to a less capable type, such as `int`, is known as a *demotion*.

Implicit demotions are not allowed; C# generates an error message.

Explicit type conversion — the cast

What if C# was wrong? What if the programmer really did want to perform integer multiplication?

You can change the type of any value-type variable through the use of the cast operator. A *cast* consists of the desired type contained in parentheses and placed immediately in front of the variable or expression in question.

Thus the following expression uses the `int * int` operator:

```
int anInt = 10;
double aDouble = 5.0;
int result = anInt * (int)aDouble;
```

The cast of `aDouble` to an `int` is known as an *explicit demotion* or *downcast*. The conversion is explicit because the programmer explicitly declared her intent — duh.

You can make an explicit conversion between any two value types, whether up or down the promotion ladder.

Avoid implicit type conversion. Make any changes in value-types explicit through the use of a cast.

Leave logical alone

C# offers no type conversion path to or from the bool type.

Assigning types

The same matching of types applies to the assignment operator.

Inadvertent type mismatches that generate compiler error messages usually occur in the assignment operator, not at the point of the actual mismatch.

Consider the following multiplication example:

```
int n1 = 10;
int n2 = 5.0 * n1;
```

The second line in this example generates an error message due to a type mismatch, but the error occurs *at the assignment* — not at the multiplication. Here's the horrible tale: To perform the multiplication, C# implicitly converts n1 to a double. C# can then perform double multiplication, the result of which is the all-powerful double.

The type of the right-hand and left-hand operators of the assignment operator must match, but the type of the left-hand operator cannot change. Because C# refuses to demote an expression implicitly, the compiler generates the following error message: Cannot implicitly convert type double to int.

C# allows this expression with an explicit cast, as follows:

```
int n1 = 10;
int n2 = (int)(5.0 * n1);
```

(The parentheses are necessary because the cast operator has very high precedence.) This works — *explicit* demotion is okay. The n1 is promoted to a double, the multiplication is performed, and the double result is demoted to an int. In this case, however, you'd have to worry about the sanity of the programmer because 5 * n1 is so much easier for both the programmer and the C# compiler.

Chapter 4

Getting into the Program Flow

● ●

In This Chapter

▶ Making decisions if you can

▶ Deciding what else to do

▶ Looping without going in a circle

▶ Using the while and do . . . while loops

▶ Using the for loop and understanding scope

● ●

Consider the following simple program:

```
using System;
namespace HelloWorld
{
  public class Program
  {
    // This is where the program starts.
    static void Main(string[] args)
    {
      // Prompt user to enter a name.
      Console.WriteLine("Enter your name, please:");
      // Now read the name entered.
      string name = Console.ReadLine();
      // Greet the user with the entered name.
      Console.WriteLine("Hello, " + name);
      // Wait for user to acknowledge the results.
      Console.WriteLine("Press Enter to terminate . . . ");
      Console.Read();
    }
  }
}
```

Beyond introducing you to a few fundamentals of C# programming, this program is almost worthless. It simply spits back out whatever you typed in. You can imagine more complicated example programs that take in input, perform some type of calculations, generate some type of output (otherwise why do the calculations?), and then exit at the bottom. However, even a program such as that can be of only limited use.

One of the key elements of any computer processor is its ability to make decisions. When I say "make decisions," I mean the processor sends the flow of execution down one path of instructions if a condition is true or down another path if the condition is not true. Any programming language must offer this fundamental capability to control the flow of execution.

The three basic types of *flow control* are the `if` statement, the loop, and the jump. (I describe one of the looping controls, the `foreach`, in Chapter 5.)

Branching Out with if and switch

The basis of all C# decision-making capability is the `if` statement (the basis of all my decisions is the `maybe`), as follows:

```
if (bool-expression)
{
    // Control goes here if the expression is true.
}
// Control passes to this statement whether the expression is true or not.
```

A pair of parentheses immediately following the keyword `if` contains some *conditional expression* of type `bool`. (See Chapter 3 for a discussion of `bool` expressions.) Immediately following the expression is a block of code set off by a pair of braces. If the expression is true, the program executes the code within the braces. If the expression is not true, the program skips the code in the braces. (If it does execute the code in braces, it ends up just after the closing brace and continues from there.)

The `if` statement is easier to understand with a concrete example:

```
// Make sure that a is not negative:
// If a is less than 0 . . .
if (a < 0)
{
    // . . . .then assign 0 to it so it won't be negative any longer.
    a = 0;
}
```

This segment of code makes sure that the variable a is nonnegative — greater than or equal to 0. The `if` statement says, "If a is less than 0, assign 0 to a." (In other words, turn a into a positive value.)

The braces are not required. C# treats `if(bool-expression) statement;` as if it had been written `if(bool-expression) {statement;}`. The general consensus (and my preference) is to always use braces for better clarity. In other words, don't ask — just do it.

Introducing the if statement

Consider a small program that calculates interest. The user enters the principal and the interest rate, and the program spits out the resulting value for each year. (This is not a sophisticated program.) The simplistic calculation appears as follows in C#:

```
// Calculate the value of the principal plus interest.
decimal interestPaid;
interestPaid = principal * (interest / 100);
// Now calculate the total.
decimal total = principal + interestPaid;
```

The first equation multiplies the principal `principal` times the interest `interest` to get the interest to be paid, `interestPaid`. (You divide by 100 because interest is usually input in percent.) The interest to be paid is then added back into the principal, resulting in a new principal, which is stored in the variable `total`.

The program must anticipate almost anything when dealing with human input. For example, you don't want to accept a negative principal or interest (well, maybe a negative interest . . .). The following `CalculateInterest` program includes checks to make sure that neither of these things happens:

```
// CalculateInterest - Calculate the interest amount paid
//      on a given principal. If either the principal or the
//      interest rate is negative, generate an error message.
using System;
namespace CalculateInterest
{
  public class Program
  {
    public static void Main(string[] args)
    {
      // Prompt user to enter source principal.
      Console.Write("Enter principal: ");
      string principalInput = Console.ReadLine();
      decimal principal = Convert.ToDecimal(principalInput);
      // Make sure that the principal is not negative.
      if (principal < 0)
      {
        Console.WriteLine("Principal cannot be negative");
        principal = 0;
      }
      // Enter the interest rate.
      Console.Write("Enter interest: ");
      string interestInput = Console.ReadLine();
      decimal interest = Convert.ToDecimal(interestInput);
```

```
    // Make sure that the interest is not negative either.
    if (interest < 0)
    {
      Console.WriteLine("Interest cannot be negative");
      interest = 0;
    }
    // Calculate the value of the principal plus interest.
    decimal interestPaid = principal * (interest / 100);
    // Now calculate the total.
    decimal total = principal + interestPaid;
    // Output the result.
    Console.WriteLine();  // Skip a line.
    Console.WriteLine("Principal   = " + principal);
    Console.WriteLine("Interest    = " + interest + "%");
    Console.WriteLine();
    Console.WriteLine("Interest paid = " + interestPaid);
    Console.WriteLine("Total       = " + total);
    // Wait for user to acknowledge the results.
    Console.WriteLine("Press Enter to terminate . . . ");
    Console.Read();
  }
}
}
```

The `CalculateInterest` program begins by prompting the user for his name using `WriteLine()` to write a `string` to the console. Tell the user exactly what you want. If possible, specify the format you want as well. Users don't respond well to uninformative prompts like >.

The example program uses the `ReadLine()` command to read in the user types; it returns the value entered, in the form of a `string`, when the user types Enter. Because the program is looking for the principal in the form of a `decimal`, the input `string` must be converted using the `Convert. ToDecimal()` command. The result is stored in `principalInput`.

The `ReadLine()`, `WriteLine()`, and `ToDecimal()` commands are all examples of *method calls.* A method call delegates some work to another part of the program, called a method. I describe method calls in detail in Chapter 8; these particular method calls are straightforward. You should be able to get at least the gist of the meaning using my extraordinarily insightful explanatory narrative. If that doesn't work, ignore my narrative. If that still doesn't work, skim through the beginning of Chapter 8.

The next line checks `principal`. If it's negative, the program outputs a polite nasty-gram, indicating that the user has fouled up. The program does the same thing for the interest rate. That done, the program performs the simplistic interest calculation outlined earlier and spits out the result, using a series of `WriteLine()` commands.

The program generates the following output with a legitimate principal and a usurious interest rate that is perfectly legal in most states:

```
Enter principal: 1234
Enter interest: 21

Principal    = 1234
Interest     = 21%

Interest paid = 259.14
Total         = 1493.14
Press Enter to terminate . . .
```

Executing the program with illegal input generates the following output:

```
Enter principal: 1234
Enter interest: -12.5
Interest cannot be negative

Principal    = 1234
Interest     = 0%

Interest paid = 0
Total         = 1234
Press Enter to terminate . . .
```

Indent the lines within an `if` clause to enhance readability. C# ignores such indentation, but it helps us humans. Most programming editors support auto-indenting, whereby the editor automatically indents as soon as you enter the `if` command. To set auto-indenting in Visual Studio, choose Tools➪Options. Then expand the Text Editor node. From there, expand C#. Finally, click Tabs. On this page, enable Smart Indenting and set the number of spaces per indent to your preference. (I use two spaces per indent for this book.) Set the Tab Size to the same value.

Examining the else statement

Some code must check for mutually exclusive conditions. For example, the following code segment stores the maximum of two numbers, a and b, in the variable `max`:

```
// Store the maximum of a and b into the variable max.
int max;
// If a is greater than b . . .
if (a > b)
{
    // . . .save a as the maximum.
```

```
        max = a;
    }
    // If a is less than or equal to b . . .
    if (a <= b)
    {
        //  . . .save b as the maximum.
        max = b;
    }
```

The second `if` statement is needless processing because the two conditions are mutually exclusive. If a is greater than b, then a can't possibly be less than or equal to b. C# defines an `else` clause for just this case. The `else` keyword defines a block of code that's executed if the `if` block is not.

The code segment to calculate the maximum now appears as follows:

```
// Store the maximum of a and b into the variable max.
int max;
// If a is greater than b . . .
if (a > b)
{
    //  . . .save a as the maximum; otherwise . . .
    max = a;
}
else
{
    //  . . .save b as the maximum.
    max = b;
}
```

If a is greater than b, the first block is executed; otherwise the second block is executed. In the end, max contains the greater of a or b.

Avoiding even the else

Sequences of `else` clauses can get confusing. Some programmers, myself included, like to avoid them when doing so doesn't cause even more confusion. You could write the maximum calculation like this:

```
// Store the maximum of a and b into the variable max.
int max;
// Start by assuming that a is greater than b.
max = a;
// If it is not . . .
if (b > a)
{
    // . . . then you can change your mind.
    max = b;
}
```

Some programmers avoid this style like the plague, and I can sympathize. (That doesn't mean I'm going to change; it just means I sympathize.) You see both this style and the "else style" in common use.

Programmers who like to be cool and cryptic often use the *ternary operator*, :?, equivalent to an if/else on one line:

```
bool informal = true;
string name = informal : "Chuck" ? "Charles";  // Returns "Chuck".
```

This evaluates the expression before the colon. If it's true, return the expression after the colon but before the question mark. If false, return the expression after the question mark. This turns an if/else into an expression.

Generally speaking, I advise using it only rarely, because it really *is* cryptic.

Nesting if statements

The CalculateInterest program warns the user of illegal input; however, continuing with the interest calculation, even if one of the values is illogical, doesn't seem quite right. It causes no real harm here because the interest calculation takes little or no time and the user can ignore the results, but some calculations aren't nearly so quick. In addition, why ask the user for an interest rate after she has already entered an invalid value for the principal? The user knows that the results of the calculation will be invalid no matter what she enters next. (You'd be amazed at how infuriating that can be to a user.)

The program should only ask the user for an interest rate if the principal is reasonable and only perform the interest calculation if both values are valid. To accomplish this, you need two if statements, one within the other.

An if statement found within the body of another if statement is called an *embedded* or *nested* statement.

The following program, CalculateInterestWithEmbeddedTest, uses embedded if statements to avoid stupid questions if a problem with the input is detected:

```
// CalculateInterestWithEmbeddedTest - Calculate the interest amount
//     paid on a given principal. If either the principal or the
//     interest rate is negative, then generate an error message
//     and don't proceed with the calculation.
using System;
namespace CalculateInterestWithEmbeddedTest
{
  public class Program
```

```csharp
{
  public static void Main(string[] args)
  {
    // Define a maximum interest rate.
    int maximumInterest = 50;
    // Prompt user to enter source principal.
    Console.Write("Enter principal: ");
    string principalInput = Console.ReadLine();
    decimal principal = Convert.ToDecimal(principalInput);
    // If the principal is negative . . .
    if (principal < 0)
    {
      // . . . generate an error message . . .
      Console.WriteLine("Principal cannot be negative");
    }
    else  // Go here only if principal was > 0: thus valid.
    {
      // . . . otherwise, enter the interest rate.
      Console.Write("Enter interest: ");
      string interestInput = Console.ReadLine();
      decimal interest = Convert.ToDecimal(interestInput);
      // If the interest is negative or too large . . .
      if (interest < 0 || interest > maximumInterest)
      {
        // . . . generate an error message as well.
        Console.WriteLine("Interest cannot be negative " +
                          "or greater than " + maximumInterest);
        interest = 0;
      }
      else  // Reach this point only if all's well.
      {
        // Both the principal and the interest appear to be legal;
        // calculate the value of the principal plus interest.
        decimal interestPaid;
        interestPaid = principal * (interest / 100);
        // Now calculate the total.
        decimal total = principal + interestPaid;
        // Output the result.
        Console.WriteLine();  // Skip a line.
        Console.WriteLine("Principal     = " + principal);
        Console.WriteLine("Interest      = " + interest + "%");
        Console.WriteLine();
        Console.WriteLine("Interest paid = " + interestPaid);
        Console.WriteLine("Total         = " + total);
      }
    }
    // Wait for user to acknowledge the results.
    Console.WriteLine("Press Enter to terminate . . . ");
    Console.Read();
  }
}
}
```

The program first reads the principal from the user. If the principal is negative, the program outputs an error message and quits. If the principal is not negative, control passes to the else clause, where the program continues executing.

The interest rate test has been improved in this sample. Here, the program requires an interest rate that's nonnegative (a mathematical law) and less than some maximum (a judiciary law — we can only wish that credit cards had an interest rate limit). This if statement uses the following compound test:

```
if (interest < 0 || interest > maximumInterest)
```

This statement is true if interest is less than 0 or greater than maximumInterest. Notice that I declare maximumInterest at the top of the program rather than *hard-code* it as a constant number here.

Define important constants at the top of your program. Giving constants a name is more descriptive than just the number. It makes the constant easy to find and easier to change. If the constant appears ten times in your code, you still have to make only one change to change them all. Chapter 7 has more to say about using constants.

Entering a correct principal but a negative interest rate generates the following output:

```
Enter principal: 1234
Enter interest: -12.5
Interest cannot be negative or greater than 50.
Press Enter to terminate . . .
```

Only when the user enters both a legal principal and a legal interest rate does the program generate the desired calculation, as follows:

```
Enter principal: 1234
Enter interest: 12.5

Principal    = 1234
Interest     = 12.5%

Interest paid = 154.250
Total        = 1388.250
Press Enter to terminate . . .
```

Running the switchboard

You often want to test a variable for numerous different values. For example, maritalStatus may be 0 for unmarried, 1 for married, 2 for divorced, 3 for widowed (I think I got them all — oh, wait), or 4 for none of your business. To differentiate among these values, you could use the following series of `if` statements:

```
if (maritalStatus == 0)
{
  // Must be unmarried . . .
  //  . . .do something . . .
}
else
{
  if (maritalStatus == 1)
  {
    // Must be married . . .
    //  . . .do something else . . .
```

And so on.

You can see that these repetitive `if` statements get old quickly. Testing for multiple cases is such a common occurrence that C# provides a special construct to decide between a set of mutually exclusive conditions. This control is called the `switch`, and it works as follows:

```
switch(maritalStatus)
{
  case 0:
          //  . . .do the unmarried stuff . . .
          break;
  case 1:
          //  . . .do the married stuff . . .
          break;
  case 2:
          //  . . .do the divorced stuff . . .
          break;
  case 3:
          //  . . .do the widowed stuff . . .
          break;
  case 4:
          //  . . .get out of my face . . .
          break;
  default:
          // Goes here if doesn't pass any of the cases;
          // this is probably an error condition.
          break;
}
```

The expression at the top of the `switch` statement is evaluated. In this case, the expression is simply the variable `maritalStatus`. The value of that expression is then compared against the value of each of the cases. Control passes to the `default` clause if no match is found.

The argument to the `switch` statement can also be a `string`, as follows:

```
string s = "Davis";
switch(s)
{
  case "Davis":
          // . . .control will actually pass here . . .
          break;
  case "Smith":
          // . . .do Smith stuff . . .
          break;
  case "Jones":
          // . . .do Jones stuff . . .
          break;
  case "Hvidsten":
          // . . .do Hvidsten stuff . . .
          break;
  default:
          // Goes here if doesn't pass any of the cases.
          break;
}
```

Using the `switch` statement involves the following severe restrictions:

✔ The argument to the `switch()` must be one of the counting types (including `char`) or a `string`. Floating-point values are excluded.

✔ The various `case` values must refer to values of the same type as the `switch` expression.

✔ The `case` values must be constant in the sense that their value must be known at compile time. (A statement such as `case x` is not legal unless x is some type of constant.)

✔ Each clause must end in a `break` statement (or some other exit command that you haven't seen yet, such as `return`). The `break` statement passes control out of the `switch`.

You can omit a break statement if two cases lead to the same actions: A single `case` clause may have more than one `case` label, as in the following example:

```
string s = "Davis";
switch(s)
{
    case "Davis":
    case "Hvidsten":
```

```
                // Do the same thing whether s is Davis or Hvidsten
                // since they're related.
                   break;
        case "Smith":
                // . . .do Smith stuff . . .
                   break;
        default:
                // Goes here if doesn't pass any of the cases.
                   break;
    }
```

This approach enables the program to perform the same operation, whether the input is Davis or Hvidsten. The `SwitchSyntaxTest` example on the Web site illustrates a variety of advice about using `switch`. The final section of this chapter supplies a small addendum to the `switch` story.

Here We Go Loop the Loop

The `if` statement enables a program to take a different path through the code being executed depending on the results of a `bool` expression. This statement allows drastically more interesting programs than a program without decision-making capability. Adding the ability to execute a set of instructions *repeatedly* adds another quantum jump in capability.

Consider the `CalculateInterest` program from the section "Introducing the if statement," earlier in this chapter. Performing this simple interest calculation with a calculator (or by hand with a piece of paper) would be much easier than writing and executing a program.

What if you could calculate the amount of principal for each of several succeeding years? That would be a lot more useful. A simple macro in a Microsoft Excel spreadsheet would still be easier, but at least you're getting closer.

What you need is a way for the computer to execute the same short sequence of instructions multiple times. This is known as a *loop*.

Looping for a while

The C# keyword `while` introduces the most basic form of execution loop, as follows:

```
while(bool-expression)
{
    // . . .repeatedly executed as long as the expression is true.
}
```

When the `while` loop is first encountered, the `bool` expression is evaluated. If the expression is true, the code within the block is executed. When the block of code reaches the closed brace, control returns to the top, and the whole process starts over again. (It's kind of the way I feel when I'm walking the dog. He and I loop around and around the yard until he . . . well, until we're finished.) Control passes beyond the closed brace the first time the `bool` expression is evaluated and turns out to be false.

If the condition is not true the first time the `while` loop is encountered, the set of commands within the braces is never executed.

Programmers often get sloppy in their speech. (Programmers are sloppy most of the time.) A programmer may say that a loop is executed until some condition is false. To me, that implies that control passes outside the loop — no matter where the program happens to be executing — as soon as the condition becomes false. This is definitely not the case. The program does not check whether the condition is still true until control specifically passes back to the top of the loop.

You can use the `while` loop to create the `CalculateInterestTable` program, a looping version of the `CalculateInterest` program. `CalculateInterestTable`, as follows, calculates a table of principals showing accumulated annual payments:

```
// CalculateInterestTable - Calculate the interest paid on a given
//      principal over a period of years.
using System;
namespace CalculateInterestTable
{
  using System;
  public class Program
    {
    public static void Main(string[] args)
    {
      // Define a maximum interest rate.
      int maximumInterest = 50;
      // Prompt user to enter source principal.
      Console.Write("Enter principal: ");
      string principalInput = Console.ReadLine();
      decimal principal = Convert.ToDecimal(principalInput);
      // If the principal is negative . . .
      if (principal < 0)
      {
        // . . . generate an error message . . .
        Console.WriteLine("Principal cannot be negative");
      }
      else  // Go here only if principal was > 0: thus valid.
      {
        // . . . otherwise, enter the interest rate.
        Console.Write("Enter interest: ");
```

```
        string interestInput = Console.ReadLine();
        decimal interest = Convert.ToDecimal(interestInput);
        // If the interest is negative or too large . . .
        if (interest < 0 || interest > maximumInterest)
        {
            // . . . generate an error message as well.
            Console.WriteLine("Interest cannot be negative " +
                              "or greater than " + maximumInterest);
            interest = 0;
        }
        else  // Reach this point only if all's well.
        {
            // Both the principal and the interest appear to be
            // legal; finally, input the number of years.
            Console.Write("Enter number of years: ");
            string durationInput = Console.ReadLine();
            int duration = Convert.ToInt32(durationInput);
            // Verify the input.
            Console.WriteLine();  // Skip a line.
            Console.WriteLine("Principal    = " + principal);
            Console.WriteLine("Interest     = " + interest + "%");
            Console.WriteLine("Duration     = " + duration + " years");
            Console.WriteLine();

            // Now loop through the specified number of years.
            int year = 1;
            while(year <= duration)
            {
                // Calculate the value of the principal plus interest.
                decimal interestPaid;
                interestPaid = principal * (interest / 100);
                // Now calculate the new principal by adding
                // the interest to the previous principal.
                principal = principal + interestPaid;
                // Round off the principal to the nearest cent.
                principal = decimal.Round(principal, 2);
                // Output the result.
                Console.WriteLine(year + "-" + principal);
                // Skip over to next year.
                year = year + 1;
            }
        }
    }
    // Wait for user to acknowledge the results.
    Console.WriteLine("\nPress Enter to terminate . . . ");
    Console.Read();
    }
  }
}
```

The output from a trial run of `CalculateInterestTable` appears as follows:

```
Enter principal: 1234
Enter interest: 12.5
Enter number of years: 10

Principal    = 1234
Interest     = 12.5%
Duration     = 10 years

1-1388.25
2-1561.78
3-1757.00
4-1976.62
5-2223.70
6-2501.66
7-2814.37
8-3166.17
9-3561.94
10-4007.18

Press Enter to terminate . . .
```

Each value represents the total principal after the number of years elapsed, assuming simple interest compounded annually. For example, the value of $1,234 at 12.5 percent is $3,561.94 after nine years.

Most of the values show two decimal places for the cents in the amount. Because trailing zeros are not displayed in some versions of C#, some values may show only a single digit — or even no digit — after the decimal point. Thus, $12.70 may be displayed as `12.7`. If so, you can fix this by using the special formatting characters described in Chapter 6. (C# 2.0 and later appear to show trailing zeros by default.)

The `CalculateInterestTable` program begins by reading the principal and interest values from the user and checking to make sure that they're valid. `CalculateInterestTable` then reads the number of years over which to iterate, and stores this value in the variable `duration`.

Before entering the `while` loop, the program declares a variable `year`, which it initializes to 1. This will be the "current year" — that is, this number changes "each year" as the program loops. If the year number contained in `year` is less than the total duration contained in `duration`, the principal for "this year" is recalculated by calculating the interest based on the "previous year." The calculated principal is output along with the current-year offset.

The statement `decimal.Round()` rounds the calculated value to the nearest fraction of a cent.

The key to the program lies in the last line within the block. The statement `year = year + 1;` increments `year` by 1. If `year` begins with the value 3, its value will be 4 after this expression. This incrementing moves the calculations along from one year to the next.

After the year has been incremented, control returns to the top of the loop, where the value `year` is compared to the requested duration. In the example run, if the current year is less than 10, the calculation continues. After being incremented 10 times, the value of `year` becomes 11, which is greater than 10, and program control passes to the first statement after the `while` loop. That is to say, the program stops looping.

Most looping commands follow this same basic principle of incrementing a counter until it exceeds a previously defined value.

The counting variable `year` in `CalculateInterestTable` must be declared and initialized before the `while` loop in which it is used. In addition, the `year` variable must be incremented, usually as the last statement within the loop. As this example demonstrates, you have to look ahead to see what variables you will need. This pattern is easier after you've written a few thousand `while` loops, like I have.

When writing `while` loops, don't forget to increment the counting variable, as I did in this example:

```
int nYear = 1;
while (nYear < 10)
{
    // . . .whatever . . .
}
```

(I left off the `year = year + 1;`.) Without the increment, `year` is always 1, and the program loops forever. This is called an *infinite loop*. The only way to exit an infinite loop is to terminate the program (or reboot). (I guess nothing is truly infinite, with the possible exception of a particle passing through the event horizon of a black hole.)

Make sure that the terminating condition can be satisfied. Usually, this means your counting variable is being incremented properly. Otherwise you're looking at an infinite loop, an angry user, bad press, and 50 years of drought.

Infinite loops are a common mistake, so don't get embarrassed when you get caught in one.

Doing the do . . . while loop

A variation of the `while` loop is the `do . . . while` loop. In this case, shown as follows, the condition is not checked until the *end* of the loop:

```
int year = 1;
do
{
    //  . . .some calculation . . .
    year = year + 1;
} while (year < duration);
```

In contrast to the while loop, the do . . . while loop is executed at least once, regardless of the value of duration.

Breaking up is easy to do

You can use two special commands to bail out of a loop: break and continue. Executing the break command causes control to pass to the first expression immediately following the loop. The similar continue command passes control straight back up to the conditional expression at the top of the loop to start over and get it right this time.

I have rarely used continue in my programming career, and I doubt that many programmers even remember that it exists. Don't forget about it completely because it may be a trick question in an interview or crossword puzzle.

For example, suppose you want to take your money out of the bank as soon as the principal exceeds a certain number of times the original amount, irrespective of how many years' duration. (After all, how much money do you really need?) You could easily accommodate this by adding the following code within the loop:

```
if (principal > (maxPower * originalPrincipal))
{
    break;
}
```

Anyone who watches *The Simpsons* as much as I do knows who maxPower is. (Hint: *D'oh!*)

The break clause is not executed until the condition within the if comparison is true — in this case, until the calculated principal is maxPower times the original principal or more. Executing the break statement passes control outside of the while(year <= duration) statement, and the program resumes execution immediately after the loop.

For a version of the interest table program with this addition, see the CalculateInterestTableWithBreak program on the Web site. (I don't include the listing here, for brevity's sake.)

An example of output from this program looks like this:

```
Enter principal: 100
Enter interest: 25
Enter number of years: 100

Principal    = 100
Interest     = 25%
Duration     = 100 years
Quit if a multiplier of 10 is reached

1-125.00
2-156.25
3-195.31
4-244.14
5-305.18
6-381.48
7-476.85
8-596.06
9-745.08
10-931.35
11-1164.19
Press Enter to terminate . . .
```

The program terminates as soon as the calculated principal exceeds $1,000 —
thank goodness, you didn't have to wait 100 years!

Looping until you get it right

The `CalculateInterestTable` program is smart enough to terminate in
the event that the user enters an invalid balance or interest amount. However,
jumping immediately out of the program just because the user mistypes
something seems a little harsh. Even my user-unfriendly accounting program
gives me three chances to get my password right before it gives up.

A combination of `while` and `break` enables the program to be a little more
flexible. The `CalculateInterestTableMoreForgiving` program demonstrates the principle as follows:

```
// CalculateInterestTableMoreForgiving - Calculate the interest paid on a
//    given principal over a period of years. This version gives the user
//    multiple chances to input the legal principal and interest.
using System;
namespace CalculateInterestTableMoreForgiving
{
  using System;
  public class Program
  {
    public static void Main(string[] args)
    {
```

```
// Define a maximum interest rate.
int maximumInterest = 50;
// Prompt user to enter source principal; keep prompting
// until you get the correct value.
decimal principal;
while(true)
{
  Console.Write("Enter principal: ");
  string principalInput = Console.ReadLine();
  principal = Convert.ToDecimal(principalInput);
  // Exit if the value entered is correct.
  if (principal >= 0)
  {
    break;
  }
  // Generate an error on incorrect input.
  Console.WriteLine("Principal cannot be negative");
  Console.WriteLine("Try again");
  Console.WriteLine();
}
// Now enter the interest rate.
decimal interest;
while(true)
{
  Console.Write("Enter interest: ");
  string interestInput = Console.ReadLine();
  interest = Convert.ToDecimal(interestInput);
  // Don't accept interest that is negative or too large . . .
  if (interest >= 0 && interest <= maximumInterest)
  {
    break;
  }
  //  . . . generate an error message as well.
  Console.WriteLine("Interest cannot be negative " +
                    "or greater than " + maximumInterest);
  Console.WriteLine("Try again");
  Console.WriteLine();
}
// Both the principal and the interest appear to be
// legal; finally, input the number of years.
Console.Write("Enter number of years: ");
string durationInput = Console.ReadLine();
int duration = Convert.ToInt32(durationInput);
// Verify the input.
Console.WriteLine();  // Skip a line.
Console.WriteLine("Principal    = " + principal);
Console.WriteLine("Interest     = " + interest + "%");
Console.WriteLine("Duration     = " + duration + " years");
Console.WriteLine();
// Now loop through the specified number of years.
int year = 1;
while(year <= duration)
{
  // Calculate the value of the principal plus interest.
```

```
        decimal interestPaid;
        interestPaid = principal * (interest / 100);
        // Now calculate the new principal by adding
        // the interest to the previous principal.
        principal = principal + interestPaid;
        // Round off the principal to the nearest cent.
        principal = decimal.Round(principal, 2);
        // Output the result.
        Console.WriteLine(year + "-" + principal);
        // Skip over to next year.
        year = year + 1;
      }
      // Wait for user to acknowledge the results.
      Console.WriteLine("Press Enter to terminate . . . ");
      Console.Read();
    }
  }
}
```

This program works largely the same way as do the previous examples,
except in the area of the user input. This time, a `while` loop replaces the `if`
statement used in previous examples to detect invalid input:

```
decimal principal;
while(true)
{
  Console.Write("Enter principal: ");
  string principalInput = Console.ReadLine();
  principal = Convert.ToDecimal(principalInput);
  // Exit when the value entered is correct.
  if (principal >= 0)
  {
    break;
  }
  // Generate an error on incorrect input.
  Console.WriteLine("Principal cannot be negative");
  Console.WriteLine("Try again");
  Console.WriteLine();
}
```

This section of code inputs a value from the user within a loop. If the value of
the text is okay, the program exits the input loop and continues. However, if
the input has an error, the user is presented with an error message, and control passes back to start over.

Think about it this way: The program continues to loop until the user gets it
right. In the worst case, it could loop until a really obtuse user dies of old age.

Notice that the conditionals have been reversed because the question is no
longer whether illegal input should generate an error message, but whether
the correct input should exit the loop. In the interest section, for example,
consider the following test:

```
principal < 0 || principal > maximumInterest
```

This test changes to the following:

```
interest >= 0 && interest <= maximumInterest
```

Clearly, `interest >= 0` is the opposite of `interest < 0`. What may not be so obvious is that the OR (`||`) operator is replaced with an AND (`&&`) operator. This says, "Exit the loop if the interest is greater than zero AND less than the maximum amount (in other words, is correct)."

By the way, how could you revise `CalculateInterestTableMoreForgiving` to let the user run calculation after calculation, entering new principal and interest figures each time until she wanted to quit? Hint: Use another `while(true)` loop with its own exit condition.

One last point to note: The `principal` variable must be declared outside of the loop due to scope rules, which I explain in the next section of this chapter.

It may sound obvious, but the expression `true` evaluates to `true`. Therefore, `while(true)` is your archetypical infinite loop. It is the embedded `break` command that exits the loop. Therefore, if you use the `while(true)` loop, make sure that your break condition can occur.

The output from an example execution of this program (showing my ignorance) appears as follows:

```
Enter principal: -1000
Principal cannot be negative
Try again

Enter principal: 1000
Enter interest: -10
Interest cannot be negative or greater than 50
Try again

Enter interest: 10
Enter number of years: 5

Principal    = 1000
Interest     = 10%
Duration     = 5 years

1-1100.0
2-1210.00
3-1331.00
4-1464.10
5-1610.51
Press Enter to terminate . . .
```

The program refuses to accept a negative principal or interest, patiently explaining the mistake on each loop.

Explain exactly what the user did wrong before looping back for further input. Showing an example may also help, especially for formatting problems. A little diplomacy can't hurt, either, as Grandma may have pointed out.

Focusing on scope rules

A variable declared within the body of a loop is *only defined within* that loop. Consider the following code snippet:

```
int days = 1;
while(days < duration)
{
    int average = value / days;
    //  . . .some series of commands . . .
    days = days + 1;
}
```

The variable `average` is not defined outside the `while` loop. Various reasons for this exist, but consider this one: The first time the loop executes, the program encounters the declaration `int average` and the variable is defined. On the second loop, the program again encounters the declaration for `average`, and were it not for the scope rules, this would be an error because the variable is already defined.

I could provide other, more convincing reasons than this one, but this should do for now.

Suffice it to say that the variable `average` goes away, as far as C# is concerned, as soon as the program reaches the closed brace — and gets redefined each time through the loop.

Experienced programmers say that the *scope* of the variable `average` is limited to the `while` loop.

Looping a Specified Number of Times with for

The `while` loop is the simplest and second most commonly used looping structure in C#. Compared to the `for` loop, however, the `while` loop is used about as often as metric tools in an American machine shop.

The `for` loop has the following structure:

```
for(initExpression; condition; incrementExpression)
{
    // . . .body of code . . .
}
```

When the `for` loop is encountered, the program first executes the `initExpression` expression. It then executes the `condition`. If the condition expression is true, the program executes the body of the loop, which is surrounded by the braces immediately following the `for` command. When the program reaches the closed brace, control passes to `incrementExpression` and then back to `condition`, where the next pass through the loop begins.

In fact, the definition of a `for` loop can be converted into the following `while` loop:

```
initExpression;
while(condition)
{
    // . . .body of code . . .
    incrementExpression;
}
```

An example

You can better see how the `for` loop works with the following example:

```
// Here is some C# expression or other.
a = 1;
// Now loop for awhile.
for(int year = 1; year < duration; year = year + 1)
{
    // . . .body of code . . .
}
// The program continues here.
a = 2;
```

Assume that the program has just executed the `a = 1;` expression. Next, the program declares the variable `year` and initializes it to 1. That done, the program compares `year` to `duration`. If `year` is less than `duration`, the body of code within the braces is executed. Upon encountering the closed brace, the program jumps back to the top and executes the `year = year + 1` clause before sliding back over to the `year < duration` comparison.

The `year` variable is undefined outside the scope of the `for` loop. The loop's scope includes the loop's heading as well as its body.

Why do you need another loop?

Why do you need the for loop if C# has an equivalent while loop? The short answer is that you don't — the for loop doesn't bring anything to the table that the while loop can't already do.

However, the sections of the for loop exist for convenience — and to clearly establish the three parts that every loop should have: the setup, exit criteria, and increment. Not only is this easier to read, but it's also easier to get right. (Remember that the most common mistakes in a while loop are forgetting to increment the counting variable and failing to provide the proper exit criteria.)

Beyond any sort of song-and-dance justification that I may make, the most important reason to understand the for loop is that it's the loop that everyone uses — and it (along with its cousin, foreach) is the one you'll see 90 percent of the time when you're reading other people's code.

The for loop is designed so the first expression initializes a counting variable and the last section increments it; however, the C# language does not enforce any such rule. You can do anything you want in these two sections — however, you would be ill-advised to do anything *but* initialize and increment the counting variable.

The increment operator is particularly popular when writing for loops. (I describe the increment operator along with other operators in Chapter 3.) The previous for loop is usually written as follows:

```
for(int year = 1; year < nDuration; year++)
{
    // . . .body of code . . .
}
```

You almost always see the postincrement operator used in a for loop instead of the preincrement operator, although the effect in this case is the same. There's no reason other than habit and the fact that it looks cooler. (Next time you want to break the ice, just haul out your C# listing full of postincrement operators to show how cool you really are. It almost never works, but it's worth a try.)

The for loop has one variation that I really can't claim to understand. If the logical condition expression is missing, it is assumed to be true. Thus for(;;) is an infinite loop.

You will see for(;;) used as an infinite loop more often than while(true). I have no idea why that's the case.

Nesting Loops

An inner loop can appear within an outer loop, as follows:

```
for( . . .some condition . . .)
{
  for( . . .some other condition . . .)
  {
    // . . .do whatever . . .
  }
}
```

The inner loop is executed to completion upon each pass through the outer loop. The loop variable (such as `year`) used in the inner `for` loop is not defined outside the inner loop's scope.

A loop contained within another loop is called a *nested* loop. Nested loops cannot "cross." For example, the following is not possible:

```
do              // Start a do..while loop.
{
  for( . . .)   // Start some for loop.
  {
  } while( . . .)  // End do..while loop.
}               // End for loop.
```

I'm not even sure what that would mean, but that doesn't matter because the compiler will tell you it's not legal anyway.

A `break` statement within a nested loop breaks out of the inner loop only. In the following example, the `break` statement exits loop B and goes back into loop A:

```
// for loop A
for( . . .some condition . . .)
{
  // for loop B
  for( . . .some other condition . . .)
  {
    // . . .do whatever . . .
    if (something is true)
    {
      break;        // Breaks out of loop B and not A.
    }
  }
}
```

C# doesn't have a `break` command that exits both loops simultaneously.

That's not as big a limitation as it sounds. In practice, the often-complex logic contained within such nested loops is better encapsulated in a method. Executing a `return` from within any of the loops exits the method — thereby bailing out of all loops, no matter how nested they may be. I describe methods and the `return` statement in Chapter 8.

The `DisplayXWithNestedLoops` example (not shown here) illustrates nesting one loop inside another to do some primitive drawing on the screen.

Don't goto Pieces

You can transfer control in an unstructured fashion by using the `goto` statement. The `goto` statement is followed by one of these items:

- ✔ A label
- ✔ A `case` in a `switch` statement
- ✔ The keyword `default`, meaning the default clause of a `switch` statement

The idea of the latter two items is to "jump" from one case to another.

The following snippet demonstrates how the `goto` statement is used:

```
// If the condition is true . . .
if (a > b)
{
  // . . .control passes unconditionally from the goto to the label.
  goto exitLabel;
}
//  . . .whatever other code goes here . . .
exitLabel:
  // Control continues here.
```

The `goto` statement is unpopular for the very reason that makes it such a powerful control: It is almost completely unstructured. Tracking the flow of control through anything larger than a trivial piece of code can be difficult if you use `goto`. (Can you say, "spaghetti code"?)

Religious wars have sprung up over the use of the `goto` statement. In fact, the C# language itself has been criticized for the very inclusion of the control. Actually, `goto` is neither all that horrible nor necessary. Because you can almost always avoid using `goto`, I recommend staying away from it, other than *occasionally* using it to link two cases within a `switch` statement, like this:

```
switch(n)  // This example gets a bit gnarly in the logic department . . .
{
  case 0:
    // Do something for the 0 case, then  . . .
    goto 3;  // Jump to another case; no break statement needed.
  case 1:
    // Do something for the 1 case.
    break;
  case 3:    // Case 0 jumps to here after doing its thing.
    // Add some case 3 stuff to what case 0 did, thus "chaining" the cases.
    break;
  default:
    // Default case.
    break;
}
```

Don't get addicted to `goto`, though. Really.

Chapter 5

Lining Up Your Ducks with Collections

In This Chapter

▶ Creating variables that contain multiple items of data: Arrays

▶ Going arrays one better with flexible "collections"

▶ New features: Array and collection initializers, and set-type collections

Simple one-value variables of the sort you've encountered in this book so far fall a bit short when it comes to dealing with lots of things of the same kind: ten ducks instead of just one. C# fills the gap with two kinds of variable that store multiple items: generally called "collections." The two species of collection are the *array* and the more general purpose *collection class*. Usually if I mean array I'll say so, and if I mean collection class, I'll just call it that. If I refer to a *collection* or a *list* I usually mean it could be either.

An array is a data type that holds a list of items, all of which must be of the same type: all `int`s, all `double`s, and so on.

C# gives you quite a collection of collection classes, and they come in various *shapes*, such as flexible *lists* (like strings of beads), *queues* (like the line to buy your *Spider-Man XII* tickets), *stacks* (like the semi-stack of junk on my desk), and more. Most collection classes are like arrays in that they can hold just apples, or just oranges. But C# also gives you a few that can hold both apples and oranges at once — which is useful only on rare occasions (and there are much better ways to manage the feat than these elderly collections).

For now, if you can master the array and the `List` collection (although this chapter does introduce two other kinds of collections), you'll do fine for most of the book. But do circle back later to pump up your collection repertoire.

The C# Array

Variables that contain single values are plenty useful. Even class structures that can describe compound objects made up of parts (like a vehicle with its engine and transmission) are critical. But you also need a construct for holding a bunch of objects, such as Bill Gates's extensive collection of vintage cars, or mine of vintage socks. The built-in class Array is a structure that can contain a series of elements of the same type (all int values, all double values, and so on, or all Vehicle objects, Motor objects, and so on — you meet these latter sorts of objects in Chapter 7).

The argument for the array

Consider the problem of averaging a set of six floating-point numbers. Each of the six numbers requires its own double storage, as follows:

```
double d0 = 5;
double d1 = 2;
double d2 = 7;
double d3 = 3.5;
double d4 = 6.5;
double d5 = 8;
```

(Averaging int variables could result in rounding errors, as described in Chapter 2.)

Computing the average of those variables might look like this:

```
double sum = d0 + d1 + d2 + d3 + d4 + d5;
double average = sum / 6;
```

Listing each element by name is tedious. Okay, maybe it's not so tedious when you have only 6 numbers to average, but imagine averaging 600 (or even 6,000,000) floating-point values.

The fixed-value array

Fortunately, you don't need to name each element separately. C# provides the array structure that can store a sequence of values. Using an array, you can put all your doubles into one variable as follows:

```
double[] doublesArray = {5, 2, 7, 3.5, 6.5, 8, 1, 9, 1, 3};
```

(You can also declare an empty array without initializing it, like this . . :

```
double[] doublesArray = new double[6];
```

... which allocates space for six `doubles` but doesn't initialize them.)

The `Array` class, on which all C# arrays are based, provides a special syntax that makes it more convenient to use. The paired brackets `[]` refer to the way you access individual elements in the array, as follows:

```
doublesArray[0] // Corresponds to d0 (that is, 5).
doublesArray[1] // Corresponds to d1 (that is, 2).
. . .
```

The 0th element of the array corresponds to d0, the 1th element to d1, the '2th' element to d2, and so on. It's common to refer to the 0th element as "`doublesArray` sub-0," the 1st element as "`doublesArray` sub-1," and so on.

The array's element numbers — 0, 1, 2, . . . — are known as the *index.*

In C#, the array index starts at 0 and not at 1. Therefore, you typically don't refer to the element at index 1 as the first element but the "oneth element" or the "element at index 1." *The first element is the zeroth element.* If you insist on using normal speech, just be aware that the first element is always at index 0 and the second element is at index 1. You Visual Basic types take note.

The `doublesArray` variable wouldn't be much of an improvement, were it not for the fact that the index of the array can be a variable. Using a `for` loop is easier than writing each element out by hand, as the following program demonstrates:

```
// FixedArrayAverage - Average a fixed array of numbers using a loop.
namespace FixedArrayAverage
{
  using System;
  public class Program
  {
    public static void Main(string[] args)
    {
      double[] doublesArray = {5, 2, 7, 3.5, 6.5, 8, 1, 9, 1, 3};
      // Accumulate the values in the array into the variable sum.
      double sum = 0;
      for (int i = 0; i < 10; i++)
      {
        sum = sum + doublesArray[i];
      }
      // Now calculate the average.
      double average = sum / 10;
```

```
        Console.WriteLine(average);
        Console.WriteLine("Press Enter to terminate...");
        Console.Read();
      }
    }
  }
```

The program begins by initializing a variable sum to 0. Then it loops through the values stored in doublesArray, adding each one to sum. By the end of the loop, sum has accumulated the sum of all the values in the array. The resulting sum is divided by the number of elements to create the average. The output from executing this program is the expected 4.6. (You can check it with your calculator.)

The variable-length array

The array used in the example program FixedArrayAverage suffers from the following two serious problems:

- The size of the array is fixed at ten elements.
- Worse yet, the elements' values are specified directly in the program.

A program that could read in a variable number of values, perhaps determined by the user during execution, would be much more flexible. It would work not only for the ten values specified in FixedArrayAverage, but also for any other set of values, regardless of their number.

The format for declaring a variable-sized array differs slightly from that of a fixed-size, fixed-value array, as follows:

```
double[] doublesArrayVariable = new double[N];   // Variable, versus ...
double[] doublesArrayFixed = new double[10];      // Fixed.
```

Here, N represents the number of elements to allocate.

The updated program VariableArrayAverage enables the user to specify the number of values to enter. (N has to come from somewhere.) Because the program retains the values entered, not only does it calculate the average, it also displays the results in a pleasant format, as shown here:

```
// VariableArrayAverage - Average an array whose size is
//    determined by the user at run time, accumulating the values
//    in an array. Allows them to be referenced as often as
//    desired. In this case, the array creates an attractive output.
namespace VariableArrayAverage
{
  using System;
  public class Program
  {
    public static void Main(string[] args)
    {
      // First read in the number of doubles the user intends to enter.
      Console.Write("Enter the number of values to average: ");
      string numElementsInput = Console.ReadLine();
      int numElements = Convert.ToInt32(numElementsInput);
      Console.WriteLine();
      // Now declare an array of that size.
      double[] doublesArray = new double[numElements]; // Here's our 'N'.
      // Accumulate the values into an array.
      for (int i = 0; i < numElements; i++)
      {
        // Prompt the user for another double.
        Console.Write("enter double #" + (i + 1) + ": ");
        string val = Console.ReadLine();
        double value = Convert.ToDouble(val);
        // Add this to the array using brackets notation.
        doublesArray[i] = value;
      }
      // Accumulate 'numElements' values from
      // The array in the variable sum.
      double sum = 0;
      for (int i = 0; i < numElements; i++)
      {
        sum = sum + doublesArray[i];
      }

      // Now calculate the average.
      double average = sum / numElements;
      // Output the results in an attractive format.
      Console.WriteLine();
      Console.Write(average + " is the average of (" + doublesArray[0]);
      for (int i = 1; i < numElements; i++)
      {
        Console.Write(" + " + doublesArray[i]);
      }
      Console.WriteLine(") / " + numElements);
      // Wait for user to acknowledge the results.
      Console.WriteLine("Press Enter to terminate...");
      Console.Read();
    }
  }
}
```

Checking array bounds

Fortunately, the `FixedArrayAverage` program (in the section "The fixed-value array") loops through all ten elements. But what if you goofed and didn't iterate through the loop properly? (*Iterate* means looping through the array one element at a time, as with a `for` loop.) You have the following two cases to consider:

What if you had only iterated through nine elements? C# would not have considered this an error. If you want to read nine elements of a ten-element array, who is C# to say any differently? Of course, the average would be incorrect, but the program wouldn't know that.

What if you had iterated through 11 (or more) elements? *Now* C# cares a lot. C# does not allow you to index beyond the end of an array, for fear that you will overwrite some important value

in memory. To test this, change the comparison in `FixedArrayAverage`'s `for` loop to the following, replacing the value 10 with 11 in the comparison, like this:

```
for(int i = 0; i < 11; i++)
```

When you execute the program, you get a dialog box with the following error message:

```
IndexOutOfRangeException was unhandled
Index was outside the bounds of the array.
```

At first glance, this error message seems imposing. However, you can get the gist rather quickly: Clearly, the `IndexOutOfRangeException` tells you that the program tried to access an array beyond the end of its *range* — accessing element 11 in a 10-element array. (In Bonus Chapter 6 on the Web site, I show you how to learn more about that error.)

Look at the following output of a sample run in which you enter five sequential values, 1 through 5, and the program calculates the average to be 3:

```
Enter the number of values to average:5

enter double #1: 1
enter double #2: 2
enter double #3: 3
enter double #4: 4
enter double #5: 5


3 is the average of (1 + 2 + 3 + 4 + 5) / 5
Press Enter to terminate...
```

The `VariableArrayAverage` program begins by prompting the user for the number of values she intends to average (that's the N I mentioned earlier). The result is stored in the `int` variable `numElements`. In the example, the number entered is 5.

The program continues by allocating an array `doublesArray` with the specified number of elements. In this case, the program allocates an array with five elements. The program loops the number of times specified by `numElements`, reading a new value from the user each time. After the last value, the program calculates the average.

Getting console output like that in this example just right is a little tricky. Follow each statement in `VariableArrayAverage` carefully as the program outputs open parentheses, equal signs, plus signs, and each of the numbers in the sequence, and compare this with the output.

The `VariableArrayAverage` program probably doesn't completely satisfy your thirst for flexibility. You don't want to have to tell the program how many numbers you want to average. What you'd really like is to enter numbers to average as long as you want — and then tell the program to average what you've entered. That's where C#'s collections come in. They give you a powerful, flexible alternative to arrays. Getting input directly from the user isn't the only way to fill up your array or other collection, either. Bonus Chapter 3 on the Web site describes how to read an arbitrary number of data items from a file.

The Length property

The `for` loop that's used to populate the array in the `VariableArray-Average` program begins as follows:

```
// Now declare an array of that size.
double[] doublesArray = new double[numElements];
// Accumulate the values into an array.
for (int i = 0; i < numElements; i++)
{
    . . .
}
```

The `doublesArray` is declared to be `numElements` items in length. Thus the clever programmer (that would be me) used a `for` loop to iterate through `numElements` items of the array.

It would be a shame and a crime to have to schlep the variable `numElements` around with `doublesArray` everywhere it goes just so you know how long it is. Fortunately, that isn't necessary. An array has a property called `Length` that contains its length. `doublesArray.Length` has the same value as `numElements`.

The following `for` loop would be preferable:

```
// Accumulate the values into an array.
for (int i = 0; i < doublesArray.Length; i++) ...
```

How do I initialize my array?

The following lines show an array with its *initializer* and then one that allocates space but doesn't initialize the elements' values:

```
double[] fixedLengthArray = {5, 2, 7, 3.5, 6.5, 8, 1, 9, 1, 3};
double[] variableLengthArray = new double[10];
```

You could do it all yourself using the following code:

```
double[] fixedLengthArray = new double[10] {5, 2, 7, 3.5, 6.5, 8, 1, 9, 1, 3};
```

Here you have specifically allocated the memory using `new`, and then followed that declaration with the initial values for the members of the array, but I think I can predict which form you'll prefer. (Hint: Line 1?)

A Loop Made foreach Array

Given an array of strings, the following loop averages their lengths:

```
public class Student   // You'll learn about classes in Chapter 7.
{
  public string name;
  public double gpa;        // Grade point average.
}
public class Program
{
  public static void Main(string[] args)
  {
    //  . . .create the array somehow . . .
    // Now average the students that you have.
    double sum = 0.0;
    for (int i = 0; i < students.Length; i++)
    {
      sum += students[i].gpa;
    }
    double avg = sum / students.Length;
    //  . . .do something with the average . . .
  }
}
```

The `for` loop iterates through the members of the array. (And yes, you can have arrays of any sort of object, not just of simple types like `doubles` and `strings`. You haven't formally met classes yet, but bear with me a bit longer.)

`students.Length` contains the number of elements in the array.

C# provides yet another loop, called `foreach`, designed specifically for iterating through collections such as the array. It works as follows:

```
// Now average the students that you have.
double sum = 0.0;
foreach (Student student in students)
{
  sum += student.gpa;  // This extracts the current student's GPA.
}
double avg = sum / students.Length;
```

The first time through the loop, the `foreach` fetches the first `Student` object in the array and stores it in the variable `student`. On each subsequent pass, the `foreach` retrieves the next element. Control passes out of the `foreach` when all the elements in the array have been processed.

Notice that no index appears in the `foreach` statement. This greatly reduces the chance of error and is simpler to write than the `for` statement, although sometimes that index is handy and you'll prefer a `for` loop.

The `foreach` is actually more powerful than it would seem from this example. This statement works on other collection types in addition to arrays. In addition, `foreach` handles multidimensional arrays (arrays of arrays, in effect), a topic I won't take up in this book. To find out all about multidimensional arrays, look up "multidimensional arrays" in Help.

Sorting Through Arrays of Data

A common programming challenge is the need to sort the elements within an array. Just because an array cannot grow or shrink in size does not mean the elements within the array cannot be moved, removed, or added. For example, the following code snippet swaps the location of two `string` elements within the array `strings`:

```
string temp = strings[i]; // Save the i'th string.
strings[i] = strings[k];  // Replace it with the kth.
strings[k] = temp;        // Replace kth with temp.
```

Here the object reference in the *i*th location in the `strings` array is saved so it is not lost when the second statement replaces it with another element. Finally, the `temp` variable is saved back into the *k*th location. Pictorially, this process looks like Figure 5-1.

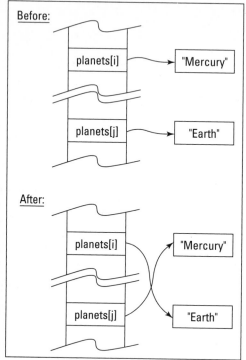

Figure 5-1:
"Swapping
two
objects"
actually
means
"swapping
references
to two
objects."

The data collections discussed in the rest of this chapter are more versatile than the array when it comes to adding and removing elements.

The following program demonstrates how to use the ability to manipulate elements within an array as part of a sort. This particular sorting algorithm is called the *bubble sort*. It's not so great on large arrays with thousands of elements, but it's simple and effective on small arrays:

```
// BubbleSortArray - Given a list of planets, sort their
//    names: First, in alphabetical order.
//    Second, by the length of their names, shortest to longest.
//    Third, longest to shortest.
//    This demonstrates using and sorting arrays, working with
//    them by array index. Two sort algorithms are used:
//    1. The Sort algorithm used by class Array's Sort() method.
//    2. The classic Bubble Sort algorithm.
using System;

namespace BubbleSortArray
{
  class Program
  {
```

```
static void Main(string[] args)
{
  Console.WriteLine("The 5 planets closest to the sun, in order: ");
  string[] planets =
    new string[] { "Mercury", "Venus", "Earth", "Mars", "Jupiter" };
  foreach (string planet in planets)
  {
    // Use the special char \t to insert a tab in the printed line.
    Console.WriteLine("\t" + planet);
  }

  Console.WriteLine("\nNow listed alphabetically: ");
  // Array.Sort() is a method on the Array class.
  // Array.Sort() does its work in-place in the planets array,
  // which leaves us without a copy of the original array. The
  // solution is to copy the old array to a new one and sort that.
  string[] sortedNames = planets;
  Array.Sort(sortedNames);
  // This demonstrates that (a) sortedNames contains the same
  // strings as planets, and (b) that they're now sorted.
  foreach (string planet in sortedNames)
  {
    Console.WriteLine("\t" + planet);
  }

  Console.WriteLine("\nList by name length - shortest first: ");
  // This algorithm is called "Bubble Sort": It's the simplest
  // but worst-performing sort. The Array.Sort() method is much
  // more efficient, but I couldn't use it directly to sort the
  // planets in order of name length because it sorts strings,
  // not their lengths.
  int outer;  // Index of the outer loop.
  int inner;  // Index of the inner loop.
  // Loop DOWN from last index to first: planets[4] to planets[0].
  for (outer = planets.Length - 1; outer >= 0; outer--)
  {
    // On each outer loop, loop through all elements BEYOND the
    // current outer element. This loop goes up, from planets[1]
    // to planets[4]. With the for loop, you can traverse the
    // array in either direction.
    for (inner = 1; inner <= outer; inner++)
    {
      // Compare adjacent elements. If the earlier one is longer
      // than the later one, swap them. This shows how you can
      // swap one array element with another when they're out of order.
      if (planets[inner - 1].Length > planets[inner].Length)
      {
        // Temporarily store one planet.
        string temp = planets[inner - 1];
        // Now overwrite that planet with the other one.
        planets[inner - 1] = planets[inner];
        // Finally, reclaim the planet stored in temp and put
```

```
            // it in place of the other.
            planets[inner] = temp;
         }
      }
   }
   foreach (string planet in planets)
   {
      Console.WriteLine("\t" + planet);
   }

   Console.WriteLine("\nNow listed longest first: ");
   // That is, just loop down through the sorted planets.
   for(int i = planets.Length - 1; i >= 0; i--)
   {
      Console.WriteLine("\t" + planets[i]);
   }

   Console.WriteLine("\nPress Enter to terminate...");
   Console.Read();
      }
   }
}
```

The program begins with an array containing the names of the first five planets out from the sun (to keep the figures small, I didn't do the outer planets, so I didn't have to decide about poor Pluto, out in the doghouse).

The program then invokes the array's own `Sort()` method. After sorting with the built-in `Sort()` method on the `Array` class, the program sorts the lengths of the planets' names using a custom sort just to amaze you.

The built-in `Sort()` method for arrays (and other collections) is, without a doubt, more efficient than the custom bubble sort. Don't roll your own unless you have good reason to.

The algorithm for the second sort works by continuously looping through the list of strings until the list is sorted. On each pass through the `sortedNames` array, the program compares each string to its neighbor. If the two are found to be out of order, the method swaps them and then flags the fact that the list was not found to be completely sorted. Figures 5-2 through 5-5 show the `planets` list after each pass.

Eventually, longer planet names "bubble" their way to the top of the list. Hence the name *bubble sort.*

Figure 5-2:
Before
starting the
bubble sort.

Mercury ◄──── And they're off and running!
Venus
Earth
Mars
Jupiter

Figure 5-3:
After pass 1
of the
bubble sort.

Earth ◄──── Earth edges its way into the lead...
Mercury
Venus
Mars
Jupiter

Figure 5-4:
After pass 2
of the
bubble sort.

Earth
Mars ◄──── Mars jumps past Mercury and Venus for second place
Mercury
Venus
Jupiter

Figure 5-5:
The next-to-
last pass
results in a
sorted list.
The final
pass
terminates
the sort
because
nothing
changes.

Earth ◄──── At the finish, it's Earth crossing the line in first place for the win...
Jupiter ◄──── ...and Jupiter noses out Mars to place.
Mars ◄──── Meanwhile, Mars struggles to show.
Mercury
Venus

Give single-item variables singular names, as in `planet` or `student`. The name of the variable should somehow include the name of the class, as in `badStudent` or `goodStudent` or `sexyCoedStudent`. Give array (or other collections) plural names, as in `students` or `phoneNumbers` or `phone-NumbersInMyPalmPilot`. As always, this tip reflects the opinion of the authors and not this book's publisher nor any of its shareholders — C# doesn't care how you name your variables.

New Feature — Using var for Arrays

Traditionally, you used one of the following forms to initialize an array — these forms are as old as C# (now going on six years old):

```
int[] numbers = new int[3];              // Size but no initializer, or ...
int[] numbers = new int[] { 1, 2, 3 }; // Initializer but no size, or ...
int[] numbers = new int[3] { 1, 2, 3 };// Size and initializer, or ...
int[] numbers = { 1, 2, 3 };              // No 'new' keyword - extreme short form.
```

Chapter 2 on variables introduces the new `var` keyword, which tells the C# compiler, "*You* figure out the variable type from the initializer expression I'm providing."

Happily, `var` works with arrays, too:

```
// myArray is an int[] with 6 elements.
var myArray = new [] { 2, 3, 5, 7, 11, 13 };  // Initializer required!
```

The new syntax has only two changes:

- ✔ Using `var` instead of the explicit type information for the `numbers` array on the left side of the assignment.
- ✔ Omitting the `int` keyword before the brackets on the right side of the assignment. That's the part that the compiler can infer.

Note that in the `var` version, the initializer is required. It's what the compiler uses to infer the type of the array elements without the `int` keyword.

Here are a few more examples:

```
var names = new [] { "John", "Paul", "George", "Ringo" };      // Strings.
var averages = new [] { 3.0, 3.34, 4.0, 2.0, 1.8 };            // Doubles.
var prez = new []{new President("FDR"), new President("JFK")};  // Presidents.
```

Notice that you can't use the extreme short form for initializing an array when you use `var`. The following won't compile:

```
var names = { "John", "Paul", "George", "Ringo" };  // Needs 'new []'.
```

The `var` way is less concise, but when used in some other situations not involving arrays, it really shines, and in some cases it's mandatory. (You can see examples in Chapter 17.)

The `UsingVarWithArraysAndCollections` example program on the Web site demonstrates `var` with array initializers. Note that you can't use `var` as a variable name now, as you could in the past. Crummy name anyway.

Loosening Up with C# Collections

Often an array is the simplest, most straightforward way to deal with a list of Students or a list of doubles. You'll also encounter many places in the .NET Framework class library that require the use of arrays.

But arrays have a couple of fairly serious limitations that will sometimes get in your way. At such times, you'll appreciate C#'s extensive repertoire of more flexible collection classes.

Although arrays have the advantage of simplicity and can have multiple dimensions, they suffer from two important limitations:

- ✔ A program must declare the size of an array when it's created. Unlike Visual Basic, C# doesn't let you change the size of an array after it's defined. What if you don't know up front how big it needs to be?

- ✔ Inserting or removing an element in the middle of an array is wildly inefficient. You have to move all the elements around to make room. In a big array, that can be a huge, time-consuming job.

Most collections, on the other hand, make it much easier to add, insert, or remove elements, and you can resize them as needed, right in midstream. In fact, they'll usually take care of resizing automatically.

If you need a multidimensional data structure, use an array. No collection allows multiple dimensions (although it's possible to create some elaborate data structures, such as collections of arrays or collections of collections).

But arrays and collections do have some things in common:

- ✔ Each can contain elements of one and only one type. You must specify that type in your code, at compile time, and once declared, the type can't change. (But see the last section of this chapter.)

- ✔ As with arrays, you can access most collections with array-like syntax using square brackets to specify an index: myList[3] = "Joe".

- ✔ Both collections and arrays have methods and properties. Thus, to find the number of elements in the following smallPrimeNumbers array, you call its Length property:

```
var smallPrimeNumbers = new [] { 2, 3, 5, 7, 11, 13 };
int numElements = smallPrimeNumbers.Length;  // Result is 6.
```

whereas with a collection, you call its Count property:

```
List<int> smallPrimes = new List<int> { 2, 3, 5, 7, 11, 13 };
int numElements = smallPrimes.Count; // Collections have a Count property.
```

Check out class `Array` in Help to see what other methods and properties it has (seven public properties and some 36 public methods).

Understanding Collection Syntax

In this section, I'll get you up and running with collection syntax and introduce the most important and most frequently used collection classes.

C#'s collection classes

Table 5-1 lists the main collection classes in C#. I find it useful to think of collections having various "shapes": the list shape, the dictionary shape, and so on.

Table 5-1	The Most Common Collection "Shapes"
Class	**Description**
`List<T>`	A dynamic array containing objects of type `T`.
`LinkedList<T>`	A linked list of objects of type `T`.
`Queue<T>`	Start at the back end of the line, end up at the front.
`Stack<T>`	Always add or delete items at the "top" of the list, like a stack of cafeteria trays.
`Dictionary<TKey, TValue>`	A structure that works like a dictionary. Look up a key (e.g., a word) and retrieve its corresponding value (e.g., definition).
`HashSet<T>`	**New:** A structure like a mathematical set, with no duplicate items. It works much like a list but provides mathematical set operations such as union and intersection.

Figuring out <T>

In the mysterious-looking `<T>` notation you see in Table 5-1, `<T>` is a placeholder for some particular data type. To bring this symbolic object to life, *instantiate* it by inserting a real type, as follows:

```
List<int> intList = new List<int>(); // Instantiating for int.
```

"Instantiate" is Geek speak for "create an object (instance) of this type."

For example, you might create different List<T> instantiations for types int, string, Student, and so on. By the way, T isn't a sacred name. You can use anything you like. For instance, <dummy> or <aType>. It's common to use T, U, V, and so on.

But notice how I expressed the Dictionary<TKey, TValue> collection in Table 5-1. Here, two types are needed, one for the dictionary's keys and one for the values associated with the keys. I cover dictionaries shortly.

If this notation seems a bit forbidding, don't worry. You get used to it.

Going generic

These modern collections are known as *generic* collections. They're generic in the sense that you can fill in a blank template, of sorts, with a type (or types) in order to create a custom collection. If the generic List<T> seems puzzling, Bonus Chapter 8 on my Web site at csharp102.info may help. That chapter discusses C#'s generic facilities in more detail. In particular, the chapter shows you how to roll your own generic collections, classes, methods, and other types.

Using Lists

Suppose you need to store a list of MP3 objects, each of which represents one item in your MP3 music collection. As an array, it might look like this:

```
MP3[] myMP3s = new MP3[50];          // Start with an empty array.
myPP3s[0] = new MP3("Norah Jones"); // Create an MP3 and add it to the array.
// ... and so on.
```

With a list collection, it looks like this:

```
List<MP3> myMP3s = new List<MP3>();   // An empty list.
myMP3s.Add(new MP3("Avril Levigne")); // Call the list's Add() method to add.
// ... and so on.
```

So what, you say? These look pretty similar, and the list doesn't appear to provide any advantage over the array. But what happens when you add the fiftieth MP3 to the array and then want to add a fifty-first? You're out of room. Your only course is to declare a new, larger array, then copy all of the MP3s from the old array into the new one. Also, if you remove an MP3 from the array, your array is left with a gaping hole. What do you put into that empty slot to take the place of the MP3 you ditched? The value null, maybe?

But the list collection sails happily on, in the face of those same obstacles. Want to add MP3 number 51? No problem. Want to junk your old Pat Boone MP3s? (Are there any?) No problem. The list takes care of healing itself up after you delete old Pat.

If your list (or array, for that matter) can contain null items, be sure to check for null when you're looping through with for or foreach. You don't want to call the Play() method on a null MP3 item. That results in an error.

The ListCollection example on the Web site shows some of the things you can do with List<T>. In the following code listing, I'll intersperse explanations with bits of code.

The code below (excerpted from the example) shows how to instantiate a new, empty list for the string type. In other words, this list that can hold only strings:

```
// List<T>: note angle brackets plus parentheses in
// List<T> declaration; T is a "type parameter",
// List<T> is a "parameterized type".
// Instantiate for string type.
List<string> nameList = new List<string>();
sList.Add("one");
sList.Add(3);                              // Compiler error here!
sList.Add(new Student("du Bois"));         // Compiler error here!
```

You add items to a List<T> via its Add() method. The code above successfully adds one string to the list, but then it runs into trouble trying to add first an integer, then a Student. The list was instantiated for strings, so the compiler rejects both attempts.

The next code fragment instantiates a completely new list for type int, then adds two int values to the list. Afterwards, the foreach loop iterates the int list, printing out the ints.

```
// Instantiate for int.
List<int> intList = new List<int>();
intList.Add(3);                           // Fine.
intList.Add(4);
Console.WriteLine("Printing intList:");
foreach(int i in intList)  // foreach just works for all collections.
{
    Console.WriteLine("int i = " + i);
}
```

The code that follows instantiates a new list to hold Students and adds two students with its Add() method. But then notice the *array* of Students, which I add to the student list using its AddRange() method. AddRange() lets you add a whole array or (almost) any other collection to the list, all at once, as here:

```
// Instantiate for Student.
List<Student> studentList = new List<Student>();
Student student1 = new Student("Vigil");
Student student2 = new Student("Finch");
studentList.Add(student1);
studentList.Add(student2);
Student[] students = { new Student("Mox"), new Student("Fox") };
studentList.AddRange(students); // Add whole array to List.
Console.WriteLine("Num students in studentList = " + studentList.Count);
```

(Don't worry about the "new Student" stuff. You'll get to that in Chapter 7.)

It's easy to convert lists to arrays and vice versa. To put an array into a list, use the list's AddRange() method as above. To convert a list to an array, call the list's ToArray() method:

```
Student[] students = studentList.ToArray();   // studentList is a List<Student>.
```

List<T> also has a number of other methods for adding items, including methods to insert one or more items anywhere in the list, and methods to remove items or clear the whole list. Note that List<T> also has a Count property. (This is one small nit that can trip you up if you're used to the Length property on arrays and strings. For collections, it's Count.)

The next snippet demonstrates several ways to search a list. IndexOf() returns the array-style index of the desired item within the list, if found, or –1 if not found. The code also demonstrates accessing an item with array-style indexing and via the Contains() method. Other searching methods include BinarySearch(), not shown.

```
// Search with IndexOf().
Console.WriteLine("Student2 at " + studentList.IndexOf(student2));
string name = studentList[3].Name;  // Access list by index.
if(studentList.Contains(student1))  // student1 is a Student object.
{
   Console.WriteLine(student1.Name + " contained in list");
}
```

The final code segment demonstrates several more List<T> operations, including sorting, inserting, and removing items:

```
studentList.Sort(); // Assumes Student implements IComparable interface (Ch 14).
studentList.Insert(3, new Student("Ross"));
studentList.RemoveAt(3);  // Deletes the third element.
Console.WriteLine("removed " + name);          // Name defined above.
```

That's only a sampling of the `List<T>` methods. You can look up the full list in Help.

To look up generic collections you have to look in the Help Index for "List<T>". If you try just "List," you'll be lost in a list of lists of lists. If you want to see information about the whole set of collection classes (well, the generic ones), search the Index for "generic collections".

Using Dictionaries

You've no doubt used Webster's or some other dictionary. It's organized as a bunch of words in alphabetical order. Associated with each word is a body of information including pronunciations, definitions, and so on. To use a dictionary, you look up a word and retrieve its information.

In C#, the dictionary "shape" differs from the list shape. Dictionaries are represented by the `Dictionary<TKey, TValue>` class. `TKey` represents the data type used for the dictionary's *keys* — think of the words in a standard dictionary, the things you look up. `TValue` represents the data type used to store the information or data associated with a key — think of the word's definitions in Webster's.

.NET dictionaries are based on the idea of a *hash table*. Imagine a group of buckets spread around the floor. When you compute a *hash*, using some *hash function*, you get a value that specifies one and only one of the buckets. That same hash will always point to the same bucket. If the hash is computed properly, you should get a good, fairly even distribution of items spread among the buckets. Thus the hash is a *key* to one of the buckets. Give the key, retrieve the bucket's contents — its *value*.

Using dictionaries is no harder in C# than in high school. The following `DictionaryExample` program (excerpts) shows a few things you can do with dictionaries. To save a little space, I show just parts of the `Main()` method.

If you find the going a bit rough here, you may want to circle back here later.

The first piece of the code just creates a new `Dictionary` that has `string` keys and `string` values. You aren't limited to strings, though. Either the key or the value, or both, can be any type. Note that the `Add()` method requires both a key and a value.

```
Dictionary<string, string> dict = new Dictionary<string, string>();
// Add(key, value).
dict.Add("C#", "cool");
dict.Add("C++", "like writing Sanskrit poetry in Morse code");
dict.Add("VB", "a simple but wordy language");
dict.Add("Java", "good, but not C#");
dict.Add("Fortran", "ANCNT");  // 6-letters-max variable name for "ancient".
dict.Add("Cobol", "even more wordy, or is it wordier, and verbose than VB");
```

The ContainsKey() method tells you whether the dictionary contains a particular key. There's a corresponding ContainsValue() method too.

```
// See if the dictionary contains a particular key.
Console.WriteLine("Contains key C# " + dict.ContainsKey("C#"));    // True.
Console.WriteLine("Contains key Ruby " + dict.ContainsKey("Ruby")); // False.
```

You can, of course, iterate the dictionary in a loop just as you can any collection. But keep in mind that the dictionary is like a list of *pairs* of things — think of each pair as some sort of object that contains both the key and the value. So to iterate the whole dictionary with foreach, you need to retrieve one of the *pairs* each time through the loop. The pairs are objects of type KeyValuePair<TKey, TValue>. In the WriteLine() call, I use the pair's Key and Value properties to extract the items. Here's what that looks like:

```
// Iterate the dictionary's contents with foreach.
// Note that you're iterating pairs of keys and values.
Console.WriteLine("\nContents of the dictionary:");
foreach (KeyValuePair<string, string> pair in dict)
{
    // Because the key happens to be a string, I can call string methods on it.
    Console.WriteLine("Key: " + pair.Key.PadRight(8) + "Value: " + pair.Value);
}
```

In the final segment of the example program, you can see how to iterate just the keys or just the values. The dictionary's Keys property returns another collection: a list-shaped collection of type Dictionary<TKey, TValue>. KeyCollection. Because our keys happen to be strings, you can iterate the keys as strings and call string methods on them. The Values property is similar. The final bit of code uses the dictionary's Count property to see how many key/value pairs it contains.

```
// List the keys, which are in no particular order.
Console.WriteLine("\nJust the keys:");
// Dictionary<TKey, TValue>.KeyCollection is a collection of just the keys,
// in this case strings. So here's how to retrieve the keys:
Dictionary<string, string>.KeyCollection keys = dict.Keys;
foreach(string key in keys)
{
    Console.WriteLine("Key: " + key);
}
```

```
// List the values, which are in same order as key collection above.
Console.WriteLine("\nJust the values:");
Dictionary<string, string>.ValueCollection values = dict.Values;
foreach (string value in values)
{
    Console.WriteLine("Value: " + value);
}
Console.Write("\nNumber of items in the dictionary: " + dict.Count);
```

Of course, that doesn't exhaust the possibilities for working with dictionaries. Look up "Dictionary<>" in the Help index for all the details.

Dictionary pairs are in no particular order, and you can't sort a dictionary. It really is just like a bunch of buckets spread around the floor.

New Feature — Array and Collection Initializers

In this section, I want to summarize initialization techniques for both arrays and collections — both old-style and new. You may want to bend the page corner.

Initializing arrays

As a reminder, given the new `var` syntax covered earlier in this chapter, an array declaration can look like either of these:

```
int[] numbers = { 1, 2, 3 };              // Shorter form - can't use var.
var numbers = new [] { 1, 2, 3 };         // Full initializer mandatory with
                var.
```

Initializing collections

Meanwhile, the traditional way to initialize a collection, such as a List<T> (or a Queue<T> or Stack<T>) back in C# 2.0 days (two years ago), was like this:

```
List<int> numList = new List<int>();      // New empty list.
numbers.Add(1);                           // Add elements one at a time.
numbers.Add(2);
numbers.Add(3);                                    // ...teeedious!
```

or, if you had the numbers in an array or another collection already, like this:

```
List<int> numList = new List<int>(numbers); // Initializing from an array, or...
List<int> numList2 = new List<int>(numList);// from another collection, or...
numList.AddRange(numbers);                   // using AddRange.
```

When initializing lists, queues, or stacks as above, you can pass in any array or *list-like* collection, including lists, queues, stacks, and the new sets, which I cover in the next section (but not dictionaries — their shape is wrong). The `MoreCollections` example on the Web site illustrates several cases of initializing one collection from another.

The new C# 3.0 collection initializers resemble the new array initializers and are much easier to use than most of the earlier forms. The new initializers look like the following:

```
List<int> numList = new List<int> { 1, 2, 3 };  // List.
int[] intArray = { 1, 2, 3 };                    // Array.
```

The key difference between the new array and collection initializers is that you still must spell out the type for collections — which means giving `List<int>` after the `new` keyword (see boldface above).

Of course, you can also use the `var` keyword with collections:

```
var list = new List<string> { "Head", "Heart", "Hands", "Health" };
```

Initializing dictionaries with the new syntax looks like this:

```
Dictionary<int, string> dict =
   new Dictionary<int, string> { { 1, "Sam" }, { 2, "Joe" } }; // Or ...
var dict2 = new Dictionary<int, int> { { 0, 1 }, { 2, 3 } };
```

Outwardly, this looks the same as for `List<T>`, but inside the outer curly braces, you see a second level of curly-brace-enclosed items, one per entry in the dictionary. Since this dictionary `dict` has integer keys and string values, each inner pair of curly braces contains one of each, separated by a comma. The key/value pairs are separated by commas as well.

Initializing sets (coming in the next section) is much like initializing lists:

```
HashSet<int> biggerPrimes = new HashSet<int> { 19, 23, 29, 31, 37, 41 };
```

The `UsingVarWithArraysAndCollections` example on the Web site demonstrates the new `var` keyword used with arrays and collections.

New Feature — Using Sets

C# 3.0 adds a new collection type called `HashSet<T>`. A *set* is an unordered collection with no duplicate items.

The set concept comes from mathematics. Think of the set of genders (female and male), the set of days in a week, the set of variations on the triangle (isosceles, equilateral, scalene, right, obtuse). Unlike math sets, C# sets can't be infinite, but they can be as large as available memory.

In common with other collections, you can do things to a set such as add items, delete items, and find items. But you can also perform several specifically set-like operations, such as *union* and *intersection*. Union joins the members of two sets into one. Intersection finds the overlap between two sets and results in a set containing the overlapping members only. So sets are good for combining things and eliminating things.

Like dictionaries, sets are implemented using hash tables. Sets are sort of dictionaries with keys but no values, making them list-like in shape. See the previous section on "Using Dictionaries" for details.

To create a `HashSet<T>`, you can do this:

```
HashSet<int> smallPrimeNumbers = new HashSet<int>();
smallPrimeNumbers.Add(2);
smallPrimeNumbers.Add(3);
```

Or, more conveniently, you can use a collection initializer:

```
HashSet<int> smallPrimeNumbers = new HashSet<int> { 2, 3, 5, 7, 11, 13 };
```

Or create the set from an existing collection of any list-like kind, including arrays:

```
List<int> intList = new List<int> { 0, 1, 2, 3, 4, 5, 6, 7 };
HashSet<int> numbers = new HashSet<int>(intList);
```

If you attempt to add an item to a hash set that the set already contains (like this, for example) . . :

```
smallPrimeNumbers.Add(2);
```

. . . the compiler doesn't treat the duplication as an error (and doesn't change the hash set, which can't have duplicates). Actually, `Add()` returns `true` if the addition occurred, `false` if it didn't. You don't have to use that fact, but it can be useful if you want to do something when an attempt is made to add a duplicate:

```
bool successful = smallPrimeNumbers.Add(2);
if(successful)
{
  // 2 was added, now do something useful.
}
// If successful is false, not added because it was already there.
```

The following example — the HashSetExample on the Web site — shows off several HashSet<T> methods but more importantly demonstrates using a HashSet<T> *as a tool for working with other collections.* You can do strictly mathematical operations with HashSet<T>, but I find its ability to combine collections in various ways very handy.

The first segment of this code starts with a List<string> and an array. Each contains color names. While you could combine the two simply by calling the list's AddRange() method (like this) . . .

```
colors.AddRange(moreColors);
```

. . . the resulting list contains some duplicates (yellow, orange). Using a HashSet<T> and the UnionWith() method, on the other hand, you can combine two collections and eliminate any duplicates in one shot, as the following example shows.

Here's the beginning of the HashSetExample on the Web site:

```
Console.WriteLine("Combining two collections with no duplicates:");
List<string> colors = new List<string> { "red", "orange", "yellow" };
string[] moreColors = { "orange", "yellow", "green", "blue", "violet" };
// Want to combine but without any duplicates.
// Following is just the first stage ...
HashSet<string> combined = new HashSet<string>(colors);
// ... now for the second stage.
// UnionWith() collects items in both lists that aren't duplicated,
// resulting in a combined collection whose members are all unique.
combined.UnionWith(moreColors);
foreach (string color in combined)
{
  Console.WriteLine(color);
}
```

The result given here contains "red", "orange", "yellow", "green", "blue", "violet". The first stage uses the colors list to initialize a new HashSet<T>. The second stage then calls the set's UnionWith() method to add in the moreColors array — but adding only the ones not already in the set. The set ends up containing just the colors in both original lists. Green, blue, and violet come from the second list. Red, orange, and yellow come from the first. The moreColors array's orange and yellow would duplicate the ones already in the set, so they're screened out.

But suppose you'd like to end up with a `List<T>` containing those colors, not a `HashSet<T>`. The next segment shows how to create a new `List<T>` initialized with the `combined` set:

```
Console.WriteLine("\nConverting the combined set to a list:");
// Initialize a new List from the combined set above.
List<string> spectrum = new List<string>(combined);
foreach(string color in spectrum)
{
    Console.WriteLine(color);
}
```

At the time I write this, the 2008 U.S. presidential campaign is in full swing, with about ten early candidates in each major party. A good many of those candidates are also members of the U.S. Senate. How can you get a list of just the candidates who are also in the Senate? `HashSet<T>`'s `IntersectWith()` method gives you the overlapping items between the candidate list and the Senate list — items in both lists, but only those items:

```
Console.WriteLine("\nFinding the overlap in two lists:");
List<string> presidentialCandidates =
    new List<string> { "Clinton", "Edwards", "Giuliani", "McCain", "Obama",
                "Romney" };
List<string> senators = new List<string> { "Alexander", "Boxer", "Clinton",
                "McCain", "Obama", "Snowe" };
HashSet<string> senatorsRunning = new HashSet<string>(presidentialCandidates);
// IntersectWith() collects items that appear in both lists, eliminates others.
senatorsRunning.IntersectWith(senators);
foreach (string senator in senatorsRunning)
{
    Console.WriteLine(senator);
}
```

The result is `"Clinton"`, `"McCain"`, `"Obama"` because those are the only ones in both lists. The opposite trick is to remove any items that appear in both of two lists so you end up with just the items in your target list that aren't duplicated in the other list. This calls for the `HashSet<T>` method `ExceptWith()`:

```
Console.WriteLine("\nExcluding items from a list:");
Queue<int> queue =
    new Queue<int>(new int[] { 0, 1, 2, 3, 4, 5, 6, 7, 8, 9, 17 });
HashSet<int> unique = new HashSet<int> { 1, 3, 5, 7, 9, 11, 13, 15 };
// ExceptWith() removes items in unique that are also in queue: 1, 3, 5, 7.
unique.ExceptWith(queue);
foreach (int n in unique)
{
    Console.WriteLine(n.ToString());
}
```

After this code, unique excludes its own items that duplicate items in queue, 1, 3, 5, 7, and 9, and also excludes items in queue that aren't in unique: 0, 2, 4, 6, 8, and 17. You end up with 11, 13, 15 in unique.

Meanwhile, the next code segment uses the SymmetricExceptWith() method to give the opposite result that you saw with IntersectWith(). Where intersection gives you the overlapping items, SymmetricExcept-With() gives you the items in both lists *that don't overlap*. The uniqueTo-One set ends up containing just 5, 3, 1, 12, 10. (My use of stacks here is a bit unorthodox, because I add all the members at once rather than *pushing* each one, and I remove a bunch at once rather than *popping* each. Those operations — pushing and popping — are the correct ways to interact with a stack.)

```
Console.WriteLine("\nFinding just the non-overlapping items in two lists:");
Stack<int> stackOne = new Stack<int>(new int[] { 1, 2, 3, 4, 5, 6, 7, 8 });
Stack<int> stackTwo = new Stack<int>(new int[] { 2, 4, 6, 7, 8, 10, 12 });
HashSet<int> nonoverlapping = new HashSet<int>(stackOne);
// SymmetricExceptWith() collects items that are in one collection but not
// the other: the items that don't overlap.
nonoverlapping.SymmetricExceptWith(stackTwo);
foreach(int n in nonoverlapping)
{
   Console.WriteLine(n.ToString());
}
Console.WriteLine("Press Enter to terminate...");
Console.Read();
}
```

Notice that all the HashSet<T> methods I've demonstrated are void methods, that is, they don't return a value. Thus the results are reflected directly in the hash set on which you call these methods: nonoverlapping in the code above.

I found the behavior of UnionWith() and IntersectWith() a bit awkward at first, because I wanted a new resulting set, with the original (input) sets remaining the same when I applied these methods. But, I'm happy to report, in Chapter 17 you'll meet the new LINQ query operators, which add versions of these methods that return a whole new set object. Combining what you see here with what you'll see there, you get the best of both worlds. More than that I'd better not say now.

When would you use HashSet<T>? Any time you're working with two or more collections and want to find things like the overlap — or create a collection that contains two other collections, or exclude a group of items from a collection — sets can be useful. Many of the HashSet<T> methods can relate sets and other collection classes. You can do more with sets, of course, so look up "HashSet<T>" in Help and play with the HashSetExample a bit.

On Not Using Old-Fashioned Collections

At the Dawn of Time, before C# 2.0, when Zarathustra spake, all collection classes were implemented as collections of type `Object`. You couldn't create a collection just for `strings` or just for `ints`. Such a collection lets you store any type of data, because all objects in C# are derived from class `Object`. Thus you can add both `ints` and `strings` to *the same collection* without getting error messages (due to C#'s inheritance and polymorphism, which I discuss in Chapters 12 and 13).

But there's a serious drawback to the `Object`-based arrangement: In order to extract the `int` that you know you put *into* a collection, you must cast the `Object` that you get out to an `int`:

```
ArrayList ints = new ArrayList();   // An old-fashioned list of Objects.
int myInt = (int)ints[0];           // Extract the first int in the list.
```

It's as if your `ints` were hidden inside Easter eggs. If you don't cast, you get errors because, for instance, `Object` doesn't support the + operation or other methods, properties, and operators that you expect on `ints`. You can work with these limitations, but this kind of code is error-prone, and it's just plain tedious to do all of that casting. (Besides, as I'll discuss in Bonus Chapter 4, working with such Easter eggs adds some processing overhead due to a phenomenon called "boxing." Too much boxing slows your program.)

And if the collection happens to contain objects of more than one type — pomegranates and basketballs, say — the problem gets tougher. Somehow, you have to detect that the object you fish out is a pomegranate or a basketball, so you can cast it correctly.

With those limitations on the older, nongeneric collections, the newer generic ones are a gale of fresh air. You never have to cast, and you always know what you're getting because you can only put one type into any given collection. But you'll still see the older collections occasionally, in code that other people write — and there are even times when you have a legitimate reason to stick apples and oranges in the same collection.

The nongeneric collections are found in the `System.Collections` and `System.Collections.Specialized` namespaces. The Specialized collections are interesting, sometimes useful oddball collections, mainly nongeneric. The modern, generic ones are found in `System.Collections.Generic`. (I explain namespaces in Bonus Chapter 1 on the Web site, and generics in Bonus Chapter 7 on my Web site at `csharp102.info`.)

Chapter 6

Pulling Strings

- -

In This Chapter

▶ Pulling and twisting a string with C# — just don't string me along

▶ Comparing strings

▶ Other string operations, such as searching, trimming, splitting, and concatenating

▶ Parsing strings read into the program

▶ Formatting output strings manually or using the String.Format() method

- -

*F*or many applications, you can treat a string like one of the built-in value-type variable types such as int or char. Certain operations that are otherwise reserved for these intrinsic types are available to strings, as follows:

```
int i = 1;          // Declare and initialize an int.
string s = "abc";   // Declare and initialize a string.
```

In other respects, shown as follows, a string is treated like a user-defined class (I cover classes in Chapter 7):

```
string s1 = new String();
string s2 = "abcd";
int lengthOfString = s2.Length;
```

Which is it — a value-type or a class? In fact, String is a class for which C# offers special treatment because strings are so widely used in programs. For example, the keyword string is synonymous with the class name String, as shown in the following code:

```
String s1 = "abcd"; // Assign a string literal to a String obj.
string s2 = s1;     // Assign a String obj to a string variable.
```

In this example, s1 is declared to be an object of class String (spelled with an uppercase *S*), while s2 is declared as a simple string (spelled with a lowercase *s*). However, the two assignments demonstrate that string and String are of the same (or compatible) types.

In fact, this same property is true of the other intrinsic variable types, to a more limited extent. Even the lowly `int` type has a corresponding class `Int32`, `double` has the class `Double`, and so on. (See Bonus Chapter 4.) The distinction here is that `string` and `String` really are the same thing.

The Union Is Indivisible, and So Are Strings

You need to know at least one thing that you didn't learn before the sixth grade: You can't change a `string` object itself after it has been created. Even though I may speak of modifying a string, C# doesn't have an operation that modifies the actual `string` object. Plenty of operations appear to modify the `string` that you're working with, but they always return the modified `string` as a new object, instead. One string becomes two.

For example, the operation `"His name is " + "Randy"` changes neither of the two strings, but generates a third string, `"His name is Randy"`. One side effect of this behavior is that you don't have to worry about someone modifying a `string` "out from under you."

Consider the following simplistic example program:

```
// ModifyString - The methods provided by class String do
//     not modify the object itself (s.ToUpper() does not
//     modify s; rather it returns a new string that has
//     been converted).
using System;
namespace ModifyString
{
  class Program
  {
    public static void Main(string[] args)
    {
      // Create a student object.
      Student s1 = new Student();
      s1.Name = "Jenny";
      // Now make a new object with the same name.
      Student s2 = new Student();
      s2.Name = s1.Name;
      // "Changing" the name in the s1 object does not
      // change the object itself because ToUpper() returns
      // a new string without modifying the original.
      s2.Name = s1.Name.ToUpper();
      Console.WriteLine("s1 - " + s1.Name + ", s2 - " + s2.Name);
      // Wait for user to acknowledge the results.
      Console.WriteLine("Press Enter to terminate...");
```

```
        Console.Read();
    }
}

// Student - We just need a class with a string in it.
class Student
{
    public String Name;
}
}
```

I won't get to a full discussion of classes until Chapter 7, but you can see that the `Student` class contains a data variable called `Name`, of type `String`. The `Student` objects `s1` and `s2` are set up so the student `Name` data in each points to the same string data. `ToUpper()` converts the string `s1.Name` to all uppercase characters. Normally, this would be a problem because both `s1` and `s2` point to the same object. However, `ToUpper()` does not change `Name` — it creates a new, independent uppercase string and stores it in the object `s2`. Now the two `Students` don't point to the same string data.

The following output of the program is simple:

```
s1 - Jenny, s2 - JENNY
Press Enter to terminate...
```

This property of strings is called *immutability* (meaning, "unchangeability").

The immutability of strings is also important for `string` constants. A string such as `"this is a string"` is a form of a `string` constant, just as 1 is an `int` constant. In the same way that I reuse my shirts to reduce the size of my wardrobe (and go easy on my bank account), a compiler may choose to combine all accesses to the single constant `"this is a string"`. Reusing `string` constants can reduce the *footprint* of the resulting program (its size on disk or in memory) but would be impossible if a `string` could be modified.

Performing Common Operations on a String

C# programmers perform more operations on strings than Beverly Hills plastic surgeons do on Hollywood hopefuls. Virtually every program uses the "addition" operator that's used on `strings`, as shown in the following example:

```
string name = "Randy";
Console.WriteLine("His name is " + name); // + means concatenate.
```

The `String` class provides this special operator. However, the `String` class also provides other, more direct methods for manipulating strings. You can see the complete list by looking up "String class" in the Help Index, and you'll meet many of the usual suspects in this chapter. Among the string-related tasks I cover here are these:

- Comparing strings — for equality or for tasks like alphabetizing
- Changing and converting strings in various ways: replacing part of a string, changing case, and converting between strings and other things
- Accessing the individual characters in a string
- Finding characters or substrings inside a string
- Handling input from the command line
- Managing formatted output
- Working efficiently with strings using the `StringBuilder`

In addition to the examples shown in the rest of this chapter, take a look at the `StringCaseChanging` and `VariousStringTechniques` examples on the Web site.

Comparing Strings

It's very common to need to compare two strings. For example, did the user input the expected value? Or maybe you have a list of strings and need to alphabetize them.

If all you need to know is whether two strings are equal (same length, same characters in the same order), you can use the == operator (or its inverse, !=, or 'not equal'):

```
string a = "programming";
string b = "Programming";
if(a == b) ... // True if we don't consider case, false otherwise.
if(a != b) ... // False if we don't consider case, true otherwise.
```

But comparing two strings for anything but equality or inequality is another matter. It doesn't work to say

```
if(a < b) ...
```

So if you need to ask, *Is string A "greater than" string B?* or *Is string A "less than" string B?*, you need another approach.

Equality for all strings: The Compare () method

Numerous operations treat a string as a single object — for example, the Compare() method. Compare(), with the following properties, compares two strings as if they were numbers:

- If the left-hand string is *greater than* the right string, Compare(*left, right*) returns 1.
- If the left-hand string is *less than* the right string, it returns –1.
- If the two strings are equal, it returns 0.

The algorithm works as follows when written in "notational C#" (that is, C# without all the details, also known as *pseudocode):*

```
compare(string s1, string s2)
{
  // Loop through each character of the strings until
  // a character in one string is greater than the
  // corresponding character in the other string.
  foreach character in the shorter string
    if (s1's character > s2's character when treated as a number)
      return 1
    if (s2's character < s1's character)
      return -1
  // Okay, every letter matches, but if the string s1 is longer,
  // then it's greater.
  if s1 has more characters left
    return 1
  // If s2 is longer, it's greater.
  if s2 has more characters left
    return -1
  // If every character matches and the two strings are the same
  // length, then they are "equal".
  return 0
}
```

Thus, "abcd" is greater than "abbd", and "abcde" is greater than "abcd". More often than not, you don't care whether one string is greater than the other, but only whether the two strings are equal.

You *do* want to know which string is "bigger" when performing a sort.

The Compare() operation returns 0 when two strings are identical. The following test program uses the equality feature of Compare() to perform a certain operation when the program encounters a particular string or strings.

BuildASentence prompts the user to enter lines of text. Each line is concatenated to the previous line to build a single sentence. This program exits if the user enters the word *EXIT*, *exit*, *QUIT*, or *quit*:

```
// BuildASentence - The following program constructs sentences
//    by concatenating user input until the user enters one of the
//    termination characters. This program shows when you need to look for
//    string equality.
using System;
namespace BuildASentence
{
  public class Program
  {
    public static void Main(string[] args)
    {
      Console.WriteLine("Each line you enter will be "
                        + "added to a sentence until you "
                        + "enter EXIT or QUIT");
      // Ask the user for input; continue concatenating
      // the phrases input until the user enters exit or
      // quit (start with an empty sentence).
      string sentence = "";
      for (; ; )
      {
        // Get the next line.
        Console.WriteLine("Enter a string ");
        string line = Console.ReadLine();
        // Exit the loop if line is a terminator.
        string[] terms = { "EXIT", "exit", "QUIT", "quit" };
        // Compare the string entered to each of the
        // legal exit commands.
        bool quitting = false;
        foreach (string term in terms)
        {
          // Break out of the for loop if you have a match.
          if (String.Compare(line, term) == 0)
          {
            quitting = true;
          }
        }
        if (quitting == true)
        {
          break;
        }
        // Otherwise, add it to the sentence.
        sentence = String.Concat(sentence, line);
        // Let the user know how she's doing.
        Console.WriteLine("\nyou've entered: " + sentence);
```

```
      }
      Console.WriteLine("\ntotal sentence:\n" + sentence);
      // Wait for user to acknowledge the results.
      Console.WriteLine("Press Enter to terminate...");
      Console.Read();
    }
  }
}
```

After prompting the user for what the program expects, the program creates an empty initial sentence string called `sentence`. From there, the program enters an "infinite" loop.

The controls `while(true)` and `for(;;)` loop forever, or at least long enough for some internal `break` or `return` to break you out. The two loops are equivalent, and in practice, you'll see them both. (Looping is covered in Chapter 4.)

`BuildASentence` prompts the user to enter a line of text, which the program reads using the `ReadLine()` method. Having read the line, the program checks to see whether it is a terminator using the boldfaced lines above.

The termination section of the program defines an array of strings called `terms` and a `bool` variable `quitting`, initialized to `false`. Each member of the `terms` array is one of the strings you're looking for. Any of these strings causes the program to quit faster than a programmer forced to write COBOL.

The program must include both `"EXIT"` and `"exit"` because `Compare()` considers the two strings different by default. (The way the program is written, these are the only two ways to spell *exit*. Strings such as `"Exit"` and `"eXit"` would not be recognized as terminators.)

The termination section loops through each of the strings in the array of target strings. If `Compare()` reports a match to any of the terminator phrases, `quitting` is set to `true`. If `quitting` remains `false` after the termination section, then if `line` is not one of the terminator strings, it is concatenated to the end of the sentence using the `String.Concat()` method. The program outputs the immediate result just so the user can see what's going on.

Iterating through an array is a classic way to look for one of various possible values. (I'll show you another way in the next section, and an even cooler way in Chapter 17.)

Here's an example run of the `BuildASentence` program:

```
Each line you enter will be added to a
sentence until you enter EXIT or QUIT
Enter a string
Programming with

You've entered: Programming with
Enter a string
 C# is fun

You've entered: Programming with C# is fun
Enter a string
 (more or less)

You've entered: Programming with C# is fun (more or less)
Enter a string
EXIT

Total sentence:
Programming with C# is fun (more or less)
Press Enter to terminate...
```

I've flagged my input in bold to make the output easier to read.

Would you like your compares with or without case?

The `Compare()` method used in the previous example considers `"EXIT"` and `"exit"` to be different strings. However, the `Compare()` method has a second version that includes a third argument. This argument indicates whether the comparison should ignore the letter case. A `true` indicates "ignore."

The following version of the lengthy termination section in the `BuildASentence` example sets `quitting` to `true` whether the string passed is uppercase, lowercase, or a combination of the two:

```
// Indicate true if passed either exit or quit,
// irrespective of case.
if (String.Compare("exit", source, true) == 0 ||
     (String.Compare("quit", source, true) == 0)
{
  quitting = true;
}
}
```

This version is simpler than the previous looping version. This code doesn't need to worry about case, and it can use a single conditional expression because it now has only two options to consider instead of a longer list: any spelling variation of QUIT or EXIT.

What If I Want to Switch Case?

You may be interested in whether all of the characters (or just one) in a string are uppercase or lowercase characters. And you may need to convert from one to the other.

Distinguishing between all-uppercase and all-lowercase strings

I almost hate to bring it up, but you can use the `switch` command (Chapter 4) to look for a particular string. Normally, you use the `switch` command to compare a counting number to some set of possible values; however, the `switch` does work on `string` objects, as well. The following version of the termination section in `BuildASentence` uses the `switch` construct:

```
switch(line)
{
  case "EXIT":
  case "exit":
  case "QUIT":
  case "quit":
    return true;
}
return false;
```

This approach works because you're comparing only a limited number of strings. The `for` loop offers a much more flexible approach for searching for string values. Using the case-less `Compare()` in the previous section gives the program greater flexibility in understanding the user.

Converting a string to upper- or lowercase

Suppose you have a string in lowercase and need to convert it to uppercase. You can use the `ToUpper()` method:

```
string lowcase = "armadillo";
string upcase = lowcase.ToUpper();  // ARMADILLO.
```

Similarly, you can convert uppercase to lowercase with `ToLower()`.

What if you want to convert just the first character in a string to uppercase? The following rather convoluted code will do it (but you'll see a better way in the last section of this chapter):

```
string name = "chuck";
string properName =
    char.ToUpper(name[0]).ToString() + name.Substring(1, name.Length - 1);
```

The idea above is to extract the first `char` in name (that's `name[0]`), convert it to a one-character string with `ToString()`, then tack on the remainder of name after removing the old lowercase first character with `Substring()`.

You can tell whether a string is uppercased or lowercased by using the following scary-looking `if` statement:

```
if (string.Compare(line.ToUpper(CultureInfo.InvariantCulture),
                   line, false) == 0) ... // True if line is all upper.
```

Here the `Compare()` method is comparing an uppercase version of `line` to `line` itself. There should be no difference if `line` is already uppercase. You can puzzle over the `CultureInfo.InvariantCulture` gizmo in Help, 'cause I'm not going to explain it here. For "is it all lowercase," stick a not (`!`) operator in front of the `Compare()` call. Alternatively, you can use a loop, as described in the next section.

The `StringCaseChanging` example on the Web site illustrates these and other techniques, including a brief explanation of "cultures."

Looping Through a String

You can access individual characters of a string in a `foreach` loop. The following code steps through the characters and writes each to the console — just another (roundabout) way to write out the string:

```
string favoriteFood = "cheeseburgers";
foreach(char c in favoriteFood)
{
  Console.Write(c);  // Could do things to the char here.
}
Console.WriteLine();
```

You could use that loop to solve the problem of deciding whether `favoriteFood` is all uppercase (see previous section):

```
bool isUppercase = true;  // Start with assumption it's uppercase.
foreach(char c in favoriteFood)
{
  if(!char.IsUpper(c))
```

```
{
    isUppercase = false;  // Disproves all uppercase, so get out.
    break;
}
}
```

At the end of the loop, isUppercase will either be true or false.

As shown in the final example in the previous section on switching case, you can also access individual characters in a string by using an array index notation:

```
char thirdChar = favoriteFood[2];   // First 'e' in "cheeseburgers".
```

Searching Strings

What if you need to find a particular word, or a particular character, inside a string? Maybe you need its index so you can use Substring(), Replace(), Remove(), or some other method on it. In this section, you'll see how to find individual characters or substrings. (I'm still using the favoriteFood variable from the previous section.)

Can 1 find it?

The simplest thing is finding an individual character with IndexOf():

```
int indexOfLetterS = favoriteFood.IndexOf('s');  // 4.
```

Class String also has other methods for finding things, either individual characters or substrings:

- ✔ IndexOfAny() takes an array of chars and searches the string for any of them, returning the index of the first one found.

    ```
    char[] charsToLookFor = { 'a', 'b', 'c' };
    int indexOfFirstFound = favoriteFood.IndexOfAny(charsToLookFor); // 0.
    ```

    That call is often written more briefly this way:

    ```
    int index = name.IndexOfAny(new char[] { 'a', 'b', 'c' });
    ```

- * LastIndexOf() finds not the first occurrence of a character but the last.

- ✔ LastIndexOfAny() works like IndexOfAny(), but starting at the end of the string.

✔ Contains() returns true if a given substring can be found within the target string:

```
if(favoriteFood.Contains("ee")) ...                    // True.
```

* And Substring() returns the string (if it's there), or empty if not:

```
string sub = favoriteFood.Substring(6, favoriteFood.Length - 6);
```

(I go into Substring() in greater detail later in the chapter.)

Is my string empty?

How can you tell if a target string is empty (" ") or has the value null (no value has been assigned yet, not even the empty string)? Use the IsNullOrEmpty() method, like this:

```
bool notThere = string.IsNullOrEmpty(favoriteFood);  // False.
```

Notice how you call IsNullOrEmpty() — **string.**IsNullOrEmpty(s).

You can set a string to the empty string in two ways:

```
string name = "";
string name = string.Empty;
```

Getting Input from the Command Line

A common task in console applications is getting the information that the user types in when you prompt her for, say, an interest rate or a name. You need to read the information in as a string (everything coming from the command line comes as a string). Then you sometimes need to *parse* the input to extract a number from it. And sometimes you need to process lots of input numbers.

Trimming excess white space

First, consider that in some cases, you don't want to mess with any white space on either end of the string. The term *white space* refers to the characters that don't normally display on the screen, for example, space, newline (or \n), and tab (\t). You may sometimes also encounter the carriage return character, \r.

You can use the Trim() method to trim off the edges of the string as follows:

```
// Get rid of any extra spaces on either end of the string.
random = random.Trim();
```

Class `String` also provides `TrimFront()` and `TrimEnd()` methods for getting more specific, and you can pass an array of `chars` to be included in the trimming along with white space. For example, you might trim a leading currency sign, such as `'$'`. Cleaning up a string can make it easier to parse. The "trim" methods return a new string.

Parsing numeric input

A program can read from the keyboard one character at a time, but you have to worry about newlines and so on. An easier approach reads a string and then *parses* the characters out of the string.

Parsing characters out of a string is another topic I don't like to mention for fear that programmers will abuse this technique. In some cases, programmers are too quick to jump down into the middle of a string and start pulling out what they find there. This is particularly true of C++ programmers because that's the only way they could deal with strings — until the addition of a string class.

The `ReadLine()` method used for reading from the console returns a `string` object. A program that expects numeric input must convert this `string`. C# provides just the conversion tool you need in the `Convert` class. This class provides a conversion method from `string` to each built-in variable type. Thus the following code segment reads a number from the keyboard and stores it in an `int` variable:

```
string s = Console.ReadLine();  // Keyboard input is string data
int n = Convert.Int32(s);       // but you know it's meant to be a number.
```

The other conversion methods are a bit more obvious: `ToDouble()`, `ToFloat()`, and `ToBoolean()`.

`ToInt32()` refers to a 32-bit, signed integer (32 bits is the size of a normal `int`), so this is the conversion method for `int`s. `ToInt64()` handles the size of a `long`.

When `Convert()` encounters an unexpected character type, it can generate unexpected results. Thus, you must know for sure what type of data you're processing and ensure that no extraneous characters are present.

Although I haven't fully discussed methods yet (see Chapters 8 and 9), here's one anyway. The following method returns `true` if the string passed to it consists of only digits. You can call this method prior to converting into a type of integer, assuming that a sequence of nothing but digits is probably a legal number.

To be really complete, you would need to include the decimal point for floating-point variables, and include a leading minus sign for negative numbers — but hey, you get the idea.

Here's the method:

```
// IsAllDigits - Return true if all the characters
//   in the string are digits.
public static bool IsAllDigits(string raw)
{
  // First get rid of any benign characters at either end;
  // if there's nothing left then we don't have a number.
  string s = raw.Trim();  // Ignore whitespace on either side.
  if (s.Length == 0) return false;
  // Loop through the string.
  for(int index = 0; index < s.Length; index++)
  {
    // A non-digit indicates that the string probably is not a number.
    if (Char.IsDigit(s[index]) == false) return false;
  }
  // No non-digits found; it's probably OK.
  return true;
}
```

The method `IsAllDigits()` first removes any harmless white space at either end of the string. If nothing is left, the string was blank and could not be an integer. The method then loops through each character in the string. If any of these characters turns out to be a nondigit, the method returns `false`, indicating that the string is probably not a number. If this method returns `true`, the probability is high that the string can be converted into an integer successfully.

The following code sample inputs a number from the keyboard and prints it back out to the console. (I omitted the `IsAllDigits()` method from the listing to save space, but I've boldfaced where this program calls it.)

```
// IsAllDigits - Demonstrate the IsAllDigits method.
using System;
namespace IsAllDigits
{
  class Program
  {
    public static void Main(string[] args)
    {
      // Input a string from the keyboard.
      Console.WriteLine("Enter an integer number");
      string s = Console.ReadLine();
      // First check to see if this could be a number.
      if (!IsAllDigits(s)) // Call our special method.
      {
        Console.WriteLine("Hey! That isn't a number");
```

```
    }
    else
    {
      // Convert the string into an integer.
      int n = Int32.Parse(s);
      // Now write out the number times 2.
      Console.WriteLine("2 * " + n + ", = " + (2 * n));
    }
    // Wait for user to acknowledge the results.
    Console.WriteLine("Press Enter to terminate...");
    Console.Read();
  }
  // IsAllDigits here.
}
}
```

The program reads a line of input from the console keyboard. If
`IsAllDigits()` returns `false`, the program alerts the user. If not, the program converts the string into a number using an alternative to
`Convert.ToInt32(aString)` — the `Int32.Parse(aString)` call. Finally,
the program outputs both the number and two times the number (the latter
to prove that the program did, in fact, convert the string as advertised).

The output from a sample run of the program appears as follows:

```
Enter an integer number
1A3
Hey! That isn't a number
Press Enter to terminate...
```

You could let `Convert` try to convert garbage and handle any exception it
may decide to throw. However, a better-than-even chance exists that it won't
throw an exception, but just return incorrect results — for example, returning
1 when presented with 1A3. It's best to validate input data yourself.

You could instead use `Int32.TryParse(s, n)`, which returns `false` if the
parse fails or `true` if it succeeds. If it does work, the converted number is
found in the second parameter, an `int` that I named n. This won't throw
exceptions. See the next section for an example.

Handling a series of numbers

Often a program receives a series of numbers in a single line from the keyboard. Using the `String.Split()` method, you can easily break the string
into a number of substrings, one for each number, and parse them separately.

The `Split()` method chops up a single string into an array of smaller strings
using some delimiter. For example, if you tell `Split()` to divide a string
using a comma (`,`) as the delimiter, `"1,2,3"` becomes three strings, `"1"`,
`"2"`, and `"3"`.

The following program uses the `Split()` method to input a sequence of numbers to be summed (again, I've omitted the `IsAllDigits()` method to save trees):

ON THE WEB

```
// ParseSequenceWithSplit - Input a series of numbers separated by commas,
//      parse them into integers and output the sum.
namespace ParseSequenceWithSplit
{
  using System;
  class Program
  {
    public static void Main(string[] args)
    {
      // Prompt the user to input a sequence of numbers.
      Console.WriteLine(
          "Input a series of numbers separated by commas:");
      // Read a line of text.
      string input = Console.ReadLine();
      Console.WriteLine();
      // Now convert the line into individual segments
      // based upon either commas or spaces.
      char[] dividers = {',', ' '};
      string[] segments = input.Split(dividers);
      // Convert each segment into a number.
      int sum = 0;
      foreach(string s in segments)
      {
        // Skip any empty segments.
        if (s.Length > 0)
        {
          // Skip strings that aren't numbers.
          if (IsAllDigits(s))
          {
            // Convert the string into a 32-bit int.
            int num = 0;
            if (Int32.TryParse(s, out num))
            {
              Console.WriteLine("Next number = {0}", num);
              // Add this number into the sum.
              sum += num;
            }
            // If parse fails, move on to next number.
          }
        }
      }
      // Output the sum.
      Console.WriteLine("Sum = {0}", sum);
      // Wait for user to acknowledge the results.
```

```
      Console.WriteLine("Press Enter to terminate...");
      Console.Read();
    }
    // IsAllDigits here.
  }
}
```

The `ParseSequenceWithSplit` program begins by reading a string from the keyboard. The program passes the `dividers` array of char to the `Split()` method to indicate that the comma and the space are the characters used to separate individual numbers. Either character will cause a split there.

The program iterates through each of the smaller "subarrays" created by `Split()` using the `foreach` loop control. The program skips any zero-length subarrays (this would result from two dividers in a row). The program next uses the `IsAllDigits()` method to make sure that the string contains a number (it won't if, for instance, you type , .3 with an extra nondigit, nonseparator character). Valid numbers are converted into integers and then added to an accumulator, sum. Invalid numbers are ignored. (I chose not to generate an error message to keep this short.)

Here's the output of a typical run:

```
Input a series of numbers separated by commas:
1,2, a, 3 4

Next number = 1
Next number = 2
Next number = 3
Next number = 4
Sum = 10
Press Enter to terminate...
```

The program splits the list, accepting commas, spaces, or both as separators. It successfully skips over the a to generate the result of 10. In a real-world program, however, you probably don't want to skip over incorrect input without comment. You almost always want to draw the user's attention to garbage in the input stream.

Joining an array of strings into one string

Class `String` also has a `Join()` method. If you have an array of strings, you can use `Join()` to concatenate all of the strings. You can even tell it to put a certain character string between each item and the next in the array:

```
string[] brothers = { "Chuck", "Bob", "Steve", "Mike" };
string theBrothers = string.Join(":", brothers);
```

The result in `theBrothers` is `"Chuck:Bob:Steve:Mike"`, with the names separated by colons. You can put any separator string between the names: `", "`, `"\t"`, `"        "`. The first item is a comma and a space. The second is a tab character. The third is a string of several spaces.

Controlling Output Manually

Controlling the output from programs is an important aspect of string manipulation. Face it: The output from the program is what the user sees. No matter how elegant the internal logic of the program may be, the user probably won't be impressed if the output looks shabby.

The `String` class provides help in directly formatting string data for output. The following sections examine the `Pad()`, `PadRight()`, `PadLeft()`, `Substring()`, and `Concat()` methods.

Using the Trim() and Pad() methods

I showed earlier how to use `Trim()` and its more specialized variants, `TrimFront()` and `TrimEnd()`.

Another common method for formatting output is to use the `Pad` methods, which add characters to either end of a string to expand the string to some predetermined length. For example, you may add spaces to the left or right of a string to left- or right-justify it, or you can add `"*"` characters to the left of a currency number, and so on.

The following small `AlignOutput` program uses both `Trim()` and `Pad()` to trim up and justify a series of names:

```
// AlignOutput - Left justify and align a set of strings
//    to improve the appearance of program output.
namespace AlignOutput
{
  using System;
  using System.Collections.Generic;
  class Program
  {
    public static void Main(string[] args)
    {
      List<string> names = new List<string> {"Christa  ",
                                             "  Sarah",
                                             "Jonathan",
                                             "Sam",
                                             " Schmekowitz "};
      // First output the names as they start out.
```

```
      Console.WriteLine("The following names are of "
                        + "different lengths");
      foreach(string s in names)
      {
        Console.WriteLine("This is the name '" + s + "' before");
      }
      Console.WriteLine();

      // This time, fix the strings so they are
      // left justified and all the same length.
      // First, copy the source array into an array that you can manipulate.
      List<string> stringsToAlign = new List<string>();
      // At the same time, remove any unnecessary spaces from either end
      // of the names.
      for (int i = 0; i < names.Count; i++)
      {
        string trimmedName = names[i].Trim();
        stringsToAlign.Add(trimmedName);
      }
      // Now find the length of the longest string so that
      // all other strings line up with that string.
      int maxLength = 0;
      foreach (string s in stringsToAlign)
      {
        if (s.Length > maxLength)
        {
          maxLength = s.Length;
        }
      }
      // Now justify all the strings to the length of the maximum string.
      for (int i = 0; i < stringsToAlign.Count; i++)
      {
        stringsToAlign[i] = stringsToAlign[i].PadRight(maxLength + 1);
      }
      // Finally output the resulting padded, justified strings.
      Console.WriteLine("The following are the same names "
                        + "normalized to the same length");
      foreach(string s in stringsToAlign)
      {
        Console.WriteLine("This is the name '" + s + "' afterwards");
      }
      // Wait for user to acknowledge.
      Console.WriteLine("\nPress Enter to terminate...");
      Console.Read();
    }
  }
}
```

AlignOutput defines a List<string> of names of uneven alignment and
length. (You could just as easily write the program to read these names from
the console or from a file.) The Main() method first displays the names as
they are. Main() then aligns the names using the Trim() and PadRight()
methods before redisplaying the resulting trimmed up strings, as follows:

```
The following names are of different lengths:
This is the name 'Christa ' before
This is the name '  Sarah' before
This is the name 'Jonathan' before
This is the name 'Sam' before
This is the name ' Schmekowitz ' before

The following are the same names rationalized to the same length:
This is the name 'Christa     ' afterwards
This is the name 'Sarah       ' afterwards
This is the name 'Jonathan    ' afterwards
This is the name 'Sam         ' afterwards
This is the name 'Schmekowitz ' afterwards
```

The alignment process begins by making a copy of the input `names` list.

The code first loops through the list, calling `Trim()` on each element to remove unneeded white space on either end. The method loops again through the list to find the longest member. The code loops one final time, calling `PadRight()` to expand each string to match the length of the longest member in the list. Note how the padded names form a neat column in the output.

`PadRight(10)` expands a string to be at least ten characters long. For example, `PadRight(10)` would add four spaces to the right of a six-character string.

Finally, the code displays the list of trimmed and padded strings for output. Voilà.

Using the Concatenate () method

You often face the problem of breaking up a string or inserting some substring into the middle of another. Replacing one character with another is most easily handled with the `Replace()` method, as follows:

```
string s = "Danger NoSmoking";
s = s.Replace(' ', '!')
```

This example converts the string into `"Danger!NoSmoking"`.

Replacing all appearances of one character (in this case, a space) with another (an exclamation mark) is especially useful when generating comma-separated strings for easier parsing. However, the more common and more difficult case involves breaking a single string into substrings, manipulating them separately, and then recombining them into a single, modified string.

The following `RemoveWhiteSpace` example program uses the `Replace()` method to remove white space (spaces, tabs, and newlines — all instances of a set of special characters) from a string:

```
// RemoveWhiteSpace - Remove any of a set of chars from a given string.
//     Use this method to remove whitespace from a sample string.
namespace RemoveWhiteSpace
{
  using System;
  public class Program
  {
    public static void Main(string[] args)
    {
      // Define the white space characters.
      char[] whiteSpace = {' ', '\n', '\t'};
      // Start with a string embedded with whitespace.
      string s = " this is a\nstring"; // Contains spaces & newline.
      Console.WriteLine("before:" + s);
      // Output the string with the whitespace missing.
      Console.Write("after:");
      // Start looking for the white space characters.
      for(;;)
      {
        // Find the offset of the character; exit the loop
        // if there are no more.
        int offset = s.IndexOfAny(whiteSpace);
        if (offset == -1)
        {
          break;
        }
        // Break the string into the part prior to the
        // character and the part after the character.
        string before = s.Substring(0, offset);
        string after  = s.Substring(offset + 1);
        // Now put the two substrings back together with the
        // character in the middle missing.
        s = String.Concat(before, after);
        // Loop back up to find next whitespace char in
        // this modified s.
      }
      Console.WriteLine(s);
      // Wait for user to acknowledge the results.
      Console.WriteLine("Press Enter to terminate...");
      Console.Read();
    }
  }
}
```

The key to this program is the boldfaced loop. This loop continually refines a string consisting of the input string, s, removing every one of a set of characters contained in the array `whiteSpace`.

The loop uses `IndexOfAny()` to find the first occurrence of any of the `chars` in the `whiteSpace` array. It doesn't return until every instance of any of those `chars` has been removed. The `IndexOfAny()` method returns the index within the array of the first white-space `char` that it can find. A return value of –1 indicates that no items in the array were found in the string.

The first pass through the loop removes the leading blank on the target string. `IndexOfAny()` finds the blank at index 0. The first `Substring()` call returns an empty string, and the second call returns the whole string after the blank. These are then concatenated with `Concat()`, producing a string with the leading blank squeezed out.

The second pass through the loop finds the space after `"this"` and squeezes that out the same way, concatenating the strings `"this"` and `"is a\nstring"`. After this pass, s has become `"thisis a\nstring"`.

The third pass finds the `\n` character and squeezes that out. On the fourth pass, `IndexOfAny()` runs out of white space characters to find and returns –1 (not found). That ends the loop.

The `RemoveWhiteSpace` program prints out a string containing several forms of white space. The program then strips out white-space characters. The output from this program appears as follows:

```
before: this is a
string
after:thisisastring
Press Enter to terminate...
```

Let's Split() that concatenate program

The `RemoveWhiteSpace` program demonstrates the use of the `Concat()` and `IndexOf()` methods; however, it doesn't use the most efficient approach. As usual, a little examination reveals a more efficient approach using our old friend `Split()`. You can find the program containing this code — now in another example of a method — on the Web site under `RemoveWhiteSpace-WithSplit`. The method that does the work is as follows:

```
// RemoveWhiteSpace - The RemoveSpecialChars method removes every
//     occurrence of the specified characters from the string.
// Note: The rest of the program is not shown here.
public static string RemoveSpecialChars(string input, char[] targets)
{
    // Split the input string up using the target
    // characters as the delimiters.
    string[] subStrings = input.Split(targets);
```

```
// output will contain the eventual output information.
string output = "";

// Loop through the substrings originating from the split.
foreach(string subString in subStrings)
{
  output = String.Concat(output, subString);
}
return output;
}
```

This version uses the Split() method to break the input string into a set of substrings, using the characters to be removed as delimiters. The delimiter is not included in the substrings created, which has the effect of removing the character(s). The logic here is much simpler and less error-prone.

The foreach loop in the second half of the program puts the pieces back together again using Concat(). The output from the program is unchanged.

Pulling the code out into a method further simplifies it and makes it clearer.

Formatting Your Strings Precisely

The String class also provides the Format() method for formatting output, especially the output of numbers. In its simplest form, Format() allows the insertion of string, numeric, or Boolean input in the middle of a format string. For example, consider the following call:

```
string myString = String.Format("{0} times {1} equals {2}", 2, 5, 2*5);
```

The first argument to Format() is known as the *format string* — the quoted string you see. The {*n*} items in the middle of the format string indicate that the *n*th argument following the format string is to be inserted at that point. {0} refers to the first argument (in this case, the value 2), {1} refers to the next (that is, 5), and so on.

This returns a string, myString. The resulting string is as follows:

```
"2 times 5 equals 10"
```

Unless otherwise directed, Format() uses a default output format for each argument type. Format() enables you to affect the output format by including *specifiers* (modifiers or controls) in the placeholders. See Table 6-1 for a listing of some of these specifiers. For example, {0:E6} says, "Output the number in exponential form, using six spaces for the fractional part."

The `Console.WriteLine()` method you've been using all along uses the same placeholder system. The first placeholder, `{0}`, takes the first variable or value listed after the format string part of the statement, and so on: given the exact same arguments as in the `Format()` call above, `Console.WriteLine()` would write the same string to the console. You also have access to the format specifiers. From now on, I'll use the formatted form of `WriteLine()` much of the time, instead of concatenating items to form the final output string with the + operator.

Table 6-1	Format Specifiers Using `String.Format()`		
Control	*Example*	*Result*	*Notes*
C — currency	`{0:C}` of 123.456	$123.45	The currency sign depends on the Region setting.
	`{0:C}` of −123.456	($123.45)	(Specify Region in Windows control panel.)
D — decimal	`{0:D5}` of 123	00123	Integers only.
E — exponential	`{0:E}` of 123.45	1.2345E+002	Also known as scientific notation.
F — fixed	`{0:F2}` of 123.4567	123.45	The number after the F indicates the number of digits after the decimal point.
N — number	`{0:N}` of 123456.789	123,456.79	Adds commas and rounds off to nearest 100th.
	`{0:N1}` of 123456.789	123,456.8	Controls the number of digits after the decimal point.
	`{0:N0}` of 123456.789	123,457	
X — hexadecimal	`{0:X}` of 123	0x7B	7B hex = 123 decimal (integers only).
`{0:0...}`	`{0:000.00}` of 12.3	012.30	Forces a 0 if a digit is not already present.
`{0:#...}`	`{0:###.##}` of 12.3	12.3	Forces the space to be left blank; no other field can encroach on the three digits to the left and two digits after the decimal point (useful for maintaining decimal-point alignment).

Control	Example	Result	Notes
	`{0:##0.0#}` of 0	0.0	Combining the # and zeros forces space to be allocated by the #s and forces at least one digit to appear, even if the number is 0.
`{0:#` or `0%}`	`{0:#00.#%}` of .1234	12.3%	The % displays the number as a percentage (multiplies by 100 and adds the % sign).
	`{0:#00.#%}` of .0234	02.3%	

These format specifiers can seem a bit bewildering. (I didn't even mention the detailed currency and date controls.) Explore the topic "format specifiers" in the Help index for more information. To help you wade through these options, the following `OutputFormatControls` program enables you to enter a floating-point number followed by a specifier sequence. The program then displays the number, using the specified `Format()` control:

```csharp
// OutputFormatControls - Allow the user to reformat input numbers
//      using a variety of format specifiers input at run time.
namespace OutputFormatControls
{
  using System;
  public class Program
  {
    public static void Main(string[] args)
    {
      // Keep looping - inputting numbers until the user
      // enters a blank line rather than a number.
      for(;;)
      {
        // First input a number - terminate when the user
        // inputs nothing but a blank line.
        Console.WriteLine("Enter a double number");
        string numberInput = Console.ReadLine();
        if (numberInput.Length == 0)
        {
          break;
        }
        double number = Double.Parse(numberInput);
        // Now input the specifier codes; split them
        // using spaces as dividers.
        Console.WriteLine("Enter the format specifiers"
                        + " separated by a blank "
```

```
                    + "(Example: C E F1 N0 0000000.00000)");
      char[] separator = {' '};
      string formatString = Console.ReadLine();
      string[] formats = formatString.Split(separator);
      // Loop through the list of format specifiers.
      foreach(string s in formats)
      {
        if (s.Length != 0)
        {
          // Create a complete format specifier
          // from the letters entered earlier.
          string formatCommand = "{0:" + s + "}";
          // Output the number entered using the
          // reconstructed format specifier.
          Console.Write(
               "The format specifier {0} results in ", formatCommand);
          try
          {
            Console.WriteLine(formatCommand, number);
          }
          catch(Exception)
          {
            Console.WriteLine("<illegal control>");
          }
          Console.WriteLine();
        }
      }
    }
    // Wait for user to acknowledge.
    Console.WriteLine("Press Enter to terminate...");
    Console.Read();
  }
}
```

The `OutputFormatControls` program continues to read floating-point numbers into a variable `numberInput` until the user enters a blank line. (Because the input is a bit tricky, I include an example for the user to imitate as part of the message asking for input.) Notice that the program does not include any tests to determine whether the input is a legal floating-point number. I just assume that the user is smart enough to know what a number looks like (a dangerous assumption!).

The program then reads a series of specifier strings separated by spaces. Each specifier is then combined with a `"{0}"` string (the number before the colon, which corresponds to the placeholder in the format string) into the variable `formatCommand`. For example, if you entered **N4**, the program would store the specifier `"{0:N4}"`. The following statement writes the number `number` using the newly constructed `formatCommand`:

```
Console.WriteLine(formatCommand, number);
```

In the case of our lowly N4, the command would be rendered as follows:

```
Console.WriteLine("{0:N4}", number);
```

Typical output from the program appears as follows (I boldfaced my input):

```
Enter a double number
12345.6789
Enter the specifiers separated by a blank (Example: C E F1 N0 0000000.00000)
C E F1 N0 0000000.00000
The format specifier {0:C} results in $12,345.68

The format specifier {0:E} results in 1.234568E+004

The format specifier {0:F1} results in 12345.7

The format specifier {0:N0} results in 12,346

The format specifier {0:0000000.00000} results in 0012345.67890


Enter a double number
.12345
Enter the specifiers separated by a blank (Example: C E F1 N0 0000000.00000)
00.0%
The format specifier {0:00.0%} results in 12.3%
Enter a double number

Press Enter to terminate...
```

When applied to the number 12345.6789, the specifier N0 adds commas in the proper place (the N part) and lops off everything after the decimal point (the 0 portion) to render 12,346 (the last digit was rounded off, not truncated).

Similarly, when applied to 0.12345, the control 00.0% outputs 12.3%. The percent sign multiplies the number by 100 and adds %. The 00.0 indicates that the output should include at least two digits to the left of the decimal point and only one digit after the decimal point. The number 0.01 is displayed as 01.0%, using the same 00.0% specifier.

The mysterious try . . . catch catches any errors that spew forth in the event you enter an illegal format command such as a D, which stands for decimal. (I cover exceptions in Bonus Chapter 2 on the Web site.)

StringBuilder: Manipulating Strings More Efficiently

Building up longer strings out of a bunch of shorter strings can cost you an arm and its elbow. Because a string, once created, can't be changed — it's immutable, as I said at the beginning of this chapter — the following

```
string s1 = "rapid";
string s2 = s1 + "ly";              // s2 = rapidly.
```

doesn't really tack an "ly" onto s1. It creates a new string composed of the combination (s1 is unchanged). Similarly, other operations that appear to modify a string, such as Substring() and Replace(), do the same.

The result is that each operation on a string produces yet another string. Suppose you need to concatenate 1000 strings into one huge one. You're going to create a new string for each concatenation:

```
string[] listOfNames = ...  // 1000 pet names.
string s = string.Empty;
for(int i = 0; i < 1000; i++)
{
   s += listOfNames[i];
}
```

To avoid such costs when you're doing lots of modifications to strings, use the companion class StringBuilder. Be sure to add the following at the top of your file:

```
using System.Text;  // Tells the compiler where to find StringBuilder.
```

Unlike String manipulations, the manipulations you do on a StringBuilder directly change the underlying string. Here's an example:

```
StringBuilder builder = new StringBuilder("012");
builder.Append("34");
builder.Append("56");
string result = builder.ToString();  // result = 0123456.
```

Create a StringBuilder instance initialized with an existing string, as just shown. Or create an empty StringBuilder with no initial value:

```
StringBuilder builder = new StringBuilder();  // Defaults to 16 characters.
```

You can also create the StringBuilder with the capacity you expect it to need, which reduces the overhead of increasing the builder's capacity frequently:

```
StringBuilder builder = new StringBuilder(256); // 256 characters.
```

Use the `Append()` method to add text to the end of the current contents. Use `ToString()` to retrieve the string inside the `StringBuilder` when you finish your modifications. Here's the `StringBuilder` version of the loop just shown, with retrieval of the final concatenated string in boldface:

```
StringBuilder sb = new StringBuilder(20000);  // Allocate a bunch.
for(int i = 0; i < 1000; i++)
{
  sb.Append(listOfNames[i]);     // Same list of names as earlier.
}
string result = sb.ToString();  // Retrieve the results.
```

`StringBuilder` has a number of other useful string manipulation methods, including `Insert()`, `Remove()`, and `Replace()`. It lacks many of `string`'s methods, though, such as `Substring()`, `CopyTo()`, and `IndexOf()`.

For example, suppose you want to uppercase just the first character of a string, as in the earlier section "Converting a string to upper- or lowercase." With `StringBuilder` it's much cleaner looking than the code I gave earlier:

```
StringBuilder sb = new StringBuilder("jones");
sb[0] = char.ToUpper(sb[0]);
string fixedString = sb.ToString();
```

This puts the lowercase string `"jones"` into a `StringBuilder`, accesses the first `char` in the `StringBuilder`'s underlying string directly with `sb[0]`, uses the `char.ToUpper()` method to uppercase the character, and reassigns the uppercased character to `sb[0]`. Finally, it extracts the improved string `"Jones"` from the `StringBuilder`.

The `BuildASentence` example presented earlier in this chapter could benefit from using a `StringBuilder`. I use `StringBuilder` quite a bit.

The `StringCaseChanging` and `VariousStringTechniques` examples on the Web site show `StringBuilder` in action.

Chapter 9 introduces a new C# feature called extension methods. The example there adds several handy methods to the `String` class. And Bonus Chapter 5 on the Web site describes how to convert between `strings`, arrays of `char`, and arrays of `byte`. Those are operations you may need to do frequently (and are shown in the `StringCaseChanging` example on the Web site).

Part III
Using Objects

In this part . . .

1t's one thing to declare a variable here or there and to add them and subtract them. It's quite another thing to write real programs that people can use — us simple people, but people nonetheless. In this part, you discover how to group data and how to operate on that data as a group. You begin to think about programs as collections of collaborating *objects* and start designing your own custom objects. These skills form the basis of all programming jobs you'll find in the classifieds. And you can't reach the heights of object-oriented programming without going airborne with a few simple objects.

Chapter 7

Showing Some Class

● ●

In This Chapter

▶ Introducing the C# class — the way to roll your own custom objects

▶ Storing data in an object

▶ Assigning and using object references

▶ Examining classes that contain classes

▶ Identifying static and instance class members

▶ Using constants in C#

● ●

*Y*ou can freely declare and use all the intrinsic data types — such as `int`, `double`, and `bool` — to store the information necessary to make your program the best that it can be. For some programs, these simple variables are enough. However, most programs need a way to bundle related data into a neat package.

As shown in Chapter 5, C# provides arrays and other collections for gathering groups of *like-typed* variables, such as `strings` or `ints`, into one structure. Take a hypothetical college, for example, that might track its students via an array. But how should such a program represent a student? A student is much more than just a name.

Some programs need to bundle pieces of data that logically belong together but aren't of the same type. A college-enrollment application handles students, each with his or her own name, rank (grade-point average), and serial number. Logically, the student's name may be a `string`, the grade-point average could be a `double`, and the serial number a `long`. That type of program needs some way to bundle these three different types of variables into a single structure called `Student`. Fortunately, C# provides a structure known as the *class* for accommodating groupings of unlike-typed variables.

What's an Object? What's a Class?

A *class* is a bundling of unlike data and functions that logically belong together into one tidy package. C# gives you the freedom to foul up your classes any way you want, but good classes are designed to represent *concepts.*

Computer science models the world via structures that represent concepts or things in the world, such as bank accounts, Tic Tac Toe games, customers, game boards, documents, and products. Analysts say that "a class maps concepts from the problem into the program." For example, suppose your problem is to build a traffic simulator. This traffic simulator is to model traffic patterns for the purpose of building streets, intersections, and high-ways. (I would really like you to build a traffic simulator that could fix the intersection in front of my house.)

Any description of a problem concerning traffic would include the term *vehicle* in its solution. Vehicles have a top speed that must be figured into the equation. They also have a weight, and some of them are clunkers. In addition, vehicles stop and vehicles go. Thus, as a concept, *vehicle* is part of the problem domain.

A good C# traffic-simulator program would necessarily include the class `Vehicle`, which describes the relevant properties of a vehicle. The C# `Vehicle` class would have properties like `topSpeed`, `weight`, and `isClunker`. (I address the `stop` and `go` parts in Chapters 8 and 9.)

Because the class is so central to C# programming, the chapters in Part IV of this book spelunk the ins and outs of classes in much more detail. This chapter gets you started.

Defining a class

An example of the class `Vehicle` may appear as follows:

```
public class Vehicle
{
  public string model;        // Name of the model.
  public string manufacturer; // Ditto.
  public int numOfDoors;      // The number of doors on the vehicle.
  public int numOfWheels;     // You get the idea.
}
```

A class definition begins with the words `public class`, followed by the name of the class — in this case, `Vehicle`.

Like all names in C#, the name of the class is case sensitive. C# doesn't enforce any rules concerning class names, but an unofficial rule holds that the name of a class starts with a capital letter.

The class name is followed by a pair of open and closed braces. Within the braces, you have zero or more *members.* The members of a class are variables that make up the parts of the class. In this example, class `Vehicle` starts with the member `string model`, which contains the name of the model of the vehicle. Were this a car, the model name could be Trouper II. (Hmm, have you ever seen or heard of a Trouper I?) The second member of this example `Vehicle` class is the `string manufacturer`. The final two properties are the number of doors and the number of wheels on the vehicle.

As with any variable, make the names of the members as descriptive as possible. Although I've added comments to the data members, that really isn't necessary. A good variable name says it all.

The `public` modifier in front of the class name makes the class universally accessible throughout the program. Similarly, the `public` modifier in front of the member names makes them accessible to everything else in the program. Other modifiers are possible. (Chapter 11 covers the topic of accessibility in more detail and shows how you can hide some members away.)

The class definition should describe the properties of the object that are salient to the problem at hand. That's a little hard to do right now because you don't know what the problem is, but you can see where I'm headed here.

What's the object?

Defining a `Vehicle` design is not the same thing as building a car. Someone has to cut some sheet metal and turn some bolts before anyone can drive an actual vehicle. A class object is declared in a similar (but not identical) fashion to declaring an intrinsic object such as an `int`.

The term *object* is used universally to mean a "thing." Okay, that isn't too helpful. An `int` variable is an `int` object. A vehicle is a `Vehicle` object. You are a reader object. I am an author . . . okay, forget that last one.

The following code segment creates a car of class `Vehicle`:

```
Vehicle myCar;
myCar = new Vehicle();
```

The first line declares a variable `myCar` of type `Vehicle`, just like you can declare a `somethingOrOther` of class `int`. (Yes, a class is a type, and all C# objects are defined as classes.) The `new Vehicle()` command creates a specific object of type `Vehicle` and stores the location into the variable `myCar`.

The `new` has nothing to do with the age of `myCar`. My car could qualify for an antique license plate if it weren't so ugly. The `new` operator creates a new block of memory in which your program can store the properties of `myCar`.

In C# terms, you say that `myCar` is an object of class `Vehicle`. You also say that `myCar` is an instance of `Vehicle`. In this context, *instance* means "an example of" or "one of." You can also use the word *instance* as a verb, as in *instantiating* a `Vehicle`. That's what *new* does.

Compare the declaration of `myCar` with that of an `int` variable called `num`:

```
int num;
num = 1;
```

The first line declares the variable `num`, and the second line assigns an already-created constant of type `int` into the location of the variable `num`.

The intrinsic `num` and the object `myCar` are stored differently in memory. The constant 1 does not occupy memory because both the CPU and the C# compiler already know what a 1 is. Your CPU doesn't have the concept of a `Vehicle`. The `new Vehicle` expression allocates the memory necessary to describe a vehicle to the CPU, to C#, to the world, and yes, to the universe!

Accessing the Members of an Object

Each object of class `Vehicle` has its own set of members. The following expression stores the number 1 into the `numberOfDoors` member of the object referenced by `myCar`:

```
myCar.numberOfDoors = 1;
```

Every C# operation must be evaluated by type as well as by value. The object `myCar` is an object of type `Vehicle`. The variable `Vehicle.number OfDoors` is of type `int` (look again at the definition of the `Vehicle` class). The constant 5 is also of type `int`, so the type of the variable on the right side of the assignment operator matches the type of the variable on the left.

Similarly, the following code stores a reference to the `strings` describing the model and manufacturer name of `myCar`:

```
myCar.manufacturer = "BMW";        // Don't get your hopes up.
myCar.model = "Isetta";            // The Urkel-mobile.
```

The Isetta was a small car built during the 1950s with a single door that opened the entire front of the car. I leave "Urkel" to you and Google.

An Example Object-Based Program

The simple `VehicleDataOnly` program does the following:

✔ Defines the class `Vehicle`

✔ Creates an object `myCar`

✔ Assigns properties to `myCar`

✔ Retrieves those values out of the object for display

The code for the `VehicleDataOnly` program is as follows:

```
// VehicleDataOnly - Create a Vehicle object, populate its
//      members from the keyboard and then write it back out.
using System;
namespace VehicleDataOnly
{
  public class Vehicle
  {
    public string model;        // Name of the model.
    public string manufacturer; // Ditto.
    public int numOfDoors;      // The number of doors on the vehicle.
    public int numOfWheels;     // You get the idea.
  }
  public class Program
  {
    static void Main(string[] args)
    {
      // Prompt user to enter her name.
      Console.WriteLine("Enter the properties of your vehicle");
      // Create an instance of Vehicle.
      Vehicle myCar = new Vehicle();
      // Populate a data member via a temporary variable.
      Console.Write("Model name = ");
      string s = Console.ReadLine();
      myCar.model = s;
      // Or you can populate the data member directly.
      Console.Write("Manufacturer name = ");
      myCar.manufacturer = Console.ReadLine();
      // Enter the remainder of the data.
      // A temp is useful for reading ints.
      Console.Write("Number of doors = ");
      s = Console.ReadLine();
      myCar.numOfDoors = Convert.ToInt32(s);
      Console.Write("Number of wheels = ");
      s = Console.ReadLine();
      myCar.numOfWheels = Convert.ToInt32(s);
      // Now display the results.
      Console.WriteLine("\nYour vehicle is a ");
```

```
    Console.WriteLine(myCar.manufacturer + " " + myCar.model);
    Console.WriteLine("with " + myCar.numOfDoors + " doors, "
                    + "riding on " + myCar.numOfWheels
                    + " wheels.");
    // Wait for user to acknowledge the results.
    Console.WriteLine("Press Enter to terminate...");
    Console.Read();
  }
 }
}
```

The program listing begins with a definition of the `Vehicle` class.

The definition of a class can appear either before or after class `Program` — it doesn't matter. However, unlike me you should adopt a style and stick with it. Bonus Chapter 1 on the Web site shows the more conventional technique of creating a separate `.cs` file to contain each class, but just put the extra class in your `Program.cs` file for now.

The program creates an object `myCar` of class `Vehicle` and then populates each of the fields by reading the appropriate data from the keyboard. (The input data isn't — but should be — checked for legality.) The program then writes `myCar`'s properties in a slightly different format.

The output from executing this program appears as follows:

```
Enter the properties of your vehicle
Model name = Metropolitan
Manufacturer name = Nash
Number of doors = 2
Number of wheels = 4

Your vehicle is a
Nash Metropolitan
with 2 doors, riding on 4 wheels
Press Enter to terminate...
```

The calls to `Write()` as opposed to `WriteLine()` leave the cursor right after the output string. This makes the user's input appear on the same line as the prompt. In addition, inserting the newline character `'\n'` in writes generates a blank line without the need to execute `WriteLine()` separately.

Discriminating Between Objects

Detroit car manufacturers can track each car they make without getting the cars confused. Similarly, a program can create numerous objects of the same class, as follows:

```
Vehicle car1 = new Vehicle();
car1.manufacturer = "Studebaker";
car1.model = "Avanti";
// The following has no effect on car1.
Vehicle car2 = new Vehicle();
car2.manufacturer = "Hudson";
car2.model = "Hornet";
```

Creating an object `car2` and assigning it the manufacturer name `Hudson` has no effect on the `car1` object (with the manufacturer name `Studebaker`).

In part, the ability to discriminate between objects is the real power of the class construct. The object associated with the Hudson Hornet can be created, manipulated, and dispensed with as a single entity, separate from other objects, including the Avanti. (These are both classic automobiles, especially the latter.)

Can You Give Me References?

The dot operator and the assignment operator are the only two operators defined on reference types, as follows:

```
// Create a null reference.
Vehicle yourCar;//Nothing assigned to yourCar yet
// Assign the reference a value.
yourCar = new Vehicle();
// Use dot to access a member.
yourCar.manufacturer = "Rambler";
// Create a new reference and point it to the same object.
Vehicle yourSpousalCar = yourCar;
```

The first line creates an object `yourCar` without assigning it a value. A reference that has not been initialized is said to point to the *null object*. Any attempt to use an uninitialized (null) reference generates an immediate error that terminates the program.

The C# compiler can catch most attempts to use an uninitialized reference and generate a warning at build time. If you somehow slip one past the compiler, accessing an uninitialized reference terminates the program immediately. You get a "null reference" message.

The second statement creates a new `Vehicle` object and assigns it to `yourCar`. The last statement in this code snippet assigns the reference `yourSpousalCar` to the reference `yourCar`. As shown in Figure 7-1, this has the effect of causing `yourSpousalCar` to refer to the same object as `yourCar`.

Figure 7-1:
The
relationship
between
two
references
to the same
object.

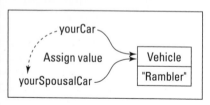

The following two calls have the same effect:

```
// Build your car.
Vehicle yourCar = new Vehicle();
yourCar.model = "Kaiser";
// It also belongs to your spouse.
Vehicle yourSpousalCar = yourCar;
// Changing one changes the other.
yourSpousalCar.model = "Henry J";
Console.WriteLine("Your car is a " + yourCar.model);
```

Executing this program would output `Henry J` and not `Kaiser`. Notice that `yourSpousalCar` does not point to `yourCar`; rather, both `yourCar` and `yourSpousalCar` refer to the same vehicle.

In addition, the reference `yourSpousalCar` would still be valid, even if the variable `yourCar` were somehow "lost" (went out of scope, for example), as shown in the following code:

```
// Build your car.
Vehicle yourCar = new Vehicle();
yourCar.model = "Kaiser";
// It also belongs to your spouse.
Vehicle yourSpousalCar = yourCar;
// When she takes your car away . . .
yourCar = null;            // yourCar now references the "null object."
//  . . .yourSpousalCar still references the same vehicle
Console.WriteLine("your car was a " + yourSpousalCar.model);
```

Executing this program generates the output `Your car was a Kaiser`, even though the reference `yourCar` is no longer valid.

The object is no longer *reachable* from the reference `yourCar`. The object does not become completely unreachable until both `yourCar` and `yourSpousalCar` are "lost" or nulled out.

At that point — well, at some unpredictable later point, anyway — C#'s *garbage collector* steps in and returns the space formerly used by that particular `Vehicle` object to the pool of space available for allocating more `Vehicles` (or `Students`, for that matter). (I say a little more about garbage collection at the end of Chapter 12.)

Making one *object variable* (a variable of a reference type, such as `Vehicle` or `Student`, rather than one of a simple type such as `int` or `double`) point to a different object — as we did here — makes storing and manipulating reference objects in arrays and collections very efficient. Each element of the array stores a reference to an object, and when you swap elements within the array, you're just moving references, not the objects themselves. References have a fixed size in memory, unlike the objects they refer to.

Classes That Contain Classes Are the Happiest Classes in the World

The members of a class can themselves be references to other classes. For example, vehicles have motors, which have power and efficiency factors, including displacement. (I suppose a bicycle doesn't have a displacement.) You could throw these factors directly into the class as follows:

```
public class Vehicle
{
    public string model;            // Name of the model.
    public string manufacturer;     // Ditto.
    public int numOfDoors;          // The number of doors on the vehicle.
    public int numOfWheels;         // You get the idea.
    // New stuff:
    public int power;               // Power of the motor [horsepower].
    public double displacement;     // Engine displacement [liter].
}
```

However, power and engine displacement are not properties of the car. For example, my son's Jeep comes with two different motor options with drastically different horsepower. The 2.4-liter Jeep is a snail while the same car outfitted with the 4.0-liter engine is quite peppy.

The motor is a concept of its own and deserves its own class, as follows:

```
public class Motor
{
    public int power;               // Power [horsepower].
    public double displacement;     // Engine displacement [liter].
}
```

You can combine this class into the `Vehicle` as follows (see boldfaced text):

```
public class Vehicle
{
  public string model;          // Name of the model.
  public string manufacturer;   // Ditto.
  public int numOfDoors;        // The number of doors on the vehicle.
  public int numOfWheels;       // You get the idea.
  public Motor motor;
}
```

Creating `myCar` now appears as follows:

```
// First create a Motor.
Motor largerMotor = new Motor();
largerMotor.power = 230;
largerMotor.displacement = 4.0;
// Now create the car.
Vehicle sonsCar = new Vehicle();
sonsCar.model = "Cherokee Sport";
sonsCar.manfacturer = "Jeep";
sonsCar.numOfDoors = 2;
sonsCar.numOfWheels = 4;
// Attach the motor to the car.
sonsCar.motor = largerMotor;
```

From the `Vehicle`, you can access the motor displacement in two stages. You can take one step at a time, as this code shows:

```
Motor m = sonsCar.motor;
Console.WriteLine("The motor displacement is " + m.displacement);
```

Or you can access it directly, as shown here:

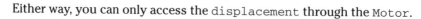
```
Console.Writeline("The motor displacement is " + sonsCar.motor.displacement);
```

Either way, you can only access the `displacement` through the `Motor`.

This example is bundled in the simple program `VehicleAndMotor` on the Web site, not shown in full here.

Generating Static in Class Members

Most data members of a class are specific to their containing object, not any other objects. Consider the `Car` class, as follows:

```
public class Car
{
  public string licensePlate;      // The license plate ID.
}
```

The license plate ID is an *object property,* meaning that it describes each object of class Car uniquely. For example, thank goodness that my car has a different license plate from yours; otherwise you may not make it out of your driveway, as shown in the following code:

```
Car myCar = new Car();
myCar.licensePlate = "XYZ123";

Car yourCar = new Car();
yourCar.licensePlate = "ABC789";
```

However, some properties exist that all cars share. For example, the number of cars built is a property of the class Car but not of any one object. These are called *class properties* and are flagged in C# with the keyword static, as follows:

```
public class Car
{
  public static int numberOfCars; // The number of cars built.
  public string licensePlate;      // The license plate ID.
}
```

Static members are not accessed through the object. Instead, you access them via the class itself, as the following code snippet demonstrates:

```
// Create a new object of class Car.
Car newCar = new Car();
newCar.licensePlate = "ABC123";
// Now increment the count of cars to reflect the new one.
Car.numberOfCars++;
```

The object member newCar.licensePlate is accessed through the object newCar, while the class (static) member Car.numberOfCars is accessed through the class Car. All Cars share the same numberOfCars member so each car contains exactly the same value as all other cars.

Class members are static members. Nonstatic members are specific to each "instance" (each individual object) and are called *instance members.* The italicized phrases are the generic way to refer to these types of members.

Defining const and readonly Data Members

One special type of static member is the `const` data member, which represents a constant. You must establish the value of a `const` variable in the declaration, and you may not change it anywhere within the program, as shown in the following code:

```
class Program
{
  // Number of days in the year (including leap day).
  public const int daysInYear = 366;  // Must have initializer.
  public static void Main(string[] args)
  {
    // This is an array, covered later in this chapter.
    int[] maxTemperatures = new int[daysInYear];
    for(int index = 0; index < daysInYear; index++)
    {
      //  . . .store the maximum temperature for each
      // day of the year . . .
    }
  }
}
```

You can use the constant `daysInYear` in place of the value `366` anywhere within your program. The `const` variable is useful because it can replace a mysterious number such as `366` with the descriptive name `daysInYear` to enhance the readability of your program.

Actually, C# provides a second way to declare constants. You can preface a variable declaration with the `readonly` modifier, like so:

```
public readonly int daysInYear = 366;  // This could also be static.
```

As with `const`, after you assign the initial value, it can't be changed. Although the reasons are too technical for this book, the `readonly` approach to declaring constants is usually preferable to `const`.

You can use `const` with class data members like those you've seen in this chapter and inside class methods. But `readonly` is not allowed in a method. Chapter 8 dives into methods.

An alternative convention also exists for naming constants. Instead of naming them like variables (as in `daysInYear`), many programmers prefer to use uppercase letters separated by underscores, as in `DAYS_IN_YEAR`. This convention separates constants clearly from ordinary read-write variables.

Chapter 8

We Have Our Methods

In This Chapter

▶ Defining a method

▶ Passing arguments to a method

▶ Getting results back — that would be nice

▶ Reviewing the `WriteLine()` method

*P*rogrammers need the ability to break large programs into smaller
chunks that are easier to handle. For example, the programs contained
in previous chapters are reaching the limit of what a person can digest at one
time.

C# lets you divide your class code into chunks known as *methods*. Properly
designed and implemented methods can greatly simplify the job of writing
complex programs.

Methods are equivalent to what other languages call functions, procedures,
or subroutines. The difference is that methods are always part of a class.

Defining and Using a Method

Consider the following example:

```
class Example
{
  public int anInt;                    // Non-static.
  public static int staticInt          // Static.
  public void InstanceMethod()         // Non-static.
  {
    Console.WriteLine("this is an instance method");
  }
  public static void ClassMethod()     // Static.
  {
    Console.WriteLine("this is a class method");
  }
}
```

The element `anInt` is a *data member*, just like those shown in Chapter 7. However, the element `InstanceMethod()` is new. `InstanceMethod()` is known as an *instance method* (duh!), which is a set of C# statements that you can execute by referencing the method's name. This is best explained by example — even I'm confused right now. (Actually, you've been seeing methods all along, starting with `Main()` and `WriteLine()`.)

Note: The distinction between static and nonstatic members is important. I cover part of that story in this chapter and continue in more detail in Chapter 9 with a focus on nonstatic, or instance, methods.

To invoke a non-static — instance — method, you need an instance of the class. To invoke a static — class — method, you call through the class name, not an instance. The following code snippet assigns a value to the object data member `anInt` and the class, or static, member `staticInt`:

```
Example example = new Example(); // Create an instance of class Example.
example.anInt = 1;               // Initialize instance member through instance.
Example.staticInt = 2;           // Initialize class member through class.
```

The following snippet defines and accesses `InstanceMethod()` and `ClassMethod()` in almost the same way:

```
Example example = new Example(); // Create an instance.
example.InstanceMethod();        // Invoke the instance method
                                 // with that instance.
Example.ClassMethod();           // Invoke the class method with the class.
// The following lines won't compile.
example.ClassMethod();           // Can't access class methods via an instance.
Example.InstanceMethod();        // Can't access instance methods via class.
```

Every instance of a class has its own private copy of any instance members. But all instances of the same class share the same class members — both data members and methods — and their values.

The expression `example.InstanceMethod()` passes control to the code contained within the method. C# follows an almost identical process for `Example.ClassMethod()`. Executing the lines just shown (after commenting out the last two lines, which won't compile) generates the following output:

```
this is an instance method
this is a class method
```

After a method completes execution, it returns control to the point where it was called. That is, control moves to the next statement after the call.

The bit of C# code given in the two example methods does nothing more than write a silly `string` to the console, but methods generally perform useful (and sometimes complex) operations such as calculating sines, concatenating two strings, sorting an array of students, or surreptitiously e-mailing your URL to Microsoft. A method can be as large and complex as you want it to be, but it's best to strive for shorter methods, using the approach described in the next section.

I usually include the parentheses when describing methods in text — as in InstanceMethod() — to make them a little easier to recognize. Otherwise I get confused trying to understand what I'm saying.

An Example Method for Your Files

In this section, I take the monolithic CalculateInterestTable programs from Chapter 4 and divide them into several reasonable methods; it's a demonstration of how the proper definition of methods can help make the program easier to write and understand. The process of dividing up working code this way is known as *refactoring*, and Visual Studio 2008 provides a handy Refactor menu that automates the most common refactorings.

I explain the exact details of the method definitions and method calls in later sections of this chapter. This example simply gives an overview.

By reading the comments *with the actual C# code removed*, you should be able to get a good idea of a program's intention. If you cannot, you aren't commenting properly. Conversely, if you can't strip out most comments and still understand the intention from the method and variable names, you aren't naming your methods clearly enough and/or making them small enough. Smaller methods are preferable, and good method names beat using comments. (That's why real-world code has far fewer comments than the example code in this book. I comment more heavily here to explain more.)

In outline form, the CalculateInterestTable program appears as follows:

```
public static void Main(string[] args)
{
    // Prompt user to enter source principal.
    // If the principal is negative, generate an error message.
    // Prompt user to enter the interest rate.
    // If the interest is negative, generate an error message.
    // Finally, prompt user to input the number of years.
    // Display the input back to the user.
    // Now loop through the specified number of years.
    while(year <= duration)
    {
        // Calculate the value of the principal plus interest.
        // Output the result.
    }
}
```

This code illustrates a good technique for planning a method. If you stand back and study the program from a distance, you can see it's divided into the following three sections:

- ✔ An initial input section in which the user inputs the principal, interest, and duration information
- ✔ A section that mirrors the input data so that the user can verify that the correct data was entered
- ✔ A final section that creates and outputs the table

These are good places to start looking for ways to refactor the program. In fact, if you further examine the input section of that program, you can see that *the same basic code* is used to input the following:

- ✔ The principal
- ✔ The interest
- ✔ The duration

That observation gives you another good place to look. Alternatively, you can write empty methods for some of those comments, and then fill them in one by one. That's called "programming by intention."

I have used this information to create the following version of the CalculateInterestTableWithMethods program:

```
// CalculateInterestTableWithMethods - Generate an interest table
//    much like the other interest table programs, but this time using a
//    reasonable division of labor among several methods.
using System;
namespace CalculateInterestTableWithMethods
{
  public class Program
  {
    public static void Main(string[] args)
    {
      // Section 1 - Input the data you will need to create the table.
      decimal principal = 0M;
      decimal interest = 0M;
      decimal duration = 0M;
      InputInterestData(ref principal, ref interest, ref duration);
      // Section 2 - Verify the data by mirroring it back to the user.
      Console.WriteLine();  // Skip a line.
      Console.WriteLine("Principal    = " + principal);
      Console.WriteLine("Interest     = " + interest + "%");
      Console.WriteLine("Duration     = " + duration + " years");
      Console.WriteLine();
      // Section 3 - Finally, output the interest table.
      OutputInterestTable(principal, interest, duration);
```

```
        // Wait for user to acknowledge the results.
        Console.WriteLine("Press Enter to terminate...");
        Console.Read();
    }
    // InputInterestData - Retrieve from the keyboard the
    //      principal, interest and duration information needed
    //      to create the future value table. (Implements Section 1.)
    public static void InputInterestData(ref decimal principal,
                                         ref decimal interest,
                                         ref decimal duration)
    {
        // 1a - Retrieve the principal.
        principal = InputPositiveDecimal("principal");
        // 1b - Now enter the interest rate.
        interest = InputPositiveDecimal("interest");
        // 1c - Finally, the duration.
        duration = InputPositiveDecimal("duration");
    }
    // InputPositiveDecimal - Return a positive decimal number
    //      from the keyboard.
    public static decimal InputPositiveDecimal(string prompt)
    {
        // Keep trying until the user gets it right.
        while(true)
        {
            // Prompt the user for input.
            Console.Write("Enter " + prompt + ":");
            // Retrieve a decimal value from the keyboard.
            string input = Console.ReadLine();
            decimal value = Convert.ToDecimal(input);
            // Exit the loop if the value entered is correct.
            if (value >= 0)
            {
                // Return the valid decimal value entered by the user.
                return value;
            }
            // Otherwise, generate an error on incorrect input.
            Console.WriteLine(prompt + " cannot be negative");
            Console.WriteLine("Try again");
            Console.WriteLine();
        }
    }
    // OutputInterestTable - Given the principal and interest
    //      generate a future value table for the number of periods
    //      indicated in duration. (Implements Section 3.)
    public static void OutputInterestTable(decimal principal,
                                           decimal interest,
                                           decimal duration)
    {
        for (int year = 1; year <= duration; year++)
        {
            // Calculate the value of the principal plus interest.
            decimal interestPaid;
```

```
    interestPaid = principal * (interest / 100);
    // Now calculate the new principal by adding
    // the interest to the previous principal.
    principal = principal + interestPaid;
    // Round off the principal to the nearest cent.
    principal = decimal.Round(principal, 2);
    // Output the result.
    Console.WriteLine(year + "-" + principal);
}
        }
    }
}
```

I have divided the `Main()` method into three clearly distinguishable parts, each marked with boldfaced comments. I further divide the first section into 1a, 1b, and 1c.

Normally you wouldn't include the comments that I have boldfaced. The listings would get rather complicated with all the numbers and letters if you did. In practice, those types of comments aren't necessary if the methods are well thought out and their names clearly express the intent of each.

Part 1 calls the method `InputInterestData()` to input the three variables the program needs to create the table: `principal`, `interest`, and `duration`. Part 2 displays these three values for verification just as the earlier versions of the program do. Part 3 outputs the table via the method `OutputInterestTable()`.

Starting at the bottom and working up, the `OutputInterestTable()` method contains an output loop with the interest-rate calculations. This is the same loop used in the in-line, nonmethod `CalculateInterestTable` program in Chapter 4. The advantage of this version, however, is that when writing this section of code, you don't need to concern yourself with any of the details of inputting or verifying the data. In writing this method, you need to think, "Given the three numbers — `principal`, `interest`, and `duration` — output an interest table," and that's it. After you're done, you can return to the line that called the `OutputInterestTable()` method and continue from there.

`OutputInterestTable()` offers a good tryout of Visual Studio 2008's Refactor menu. Take these steps to give it a whirl:

1. **Using the** `CalculateInterestTableMoreForgiving` **example from Chapter 4 as a starting point, select the code from the declaration of the** `year` **variable through the end of the** `while` **loop:**

```
int year = 0;          // You grab the loop variable
while(year <= duration)  // and the entire while loop.
{
   //...
}
```

2. Choose Refactor⇨Extract Method.

3. In the Extract Method dialog box, type OutputInterestTable. **Examine the Preview Method Signature box.**

Notice that the proposed signature for the new method begins with the private static keywords and includes principal, interest, and duration in the parentheses. (I introduce private, an alternative to public, in Chapter 11. For now, you can make the method public after the refactoring if you like.)

```
private static decimal OutputInterestTable(decimal principal,
    decimal interest, int duration)
```

4. Click OK, then Apply to complete the Extract Method refactoring.

The code you selected in Step 1 above has been moved to a new method located below Main(), called OutputInterestTable(). In the spot that it formerly occupied, you see the following method call:

```
principal = OuputInterestTable(principal, interest, duration);
```

The Preview Changes window shows two panes so you can preview exactly what will change. The top pane shows the code you're fixing, as it is now. The lower pane shows it as it will look when changed. For more sweeping refactorings, each pane may have numerous lines. You can select or deselect them individually to determine which specific elements will actually be refactored.

If, after doing a refactoring, you suffer "buyer's remorse," click Undo.

Suppose the previous refactoring had done something you didn't like, such as not including principal as a parameter. (This is possible, which means that you must always check a refactoring to be certain it's what you want.)

In fact, that happened to me for some reason the first time I wrote this section (keep in mind that I'm writing this based on beta software). Instead of making principal one of the parameters, the Extract Method refactoring made it a local variable. To move it up into the parameter list, you could use the Promote Local Variable To Parameter refactoring. But before you do that, you'd need to initialize the local variable principal (the promotion refactoring won't work if the variable is uninitialized):

```
decimal principal = 0M;  // M means decimal.
```

To carry out the Promote Local Variable to Parameter refactoring, you'd right-click the local principal variable's name and click Promote Local Variable To Parameter. This moves the local variable definition up to the parameter list:

```
private static decimal OutputInterestTable(decimal interest,
                                           int duration,
                                           decimal principal) ...
```

However, it's at the end of the list, and you'd like it at the beginning. You could use the Reorder Parameters refactoring to fix that.

To carry out Reorder Parameters, right-click the new `principal` parameter and click Reorder Parameters. In the dialog box, click the line with `principal` to select it. Then click the ↑ button twice to move `principal` to the top of the list. Click OK.

The result of all of this refactoring consists of the following two pieces:

- ✔ A new `private static` method below `Main()`, called `OutputInterestTable()`
- ✔ The following line of code within `Main()` where the extracted code was:

```
principal = OutputInterestTable(principal, interest, duration);
```

Pretty cool! The same divide-and-conquer logic holds for `InputInterestData()`. However, that refactoring is more complex, so I do it by hand and don't show the steps. The full art of refactoring is beyond the scope of this book, though you can find an introduction on my Web site at `csharp102.info`. Experiment with the Refactor menu and use it often for better factored code. But always check the results.

For `InputInterestData()`, you can focus solely on inputting the three decimal values. However, in this case, you realize that inputting each decimal involves identical operations on three different input variables. The `InputPositiveDecimal()` method bundles these operations into a set of general code that you can apply to principal, interest, and duration alike. Notice that the three `while` loops that take input in the original program get collapsed into one `while` loop inside `InputPositiveDecimal()`. This reduces code duplication.

Duplicating code is always a bad thing. Refactoring folks call it the worst "code smell."

This `InputPositiveDecimal()` method displays the prompt it was given and awaits input from the user. The method returns the value to the caller if it is not negative. If the value is negative, the method outputs an error message and loops back to try again.

From the user's standpoint, the modified program acts exactly the same as the in-line version in Chapter 4, which is just the point:

```
Enter principal:100
Enter interest:-10
interest cannot be negative
Try again

Enter interest:10
Enter duration:10

Principal    = 100
Interest     = 10%
Duration     = 10 years


1-110.0
2-121.00
3-133.10
4-146.41
5-161.05
6-177.16
7-194.88
8-214.37
9-235.81
10-259.39
Press Enter to terminate...
```

I've taken a lengthy, somewhat difficult program and refactored it into
smaller, more understandable pieces — while reducing some duplication. As
we say in my neck of the woods, "You can't beat that with a stick."

Having Arguments with Methods

A method such as the following example is about as useful as my co-author's
hairbrush because no data passes into or out of the method:

```
public static void Output()
{
   Console.WriteLine("this is a method");
}
```

Compare this example to real-world methods that actually do something. For
example, the mathematical sine operation requires some type of input —
after all, you have to take the sine of something. Similarly, to concatenate two
strings into one, you need two strings. So the Concatenate() method
requires at least two strings as input. "Gee, Wally, that sounds logical." You
need some way to get data into and out of a method.

Why bother with methods?

When FORTRAN introduced the function concept — methods, in C# — during the 1950s, the sole purpose was to avoid duplication of code by combining similar sections into a common element. Suppose you were to write a program that needed to calculate ratios in multiple places. Your program could call the `CalculateRatio()` method when needed, more or less for the sole purpose of avoiding duplicating code. The savings may not seem so important for a method as small as `CalculateRatio()`, but methods can grow to be much larger. Besides, a common method like `WriteLine()` may be invoked in hundreds of different places.

Quickly, a second advantage became obvious: It is easier to code a single method correctly — and doubly easier if the method is small. The `CalculateRatio()` method includes a check to make sure that the denominator is not zero. If you repeat the calculation code throughout your program, you could easily remember this test in some cases — and in other places, forget.

Not so obvious is a third advantage: A carefully crafted method reduces the complexity of the program. A well-defined method should stand for some concept. You should be able to describe the purpose of the method without using the words *and* or *or*. The method should do one thing.

A method like `CalculateSin()` is an ideal example. The programmer who has been tasked with this assignment can implement this complex operation without worrying about how it may be used. The applications programmer can use `CalculateSin()` without worrying about how this operation is performed internally. This greatly reduces the number of things that the applications programmer has to worry about. By reducing the number of "variables," a large job gets accomplished by implementing two smaller, easier jobs.

Large programs (such as word processors) are built up from many layers of methods at ever-increasing levels of abstraction. For example, a `RedisplayDocument()` method would undoubtedly call a `Reparagraph()` method to redisplay the paragraphs within the document. `Reparagraph()` would need to invoke a `CalculateWordWrap()` method to decide where to wrap the lines that make up the paragraph. `CalculateWordWrap()` would have to call a `LookUpWordBreak()` method to decide where to break a word at the end of the line, to make the sentences wrap more naturally. Each of these methods was described in a single, simple sentence. (Notice, also, how well-named these methods are.)

Without the ability to *abstract* complex concepts, writing programs of even moderate complexity would become almost impossible — let alone creating an operating system such as Windows Vista, a utility such as WinZip, a word processor like WordPerfect, or a game such as Halo, to name a few examples.

Passing an argument to a method

The values you input to a method are called the *method arguments* (also called *parameters*). Most methods require some type of arguments if they're going to do something. In this way, methods remind me of my son: We need to have an argument before he'll do anything. You pass arguments to a method by listing them in the parentheses that follow the method name. Consider the following small addition to the earlier `Example` class:

```
public class Example
{
   public static void Output(string someString)
   {
      Console.WriteLine("Output() was passed the argument: " + someString);
   }
}
```

I could invoke this method from within the same class as follows:

```
Output("Hello");
```

I would get the following not-too-exciting output:

```
Output() was passed the argument: Hello
```

The program passes a reference to the `string` `"Hello"` to the method `Output()`. The method receives the reference and assigns it the name `someString`. The `Output()` method can use `someString` within the method just as it would any other `string` variable.

I can change the example in one minor way:

```
string myString = "Hello";
Output(myString);
```

This code snippet assigns the variable `myString` to reference the `string` `"Hello"`. The call `Output(myString)` passes the object referenced by `myString`, which is your good old friend `"Hello"`. Figure 8-1 depicts this process. From there, the effect is the same as before.

Technically, the placeholders you specify for arguments when you write a method — for example, `someString` in `Output()` — are called *parameters*. The values you pass to a method via a parameter are *arguments*. But I'll just use the terms more or less interchangeably everywhere.

Figure 8-1:
The call
`Output`
`(my`
`String)`
copies the
value of
`myString`
to `some`
`String`.

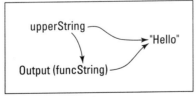

Bonus Chapter 5 covers a similar idea: passing arguments to a program. For example, you may have noticed that `Main()` usually takes an array argument.

Passing multiple arguments to methods

When I ask my daughter to wash the car, she usually gives me more than just a single argument. Because she has lots of time on the couch to think about it, she can keep several at the ready.

You can define a method with multiple arguments of varying types. Consider the following example method `AverageAndDisplay()`:

```
// AverageAndDisplay - Demonstrate argument passing.
using System;
namespace Example
{
  public class Program
  {
    public static void Main(string[] args)
    {
      // Access the member method.
      AverageAndDisplay("grade 1", 3.5, "grade 2", 4.0);
      // Wait for user to acknowledge.
      Console.WriteLine("Press Enter to terminate...");
      Console.Read();
    }
    // AverageAndDisplay - Average two numbers with their
    //    labels and display the results.
    public static void AverageAndDisplay(string s1, double d1,
                                         string s2, double d2)
    {
      double average = (d1 + d2) / 2;
      Console.WriteLine("The average of " + s1
                + " whose value is " + d1
                + " and "            + s2
                + " whose value is " + d2
                + " is " + average);
    }
  }
}
```

Executing this simple program generates the following output:

```
The average of grade 1 whose value is 3.5 and grade 2 whose value is 4 is 3.75
Press Enter to terminate...
```

The method `AverageAndDisplay()` is declared with several parameters in the order in which arguments are to be passed to them.

As usual, execution of the example program begins with the first statement after `Main()`. The first noncomment line in `Main()` invokes the method `AverageAndDisplay()`, passing the two `string`s "grade 1" and "grade 2" and the two `double` values 3.5 and 4.0.

The method `AverageAndDisplay()` calculates the average of the two `double` values, d1 and d2, passed to it along with their names contained in s1 and s2, and the calculated average is stored in `average`.

Changing the value of an argument inside the method can lead to confusion and errors. It's wiser to assign it to a temporary variable and modify that.

Matching argument definitions with usage

Each argument in a method call must match the method definition in both type *and order.* The following is illegal and generates a build-time error:

```
// AverageWithCompilerError - This version does not compile!
using System;
namespace Example
{
  public class Program
  {
    public static void Main(string[] args)
    {
      // Access the member method.
      AverageAndDisplay("grade 1", "grade 2", 3.5, 4.0);
      // Wait for user to acknowledge.
      Console.WriteLine("Press Enter to terminate...");
      Console.Read();
    }
    // AverageAndDisplay - Average two numbers with their
    //     labels and display the results.
    public static void AverageAndDisplay(string s1, double d1,
                                         string s2, double d2)
    {
      // var ok here, but it's really double - see Ch 2.
      var average = (d1 + d2) / 2;
      Console.WriteLine("The average of "  + s1
                  + " whose value is " + d1
                  + " and "            + s2
                  + " whose value is " + d2
                  + " is " + average);

    }
  }
}
```

C# can't match the type of each argument in the call to AverageAnd Display() with the corresponding argument in the method definition. The string "grade 1" matches the first string in the method definition; however, the method definition calls for a double as its second argument rather than the string that's passed.

You can easily see that I simply transposed the second and third arguments. That's what I hate about computers — they take me too literally. I know what I *said*, but it's obvious what I *meant!*

To fix the problem, swap the second and third arguments.

Overloading a method does not mean giving it too much to do

You can give two methods within a given class the same name *as long as* their arguments differ. This is called *overloading* the method name.

The following example demonstrates overloading:

```
// AverageAndDisplayOverloaded - This version demonstrates that
//    the AverageAndDisplay method can be overloaded.
using System;
namespace AverageAndDisplayOverloaded
{
  public class Program
  {
    public static void Main(string[] args)
    {
      // Access the first version of the method.
      AverageAndDisplay("my GPA", 3.5, "your GPA", 4.0);
      Console.WriteLine();
      // Access the second version of the method.
      AverageAndDisplay(3.5, 4.0);
      // Wait for user to acknowledge.
      Console.WriteLine("Press Enter to terminate...");
      Console.Read();
    }
    // AverageAndDisplay - Average two numbers with their
    //    labels and display the results.
    public static void AverageAndDisplay(string s1, double d1,
                                         string s2, double d2)
    {
      double average = (d1 + d2) / 2;
      Console.WriteLine("The average of " + s1
                     + " whose value is " + d1);
      Console.WriteLine("and "            + s2
                     + " whose value is " + d2
```

```
                    + " is " + average);
    }
    public static void AverageAndDisplay(double d1, double d2)
    {
        double average = (d1 + d2) / 2;
        Console.WriteLine("The average of " + d1
                + " and "            + d2
                + " is " + average);
    }
  }
}
```

This program defines two versions of `AverageAndDisplay()`. The program invokes one and then the other by passing the proper arguments. C# can tell which method the program wants by comparing the call with the definition. The program compiles properly and generates the following output when executed:

```
The average of my GPA whose value is 3.5
and your GPA whose value is 4 is 3.75

The average of 3.5 and 4 is 3.75
Press Enter to terminate..
```

In general, C# does not allow two methods in the same class to have the same name unless the number and/or type of the methods' arguments differ. Thus C# differentiates between the two methods `AverageAndDisplay-(string, double, string, double)` and `AverageAndDisplay(double, double)`. When you say it that way, it's clear that the two methods are different.

Implementing default arguments

Often, you want to supply two (or more) versions of a method, as follows:

- ✔ One version would be the complicated version that provides complete flexibility but requires numerous arguments from the calling routine, several of which the user may not even understand.

In practice, references to the "user" of a method often mean the programmer who is making use of the method. *User* does not always refer to the ultimate user of the program. Another term for the kind of user meant here is *client*. (Often the client is you.)

- ✔ A second version of the method would provide acceptable, if somewhat bland, performance by assuming default values for some of the arguments.

You can easily implement default arguments using method overloading. Consider the following pair of `DisplayRoundedDecimal()` methods:

```
// MethodsWithDefaultArguments - Provide variations of the same methods,
//    some with default arguments, by overloading the method name.
using System;
namespace MethodsWithDefaultArguments
{
  public class Program
  {
    public static void Main(string[] args)
    {
      // Access the member method.
      Console.WriteLine(DisplayRoundedDecimal(12.345678M, 3));
      // Wait for user to acknowledge.
      Console.WriteLine("Press Enter to terminate...");
      Console.Read();
    }
    // DisplayRoundedDecimal - Convert a decimal value into a string
    //    with the specified number of signficant digits.
    public static string DisplayRoundedDecimal(decimal value,
                                   int numberOfSignificantDigits)
    {
      // First round the number off to the specified number
      // of significant digits.
      decimal roundedValue =
                  decimal.Round(value,
                              numberOfSignificantDigits);
      // Convert that to a string.
      string s = Convert.ToString(roundedValue);
      return s;
    }
    public static string DisplayRoundedDecimal(decimal value)
    {
      // Invoke DisplayRoundedDecimal(decimal, int) specifying.
      // The default number of digits.
      string s = DisplayRoundedDecimal(value, 2);
      return s;
    }
  }
}
```

The `DisplayRoundedDecimal(decimal, int)` method converts the `decimal` value provided into a `string` with the specified number of digits after the decimal point. Because decimals are often used to display monetary values, the most common choice is two digits after the decimal point. Therefore the `DisplayRoundedDecimal(decimal)` method provides the same conversion service — but defaults the number of significant digits to two, thereby saving the user from even worrying about the meaning of the second argument.

Notice that the generic `(decimal)` version of the method actually calls the more specific `(decimal, int)` version to perform its magic. This is more common than not, because it reduces duplication. The generic methods simply provide arguments that the programmer doesn't have the inclination to look up in the documentation, and shouldn't have to unless she needs them.

Providing default arguments is more than just saving a lazy programmer a tiny bit of effort. Programming requires lots of concentration. Unnecessary trips to the reference documentation to look up the meaning of normally defaulted arguments distract the programmer from the main job at hand — thereby making the job more difficult, wasting time, and increasing the likelihood of mistakes. The author of the method understands the relationship between the arguments — and therefore bears the onus of providing friendlier, overloaded versions of methods.

Visual Basic 6.0 and C/C++ programmers take note: In C#, overloaded methods are the only way to implement default arguments. C# also doesn't allow optional arguments. Do it all with overloads.

Passing Value-Type and Reference-Type Arguments

The basic variable types such as `int`, `double`, and `decimal` are known as *value-type* variables. You can pass value-type variables to a method in one of two ways. The default form is to *pass by value.* An alternate form is to *pass by reference.* (Bonus Chapter 4 gives a full discussion of value- and reference-types.)

Programmers can get sloppy in their speech. In referring to value-types, when a programmer says "passing a variable to a method," that usually means "pass the value of a variable to a method."

Passing value-type arguments by value

Unlike object references, value-type variables such as an `int` or a `double` are normally *passed by value,* which means that *a copy of the value* contained within the variable is passed to the method and not the variable itself.

Pass by value has the effect that changing the value of a value-type variable within a method does not change the value of that variable in the calling program. This is demonstrated in the following code:

```
// PassByValue - Demonstrate pass-by-value semantics.
using System;
namespace PassByValue
{
  public class Program
  {
    // Update - Try to modify the values of the arguments
```

```
//    passed to it; note that you can declare methods
//    in any order in a class.
public static void Update(int i, double d)
{
  i = 10;
  d = 20.0;
}
public static void Main(string[] args)
{
    // Declare two variables and initialize them.
    int i = 1;
    double d = 2.0;
    Console.WriteLine("Before the call to Update(int, double):");
    Console.WriteLine("i = " + i + ", d = " + d);
    // Invoke the Update method.
    Update(i, d);
    // Notice that the values 1 and 2.0 have not changed.
    Console.WriteLine("After the call to Update(int, double):");
    Console.WriteLine("i = " + i + ", d = " + d);
    // Wait for user to acknowledge.
    Console.WriteLine("Press Enter to terminate...");
    Console.Read();
  }
 }
}
```

Executing this program generates the following output (highlight added):

```
Before the call to Update(int, double):
i = 1, d = 2
After the call to Update(int, double):
i = 1, d = 2
Press Enter to terminate...
```

The call to Update() copies the *values* 1 and 2.0 into the method arguments, not a reference to the variables i and d. Thus changing their value within the method no more affects the value of the variables back in the calling routine than asking for ice water at an English pub. The method changes the copies.

Passing value-type arguments by reference

Passing a value-type argument to a method *by reference* is advantageous sometimes, too — in particular, when the caller wants to give the method the ability to change the value of the variable. The following PassByReference program demonstrates this capability.

C# gives the programmer the pass-by-reference capability via the `ref` and `out` keywords. The following slight modification to the example `PassByValue` program snippet from the previous section demonstrates the point:

ON THE WEB

```
// PassByReference - Demonstrate pass-by-reference semantics.
using System;
namespace PassByReference
{
  public class Program
  {
    // Update - Try to modify the values of the arguments
    //     passed to it; note ref and out parameters.
    public static void Update(ref int i, out double d)
    {
      i = 10;
      d = 20.0;
    }
    public static void Main(string[] args)
    {
      // Declare two variables and initialize them.
      int i = 1;
      double d;
      Console.WriteLine("Before the call to Update(ref int, out double):");
      Console.WriteLine("i = " + i + ", d is not initialized");
      // Invoke the Update method.
      Update(ref i, out d);
      // Notice that i now equals 10 and d equals 20.
      Console.WriteLine("After the call to Update(ref int, out double):");
      Console.WriteLine("i = " + i + ", d = " + d);
      // Wait for user to acknowledge.
      Console.WriteLine("Press Enter to terminate...");
      Console.Read();
    }
  }
}
```

The `ref` keyword indicates that C# should pass a reference to `i` and not just the value contained within this variable. Consequently, changes made within the method are exported back out of the calling routine.

In a similar vein, the `out` keyword says, "Pass back by reference, but I don't care what the initial value is because I'm going to overwrite it anyway." (That's a lot to pack into three words!) The `out` keyword is applicable when the method is only returning a value to the caller.

Executing the program generates the following output (highlight added):

```
Before the call to Update(ref int, out double):
i = 1, d is not initialized
After the call to Update(ref int, out double):
i = 10, d = 20
Press Enter to terminate...
```

An `out` argument is always `ref`, though you don't say `ref out`. Also, you must pass *variables* to both `ref` and `out`. Passing literal values, such as 2, generates compiler errors. You need an object to refer back to — a variable.

Notice that the initial values of `i` and `d` are overwritten in the method `Update()`. After they are back in `Main()`, these variables retain their *modified* values. Compare this to the `PassByValue()` method in which the variables do not retain their modified values.

Passing reference-type arguments

Passing value-types makes a copy of the data being passed; passing *reference types* — such as `string`, `Student`, or `Car` — works differently. You can think of a reference as an "address" or a "pointer" to where the object is located in memory. So when you pass a reference, you're passing a copy of the pointer — and you don't use the `ref` or `out` keywords. The argument still points to the same object, *not to a copy of it*. Anything you do to the passed reference inside the method alters the original object (if it's alterable — recall that strings are not), *not a copy of it*. Passing a string actually does make a copy of the original string.

Don't pass a variable to a method by reference twice simultaneously

Do not, under any but the most dire circumstance, pass the same variable by reference twice in the same method call. This is more difficult to describe than it is to demonstrate. Consider the following `Update()` method:

```
// PassByReferenceError - Demonstrate a potential error situation
//    when calling a method using reference arguments.
using System;
namespace PassByReferenceError
{
  public class Program
  {
    // Update - Try to modify the values of the arguments
    //    passed to it by reference.
    public static void DisplayAndUpdate(ref int var1, ref int var2)
    {
      Console.WriteLine("The initial value of var1 is " + var1);
      var1 = 10;
      Console.WriteLine("The initial value of var2 is " + var2);
      var2 = 20;
    }
    public static void Main(string[] args)
```

```
{
    // Declare two variables and initialize them.
    int n = 1;
    Console.WriteLine("Before the call to Update(ref n, ref n):");
    Console.WriteLine("n = " + n);
    Console.WriteLine();
    // Invoke the method.
    DisplayAndUpdate(ref n, ref n);  // Bad idea!
    // Notice that n changes in an unexpected way.
    Console.WriteLine();
    Console.WriteLine("After the call to Update(ref n, ref n):");
    Console.WriteLine("n = " + n);
    // Wait for user to acknowledge.
    Console.WriteLine("Press Enter to terminate...");
    Console.Read();
    }
  }
}
```

`Update(ref int, ref int)` is now declared to accept two `int` arguments *by reference*, which, in and of itself, is not a problem. The problem arises when the `Main()` method invokes `Update()` passing the same *variable* in both arguments. Within the method, `Update()` modifies `var1`, which references back to `n` from its initial value of 1 to the new value of 10. By the time `Update()` gets around to modifying `var2`, the value of `n` to which it refers has already been modified from its initial value of 1 to the new value of 10.

This is shown in the following example output:

```
Before the call to Update(ref n, ref n):
n = 1

The initial value of var1 is 1
The initial value of var2 is 10

After the call to Update(ref n, ref n):
n = 20
Press Enter to terminate...
```

Exactly what's going on in this interplay between `n`, `var1`, and `var2` is about as obvious as an exotic bird's mating dance. Neither the user programmer nor the `Update()` method's author can anticipate this bizarre result. In other words, don't do it.

You can pass a single value as more than one argument in a single method call if all variables are passed by value.

Why do some arguments come out but they don't go in?

C# is careful about keeping the programmer from doing something stupid. One of the stupid things that programmers do is forget to initialize a variable before they use it for the first time. (This is particularly true of counting variables.) C# generates an error when you try to use a variable that you've declared but not initialized:

```
int variable;
Console.WriteLine("this is an error " + variable);
variable = 1;
Console.WriteLine("but this is not " + variable);
```

However, C# cannot keep track of variables from within a method:

```
void SomeMethod(ref int variable)
{
  Console.WriteLine("is this an error or not? " + variable);
}
```

How can `SomeMethod()` know whether `variable` was initialized before being passed in the call? It can't. Instead, C# tracks the variable in the call — for example, the following call generates a compiler error:

```
int uninitializedVariable;
SomeMethod(ref uninitializedVariable);
```

If C# were to allow this call, `SomeMethod()` would have been passed a reference to an uninitialized (that is, *garbage*) variable. The `out` keyword lets both sides agree that the variable has not yet been assigned a value. The following example compiles just fine:

```
int uninitializedVariable;
SomeMethod(out uninitializedVariable);
```

By the way, passing an initialized variable as an `out` argument is legal:

```
int initializedVariable = 1;
SomeMethod(out initializedVariable);
```

The value in `initializedVariable` gets blown away within `SomeMethod()`, but there's no danger of garbage being passed about.

Returning Values after Christmas

Many real-world operations create values to return to the caller. For example, `Sin()` accepts an argument and returns the trigonometric sine. A method can return a value to the caller in two ways. The most common is via the `return` statement; however, a second method uses the *call-by-reference* feature.

Returning a value via return postage

The following code snippet demonstrates a small method that returns the average of its input arguments:

```
public class Example
{
  public static double Average(double d1, double d2)
  {
    double average = (d1 + d2) / 2;
    return average;
  }
  public static void Main(string[] args)
  {
    double v1 = 1.0;
    double v2 = 3.0;
    double averageValue = Average(v1, v2);
    Console.WriteLine("The average of " + v1
                + " and " + v2 + " is "
                + averageValue);
    // This also works.
    Console.WriteLine("The average of " + v1
                + " and " + v2 + " is "
                + Average(v1, v2));
  }
}
```

Notice first that I declare the method as `public static double Average()` — the `double` in front of the name refers to the fact that the `Average()` method returns a double-precision value to the caller.

The `Average()` method applies the names `d1` and `d2` to the double values passed to it. It creates a variable `average` to which it assigns the average of `d1` and `d2`. It then returns the value contained in `average` to the caller.

People sometimes say that "the method returns `average`." This is a careless but common shorthand. Saying that `average` or any other variable is passed or returned anywhere is imprecise. In this case, the *value* contained within `average` is returned to the caller.

The call to `Average()` from the `Test()` method appears the same as any other method call; however, the `double` value returned by `Average()` via the `return` keyword is stored into the variable `averageValue`.

A method that returns a value, such as `Average()`, cannot return to the caller merely by encountering the closed brace of the method. If it did, how would C# know what value to return? You need a `return` statement.

Returning a value using pass-by-reference

A method can also return one or more values to the calling routine via the ref and out keywords. Consider the Update() example described in the section "Passing value-type arguments by reference," earlier in this chapter:

```
// Update - Try to modify the values of the arguments passed to it.
public static void Update(ref int i, out double d)
{
  i = 10;
  d = 20.0;
}
```

The method is declared void because it does not return a value to the caller; however, because the variable i is declared ref and the variable d is declared out, any changes made to those variables within Update() retain their values in the calling method. In other words, they're passed back to the caller.

When do I return and when do I out?

You may be thinking, "A method can return a value to the caller, or it can use out (or ref, for that matter) to return a value to the caller. When do I use return and when do I use out?" After all, you could have written the Average() method as follows:

```
public class Example
{
  // Note: prefer putting 'out' parameters last.
  public static void Average(double 1, double d2, out double results)
  {
    results = (d1 + d2) / 2;
  }
  public static void Test()
  {
    double v1 = 1.0;
    double v2 = 3.0;
    double averageValue;
    Average(v1, v2, averageValue);
    Console.WriteLine("The average of " + v1
                    + " and " + v2 + " is "
                    + averageValue;
  }
}
```

Typically, you return a value to the caller via the `return` statement rather than via the `out` directive, even though it's hard to argue with the results.

Outing a value-type variable such as a `double` requires a somewhat inefficient extra process known as *boxing*, which I describe in Bonus Chapter 4. However, efficiency should not usually be a driving factor in your decision.

Typically, you use the `out` keyword when a method returns more than one value to the caller — for example:

```
public class Example
{
   public static void AverageAndProduct(double d1, double d2, out double
                                         average, out double product)

   {
      average = (d1 + d2) / 2;
      product = d1 * d2;
   }
}
```

Returning multiple values from a single method doesn't happen as often as you may think. A method that returns multiple values usually does so by returning a single class object that encapsulates multiple values or by returning an array of values. Both approaches result in clearer code.

Defining a method with no value

The declaration `public static double Average(double, double)` declares a method `Average()` that returns the average of its arguments as a `double`. The number returned had better be the average of the input values or someone has some serious explaining to do.

Some methods don't need to return a value to the caller. An earlier example method `AverageAndDisplay()` displays the average of its input arguments but doesn't return that average to the caller. That may not be such a good idea, but mine is not to question. Rather than leave the return type blank, a method like `AverageAndDisplay()` is declared as follows:

```
public void AverageAndDisplay(double, double)
```

The keyword `void`, where the return type would normally go, means the *nontype*. That is, the declaration `void` indicates that the `AverageAndDisplay()` method returns no value to the caller. (Regardless, every method declaration specifies a return type, even if it's `void`.)

A method that returns no value is referred to as a *void method*. That doesn't mean the method is empty or that it's used for some medical or astronautical purposes. It simply refers to the initial keyword. By comparison, a method that returns some value is known as a *nonvoid method*.

A nonvoid method must pass control back to the caller by executing a `return` followed by the value to return to the caller. A `void` method has no value to return. A `void` method returns when it encounters a `return` with no value attached. Or, by default (if no `return` exists), a `void` method exits automatically when control reaches the closing brace of the method.

Consider the following `DisplayRatio()` method:

```
public class Example
{
  public static void DisplayRatio(double numerator,
                                  double denominator)
  {
    // If the denominator is zero . . .
    if (denominator == 0.0)
    {
      //  . . .output an error message and . . .
      Console.WriteLine("The denominator of a ratio cannot be 0");
      //  . . .return to the caller.
      return;  // An early return due to the error.
    }
    // This is only executed if denominator is non-zero.
    double ratio = numerator / denominator;
    Console.WriteLine("The ratio of " + numerator
                + " over " + denominator
                + " is " + ratio);
  } // If the denominator isn't zero, the method exits here.
}
```

The `DisplayRatio()` method first checks whether the `denominator` value is zero, as follows:

- If it is zero, the program displays an error message and returns to the caller without attempting to calculate a ratio. Doing so would divide the numerator value by zero and cause a CPU processor fault, also known by the more descriptive name *processor upchuck*.

- If `denominator` is nonzero, the program displays the ratio. The closed brace immediately following the `WriteLine()` is the closed brace of the `DisplayRatio()` method and, therefore, acts as the return point for the program.

Null and zero references

A reference variable, as opposed to a value-type variable (see Bonus Chapter 4), is assigned the default value `null` when created. However, a null reference is not the same thing as a reference to zero. For example, the following two references are completely different:

```
class Example
{
  int value;
}

// Create a null reference ref1.
Example ref1;  // Has the value null.

// Now create a reference to a zero object.
Example ref2 = new Example();
ref2.value = 0;
```

The variable `ref1` is about as empty as my wallet. That variable points to the null object — that is, it points to no object. By comparison, `ref2` points to an object whose value is zero.

This difference is much less clear in the following example:

```
string s1;       // Has the value null.
string s2 = "";
```

This is essentially the same case: `s1` points to the null *object*, while `s2` points to an *empty string* (in programmer slang, an empty string is sometimes called a *null string* — a bit confusing). The difference is significant, as the following code shows:

```
// Test.
namespace Test
{
  using System;
  public class Program
  {
    public static void Main(string[] args)
    {
      Console.WriteLine("This program exercises the method TestString()");
      Console.WriteLine();
      Example exampleObject = new Example();
      Console.WriteLine("Pass a null object:");
      string s = null;
      exampleObject.TestString(s);
      Console.WriteLine();
      // Now pass the method a "null (empty) string."
      Console.WriteLine("Pass an empty string:");
      exampleObject.TestString("");
      Console.WriteLine();
```

(continued)

(continued)

```
        // Finally, pass a real string.
        Console.WriteLine("Pass a real string:");
        exampleObject.TestString("test string");
        Console.WriteLine();
        // Wait for user to acknowledge the results.
        Console.WriteLine("Press Enter to terminate...");
        Console.Read();
    }
}
class Example
{
  public void TestString(string test)
  {
    // First test for a null string object (do this test first!).
    if (test == null)
    {
      Console.WriteLine("test is null");
      return;
    }
    // At this point, you know test doesn't point to the null object
    // but it could still point to an empty string.
    // Check to see if test points to a "null (empty) string."
    if (String.Compare(test, "") == 0)
    {
      Console.WriteLine("test references an empty string");
      return;
    }
    // Okay, output the string.
    Console.WriteLine("test refers to: '" + test + "'");
  }
}
}
```

The method `TestString()` uses the comparison `test == null` to test for a null string object. `TestString()` can use the `Compare()` method to test for an empty string. (`Compare()` returns a 0 if the two `strings` passed to it are equal.) Chapter 6 explains `string` comparison in detail.

The output from this program is as follows:

```
This program exercises the method TestString()
Pass a null object:
test is null
Pass an empty string:
test references an empty string
Pass a real string:
test refers to: 'test string'
Press Enter to terminate...
```

The WriteLine() method

You may have noticed that the `WriteLine()` construct that you've been using in the programs so far is nothing more than a method call that's invoked with something called a `Console` class, as follows:

```
Console.WriteLine("this is a method call");
```

`WriteLine()` is one of many predefined methods provided by the .NET Framework library. `Console` is a predefined class that refers to the application console (also known as the Command Prompt or Command Window).

The argument to the `WriteLine()` method that you've been using in previous examples is a single `string`. The + operator enables the programmer to combine `string`s, or to combine a `string` and an intrinsic variable before the sum is passed to `WriteLine()`, as follows:

```
string s = "Sarah"
Console.WriteLine("My name is " + s + " and
        my age is " + 3);
```

All that `WriteLine()` sees in this case is "My name is Sarah and my age is 3."

A second form of `WriteLine()` provides a more flexible set of arguments, as follows:

```
Console.WriteLine("My name is {0} and my age
        is {1}.", "Sarah", 3);
```

The first argument is called a format string. Here, the `string` `"Sarah"` is inserted where the symbol {0} appears — zero refers to the first argument after the format string. The integer 3 is inserted at the position marked by {1}. This form is more efficient than the previous example because concatenating `string`s is not as easy as it sounds. It's a time-consuming business.

It wouldn't be much to write home about if that were the only difference. However, this second form of `WriteLine()` also provides a number of controls on the output format. I describe these format controls in Chapter 6.

Chapter 9

Let Me Say This about this

*T*his chapter moves from the static methods that Chapter 8 emphasized to the nonstatic methods of a class. Static methods belong to the whole class, while nonstatic methods belong to each instance created from the class. There are important differences between static and nonstatic class members.

Passing an Object to a Method

You pass object references as arguments to methods in the same way that you pass value-type variables, with one difference: You always pass objects by reference. (Drop back to Chapter 8 if "by reference" sounds like Martian.)

The following small program demonstrates how you pass objects — to methods, that is:

```
// PassObject - Demonstrate how to pass an object to a method.
using System;
namespace PassObject
{
  public class Student
  {
    public string name;
  }
  public class Program
  {
    public static void Main(string[] args)
```

```
    {
        Student student = new Student();
        // Set the name by accessing it directly.
        Console.WriteLine("The first time:");
        student.name = "Madeleine";
        OutputName(student);
        // Change the name using a method.
        Console.WriteLine("After being modified:");
        SetName(student, "Willa");
        OutputName(student);
        // Wait for user to acknowledge.
        Console.WriteLine("Press Enter to terminate...");
        Console.Read();
    }
    // OutputName - Output the student's name.
    public static void OutputName(Student student)
    {
        // Output current student's name.
        Console.WriteLine("Student's name is {0}", student.name);
    }
    // SetName - Modify the student object's name.
    public static void SetName(Student student, string name)
    {
        student.name = name;
    }
}
}
```

The program creates a `student` object consisting of nothing but a name. (We like to keep 'em simple down here.) The program first sets the name of the `student` directly and passes the *student object* to the output method `OutputName()`. `OutputName()` displays the name of any `Student` object it receives.

The program then updates the name of the `student` by calling `SetName()`. Because all reference-type objects are passed by reference in C#, the changes made to `student` are retained back in the calling method. When `Main()` outputs the `student` object again, the name has changed, as shown in the following code:

```
The first time:
Student's name is Madeleine
After being modified:
Student's name is Willa
Press Enter to terminate...
```

The `SetName()` method can change the name within the `Student` object and make it stick.

You don't use the `ref` keyword when passing a *reference-type* object. Yet the effect is that the object's contents can be modified *through the reference*. However, if `SetName()` tried to assign a whole new `Student` object to its `Student` parameter, this wouldn't affect the original `Student` object outside the method, as the following code shows:

```
Student student = new Student();
SetName(student, "Pam");
Console.WriteLine(student.name);  // Still "Pam".
...
// A revised SetName():
public static void SetName(Student student, string name)
{
  student = new Student(); // Doesn't replace student outside SetName().
  student.Name = name;
}
```

Defining Methods

A class is supposed to collect the elements that describe a real-world object or concept. For example, a `Vehicle` class may contain data elements for maximum velocity, weight, carrying capacity, and so on. However, a `Vehicle` has active properties — *behaviors* — as well: the ability to start, to stop, and the like. These are described by the methods that go with that vehicular data. These methods are just as much a part of the `Vehicle` class as the data elements.

Defining a static method

For example, you could rewrite the program from the previous section in a slightly better way as follows:

```
// StudentClassWithMethods - Demonstrate putting methods that
//    operate on a class's data inside the class. A class is
//    responsible for its own data and any operations on it.
using System;
namespace StudentClassWithMethods
{
  // Now the OutputName and SetName methods are members of
  // class Student, not class Program.
  public class Student
  {
    public string name;
    // OutputName - Output the student's name.
    public static void OutputName(Student student)
    {
```

```
        // Output current student's name.
        Console.WriteLine("Student's name is {0}", student.name);
    }
    // SetName - Modify the student object's name.
    public static void SetName(Student student, string name)
    {
        student.name = name;
    }
}
public class Program
{
    public static void Main(string[] args)
    {
        Student student = new Student();
        // Set the name by accessing it directly.
        Console.WriteLine("The first time:");
        student.name = "Madeleine";
        Student.OutputName(student); // Method now belongs to Student.
        // Change the name using a method.
        Console.WriteLine("After being modified:");
        Student.SetName(student, "Willa");
        Student.OutputName(student);
        // Wait for user to acknowledge.
        Console.WriteLine("Press Enter to terminate...");
        Console.Read();
    }
}
```

Other than its name, this program has only one significant change from the
`PassObject` program in the previous section: I put the `OutputName()` and
`SetName()` methods in the `Student` class.

TIP

Instead of "in" the class, many programmers speak of members "on" the class.

Because of that change, `Main()` must reference the `Student` class in the
calls to `SetName()` and `OutputName()`. The methods are now members of
the class `Student` and not `Program`, the class in which `Main()` resides.

This is a small but significant step. Placing `OutputName()` within the class
leads to a higher level of reuse: Outside methods that need to display the
object can find `OutputName()` right there as part of the class. It doesn't
have to be written separately by each program using the `Student` class.

This is also a better solution on a philosophical level. Class `Program` should-
n't need to worry about how to initialize the name of a `Student` object nor
about how to output important material. The `Student` class should contain
that information. *Objects are responsible for themselves.*

In fact, `Main()` should not initialize the name to Madeleine in the first place. It should call `SetName()` instead.

From within `Student`, one member method can invoke another without explicitly applying the class name. `SetName()` could invoke `OutputName()` without needing to reference the class name. If you leave off the class name, C# assumes that the method being accessed is in/on the same class.

Defining an instance method

Although `OutputName()` and `SetName()` are static methods, they could as easily be nonstatic, or *instance*, methods.

All static members of a class are called *class members*, and all nonstatic members are called *instance members*. This includes methods.

The nonstatic *data members* of an object — an *instance* of a class — are accessed with the object and not with the class. Thus, you may say the following:

```
Student student = new Student(); // Create an instance of Student.
student.name = "Madeleine";      // Access the member via the instance.
```

C# enables you to invoke nonstatic member *methods* in the same way:

```
student.SetName("Madeleine");
```

The following example demonstrates this technique:

```
// InvokeMethod - Invoke a member method through the object.
using System;
namespace InvokeMethod
{
  class Student
  {
    // The name information to describe a student.
    public string firstName;
    public string lastName;
    // SetName - Save name information. (Non-static.)
    public void SetName(string fName, string lName)
    {
      firstName = fName;
      lastName  = lName;
    }
    // ToNameString - Convert the student object into a
    //    string for display. (Non-static.)
    public string ToNameString()
    {
```

```
        string s = firstName + " " + lastName;
        return s;
    }
}
public class Program
{
    public static void Main()
    {
        Student student = new Student();
        student.SetName("Stephen", "Davis"); // Call instance method.
        Console.WriteLine("Student's name is "
                            + student.ToNameString());
        // Wait for user to acknowledge.
        Console.WriteLine("Press Enter to terminate...");
        Console.Read();
    }
}
}
```

The output from this program is this simple line:

```
Student's name is Stephen Davis
```

Other than having a much shorter name, this program is very similar to the earlier `StudentClassWithMethods` program. This version uses *nonstatic* methods to manipulate both a first and a last name.

The program begins by creating a new `Student` object, `student`. The program then invokes the `SetName()` method, which stores the two `strings` `"Stephen"` and `"Davis"` into the data members `firstName` and `lastName`. Finally, the program calls the member method `ToNameString()`, which returns the name of the `student` by concatenating the two `strings`.

Look again at the `SetName()` method that updates the first and last name fields in the `Student` object. Which object does `SetName()` modify? To see how it works, consider the following example:

```
Student christa = new Student();    // Here's one student.
Student sarah = new Student();       // And here's a completely different one.
christa.SetName("Christa", "Smith");
sarah.SetName("Sarah", "Jones");
```

The first call to `SetName()` updates the first and last name of the `christa` object. The second call updates the `sarah` object.

Thus, C# programmers say that a method operates on the *current* object. In the first call, the current object is `christa`; in the second, it's `sarah`.

Expanding a method's full name

A subtle but important problem exists with my description of method names. To see the problem, consider the following example code snippet:

```
public class Person
{
  public void Address()
  {
    Console.WriteLine("Hi");
  }
}
public class Letter
{
  string address;
  // Store the address.
  public void Address(string newAddress)
  {
    address = newAddress;
  }
}
```

Any subsequent discussion of the Address() method is now ambiguous. The Address() method within Person has nothing to do with the Address() method in Letter. If my programmer friend tells me to access the Address() method, which Address() does he mean?

The problem lies not with the methods themselves, but with my description. In fact, no Address() method exists as an independent entity — only a Person.Address() and a Letter.Address() method. Attaching the class name to the beginning of the method name clearly indicates which method is intended.

This description is very similar to people's names. Within my family, I am known as Stephen. (Actually, within my family, I am known by my middle name, but you get the point.) There are no other Stephens within my family (at least not within my close family). However, there are two other Stephens where I work.

If I'm at lunch with some coworkers and the other two Stephens aren't present, the name *Stephen* clearly refers to me. Back in the trenches (or cubicles), yelling out "Stephen" is ambiguous because it could refer to any one of us. In that context, you need to yell out "Stephen Davis" as opposed to "Stephen Williams" or "Stephen Leija."

Thus, you can consider Address() to be the first name or nickname of a method, with its class as the family name.

Accessing the Current Object

Consider the following `Student.SetName()` method:

```
class Student
{
  // The name information to describe a student.
  public string firstName;
  public string lastName;
  // SetName - Save name information.
  public void SetName(string firstName, string lastName)
  {
    firstName = firstName;
    lastName  = lastName;
  }
}
public class Program
{
  public static void Main()
  {
    Student student1 = new Student();
    student1.SetName("Joseph", "Smith");
    Student student2 = new Student();
    student2.SetName("John", "Davis");
  }
}
```

The method `Main()` uses the `SetName()` method to update first `student1` and then `student2`. But you don't see a reference to either `Student` object *within `SetName()` itself*. In fact, no reference to a `Student` object exists. A method is said to operate on "the current object." How does a method know which one is the current object? Will the real current object please stand up?

The answer is simple. The current object is passed as an implicit argument in the call to a method — for example:

```
student1.SetName("Joseph", "Smith");
```

This call is equivalent to the following:

```
Student.SetName(student1, "Joseph", "Smith"); // Equivalent call,
                                 // (but this won't build properly).
```

I'm not saying you can invoke `SetName()` in two different ways, just that the two calls are semantically equivalent. The object identifying the current object — the hidden first argument — is passed to the method, just like other arguments. Leave that up to the compiler.

Passing an object implicitly is pretty easy to swallow, but what about a reference from one method to another? The following code illustrates calling one method from another:

```
public class Student
{
  public string firstName;
  public string lastName;
  public void SetName(string firstName, string lastName)
  {
    SetFirstName(firstName);
    SetLastName(lastName);
  }
  public void SetFirstName(string name)
  {
    firstName = name;
  }
  public void SetLastName(string name)
  {
    lastName = name;
  }
}
```

No object appears in the call to SetFirstName(). The current object continues to be passed along silently from one method call to the next. An access to any member from within an object method is assumed to be with respect to the current object. The upshot is that a method "knows" which object it belongs to. "Current object" (or "current instance") means something like "me."

What is the this keyword?

Unlike most arguments, the current object does not appear in the method argument list, so it is not assigned a name by the programmer. Instead, C# assigns this object the not-very-imaginative name this, useful in the few situations where you need to refer directly to the current object.

this is a C# keyword, and it may not be used for any other purpose, at least not without the express written permission of the National Football League.

Thus you could write the previous example as follows:

```
public class Student
{
  public string firstName;
  public string lastName;
  public void SetName(string firstName, string lastName)
  {
    // Explicitly reference the "current object" referenced by this.
```

```
      this.SetFirstName(firstName);
      this.SetLastName(lastName);
   }
   public void SetFirstName(string name)
   {
      this.firstName = name;
   }
   public void SetLastName(string name)
   {
      this.lastName = name;
   }
}
```

Notice the explicit addition of the keyword `this`. Adding `this` to the member references doesn't add anything because `this` is assumed. However, when `Main()` makes the following call, `this` references `student1` throughout `SetName()` and any other method that it may call:

```
student1.SetName("John", "Smith");
```

When is this explicit?

You don't normally need to refer to `this` explicitly because it is understood where necessary by the compiler. However, two common cases require `this`. You may need it when initializing data members, as follows:

```
class Person
{
   public string name;   // This is this.name below.
   public int id;        // And this is this.id below.
   public void Init(string name, int id)  // These are method arguments.
   {
      this.name = name;   // Argument names same as data member names.
      this.id = id;
   }
}
```

The arguments to the `Init()` method are named `name` and `id`, which match the names of the corresponding data members. This makes the method easy to read because you know immediately which argument is stored where. The only problem is that the name `name` in the argument list obscures the name of the data member. The compiler will complain about it.

The addition of `this` clarifies which `name` is intended. Within `Init()`, the name `name` refers to the method argument, but `this.name` refers to the data member.

You also need `this` when storing the current object for use later or by some other method. Consider the following example program `ReferencingThisExplicitly`:

```
// ReferencingThisExplicitly - Demonstrates how to explicitly use
//     the reference to 'this'.
using System;
namespace ReferencingThisExplicitly
{
  public class Program
  {
    public static void Main(string[] strings)
    {
      // Create a student.
      Student student = new Student();
      student.Init("Stephen Davis", 1234);
      // Now enroll the student in a course.
      Console.WriteLine
              ("Enrolling Stephen Davis in Biology 101");
      student.Enroll("Biology 101");
      // Display student course.
      Console.WriteLine("Resulting student record:");
      student.DisplayCourse();
      // Wait for user to acknowledge the results.
      Console.WriteLine("Press Enter to terminate...");
      Console.Read();
    }
  }
  // Student - Our class for university students.
  public class Student
  {
    // All students have a name and id.
    public string _name;
    public int _id;
    // The course in which the student is enrolled.
    CourseInstance _courseInstance;
    // Init - Initialize the student object.
    public void Init(string name, int id)
    {
      this._name = name;
      this._id = id;
      _courseInstance = null;
    }
    // Enroll - Enroll the current student in a course.
    public void Enroll(string courseID)
    {
      _courseInstance = new CourseInstance();
      _courseInstance.Init(this, courseID);    // Here's the explicit reference.
    }
    // Display the name of the student and the course.
    public void DisplayCourse()
    {
      Console.WriteLine(_name);
```

```
      _courseInstance.Display();
    }
  }
// CourseInstance - A combination of a student with
//     a university course.
public class CourseInstance
{
  public Student _student;
  public string _courseID;
  // Init - Tie the student to the course.
  public void Init(Student student, string courseID)
  {
    this._student = student;
    this._courseID = courseID;
  }
  // Display - Output the name of the course.
  public void Display()
  {
    Console.WriteLine(_courseID);
  }
  }
}
```

This program is fairly mundane. The Student object has room for a name, an ID, and a single instance of a university course (not a very industrious student). Main() creates the student instance and then invokes Init() to initialize the instance. At this point, the _courseInstance reference is set to null because the student is not yet enrolled in a class.

The Enroll() method enrolls the student by initializing _courseInstance with a new object. However, the CourseInstance.Init() method takes an instance of Student as its first argument along with the course ID as the second argument. Which Student should you pass? Clearly, you need to pass the current Student — the Student referred to by this. (Thus you can say that Enroll() enrolls this student in the CourseInstance.)

Some programmers (and that includes me) like to differentiate data members from other variables more clearly by prefixing an underscore to the name of each data member, like this: _name. You'll see me adopt this convention most of the time, but of course, it's only a convention, and you may do as you like. If you use the convention, you won't need to preface the item with this, as in this._id. It's completely unambiguous with just the underscore prefix.

What happens when I don't have this?

Mixing class (static) methods and instance (nonstatic) methods is like mixing sheepmen and ranchers. Fortunately, C# gives you some ways around the problems between the two. To see the problem, consider the following program snippet MixingStaticAndInstanceMethods:

ON THE WEB

```
// MixingStaticAndInstanceMethods - Mixing class (static) methods
//    and instance (non-static) methods can cause problems.
using System;
namespace MixingStaticAndInstanceMethods
{
  public class Student
  {
    public string _firstName;
    public string _lastName;
    // InitStudent - Initialize the student object.
    public void InitStudent(string firstName, string lastName)
    {
      _firstName = firstName;
      _lastName = lastName;
    }
    // OutputBanner (static) - Output the introduction.
    public static void OutputBanner()
    {
      Console.WriteLine("Aren't we clever:");
      // Console.WriteLine(? what student do we use ?); fl The problem!
    }
    // OutputBannerAndName (non-static) - Output intro.
    public void OutputBannerAndName()
    {
      // The class Student is implied but no this
      // object is passed to the static method.
      OutputBanner();
      // The current Student object is passed explicitly.
      OutputName(this);
    }
    // OutputName - Output the student's name.
    public static void OutputName(Student student)
    {
      // Here the Student object is referenced explicitly.
      Console.WriteLine("Student's name is {0}",
                        student.ToNameString());
    }
    // ToNameString - Fetch the student's name.
    public string ToNameString()
    {
      // Here the current object is implicit -
      // this could have been written:
      // return this._firstName + " " + this._lastName;
      return _firstName + " " + _lastName;
    }
  }
  public class Program
  {
    public static void Main(string[] args)
    {
      Student student = new Student();
      student.InitStudent("Madeleine", "Cather");
```

```
        // Output the banner and name statically.
        Student.OutputBanner();
        Student.OutputName(student);
        Console.WriteLine();
        // Output the banner and name again using instance.
        student.OutputBannerAndName();
        // Wait for user to acknowledge.
        Console.WriteLine("Press Enter to terminate...");
        Console.Read();
      }
    }
  }
```

Start at the bottom of the program with Main() so that you can better see the problems. The program begins by creating a Student object and initializing its name. The simpleton program now wants to do nothing more than output the name preceded by a short message and banner.

Main() first outputs the banner and message using the class or static method approach. The program invokes the OutputBanner() method for the banner line and the OutputName() method to output the message and the student name. The method OutputBanner() outputs a simple message to the console. Main() passes the student object as an argument to OutputName() so that it can display the student's name.

Next, Main() uses the instance method approach to outputting the banner and message by calling student.OutputBannerAndName().

OutputBannerAndName() first invokes the static method Output-Banner(). The class Student is assumed. No object is passed because the static OutputBanner does not need one. Next, OutputBannerAndName() calls the OutputName() method. OutputName() is also a static method, but it takes a Student object as its argument. OutputBannerAndName() passes this for that argument.

A more interesting case is the call to ToNameString() from within OutputName(). OutputName() is declared static and therefore has no this. It does have an explicit Student object, which it uses to make the call.

The OutputBanner() method would probably like to call ToNameString() as well; however, it has no Student object to use. It has no this reference because it is a static method and it was not passed an object explicitly. Note the first boldfaced line in the code: The static method cannot call the instance method.

A static method cannot call a nonstatic method without explicitly providing an object. No object, no call. In general, static methods cannot access any nonstatic items in the class. But nonstatic (instance) methods can access static as well as instance items: static data members and static methods.

New Feature: Extension Methods

As described in Chapter 6, class `String` has a very nice collection of methods and properties — it's well worth spending some time browsing them in Help. But (of course) it doesn't do everything you might like. What class written by someone else does?

Happily, C# 3.0 now lets you extend a class by adding your own methods to it — all without having access to the source code for the class. The new Extension Methods feature lets you do that even if only within the confines of your program. An *extension method* pretends it belongs to the class it's extending, even though the designers of that class never envisioned the method. And the compiler goes along with the gag.

So what's missing from `String`? Here are a few possibilities:

- ✔ Visual Basic folks coming to C# may miss their `Left()`, `Mid()`, and `Right()` functions, which extract specified portions of a string, returning the extracted substring. (Heck, I'm not much of a VBer, but I miss them.)

- ✔ Folks coming to C# from Ruby, Perl, and other "dynamic" languages may miss things like the ability to grab a "slice" out of a string — a range of characters from anywhere within the string. To slice is nice.

You may already be thinking of more things to add yourself, but these examples will be plenty here. I'll get to the "why" in a moment.

As a first example, let's please the Basic crowd by adding a `Left()` method to class `String`:

```
public static class MyStringExtensions
{
  public static string Left(this string target, int numberOfCharsToGet)
  {
    return target.Substring(0, numberOfCharsToGet);
  }
}
```

What are you seeing? First, note that both the class and the method are declared as `static`. (Static *classes* were added in C# 2.0 a couple of years ago. All members of a static class must be static.) The class is just a holding place for any extension methods you write for `String`. (You could put extension methods for some other class here too.) Next, note the first parameter to the `Left()` method, which is preceded by our new friend, the `this` keyword. A very unusual place for `this`.

When the compiler sees this arrangement, it interprets `Left()` as an extension method to class `String`. The `this` keyword tips off the compiler that what it has here is an extension method — and the type of that first parameter names the class that is to be extended. Here, that's `String` (also known as `string`).

With this extension code somewhere in your solution, you can make calls like the following:

```
string target = "0123456789";  // A string composed of digit characters.
string leftThreeChars = target.Left(3);  // Result is "012".
```

Notice the syntax, which I modeled on the `Left()` function in Visual Basic 6.0: you're calling this `Left()` method on the target string exactly as you would call `String`'s predefined `Substring()` method:

```
target.Left(3);  // Get the leftmost three chars in target.
```

The parameter to `Left()` specifies the length of the substring — the number of characters you want. Because it's `Left()`, the substring starts at 0.

That's how it works. Under the hood, I implemented `Left()` using `String`'s `Substring()` method. Compare the simplicity of the extension method call with the somewhat more complicated `Substring()` method call:

```
target.Left(3)
target.Substring(0, 3)  // Params are start-index and length - I always forget.
```

It's not a huge gain, but the next example yields a somewhat bigger payoff.

Adding a `Right()` method to `String` looks much like adding `Left()`:

```
public static class MyStringExtensions
{
  public static string Left(this string target, int numberOfCharsToGet)
  ...
  public static string Right(this string target, int numberOfCharsToGet)
  {
    return target.Substring(target.Length - numberOfCharsToGet,
            numberOfCharsToGet);
  }
}
```

Notice how much easier it is to call `Right()` than to use `Substring()`:

```
string rightPart = target.Right(2);  // Returns the last two chars: "89".
string rightPart = target.Substring(target.Length - 2, 2);
```

With `Right()`, you don't have to stop and reason out how to compute the starting index as you do in `Substring()`. `Right()` takes care of that for you, so calling `Right()` is perfectly natural, especially if you're a veteran VB jockey. Just pass the number of characters you want to retrieve from the right end of the target string.

I'll leave implementing a `Mid()` method to you. Just note that as with the others, `String` already owns a method, `Substring()`, that lets you get the effect of all three Visual Basic–derived methods. But extension methods hide some of the trickier calculations and save you that extra little smidgen of time.

For a final example, I'll please the Ruby/Perl crowd with a `Slice()` method. In Ruby, you take a slice of a string, as in these examples:

```
target = "hello world"  // This is in Ruby, not C#!
target.slice(1..3)    // Returns "ell", a "range" of those indexes.
target.slice(-3, 3)   // Returns "orl", starting from right end of string.
target.slice("wo")    // Return the substring, or 'nil' if not found in target.
```

Ruby's `slice()` method is very powerful, and it's built into the language. You can use ranges of indexes (that's the `1..3` syntax); a starting index (from either end of the string) plus a character count; a substring; or a regular expression (not shown; you can Google "regular expressions" — C# has them too). And that's just the green stuff on the carrot. Ruby's `slice()` is like one of those infomercials on TV: "It slices, it dices, it juliennes — only $19.95." (Some would argue that Swiss Army knives like `slice()` tend to give Ruby a kitchen-sink effect, significantly steepening the learning curve, but Ruby enthusiasts love it.) Ruby has the equivalent of extension methods, too.

Implementing all of those formats in C# would require several overloaded methods (I explain overloads in Chapter 8), some of them pretty tricky to write, but I'm going to limit myself to just one simple version here.

You can see the extension methods in this chapter in action (including some not shown here) in the `StringExtensions` example program on the Web site.

This simple `Slice()` method extends `String` to extract a range of characters from a starting index through an ending index. The indexes must be positive numbers. It's another simplification of `Substring()`:

```
public static MyStringExtensions
{
  ...
  public static string Slice(this string target, int startIndex, int endIndex)
  {
    return target.Substring(startIndex, endIndex - startIndex + 1);
  }
}
```

The calculation in the body of `Slice()` is just the sort of `Substring()` call I mess up with great regularity, so I'm forced to stop and think it through (and then to test it thoroughly). But calling `Slice()` with a starting index and an ending index (not a character count, as in Ruby) is much easier:

```
string theSlice = target.Slice(6, 8);   // "6 through 8" - returns "678".
```

Just remember that this is an *inclusive* range: the result includes both the starting and ending characters.

You can put your extension methods in a class library, as described in Bonus Chapter 1, and use that library's .DLL file in other programs. It's not quite the same as actually adding the methods by editing the `String` class source code, but pretty doggone close.

If you add an extension method to class `Object`, the root object that sits at the beginning of the .NET class library, every type in C# inherits that method!

Chapter 10

Object-Oriented Programming — What's It All About?

In This Chapter

▶ Making nachos

▶ Reviewing the basics of object-oriented programming

▶ Getting a handle on abstraction and classification

▶ Understanding why object-oriented programming is important

*T*his chapter answers the musical question, "What are the concepts behind object-oriented programming and how do they differ from the procedural concepts covered in Part II of this book?"

Object-Oriented Concept #1 — Abstraction

Sometimes when my son and I are watching football, I whip up a terribly unhealthy batch of nachos. I dump some chips on a plate; throw on some beans, cheese, and lots of jalapeños; and nuke the whole mess in the microwave oven for a few minutes.

To use my microwave, I open the door, throw the stuff in, and punch a few buttons on the front. After a few minutes, the nachos are done. (I try not to stand in front of the microwave while it's working lest my eyes start glowing in the dark.)

Now think for a minute about all the things I don't do to use my microwave:

- ✔ I don't rewire or change anything inside the microwave to get it to work. The microwave has an interface — the front panel with all the buttons and the little time display — that lets me do everything I need.

- ✔ I don't have to reprogram the software used to drive the little processor inside my microwave, even if I cooked a different dish the last time I used the microwave.

- ✔ I don't look inside my microwave's case.

- ✔ Even if I were a microwave designer and knew all about the inner workings of a microwave, including its software, I still wouldn't think about all that stuff while I was using it to heat my nachos.

These are not profound observations. You can deal with only so much stress in your life. To reduce the number of things that you deal with, you work at a certain level of detail. In object-oriented (OO) computerese, the level of detail at which you are working is called the *level of abstraction*. To introduce another OO term while I have the chance, I *abstract away* the details of the microwave's innards.

Happily, computer scientists — and thousands of geeks — have invented object orientation and numerous other concepts that reduce the level of complexity at which programmers have to work. Using powerful abstractions makes the job simpler and far less error-prone than it used to be. In a sense, that's what the past half century or so of computing progress has been about: managing ever-more-complex concepts and structures with ever fewer errors.

When I'm working on nachos, I view my microwave oven as a box. (As I'm trying to knock out a snack, I can't worry about the innards of the microwave oven and still follow the Cowboys on the tube.) As long as I use the microwave only through its interface (the keypad), nothing I can do should cause the microwave to enter an inconsistent state and crash or, worse, turn my nachos — or my house — into a blackened, flaming mass.

Preparing procedural nachos

Suppose I were to ask my son to write an algorithm for how Dad makes nachos. After he understood what I wanted, he would probably write, "Open a can of beans, grate some cheese, cut the jalapeños," and so on. When he came to the part about microwaving the concoction, he would write something like, "Cook in the microwave for five minutes" (on a good day).

That description is straightforward and complete. But it's not the way a procedural programmer would code a program to make nachos. Procedural programmers live in a world devoid of objects such as microwave ovens and other appliances. They tend to worry about flow charts with their myriad procedural paths. In a procedural solution to the nachos problem, the flow of control would pass through my finger to the front panel and then to the internals of the microwave. Pretty soon, flow would be wiggling around through complex logic paths about how long to turn on the microwave tube and whether to sound the "come and get it" tone.

In that world of procedural programming, you can't easily think in terms of levels of abstraction. There are no objects and no abstractions behind which to hide inherent complexity.

Preparing object-oriented nachos

In an object-oriented approach to making nachos, I would first identify the types of objects in the problem: chips, beans, cheese, jalapeños, and an oven. Then, I would begin the task of modeling those objects in software, without regard for the details of how they will be used in the final program. For example, I can model cheese as an object pretty much in isolation from the other objects, and then combine it with the beans, the chips, the jalapeños, and the oven and make them interact. (And I may decide that some of these objects don't need to be objects in the software: cheese, for instance.)

While I do that, I'm said to be working (and thinking) at the level of the basic objects. I need to think about making a useful oven, but I don't have to think about the logical process of making nachos — yet. After all, the microwave designers didn't think about the specific problem of my making a snack. Rather, they set about solving the problem of designing and building a useful microwave.

After I have successfully coded and tested the objects I need, I can ratchet up to the next level of abstraction. I can start thinking at the nacho-making level, rather than the microwave-making level.

At this point, I can pretty much translate my son's instructions directly into C# code.

Object-Oriented Concept #2 — Classification

Critical to the concept of abstraction is that of classification. If I were to ask my son, "What's a microwave?" he would probably say, "It's an oven that. . . ." If I then asked, "What's an oven?" he might reply, "It's a kitchen appliance that. . . ." If I then asked "What's a kitchen appliance?" he would probably say, "Why are you asking so many stupid questions?"

The answers my son gave stem from his understanding of our particular microwave as an example of the type of things called microwave ovens. In addition, my son sees microwave ovens as just a special type of oven, which itself is just a special type of kitchen appliance.

In object-oriented computerese, my microwave is an *instance* of the class `microwave`. The class `microwave` is a *subclass* of the class `oven`, and the class `oven` is a subclass of the class `kitchen appliance`.

Humans classify. Everything about our world is ordered into taxonomies. We do this to reduce the number of things we have to remember. Take, for example, the first time you saw an SUV. The advertisement probably called the SUV "revolutionary, the likes of which have never been seen." But you and I know that just isn't so. I like the looks of some SUVs (others need to go back to take another crack at it), but hey, an SUV is a car. As such, it shares all (or at least most of) the properties of other cars. It has a steering wheel, seats, a motor, brakes, and so on. I bet I could even drive one without reading the user's manual first.

I don't have to clutter my limited storage with all the things that an SUV has in common with other cars. All I have to remember is "an SUV is a car that . . ." and tack on those few things that are unique to an SUV (like the price tag). I can go further. Cars are a subclass of wheeled vehicles along with other members, such as trucks and pickups. Maybe wheeled vehicles are a subclass of vehicles, which include boats and planes — and so on.

Why Classify?

Why should you classify? It sounds like a lot of trouble. Besides, people have been using the procedural approach for so long, why change now?

Designing and building a microwave oven specifically for this one problem may seem easier than building a separate, more generic oven object. Suppose, for example, that I want to build a microwave to cook nachos and nachos only. I would not need to put a front panel on it, other than a START button. I always cook nachos the same amount of time. I could dispense with all that DEFROST and TEMP COOK nonsense. The oven only needs to hold one flat, little plate. Three cubic feet of space would be wasted on nachos.

For that matter, I can dispense with the concept of "microwave oven" altogether. All I really need is the guts of the oven. Then, in the recipe, I put the instructions to make it work: "Put nachos in the box. Connect the red wire to the black wire. Bring the radar tube up to about 3,000 volts. Notice a slight hum. Try not to stand too close if you intend to have children." Stuff like that.

But the procedural approach has the following problems:

✔ **It's too complex.** I don't want the details of oven-building mixed into the details of nacho-building. If I can't define the objects and pull them out of the morass of details to deal with separately, I must deal with all the complexities of the problem at the same time.

✔ **It's not flexible.** Someday I may need to replace the microwave oven with some other type of oven. I should be able to do so as long as the two ovens have the same interface. Without being clearly delineated and developed separately, one object type can't be cleanly removed and replaced with another.

✔ **It's not reusable.** Ovens are used to make lots of different dishes. I don't want to create a new oven every time I encounter a new recipe. Having solved a problem once, I'd like to be able to reuse the solution in other places within my program. If I'm really lucky, I may be able to reuse it in future programs as well.

Object-Oriented Concept #3 — Usable Interfaces

An object must be able to project an external interface that is sufficient but as simple as possible. This is sort of the reverse of Concept #4 (described in the next section). If the device interface is insufficient, users may start ripping the top off the device, in direct violation of the laws of God and Society — or at least the liability laws of the Great State of Texas. And believe me, you do not want to violate the laws of the Great State of Texas. On the flip side, if the device interface is too complex, no one will buy the device — or at least, no one will use all its features.

People complain constantly that their VCRs are too complex (this is less of a problem with today's on-screen controls). These devices have too many buttons with too many different functions. Often the same button has different functions, depending on the state of the machine. In addition, no two VCRs seem to have the same interface. For whatever reason, the VCR projects an interface that is too difficult and too nonstandard for most people to use beyond the bare basics.

Compare this with an automobile. It would be difficult to argue that a car is less complicated than a VCR. However, people don't seem to have much trouble driving them.

All automobiles offer more or less the same controls in more or less the same place. For example (this is a true story), my sister once had a car — need I say, a French car — with the headlight control on the left-hand side of the steering wheel, where the turn signal handle normally would be. You pushed down on the light lever to turn off the lights, and you raised the lever to turn them on. This may seem like a small difference, but I never did learn to turn left in that car at night without turning off the lights.

Well-designed autos do not use the same control to perform more than one operation, depending on the state of the car. I can think of only one exception to this rule: Some buttons on most cruise controls are overloaded with multiple functions.

Object-Oriented Concept #4 — Access Control

A microwave oven must be built so that no combination of keystrokes that you can enter on the front keypad can cause the oven to hurt you. Certainly, some combinations don't do anything. However, no sequence of keystrokes should do the following:

- ✔ **Break the device:** You may be able to put the device into some sort of strange state in which it won't do anything until you reset it (say, by throwing an internal breaker). However, you shouldn't be able to break the device by using the front panel — unless, of course, you throw it to the ground in frustration. The manufacturer of such a device would probably have to send out some type of fix for a device like that.

- ✔ **Cause the device to catch fire and burn down the house:** Now, as bad as it may be for the device to break itself, catching fire is much worse. We live in a litigious society. The manufacturer's corporate officers would likely end up in jail, especially if I have anything to say about it.

However, to enforce these two rules, you have to take some responsibility. You can't make modifications to the inside of the device.

Almost all kitchen devices of any complexity, including microwave ovens, have a small seal to keep consumers from reaching inside the device. If that seal is broken, indicating that the cover of the device has been removed, the manufacturer no longer bears responsibility. If you modify the internals of an oven, you are responsible if it subsequently catches fire and burns down the house.

Similarly, a class must be able to control access to its data members. No sequence of calls to class members should cause your program to crash. The class cannot possibly ensure this if external elements have access to the internal state of the class. The class must be able to keep critical data members inaccessible to the outside world.

How Does C# Support Object-Oriented Concepts?

Okay, how does C# implement object-oriented programming? In a sense, this is the wrong question. C# is an object-oriented language; however, it doesn't implement object-oriented programming — the programmer does. You can certainly write a non-object-oriented program in C# or any other language (by, for instance, writing all of Microsoft Word in `Main()`). Something like "you can lead a horse to water" comes to mind. But you can easily write an object-oriented program in C#.

C# provides the following features necessary for writing object-oriented programs:

- ✔ **Controlled access:** C# controls the way in which class members can be accessed. C# keywords enable you to declare some members wide open to the `public` while `internal` members are `protected` from view and some secrets are kept `private`. Notice the little hints. Access control secrets are revealed in Chapter 11.

- ✔ **Specialization:** C# supports specialization through a mechanism known as *class inheritance*. One class inherits the members of another class. For example, you can create a `Car` class as a particular type of `Vehicle`. Chapter 12 specializes in specialization.

- ✔ **Polymorphism:** This feature enables an object to perform an operation the way it wants to. The `Rocket` type of `Vehicle` may implement the `Start` operation much differently from the way the `Car` type of `Vehicle` does. At least, I hope it does every time I turn the key in my car — with my car you never know. But all `Vehicles` have a Start operation, and you can rely on that. (Chapter 13 finds its own way of describing polymorphism.)

- ✔ **Indirection.** Objects frequently use the services of other objects — by calling their public methods. But classes can "know too much" about the classes they use. The two classes are then said to be "too tightly coupled," which makes the using class too dependent on the used class. The design is too brittle — liable to break if you make changes. But change is inevitable in software, so it's best to find more *indirect* ways to connect the two classes. That's where the C# `interface` construct comes in. (You can get the scoop on interfaces in Chapter 14.)

Part IV
Object-Oriented Programming

The 5th Wave   By Rich Tennant

"I understand you've found a system to reduce
the number of complaints we receive by 50 percent."

In this part . . .

Object-oriented programming is the most hyped term in the programming world — dot-com and business-to-business e-commerce eclipsed it for a year or two, but their high-flying fortunes have 'er, subsided, since the dot-com crash of 2001.

C++ claims to be object-oriented — that's what differenti-ated it from good ol' C. Java is definitely object-oriented, as are a hundred or so other languages that were invented during the last ten years. But what is *object-oriented?* Do I have it? Can I get it? Do I want it?

Part IV demonstrates the features of C# that make it object-oriented. Not only will you be programming objects, but you'll also take possession of the keys to powerful, flexible program designs — all right here in Part IV!

Speaking of flying high, in Part IV you'll discover the great door into eternal happiness: *interfaces*. Okay, that's a bit over the top, I admit. But interfaces are a powerful tool for making your objects more general and flexible, and along with the abstract classes you meet in Chapter 13, inter-faces are the key to advanced program designs. So pay attention, please!

Chapter 11

Holding a Class Responsible

A class must be held responsible for its actions. Just as a microwave oven shouldn't burst into flames if you press the wrong key, a class shouldn't allow itself to roll over and die when presented with incorrect data.

To be held responsible for its actions, a class must ensure that its initial state is correct, and control its subsequent state so that it remains valid. C# provides both of these capabilities.

Restricting Access to Class Members

Simple classes define all their members as `public`. Consider a `BankAccount` program that maintains a `balance` data member to retain the balance in each account. Making that data member `public` puts everyone on the honor system.

I don't know about your bank, but my bank is not nearly so forthcoming as to leave a pile of money and a register for me to mark down every time I add money to or take money away from the pile. After all, I may forget to mark my withdrawals in the register. I'm not as young as I used to be — my memory is beginning to fade.

Controlling access avoids little mistakes like forgetting to mark a withdrawal here or there. It also manages to avoid some really big mistakes with withdrawals.

I know exactly what you procedural types out there are thinking: "Just make a rule that other classes can't access the balance data member directly, and that's that." That approach may work in theory, but in practice it never does. People start out with good intentions (like my intentions to workout every day), but those good intentions get crushed under the weight of schedule pressures to get the product out the door. Speaking of weight. . . .

A public example of public BankAccount

The following example BankAccount class declares all its methods public but declares its data members, including _accountNumber and _balance, to be private. Note that I've left it in an incorrect state to make a point. The following code won't compile correctly yet.

```
// BankAccount - Create a bank account using a double variable
//    to store the account balance (keep the balance in a private
//    variable to hide its implementation from the outside world).
// Note: Until you correct it, this program fails to compile
// because Main() refers to a private member of class BankAccount.
using System;
namespace BankAccount
{
  public class Program
  {
    public static void Main(string[] args)
    {
      Console.WriteLine("This program doesn't compile in its present state.");
      // Open a bank account.
      Console.WriteLine("Create a bank account object");
      BankAccount ba = new BankAccount();
      ba.InitBankAccount();
      // Accessing the balance via the Deposit() method is OK -
      // Deposit() has access to all of the data members.
      ba.Deposit(10);
      // Accessing the data member directly is a compile time error.
      Console.WriteLine("Just in case you get this far the following is "
                        + "supposed to generate a compile error");
      ba._balance += 10;
      // Wait for user to acknowledge the results.
      Console.WriteLine("Press Enter to terminate...");
      Console.Read();
    }
  }

  // BankAccount - Define a class that represents a simple account.
  public class BankAccount
  {
    private static int _nextAccountNumber = 1000;
    private int _accountNumber;
```

```
   // Maintain the balance as a double variable.
   private double _balance;
   // Init - Initialize a bank account with the next
   //    account id and a balance of 0.
   public void InitBankAccount()
   {
     _accountNumber = ++_nextAccountNumber;
     _balance = 0.0;
   }
   // GetBalance - Return the current balance.
   public double GetBalance()
   {
     return _balance;
   }
   // AccountNumber.
   public int GetAccountNumber()
   {
     return _accountNumber;
   }
   public void SetAccountNumber(int accountNumber)
   {
     this._accountNumber = accountNumber;
   }
   // Deposit - Any positive deposit is allowed.
   public void Deposit(double amount)
   {
     if (amount > 0.0)
     {
       _balance += amount;
     }
   }
   // Withdraw - You can withdraw any amount up to the
   //    balance; return the amount withdrawn.
   public double Withdraw(double withdrawal)
   {
     if (_balance <= withdrawal)
     {
       withdrawal = _balance;
     }
     _balance -= withdrawal;
     return withdrawal;
   }
   // GetString - Return the account data as a string.
   public string GetString()
   {
     string s = String.Format("#{0} = {1:C}",
                           GetAccountNumber(), GetBalance());
     return s;
   }
 }
}
```

In this code, `_balance -= withdrawal` is the same as `_balance = _balance - withdrawal`. C# programmers tend to use the shortest notation available.

Marking a member `public` makes that member available to any other code within your program.

The `BankAccount` class provides an `InitBankAccount()` method to initialize the members of the class, a `Deposit()` method to handle deposits, and a `Withdraw()` method to perform withdrawals. The `Deposit()` and `Withdraw()` methods even provide some rudimentary rules like "you can't deposit a negative number" and "you can't withdraw more than you have in your account" — both good rules for a bank, I'm sure you'll agree. However, everyone's on the honor system as long as `_balance` is accessible to external methods. (In this context, *external* means "external to the class but within the same program.") That can be a problem on big programs written by teams of programmers. It can even be a problem for you (and me), given general human fallibility.

Well-written code with rules that the compiler can enforce saves us all from the occasional bullet to the big toe.

Before you get too excited, however, notice that the program doesn't build. Attempts to do so generate the following error message:

```
'BankAccount.BankAccount._balance' is inaccessible due to its protection level.
```

I don't know why it doesn't just come out and say, "Hey, this is private so keep your mitts off," but that's essentially what it means. The statement `ba._balance += 10;` is illegal because `_balance` is not accessible to `Main()`, a method outside the `BankAccount` class. Replacing this line with `ba.Deposit(10)` solves the problem. The `BankAccount.Deposit()` method is public and therefore accessible to `Main()` and other parts of your program.

The default access type is `private`. *Forgetting to declare a class member's access type explicitly is the same as declaring it `private`.* However, you should include the `private` keyword to remove any doubt. Good programmers make their intentions explicit, which is another way to reduce errors.

Jumping ahead — other levels of security

This section depends on some knowledge of inheritance (Chapter 12) and namespaces (Bonus Chapter 1 on the Web site). You can skip it for now if you want but just know that it's here when you need it.

C# provides the following levels of security:

- ✔ A `public` member is accessible to any class in the program.

- ✔ A `private` member is accessible only from the current class.

- ✔ A `protected` member is accessible from the current class and any of its subclasses. See Chapter 12.

- ✔ An `internal` member is accessible from any class within the same program module or assembly.

    A C# "module" or *assembly* is a separately compiled piece of code, either an executable program in an `.EXE` file or a supporting library module in a `.DLL` file. A single namespace can extend across multiple assemblies. (Bonus Chapter 1 on the Web site explains C# assemblies and namespaces and gets into access levels besides `public` and `private`.)

- ✔ An `internal protected` member is accessible from the current class and any subclass, and from classes within the same module.

Keeping a member hidden by declaring it `private` offers the maximum amount of security. However, in many cases, you don't need that level of security. After all, the members of a subclass already depend on the members of the base class, so `protected` offers a nice, comfortable level of security.

Why Worry about Access Control?

Declaring the internal members of a class `public` is a bad idea for at least these reasons:

- ✔ **With all data members `public`, you can't easily determine when and how data members are getting modified.** Why bother building safety checks into the `Deposit()` and `Withdraw()` methods? In fact, why bother with these methods at all? Any method of any class can modify these elements at any time. If other methods can access these data members, they almost certainly will.

    Your `BankAccount` program may execute for an hour or so before you notice that one of the accounts has a negative balance. The `Withdraw()` method would have made sure this didn't happen. Obviously, some other method accessed the balance without going through `Withdraw()`. Figuring out which method is responsible and under what conditions is a difficult problem.

- ✔ **Exposing all the data members of the class makes the interface too complicated.** As a programmer using the `BankAccount` class, you *don't want* to know about the internals of the class. You just need to know that you can deposit and withdraw funds. It's like a candy machine with 50 buttons versus one with just a few buttons — the ones you need.

✔ **Exposing internal elements leads to a distribution of the class rules.** For example, my `BankAccount` class does not allow the balance to go negative under any circumstances. That's a required *business rule* that should be isolated within the `Withdraw()` method. Otherwise you have to add this check everywhere the balance is updated.

What happens when the bank decides to change the rules so that "valued customers" are allowed to carry a slightly negative balance for a short period to avoid unintended overdrafts? You now have to search through the program to update every section of code that accesses the balance to make sure the safety checks are changed.

Don't make your classes and methods any more accessible than necessary. This isn't so much paranoia about snoopy hackers as a prudent step that helps reduce errors as you code. Use `private` if possible, and then escalate to `protected`, `internal`, `internal protected`, or `public` as necessary.

Accessor methods

If you look more carefully at the `BankAccount` class, you see a few other methods. One, `GetString()`, returns a `string` version of the account fit for presentation to any `Console.WriteLine()` for display. However, displaying the contents of a `BankAccount` object may be difficult if the contents are inaccessible. Also, using the "Render unto Caesar" policy, the class should have the right to decide how it gets displayed.

In addition, you see two "getter" methods, `GetBalance()` and `GetAccount Number()`, and one "setter" method, `SetAccountNumber()`. You may wonder why I would bother to declare a data member like `_balance` `private` but provide a `public` `GetBalance()` method to return its value. I actually have two reasons, as follows:

✔ `GetBalance()` **does not provide a way to modify _balance — it merely returns its value.** This makes the balance read-only. To use the analogy of an actual bank, you can look at your balance any time you want; you just can't take money out of your account without going through the bank's withdrawal mechanism.

✔ `GetBalance()` **hides the internal format of the class from external methods.** `GetBalance()` may go through an extensive calculation, reading receipts, adding account charges, and accounting for anything else your bank may want to subtract from your balance. External methods don't know and don't care. Of course, you care what fees are being charged. You just can't do anything about them, short of changing banks.

Finally, `GetBalance()` provides a mechanism for making internal changes to the class without the need to change the users of `BankAccount`. If the FDIC mandates that your bank store deposits differently, that shouldn't change the way you access your account.

Access control to the rescue — an example

The following `DoubleBankAccount` program demonstrates a potential flaw in the `BankAccount` program. The entire program is on your Web site; however, the following listing shows just `Main()` — the only portion of the program that differs from the earlier `BankAccount` program:

```
// DoubleBankAccount - Create a bank account using a double variable
//     to store the account balance (keep the balance in a private
//     variable to hide its implementation from the outside world).
using System;
namespace DoubleBankAccount
{
  public class Program
  {
    public static void Main(string[] args)
    {
      // Open a bank account.
      Console.WriteLine("Create a bank account object");
      BankAccount ba = new BankAccount();
      ba.InitBankAccount();
      // Make a deposit.
      double deposit = 123.454;
      Console.WriteLine("Depositing {0:C}", deposit);
      ba.Deposit(deposit);
      // Account balance.
      Console.WriteLine("Account = {0}", ba.GetString());
      // Here's the problem.
      double fractionalAddition = 0.002;
      Console.WriteLine("Adding {0:C}", fractionalAddition);
      ba.Deposit(fractionalAddition);
      // Resulting balance.
      Console.WriteLine("Resulting account = {0}", ba.GetString());
      // Wait for user to acknowledge the results.
      Console.WriteLine("Press Enter to terminate...");
      Console.Read();
    }
  }
}
```

The `Main()` method creates a bank account and then deposits $123.454, an amount that contains a fractional number of cents. `Main()` then deposits a small fraction of a cent to the balance and displays the resulting balance.

The output from this program appears as follows:

```
Create a bank account object
Depositing $123.45
Account = #1001 = $123.45
Adding $0.00
Resulting account = #1001 = $123.46
Press Enter to terminate...
```

Users start to complain. "I just can't reconcile my checkbook with my bank statement." Personally, I'm happy if I can get to the nearest $100, but some people insist that their account match to the penny. Apparently, the program has a bug.

The problem, of course, is that $123.454 shows up as $123.45. To avoid the problem, the bank decides to round deposits and withdrawals to the nearest cent. Deposit $123.454, and the bank takes that extra 0.4 cent. On the other side, the bank gives up enough 0.4 cents that everything balances out in the long run. Well, in theory.

The easiest way to do this is by converting the bank accounts to `decimal` and using the `Decimal.Round()` method, as shown in the following `DecimalBankAccount` program:

```
// DecimalBankAccount - Create a bank account using a decimal
//      variable to store the account balance.
using System;
namespace DecimalBankAccount
{
  public class Program
  {
    public static void Main(string[] args)
    {
      // Open a bank account.
      Console.WriteLine("Create a bank account object");
      BankAccount ba = new BankAccount();
      ba.InitBankAccount();
      // Make a deposit.
      double deposit = 123.454;
      Console.WriteLine("Depositing {0:C}", deposit);
      ba.Deposit(deposit);
      // Account balance.
      Console.WriteLine("Account = {0}", ba.GetString());
      // Now add in a very small amount.
      double fractionalAddition = 0.002;
      Console.WriteLine("Adding {0:C}", fractionalAddition);
      ba.Deposit(fractionalAddition);
      // Resulting balance.
      Console.WriteLine("Resulting account = {0}", ba.GetString());
      // Wait for user to acknowledge the results.
      Console.WriteLine("Press Enter to terminate...");
      Console.Read();
    }
  }
  // BankAccount - Define a class that represents a simple account.
  public class BankAccount
  {
    private static int _nextAccountNumber = 1000;
    private int _accountNumber;
    // Maintain the balance as a single decimal variable.
```

```
private decimal _balance;
// Init - Initialize a bank account with the next
//     account id and a balance of 0.
public void InitBankAccount()
{
  _accountNumber = ++_nextAccountNumber;
  _balance = 0;
}
// GetBalance - Return the current balance.
public double GetBalance()
{
  return (double)_balance;
}
// AccountNumber.
public int GetAccountNumber()
{
  return _accountNumber;
}
public void SetAccountNumber(int accountNumber)
{
  this._accountNumber = accountNumber;
}
// Deposit - Any positive deposit is allowed.
public void Deposit(double amount)
{
  if (amount > 0.0)
  {
    // Round off the double to the nearest cent before depositing.
    decimal temp = (decimal)amount;
    temp = Decimal.Round(temp, 2);
    _balance += temp;
  }
}
// Withdraw - You can withdraw any amount up to the
//     balance; return the amount withdrawn.
public double Withdraw(double withdrawal)
{
  // Convert to decimal and work with the decimal version.
  decimal decWithdrawal = (decimal)withdrawal;
  if (_balance <= decWithdrawal)
  {
    decWithdrawal = _balance;
  }
  _balance -= decWithdrawal;
  return (double)decWithdrawal;  // Return a double.
}
// GetString - Return the account data as a string.
public string GetString()
{
  string s = String.Format("#{0} = {1:C}",
                          GetAccountNumber(), GetBalance());
  return s;
}
}
}
```

I've converted all the internal representations to `decimal` values, a type better adapted to handling bank account balances than `double` in any case. The `Deposit()` method now uses the `Decimal.Round()` method to round the deposit amount to the nearest cent before making the deposit. The output from the program is now as expected:

```
Create a bank account object
Depositing $123.45
Account = #1001 = $123.45
Adding $0.00
Resulting account = #1001 = $123.45
Press Enter to terminate...
```

So what?

You could argue that I should have written the `BankAccount` program using `decimal` input arguments to begin with, and I would probably agree. But the point is that I didn't. Other applications were written using `double` as the form of storage. A problem arose. The `BankAccount` class was able to fix the problem internally with no changes to the application software. (Notice that the class's public interface didn't change: `Balance()` and `Withdraw()` still return doubles, and `Deposit()` and `Withdraw()` still take a `double` parameter.)

I repeat: Applications *using* class `BankAccount` didn't have to change.

In this case, the only calling method potentially affected was `Main()`, but the effects could have extended to dozens of methods that accessed bank accounts, and those methods could have been spread over hundreds of assemblies. None of those methods would have to change, because the fix was within the confines of the `BankAccount` class, whose *public interface* (its public methods) didn't outwardly change. This would not have been possible if the internal members of the class had been exposed to external methods.

Internal changes to a class still require some retesting of other code, even though you didn't have to modify that code.

Defining Class Properties

The `GetX()` and `SetX()` methods demonstrated in the `BankAccount` programs are called *access methods,* or simply *accessors.* Although they signify good programming habits in theory, access methods can get clumsy in practice. For example, the following code is necessary to increment `_accountNumber` by 1:

```
SetAccountNumber(GetAccountNumber() + 1);
```

C# defines a construct called a *property,* which makes using access methods much easier. The following code snippet defines a read-write property, AccountNumber (it's both a getter and a setter):

```
public int AccountNumber          // No parentheses here.
{
  get{ return _accountNumber; }   // The "read" part. Curly braces & semicolon.
  set{ _accountNumber = value; }  // The "write" part. 'value' is a keyword.
}
```

The get section is called whenever the property is read, while the set section is invoked on the write. The following Balance property is read-only because only the get section is defined (using a less compact notation):

```
public double Balance
{
  get
  {
    return (double)_balance;
  }
}
```

In use, these properties appear as follows:

```
BankAccount ba = new BankAccount();
// Set the account number property.
ba.AccountNumber = 1001;
// Get both properties.
Console.WriteLine("#{0} = {1:C}", ba.AccountNumber, ba.Balance);
```

The properties AccountNumber and Balance look very much like public data members, both in appearance and in use. However, properties enable the class to protect internal members (Balance is a read-only property) and hide their implementation (the underlying _balance data member is private). Notice that Balance performs a conversion — it could have performed any number of calculations. Properties aren't necessarily one-liners.

By convention, the names of properties begin with a capital letter. Note that properties don't have parentheses: Balance, not Balance().

Properties are not necessarily inefficient. The C# compiler can optimize a simple accessor to the point that it generates no more machine code than accessing the data member directly. This is important, not only to an application program but also to C# itself. The C# library uses properties throughout, and you should too.

Use properties to access class data members, *even from methods in the same class.*

Static properties

A static (class) data member may be exposed through a static property, as shown in the following simplistic example (note the compact layout):

```
public class BankAccount
{
  private static int _nextAccountNumber = 1000;
  public static int NextAccountNumber { get { return _nextAccountNumber; } }
  // . . .
}
```

The NextAccountNumber property is accessed through the class as follows, because it isn't an instance property (it's declared *static*):

```
// Read the account number property.
int value = BankAccount.NextAccountNumber;
```

(Here value is outside the context of a property, so it's not a reserved word.)

Properties with side effects

A get operation can perform extra work other than simply retrieving the associated property, as shown in the following code:

```
public static int AccountNumber
{
  // Retrieve the property and set it up for the
  // next retrieval by incrementing it.
  get{ return ++_nextAccountNumber; }
}
```

This property increments the static account number member before returning the result. This probably is not a good idea, however, because the user of the property gets no clue that anything is happening other than the actual reading of the property. The incrementation is a *side effect.*

Like the accessor methods that they mimic, properties should not change the state of the class other than, say, setting a data member's value. In general, both properties and methods should avoid side effects because they can lead to subtle bugs. Change a class as directly and explicitly as possible.

New Feature: Let the compiler write properties for you

Most of the properties described in the previous section are utterly routine, and writing them is tedious (though simple):

```
private string _name;  // An underlying data member for the property.
public string Name { get { return _name; } set { _name = value; } }
```

Because you write that same boilerplate code over and over, the C# 3.0 compiler will now do it for you. All you have to write for the property above (including the private data member) is this:

```
public string Name { get; set; }
```

This is sort of equivalent to

```
private string <somename>;  // What's <somename>? Don't know or care.
public string Name { get { return <somename>; } set { <somename> = value; } }
```

The compiler creates a mysterious data member that shall be nameless along with the accessor boilerplate code. The AccessorPropertyShortcuts example on the Web site illustrates this usage. This style encourages using the property even inside other members of its containing class because the property name is all you know. For that reason, you must have both get and set. You can initialize such properties using the property syntax:

```
public int AnInt { get; set; } // Compiler provides a private variable.
. . .
AnInt = 2; // Initialize compiler-written instance variable via property.
```

Accessors with access levels

Accessor properties don't necessarily have to be declared public. You can declare them at any level appropriate, even private, if the accessor is used only inside its class. (The upcoming example marks the Name property internal.)

You can even adjust the access levels of the get and set portions of an accessor individually. For example, suppose you don't want to expose the set accessor outside of your class — it's for internal use only. You can write the property like this:

```
internal string Name { get; private set; }
```

The `AccessorPropertyShortcuts` example on the Web site illustrates this usage.

Getting Your Objects Off to a Good Start — Constructors

Controlling class access is only half the problem. *An object needs a good start in life if it is to grow.* A class can supply an initialization method that the application calls to get things started, but what if the application forgets to call the method? The class starts out with garbage, and the situation doesn't get any better after that. If you're going to hold the class accountable, you have to make sure that it gets a chance to start out correctly.

C# solves that problem by calling the initialization method for you — for example:

```
MyObject mo = new MyObject();
```

In other words, this statement not only grabs an object out of a special memory area, but it also initializes that object's members.

Don't confuse the terms *class* and *object*. `Cat` is a class. My cat `Striper` is an object of class `Cat`.

The C#-Provided Constructor

C# is pretty good at keeping track of whether a variable has been initialized and doesn't allow you to use an uninitialized variable. For example, the following code generates a compile-time error:

```
public static void Main(string[] args)
{
  int n;
  double d;
  double  calculatedValue = n + d;
}
```

C# tracks the fact that the *local variables* n and d haven't been assigned a value and doesn't allow them to be used in the expression. Compiling this tiny program generates the following compiler errors:

```
Use of unassigned local variable 'n'
Use of unassigned local variable 'd'
```

By comparison, C# provides a *default constructor* that initializes the *data members* of an object to 0 for numbers, `false` for Booleans, and `null` for object references. Consider the following simple example program:

```
using System;
namespace Test
{
  public class Program
  {
    public static void Main(string[] args)
    {
      // First create an object.
      MyObject localObject = new MyObject();
      Console.WriteLine("localObject.n is {0}", localObject.n);
      if (localObject.nextObject == null)
      {
        Console.WriteLine("localObject.nextObject is null");
      }
      // Wait for user to acknowledge the results.
      Console.WriteLine("Press Enter to terminate...");
      Console.Read();
    }
  }
  public class MyObject
  {
    internal int n;
    internal MyObject nextObject;
  }
}
```

This program defines a class `MyObject`, which contains both a simple data member n of type `int` and a reference to an object, `nextObject` (both declared `internal`). The `Main()` method creates a `MyObject` and then displays the initial contents of n and `nextObject`.

The output from executing the program appears as follows:

```
localObject.n is 0
localObject.nextObject is null
Press Enter to terminate...
```

When the object is created, C# executes some small piece of code that the compiler provides to initialize the object and its members. Left to their own devices, the data members `localObject.n` and `nextObject` would contain random, garbage values.

The code that initializes values when they are created is called the *default constructor.* It "constructs" the class, in the sense of initializing its members. Thus C# ensures that an object starts life in a known state: all zeros. This affects only data members of the class, not local variables in a method.

Replacing the Default Constructor

Although the compiler will initialize all instance variables to zeros automatically, for many classes (probably most classes), all zeros is not a valid state. Consider the following BankAccount class from earlier in this chapter:

```
public class BankAccount
{
  private int _accountNumber;
  private double _balance;
  // . . .other members
}
```

Although an initial balance of zero is probably okay, an account number of 0 definitely is not the hallmark of a valid bank account.

So far, our BankAccount class includes the InitBankAccount() method to initialize the object. However, this approach puts too much responsibility on the application software using the class. If the application fails to invoke the InitBankAccount() method, the bank account methods may not work, through no fault of their own.

A class should not rely on external methods like InitBankAccount() to start the object in a valid state.

To get around this problem, you can have your class provide its own explicit *class constructor* that C# calls automatically when the object is created. The constructor could have been called Init(), Start(), or Create(), but C# *requires the constructor to carry the name of the class.* Thus a constructor for the BankAccount class appears as follows:

```
public void Main(string[] args)
{
  BankAccount ba = new BankAccount();  // This invokes the constructor.
}
public class BankAccount
{
  // Bank accounts start at 1000 and increase sequentially from there.
  private static int _nextAccountNumber = 1000;
  // Maintain the account number and balance for each object.
  private int _accountNumber;
  private double _balance;
  // BankAccount constructor - Here it is, ta daa!
  public BankAccount()    // Parentheses, possible arguments, no return type.
  {
    _accountNumber = ++_nextAccountNumber;
    _balance = 0.0;
  }
  // . . . other members . . .
}
```

The contents of the `BankAccount` constructor are the same as those of the original `Init...()` method. However, the way you declare and use the constructor differs as follows:

- ✔ The constructor always carries the same name as the class.
- ✔ The constructor can take parameters (or not).
- ✔ The constructor never has a return type, not even `void`.
- ✔ `Main()` does not need to invoke any extra method to initialize the object when it is created; no `Init()` is necessary.

If you provide your own constructor, C# no longer supplies a default constructor. Your constructor replaces the default and becomes the only way to create an instance of your class.

Constructing something

Try one of these constructor thingies. Consider the following program, `DemonstrateCustomConstructor`:

```
// DemonstrateCustomConstructor - Demonstrate how you can replace the
//    default constructor that C# provides with your own custom constructor.
//    Creates a class with a constructor and then steps through a few
//               scenarios.
using System;
namespace DemonstrateCustomConstructor
{
  // MyObject - Create a class with a noisy custom constructor
  //    and an internal data object.
  public class MyObject
  {
    // This data member is a property of the class (it's static).
    private static MyOtherObject _staticObj = new MyOtherObject();
    // This data member is a property of each instance.
    private MyOtherObject _dynamicObj;
    // Constructor (a real chatterbox).
    public MyObject()
    {
      Console.WriteLine("MyObject constructor starting");
      Console.WriteLine("(Static data member constructed before " +
                        "this constructor)");
      Console.WriteLine("Now create nonstatic data member dynamically:");
      _dynamicObj = new MyOtherObject();
      Console.WriteLine("MyObject constructor ending");
    }
  }
  // MyOtherObject - This class also has a noisy constructor but
  //    no internal members.
```

```
public class MyOtherObject
{
  public MyOtherObject()
  {
    Console.WriteLine("MyOtherObject constructing");
  }
}
public class Program
{
  public static void Main(string[] args)
  {
    Console.WriteLine("Main() starting");
    Console.WriteLine("Creating a local MyObject in Main():");
    MyObject localObject = new MyObject();
    // Wait for user to acknowledge the results.
    Console.WriteLine("Press Enter to terminate...");
    Console.Read();
  }
}
```

Executing this program generates the following output:

```
Main() starting
Creating a local MyObject in Main():
MyOtherObject constructing
MyObject constructor starting
(Static data member constructed before this constructor)
Now create nonstatic data member dynamically:
MyOtherObject constructing
MyObject constructor ending
Press Enter to terminate...
```

The following steps reconstruct what just happened here:

1. The program starts, and `Main()` outputs the initial message and announces that it's about to create a local `MyObject`.

2. `Main()` creates a `localObject` of type `MyObject`.

3. `MyObject` contains a static member `_staticObj` of class `MyOtherObject`.

   All static data members are initialized before the first `MyObject()` constructor runs. In this case, C# populates `_staticObj` with a newly created `MyOtherObject` before passing control to the `MyObject` constructor. This step accounts for the third line of output.

4. The constructor for `MyObject` is given control. It outputs the initial message, `MyObject constructor starting` and then notes that the static member was already constructed before the `MyObject()` constructor began: `(Static data member constructed before this constructor)`.

5. After announcing its intention with `Now create nonstatic data member dynamically`, the `MyObject` constructor creates an object of class `MyOtherObject` using the `new` operator, generating the second `MyOtherObject constructing` message as the `MyOtherObject` constructor is called.

6. Control returns to the `MyObject` constructor, which returns to `Main()`.

7. Job well done!

Executing the constructor from the debugger

It's illuminating to execute the same program from the debugger as follows:

1. **Rebuild the program: Choose Build⇨Build DemonstrateCustomConstructor.**

2. **Before you start executing the program from the debugger, set a breakpoint at the `Console.WriteLine()` call in the `MyOtherObject` constructor.**

   To set a breakpoint, click in the gray trough on the left side of the editor window, next to the line at which you want to stop.

   Figure 11-1 shows my display with the breakpoint set: The dark ball is in the trough.

3. **Rather than choosing Debug⇨Start Debugging, choose Debug⇨Step Into (or, better yet, press F11).**

   Your menus, toolbars, and windows should change a bit, and then a bright yellow highlight appears on the opening curly brace in `Main()`.

4. **Press F11 three more times and lightly rest the mouse pointer on the `localObject` variable (without clicking).**

   You're about to call the `MyObject` constructor. Your display should now look like that shown in Figure 11-2. You can see that `localObject` is currently `null` under the cursor. The Locals window just below shows the same thing. (If Locals isn't visible, choose Debug⇨Windows⇨Locals to display it.)

5. **Press F11 one more time.**

   The program executes up to the breakpoint in `MyOtherObject`, as shown by the yellow bar in Figure 11-3. How did you reach this point? The last call in `Main()` invoked the constructor for `MyObject`. But before that constructor begins to execute, C# initializes the static data member in class `MyObject`. That data member is of type `MyOtherObject`, so initializing it means invoking *its* constructor — which lands you at the breakpoint.

(Without the breakpoint, you wouldn't see the debugger stop there, although the constructor would indeed execute, as you could confirm by checking to make sure that the constructor's message shows up in the console window.)

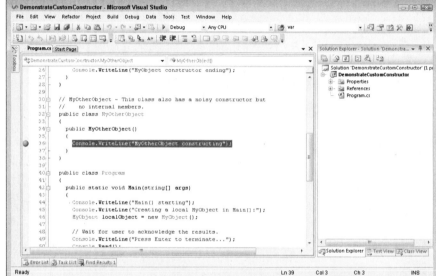

Figure 11-1:
The highlighting in the MyOther Object constructor indicates the presence of a breakpoint.

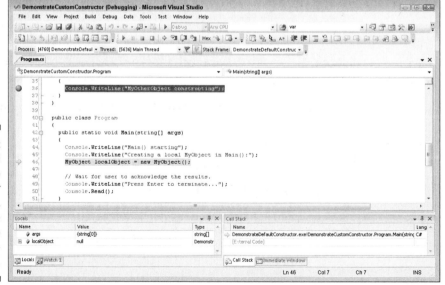

Figure 11-2:
The Visual Studio debugger display, right before jumping into constructor-ville.

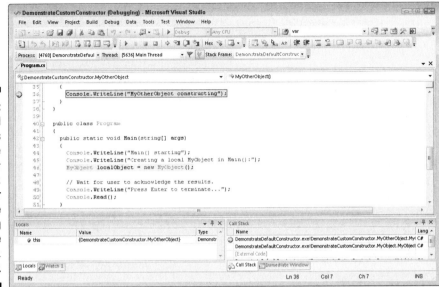

Figure 11-3:
Control
passes
to the
MyOther
Object
constructor
before
heading
into the
MyObject
constructor.

6. **Press F11 twice more, and you're stopped at the static data member, `_staticObj`, as shown in Figure 11-4.**

   It was that object's constructor that you just stepped out of.

7. **Continue pressing F11 as you walk through the program.**

   The first time you press F11, you stop at the beginning of the `MyObject` constructor, at last. Note that you step into the `MyOtherObject` constructor a second time when the `MyObject` constructor creates the other `MyObject` data member, the nonstatic one called `_dynamicObj`.

   Remember to continue through the `Console.Read()` statement back in `Main()`. After viewing the console window, you can press Enter to close it.

Bonus Chapter 6 on the Web site gives you a thorough tour of the debugger.

Initializing an object directly with an initializer

Besides letting you initialize data members in a constructor, C# enables you to initialize data members directly by using *initializers*.

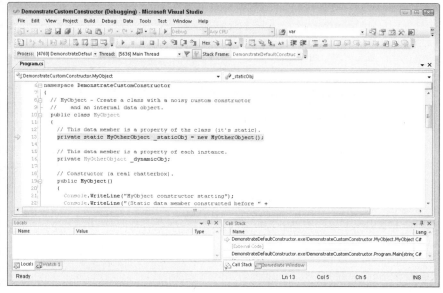

Figure 11-4:
Having
stepped
through the
`MyOther
Object`
constructor,
you're back
where the
constructor
was
invoked.

Thus I could have written the `BankAccount` class as follows:

```
public class BankAccount
{
    // Bank accounts start at 1000 and increase sequentially from there.
    private static int _nextAccountNumber = 1000;
    // Maintain the account number and balance for each object.
    private int _accountNumber = ++_nextAccountNumber;
    private double _balance = 0.0;
    // . . . other members . . .
}
```

Here's the initializer business. Both `_accountNumber` and `_balance` are assigned a value *as part of their declaration*. This has the same effect as a constructor but without having to do the work in the constructor.

Be very clear about exactly what's happening. You may think that this statement sets `_balance` to 0.0 right now. However, `_balance` exists only as a part of an object. Thus the assignment is not executed until a `BankAccount` object is created. In fact, this assignment is executed every time an object is created.

Note that the static data member `_nextAccountNumber` is initialized the first time the `BankAccount` class is accessed — as your tour in the debugger showed, that's the first time you access any method or property of the object owning the static data member, including the constructor.

Once initialized, the static member is not reinitialized each time you construct a `BankAccount` instance. That's different from the nonstatic members.

Initializers are executed in the order of their appearance in the class declaration. If C# encounters both initializers and a constructor, the initializers are executed *before the body of the constructor.*

Seeing that construction stuff with initializers

In the `DemonstrateCustomConstructor` program, move the call `new MyOtherObject()` from the `MyObject` constructor to the declaration itself, as follows (see the bold text), modify the second `WriteLine()` statement as shown, and then rerun the program:

```
public class MyObject
{
  // This member is a property of the class (it's static).
  private static MyOtherObject _staticObj = new MyOtherObject();
  // This member is a property of each instance.
  private MyOtherObject _dynamicObj = new MyOtherObject();  // <- Here.
  public MyObject()
  {
    Console.WriteLine("MyObject constructor starting");
    Console.WriteLine(
      "Both data members initialized before this constructor)");
    // _dynamicObj construction was here, now moved up.
    Console.WriteLine("MyObject constructor ending");
  }
}
```

Compare the following output from this modified program with the output from its predecessor, `DemonstrateCustomConstructor`:

```
Main() starting
Creating a local MyObject in Main():
MyOtherObject constructing
MyOtherObject constructing
MyObject constructor starting
(Both data members initialized before this constructor)
MyObject constructor ending
Press Enter to terminate...
```

You can find the entire program (after these changes) on the Web site, under the illustrious name of `DemonstrateConstructorWithInitializer`.

New Feature — Initializing an object without a constructor

Suppose you have a little class to represent a Student:

```
public class Student
{
  public string Name { get; set; }
  public string Address { get; set; }
  public double GradePointAverage { get; set; }
}
```

A Student object has three public properties, Name, Address, and GradePointAverage, which specify the student's basic information.

Normally, when you create a new Student object, you have to initialize its Name, Address, and GradePointAverage properties like this:

```
Student randal = new Student();
randal.Name = "Randal Sphar";
randal.Address = "123 Elm Street, Truth or Consequences, NM 00000";
randal.GradePointAverage = 3.51;
```

Yes, Virginia, there is a Truth or Consequences, New Mexico. My nephew Randal was actually born there.

If Student had a constructor, you could do something like the following:

```
Student randal = new Student
  ("Randal Sphar", "123 Elm Street, Truth or Consequences, NM, 00000", 3.51);
```

but, sadly, Student lacks a constructor, other than the default one that C# supplies automatically — which takes no parameters.

In C# 3.0, you can simplify that initialization with something that looks suspiciously like a constructor — well, sort of:

```
Student randal = new Student
  { Name = "Randal Sphar",
    Address = "123 Elm Street, Truth or Consequences, NM 00000",
    GradePointAverage = 3.51
  };
```

How are the last two examples different? The first one, using a constructor, shows *parentheses* containing two strings and one double value separated by commas. The second one, using the new object-initializer syntax, has instead *curly braces* containing three *assignments* separated by commas. The syntax works something like this:

```
new LatitudeLongitude
  { assignment to Latitude, assignment to Longitude  };
```

The new object-initializer syntax lets you assign to any accessible *set* properties of the LatitudeLongitude object in a code block (the curly braces). The block is designed to initialize the object. Note that you can only set accessible properties this way, not private ones, and you can't call any of the object's methods or do any other work in the initializer.

The new syntax is much more concise: one statement versus three. And it simplifies creating initialized objects that don't let you do so through a constructor. (I broke the Student example into multiple lines only to fit it on the page — and that was only because Truth or Consequences is so long. If you lived there, it would seem even longer.)

Does the new object-initializer syntax gain you anything besides convenience? Not much, but convenience when you're coding is high on any programmer's list. So is brevity. Besides, the feature becomes essential when we get to anonymous classes, in Chapter 17.

Use this feature to your heart's content. I'll start using it frequently myself throughout the rest of this book.

Look up "object initializer" in Help for the language-lawyery stuff concerning what kinds of properties it works with.

The ObjectInitializers example program on the Web site demonstrates object initializers.

Overloading the Constructor (Is That Like Overtaxing a Carpenter?)

You can overload constructors, just as you can overload any other method.

Overloading a method means defining two methods with the same name but with different types of arguments. (See Chapter 8 for details.)

Suppose you wanted to provide the following three ways to create a BankAccount: one with a zero balance (like mine most of the time) and two more variations for a bank account with some initial value:

```
// BankAccountWithMultipleConstructors - Provide our trusty bank account
```

```
//    with a number of constructors, one for every occasion.
using System;
namespace BankAccountWithMultipleConstructors
{
  using System;
  public class Program
  {
    public static void Main(string[] args)
    {
      // Create three bank accounts with valid initial values.
      BankAccount ba1 = new BankAccount();            // Use constructor 1.
      Console.WriteLine(ba1.GetString());
      BankAccount ba2 = new BankAccount(100);         // Use constructor 2.
      Console.WriteLine(ba2.GetString());
      BankAccount ba3 = new BankAccount(1234, 200);  // Use constructor 3.
      Console.WriteLine(ba3.GetString());
      // Wait for user to acknowledge the results.
      Console.WriteLine("Press Enter to terminate...");
      Console.Read();
    }
  }
  // BankAccount - Simulate a simple bank account.
  public class BankAccount
  {
    // Bank accounts start at 1000 and increase sequentially from there.
    private static int _nextAccountNumber = 1000;
    // Maintain the account number and balance.
    private int _accountNumber;
    // Back to the double version - we don't care for this example since
    // it's just about the constructors.
    private double _balance;
    // Provide a series of constructors depending upon the need.
    public BankAccount()  // You create this one, not automatic.
    {
      _accountNumber = ++_nextAccountNumber;
      _balance = 0.0;
    }
    public BankAccount(double initialBalance)
    {
      // Repeat some of the code from the default constructor.
      _accountNumber = ++_nextAccountNumber;
      // Now the code unique to this constructor.
      // Start with an initial balance as long as it's positive.
      if (initialBalance < 0)
      {
        initialBalance = 0;
      }
      _balance = initialBalance;
    }
    public BankAccount(int initialAccountNumber, double initialBalance)
    {
      // Ignore negative account numbers.
      if (initialAccountNumber <= 0)
```

```
      {
        initialAccountNumber = ++_nextAccountNumber;
      }
      _accountNumber = initialAccountNumber;
      // Start with an initial balance as long as it's positive.
      if (initialBalance < 0)
      {
        initialBalance = 0;
      }
      _balance = initialBalance;
    }
    public string GetString()
    {
      return String.Format("#{0} = {1:N}", _accountNumber, _balance);
    }
  }
}
```

C# no longer provides a default constructor for you if you define your own constructor, no matter what type it might be. Thus you have to provide the parameterless constructor in the preceding code *because you provided the others*. It's the only way you get the parameterless version.

This version of the program, named `BankAccountWithMultiple Constructors`, provides the following three constructors:

✔ The first constructor assigns an account ID and sets a balance of 0.

✔ The second constructor assigns an account ID but initializes the account with a positive balance. Negative balances are ignored.

✔ The third constructor allows the user to specify a positive account number and a positive balance.

`Main()` creates a different bank account using each of the three constructors and then outputs the objects that are created. The output from executing the program is as follows:

```
#1001 = 0.00
#1002 = 100.00
#1234 = 200.00
Press Enter to terminate...
```

A real-world class would perform a good deal more testing of the input parameters to the constructors, to make sure that they're legal.

You differentiate constructors by using the same rules that apply to methods. The first object to be constructed in `Main()` — `ba1` — is created with no arguments and thus is vectored to the parameterless constructor `Bank Account()` (still called the "default" constructor, but no longer generated automatically by C#) to receive the default account ID and a balance of 0. The second account, ba2, is sent to the BankAccount(double) constructor to get the next bank account ID, but is created with an initial value of 100. The third little piggie, ba3, goes for the full-meal deal with bacon, BankAccount (int, double), and gets his own bank account ID and an initial balance.

Avoiding Duplication among Constructors

Like a typical soap opera script, the three BankAccount constructors have significant amounts of duplication. As you can imagine, the situation would get much worse in real-world classes that may have many constructors and even more data elements to initialize. In addition, the tests on input data can get more involved in a real-world class than on a Yahoo! Web page. Duplicating these business rules is both tedious and error-prone. The checks can easily get out of synch. For example, through a coding error, two constructors may apply different sets of rules against the balance. Such errors are very difficult to find.

It's an example of the DRY principle: "Don't repeat yourself." Duplication is the greatest evil in code.

You would *like* to have one constructor call the other, but constructors are not methods — you can't just call them. However, you can create some alternative method that does the actual construction and pass control to it, as demonstrated in this BankAccountConstructorsAndMethod program:

```
// BankAccountContructorsAndMethod - Call an initialization method from
//            each constructor.
using System;
namespace BankAccountContructorsAndMethod
{
  using System;
  public class Program
  {
    public static void Main(string[] args)
    {
      // Create three bank accounts with valid initial values.
      BankAccount ba1 = new BankAccount();
      Console.WriteLine(ba1.GetString());
      BankAccount ba2 = new BankAccount(100);
      Console.WriteLine(ba2.GetString());
      BankAccount ba3 = new BankAccount(1234, 200);
      Console.WriteLine(ba3.GetString());
      // Wait for user to acknowledge the results.
      Console.WriteLine("Press Enter to terminate...");
      Console.Read();
    }
```

```
}
// BankAccount - Simulate a simple bank account.
public class BankAccount
{
  // Bank accounts start at 1000 and increase sequentially from there.
  private static int _nextAccountNumber = 1000;
  // Maintain the account number and balance.
  private int _accountNumber;
  private double _balance;
  // Place all the real initialization code in a separate,
  // conventional method, called from constructors.
  public BankAccount() // You create this one, not automatic.
  {
    Init(++_nextAccountNumber, 0.0);
  }
  public BankAccount(double initialBalance)
  {
    Init(++_nextAccountNumber, initialBalance);
  }
  public BankAccount(int initialAccountNumber, double initialBalance)
  {
    // Really should validate initialAccountNumber here so it (a) doesn't
    // duplicate existing numbers and (b) is 1000 or greater.
    Init(initialAccountNumber, initialBalance);
  }
  // All three constructors call this initialization method.
  private void Init(int initialAccountNumber, double initialBalance)
  {
    _accountNumber = initialAccountNumber;
    // Start with an initial balance as long as it's positive.
    if (initialBalance < 0)
    {
      initialBalance = 0;
    }
    _balance = initialBalance;
  }
  public string GetString()
  {
    return String.Format("#{0} = {1:N}", _accountNumber, _balance);
  }
}
}
```

Here an `Init()` method does the work of construction. However, this approach isn't exactly kosher for several reasons — not the least of which is the fact that you are now calling a method of the object before the object has been fully constructed. That's a dangerous thing to do.

Fortunately, this approach isn't necessary. One constructor can refer to another, using a variation of the `this` keyword (the preferred approach), as follows:

```
//BankAccountContructorsAndThis - "Chain" the three
//    constructors to localize all initialization.
using System;
namespace BankAccountContructorsAndThis
{
  using System;
  public class Program
  {
    public static void Main(string[] args)
    {
      // Create three bank accounts with valid initial values.
      BankAccount ba1 = new BankAccount();
      Console.WriteLine(ba1.GetString());
      BankAccount ba2 = new BankAccount(100);
      Console.WriteLine(ba2.GetString());
      BankAccount ba3 = new BankAccount(1234, 200);
      Console.WriteLine(ba3.GetString());
      // Wait for user to acknowledge the results.
      Console.WriteLine("Press Enter to terminate...");
      Console.Read();
    }
  }
  // BankAccount - Simulate a simple bank account.
  public class BankAccount
  {
    // Bank accounts start at 1000 and increase sequentially from there.
    private static int _nextAccountNumber = 1000;
    // Maintain the account number and balance.
    private int _accountNumber;
    private double _balance;
    // Invoke the most specific constructor by providing
    // default values for the missing arguments.
    public BankAccount() : this(0, 0) {}
    public BankAccount(double initialBalance) : this(0, initialBalance) {}
    // The most specific constructor does all of the real work.
    public BankAccount(int initialAccountNumber, double initialBalance)
    {
      // Ignore negative account numbers; a zero account
      // number indicates that we should use the next available.
      if (initialAccountNumber <= 0)
      {
        initialAccountNumber = ++_nextAccountNumber;
      }
      _accountNumber = initialAccountNumber;
      // Start with an initial balance as long as it's positive.
      if (initialBalance < 0)
      {
```

```
      initialBalance = 0;
    }
    _balance = initialBalance;
  }
  public string GetString()
  {
    return String.Format("#{0} = {1:N}", _accountNumber, _balance);
  }
}
}
```

This version of `BankAccount` provides the same three constructors as the previous version; however, rather than repeat the same tests in each constructor, both of the simpler constructors invoke the most flexible constructor, providing defaults for the missing arguments. `Init()` is now gone.

Creating an object using the default constructor invokes the following `BankAccount()` constructor:

```
BankAccount ba1 = new BankAccount();  // No parameters.
```

The `BankAccount()` constructor immediately passes control to the `BankAccount(int, double)` constructor, passing it the default values 0 and 0.0, as follows — it's *constructor chaining*:

```
public BankAccount() : this(0, 0) {}
```

Note that because the constructor has an empty body, you can write it all on one line, with the empty body as a pair of curly braces.

The all-powerful third constructor has been updated to look for a zero bank account ID and to supply a valid one instead. This is where the action is.

Control returns to the default constructor after the invoked constructor has completed. The body of the default constructor is empty in this case.

Creating a bank account with a balance but a default account ID goes down the following constructor chain:

```
public BankAccount(double d) : this(0, d) {}
```

Being Object-Stingy

You can't construct an object without a constructor of some sort. If you define your own constructor, C# takes its constructor away. Combining these two facts, you can create a class that can only be instantiated locally.

For example, only methods that are defined within the same assembly as BankAccount can create a BankAccount object with the constructor declared internal, as in the bold text that follows (see Bonus Chapter 1 on the Web site for more on assemblies and the internal keyword):

```
// BankAccount - Simulate a simple bank account.
public class BankAccount
{
  // Bank accounts start at 1000 and increase sequentially from there.
  private static int _nextAccountNumber = 1000;
  // Maintain the account number and balance.
  private int _accountNumber;
  double _balance;
  internal BankAccount()    // Here's the internal, not public, constructor.
  {
    _accountNumber = ++_nextAccountNumber;
    _balance = 0;
  }
  public string GetString()
  {
    return String.Format("#{0} = {1:N}", _accountNumber, _balance);
  }
}
```

Speaking of the internal keyword, I haven't really said much in this chapter about the access-level keywords other than public and private — namely internal, protected, and protected internal. Bonus Chapter 1 on the Web site gives those very handy access protectors a good workout.

Chapter 12

Inheritance — Is That All I Get?

*O*bject-oriented programming is based on four principles: the ability to control access (encapsulation), the ability to inherit from other classes, the ability to respond appropriately (polymorphism), and the ability to refer from one object to another indirectly (interfaces).

Inheritance is a common concept. I am a human, except when I first wake up. I inherit certain properties from the class Human, such as my ability to converse, more or less, and my dependence on air, food, and carbohydrate-based beverages with lots of caffeine. The class Human inherits its dependencies on air, water, and nourishment from the class Mammal, which inherits from the class Animal.

The ability to pass down properties is a powerful one. It enables you to describe things in an economical way. For example, if my son asks, "What's a duck?" I can say, "It's a bird that goes quack." Despite what you may think, that answer conveys a considerable amount of information. My son knows what a bird is, and now he knows all those same things about a duck plus the duck's additional property of "quackness."

Object-oriented languages express this inheritance relationship by allowing one class to inherit properties from another. This feature enables object-oriented languages to generate a model that's closer to the real world than the model generated by languages that don't support inheritance.

Inheriting a Class

In the following `InheritanceExample` program, the class `SubClass` inherits from the class `BaseClass`:

```
// InheritanceExample - Provide the simplest possible
//     demonstration of inheritance.
using System;
namespace InheritanceExample
{
  public class BaseClass
  {
    public int _dataMember;
    public void SomeMethod()
    {
      Console.WriteLine("SomeMethod()");
    }
  }
  public class SubClass : BaseClass
  {
    public void SomeOtherMethod()
    {
      Console.WriteLine("SomeOtherMethod()");
    }
  }
  public class Program
  {
    public static void Main(string[] args)
    {
      // Create a base class object.
      Console.WriteLine("Exercising a base class object:");
      BaseClass bc = new BaseClass();
      bc._dataMember = 1;
      bc.SomeMethod();
      // Now create a subclass object.
      Console.WriteLine("Exercising a subclass object:");
      SubClass sc = new SubClass();
      sc._dataMember = 2;
      sc.SomeMethod();
      sc.SomeOtherMethod();
      // Wait for user to acknowledge the results.
      Console.WriteLine("Press Enter to terminate...");
      Console.Read();
    }
  }
}
```

The class `BaseClass` is defined with a data member and a simple method, `SomeMethod()`. `Main()` creates and exercises the `BaseClass` object `bc`.

Inheritance is amazing

To make sense of our surroundings, humans build extensive taxonomies. For example, Fido is a special case of dog, which is a special case of canine, which is a special case of mammal — and so it goes. This ability to classify things shapes our understanding of the world.

In an object-oriented language like C#, you say that the class Student inherits from the class Person. You also say that Person is a base class of Student, and Student is a subclass of Person. Finally, you say that a Student IS_A Person. (Using all caps is a common way of expressing this unique relationship — I didn't make this up.)

Notice that the IS_A property is not reflexive: Although Student IS_A Person, the reverse

is not true. A Person IS_NOT_A Student. A statement like this always refers to the general case. It could be that a particular Person is, in fact, a Student — but lots of people who are members of the class Person are not members of the class Student. In addition, the class Student has properties it does not share with the class Person. For example, Student has a grade-point average, but the ordinary Person quite happily does not.

The inheritance property is transitive. For example, if I define a new class Graduate Student as a subclass of Student, GraduateStudent is also a Person. It must be that way: If a GraduateStudent IS_A Student and a Student IS_A Person, a GraduateStudent IS_A Person. Q.E.D.

The class SubClass inherits from that class by placing the name of the class, BaseClass, after a colon in the class definition:

```
public class SubClass : BaseClass
```

SubClass gets all the members of BaseClass as its own, plus any members that it may add to the pile. Main() demonstrates that SubClass now has a data member, _dataMember, and a member method, SomeMethod(), to join the brand-new member of the family, little method SomeOtherMethod() — and what a joy it is, too.

The program produces the following expected output — actually, I'm sort of surprised whenever one of my programs works as expected:

```
Exercising a base class object:
SomeMethod()
Exercising a subclass object:
SomeMethod()
SomeOtherMethod()
Press Enter to terminate...
```

Why Do You Need Inheritance?

Inheritance serves several important functions. You may think that inheritance reduces the amount of typing. In a way it does — you don't need to repeat the properties of a `Person` when you're describing a `Student` class. A more important, related issue is that major buzzword, *reuse*. Software scientists have known for some time that starting from scratch with each new project and rebuilding the same software components makes little sense.

Compare the situation in software development to that of other industries. How many car manufacturers start by building their own wrenches and screw-drivers before they construct a car? And even if they did, how many would start over completely, building all new tools for the next model? Practitioners in other industries have found that starting with existing screws, bolts, nuts, and even larger off-the-shelf components such as motors and compressors makes more sense than starting from scratch.

Inheritance enables you to tweak existing software components. You can adapt existing classes to new applications without making internal modifications. The existing class is inherited into — programmers often say, *extended* by — a new subclass that contains the necessary additions and modifications. If someone else wrote the base class, you may not be able to modify it, so inheritance can save the day.

This capability carries with it a third benefit of inheritance. Suppose you inherit from — extend — some existing class. Later, you find that the base class has a bug you must correct. If you've modified the class to reuse it, you must manually check for, correct, and retest the bug in each application separately. If you've inherited the class without changes, you can generally stick the updated class into the other application without much hassle.

But the biggest benefit of inheritance is that it describes the way life is. Things inherit properties from each other. There's no getting around it. Basta! — as my Italian grandmother would say.

A More Involved Example — Inheriting from a BankAccount Class

A bank maintains several types of accounts. One type, the savings account, has all the properties of a simple bank account plus the ability to accumulate interest. The following `SimpleSavingsAccount` program models this relationship in C#.

The version of this program on the Web site includes some modifications from the next section of this chapter, so it's a bit different from the code listing shown here.

```
// SimpleSavingsAccount - Implement a SavingsAccount as a form of
//    bank account; don't use any virtual methods
//    (Chapter 13 explains virtual methods).
using System;
namespace SimpleSavingsAccount
{
  // BankAccount - Simulate a bank account, each of which
  //    carries an account ID (which is assigned
  //    upon creation) and a balance.
  public class BankAccount      // The base class.
  {
    // Bank accounts start at 1000 and increase sequentially from there.
    public static int _nextAccountNumber = 1000;
    // Maintain the account number and balance for each object.
    public int _accountNumber;
    public decimal _balance;
    // Init - Initialize a bank account with the next account ID and the
    //    specified initial balance (default to zero).
    public void InitBankAccount()
    {
      InitBankAccount(0);
    }
    public void InitBankAccount(decimal initialBalance)
    {
      _accountNumber = ++_nextAccountNumber;
      _balance = initialBalance;
    }
    // Balance property.
    public decimal Balance
    {
      get { return _balance;}
    }
    // Deposit - any positive deposit is allowed.
    public void Deposit(decimal amount)
    {
      if (amount > 0)
      {
        _balance += amount;
      }
    }
    // Withdraw - You can withdraw any amount up to the
    //    balance; return the amount withdrawn.
    public decimal Withdraw(decimal withdrawal)
    {
      if (Balance <= withdrawal) // Use Balance property.
      {
        withdrawal = Balance;
      }
```

```csharp
      _balance -= withdrawal;
      return withdrawal;
    }
    // ToString - Stringify the account.
    public string ToBankAccountString()
    {
      return String.Format("{0} - {1:C}",
        _accountNumber, Balance);
    }
  }
// SavingsAccount - A bank account that draws interest.
public class SavingsAccount : BankAccount    // The subclass.
{
    public decimal _interestRate;
    // InitSavingsAccount - Input the rate expressed as a
    //     rate between 0 and 100
    public void InitSavingsAccount(decimal interestRate)
    {
      InitSavingsAccount(0, interestRate);
    }
    public void InitSavingsAccount(decimal initialBalance, decimal interestRate)
    {
      InitBankAccount(initialBalance);  // Note call to base class.
      this._interestRate = interestRate / 100;
    }
    // AccumulateInterest - Invoke once per period.
    public void AccumulateInterest()
    {
      _balance = Balance + (decimal)(Balance * _interestRate);
    }
    // ToString - Stringify the account.
    public string ToSavingsAccountString()
    {
      return String.Format("{0} ({1}%)",
        ToBankAccountString(), _interestRate * 100);
    }
  }
public class Program
{
  public static void Main(string[] args)
  {
    // Create a bank account and display it.
    BankAccount ba = new BankAccount();
    ba.InitBankAccount(100M); // M suffix indicates decimal.
    ba.Deposit(100M);
    Console.WriteLine("Account {0}", ba.ToBankAccountString());
    // Now a savings account.
    SavingsAccount sa = new SavingsAccount();
    sa.InitSavingsAccount(100M, 12.5M);
    sa.AccumulateInterest();
    Console.WriteLine("Account {0}", sa.ToSavingsAccountString());
    // Wait for user to acknowledge the results.
```

```
        Console.WriteLine("Press Enter to terminate...");
        Console.Read();
      }
    }
  }
```

The BankAccount class is not unlike some of those appearing in other chapters of this book. It begins with an overloaded initialization method InitBank Account(): one for accounts that start out with an initial balance and another for which an initial balance of zero will just have to do. Notice that this version of BankAccount doesn't take advantage of the latest and greatest constructor advances. By the end of this chapter, that will all be cleaned up, in the final version of BankAccount, and you'll see why I chose to drop back ten yards here.

The Balance property allows others to read the balance without giving them the ability to modify it. The Deposit() method accepts any positive deposit. Withdraw() lets you take out as much as you want, as long as you have enough in your account — my bank's nice, but it's not that nice. ToBankAccount String() creates a string that describes the account.

The SavingsAccount class inherits all that good stuff from BankAccount. To that, it adds an interest rate and the ability to accumulate interest at regular intervals.

Main() does about as little as it can. It creates a BankAccount, displays the account, creates a SavingsAccount, accumulates one period of interest, and displays the result, with the interest rate in parentheses, as follows:

```
Account 1001 - $200.00
Account 1002 - $112.50 (12.500%)
Press Enter to terminate...
```

Notice that the InitSavingsAccount() method invokes InitBank Account(). This initializes the bank account–specific data members. The InitSavingsAccount() method could have initialized these members directly; however, it is better practice to allow the BankAccount to initialize its own members. A class should be responsible for itself.

IS_A versus HAS_A — I'm So Confused

The relationship between SavingsAccount and BankAccount is the fundamental IS_A relationship seen with inheritance. In the following sections, I show you why and then show you what the alternative, the HAS_A relationship, would look like.

The IS_A relationship

The IS_A relationship between `SavingsAccount` and `BankAccount` is demonstrated by the following modification to the class `Program` in the `SimpleSavingsAccount` program from the preceding section:

```
public class Program
{
  // We add this:
  // DirectDeposit - Deposit my paycheck automatically.
  public static void DirectDeposit(BankAccount ba, decimal pay)
  {
    ba.Deposit(pay);
  }
  public static void Main(string[] args)
  {
    // Create a bank account and display it.
    BankAccount ba = new BankAccount();
    ba.InitBankAccount(100M);
    DirectDeposit(ba, 100M);
    Console.WriteLine("Account {0}", ba.ToBankAccountString());
    // Now a savings account.
    SavingsAccount sa = new SavingsAccount();
    sa.InitSavingsAccount(12.5M);
    DirectDeposit(sa, 100M);
    sa.AccumulateInterest();
    Console.WriteLine("Account {0}", sa.ToSavingsAccountString());
    // Wait for user to acknowledge the results.
    Console.WriteLine("Press Enter to terminate...");
    Console.Read();
  }
}
```

In effect, nothing has changed. The only real difference is that all deposits are now being made through the local method `DirectDeposit()`, which isn't part of class `BankAccount`. The arguments to this method are the bank account and the amount to deposit.

Notice (here comes the good part) that `Main()` could pass either a bank account or a savings account to `DirectDeposit()` because a `Savings Account` IS_A `BankAccount` and is accorded all the rights and privileges thereto. Because `SavingsAccount` IS_A `BankAccount`, you can assign a `SavingsAccount` to a `BankAccount`-type variable or method argument.

Gaining access to BankAccount through containment

The class `SavingsAccount` could have gained access to the members of `BankAccount` in a different way, as shown in the following code, where the key lines are shown in boldface:

```
// SavingsAccount - A bank account that draws interest.
public class SavingsAccount_    // Notice the underscore: this is not
                                // the SavingsAccount class.
{
  public BankAccount _bankAccount;  // Notice this, the contained BankAccount.
  public decimal _interestRate;
  // InitSavingsAccount - Input the rate expressed as a
  //    rate between 0 and 100.
  public void InitSavingsAccount(BankAccount bankAccount, decimal interestRate)
  {
    this._bankAccount = bankAccount;
    this._interestRate = interestRate / 100;
  }
  // AccumulateInterest - Invoke once per period.
  public void AccumulateInterest()
  {
    _bankAccount._balance = _bankAccount.Balance
                  + (_bankAccount.Balance * interestRate);
  }
  // Deposit - Any positive deposit is allowed.
  public void Deposit(decimal amount)
  {
    // Delegate to the contained BankAccount object.
    _bankAccount.Deposit(amount);
  }
  // Withdraw - You can withdraw any amount up to the
  //    balance; return the amount withdrawn.
  public double Withdraw(decimal withdrawal)
  {
    return _bankAccount.Withdraw(withdrawal);
  }
}
```

In this case, the class `SavingsAccount_` *contains* a data member _bank Account (as opposed to inheriting from `BankAccount`). The _bankAccount object contains the balance and account number information needed by the savings account. The `SavingsAccount_` class retains the data unique to a savings account and *delegates* to the contained `BankAccount` object as needed. That is, when the `SavingsAccount` needs, say, the balance, it asks the contained `BankAccount` for it.

In this case, you say that the `SavingsAccount_` HAS_A `BankAccount`. Hard-core object-oriented jocks say that `SavingsAccount` *composes* a `Bank Account`. That is, `SavingsAccount` is partly *composed of* a `BankAccount`.

The HAS_A relationship

The HAS_A relationship is fundamentally different from the IS_A relationship. This difference doesn't seem so bad in the following example application-code segment:

```
// Create a new savings account.
BankAccount ba = new BankAccount()
SavingsAccount_ sa = new SavingsAccount_(); // HAS_A version of SavingsAccount.
sa.InitSavingsAccount(ba, 5);
// And deposit 100 dollars into it.
sa.Deposit(100M);
// Now accumulate interest.
sa.AccumulateInterest();
```

The problem is that this modified `SavingsAccount_` cannot be used as a `BankAccount` because it doesn't inherit from `BankAccount`. Instead, it *contains* a `BankAccount` — not the same thing at all. For example, the following code example fails:

```
// DirectDeposit - Deposit my paycheck automatically.
void DirectDeposit(BankAccount ba, int pay)
{
   ba.Deposit(pay);
}
void SomeMethod()
{
   // The following example fails.
   SavingsAccount_ sa = new SavingsAccount_();
   DirectDeposit(sa, 100);
   // . . . continue . . .
}
```

`DirectDeposit()` can't accept a `SavingsAccount_` in lieu of a `Bank Account`. No obvious relationship between the two exists as far as C# is concerned because inheritance isn't involved. Don't think, though, that this makes containment a bad idea. You just have to approach things a bit differently to use it.

When to IS_A and When to HAS_A?

The distinction between the IS_A and HAS_A relationships is more than just a matter of software convenience. This relationship has a corollary in the real world.

For example, a Ford Explorer IS_A car (when it's upright, that is). An Explorer HAS_A motor. If your friend says, "Come on over in your car," and you show up in an Explorer, he has no grounds for complaint. He may have a complaint if you show up carrying your Explorer's engine in your arms, however. (Or at least *you* will.)

The class `Explorer` should extend the class `Car`, not only to give `Explorer` access to the methods of a `Car` but also to express the fundamental relationship between the two.

Unfortunately, the beginning programmer may have `Car` inherit from `Motor`, as an easy way to give the `Car` class access to the members of `Motor`, which the `Car` needs to operate. For example, `Car` can inherit the method `Motor.Go()`. However, this example highlights one of the problems with this approach. Even though humans get sloppy in their speech, making a car go is not the same thing as making a motor go. The car's "go" operation certainly relies on that of the motor, but they aren't the same thing — you also have to put the transmission in gear, release the brake, and so on.

Perhaps even more than that, inheriting from `Motor` misstates the facts. A car simply is not a type of motor.

Elegance in software is a goal worth achieving in its own right. It enhances understandability, reliability, and maintainability, plus it cures indigestion and gout.

The hard-core object-oriented jocks recommend preferring HAS_A over IS_A for simpler program designs. But use inheritance when it makes sense, as it probably does in the `BankAccount` hierarchy.

Other Features That Support Inheritance

C# implements a set of features designed to support inheritance. I discuss these features in the following sections.

Substitutable classes

A program can use a subclass object where a base class object is called for. In fact, you've already seen this in one example. `SomeMethod()` can pass a `SavingsAccount` object to the `DirectDeposit()` method, which expects a `BankAccount` object.

You can make this conversion more explicit as follows:

```
BankAccount ba;
SavingsAccount sa = new SavingsAccount(); // Our original, not SavingsAccount_.
// OK:
ba = sa;                    // Implicitly converting subclass to base class.
ba = (BankAccount)sa;       // But the explicit cast is preferred.
// Not OK:
sa = ba;                    // ERROR: Implicitly converting base class to subclass.
sa = (SavingsAccount)ba;    // An explicit cast is allowed, however.
```

The first line stores a `SavingsAccount` object into a `BankAccount` variable. C# converts the object for you. The second line uses a cast to explicitly convert the object.

The final two lines attempt to convert the `BankAccount` object back into a `SavingsAccount`. You can do this explicitly, but C# won't do it for you. It's just like trying to convert a larger numeric type, such as `double`, to a smaller one, such as `float`. C# won't do it implicitly because the process involves a loss of data.

The IS_A property is not reflexive. That is, even though an Explorer is a car, a car is not necessarily an Explorer. Similarly, a `BankAccount` is not necessarily a `SavingsAccount`, so the implicit conversion is not allowed. The final line is allowed because the programmer has indicated her willingness to "chance it." She must know something.

Invalid casts at run time

Generally, casting an object from `BankAccount` to `SavingsAccount` is a dangerous operation. Consider the following example:

```
public static void ProcessAmount(BankAccount bankAccount)
{
    // Deposit a large sum to the account.
    bankAccount.Deposit(10000.00M);
    // If the object is a SavingsAccount, collect interest now.
    SavingsAccount savingsAccount = (SavingsAccount)bankAccount;
    savingsAccount.AccumulateInterest();
}
```

```
public static void TestCast()
{
  SavingsAccount sa = new SavingsAccount();
  ProcessAmount(sa);
  BankAccount ba = new BankAccount();
  ProcessAmount(ba);
}
```

ProcessAmount() performs a few operations, including invoking the AccumulateInterest() method. The cast of ba to a SavingsAccount is necessary because the bankAccount parameter is declared to be a Bank Account. The program compiles properly because all type conversions are via explicit cast.

All goes well with the first call to ProcessAmount() from within TestCast(). The SavingsAccount object sa is passed to the ProcessAmount() method. The cast from BankAccount to SavingsAccount causes no problem because the ba object was originally a SavingsAccount anyway.

The second call to ProcessAmount() is not so lucky, however. The cast to SavingsAccount cannot be allowed. The ba object does not have an AccumulateInterest() method.

An incorrect conversion generates an error during the execution of the program (a so-called *run-time error*). Run-time errors are much more difficult to find and fix than compile-time errors. Worse, they can happen to a user other than you. Users tend not to appreciate this.

Avoiding invalid conversions with the is operator

The ProcessAmount() method would be okay if it could ensure that the object passed to it is actually a SavingsAccount object before performing the conversion. C# provides two keywords for this purpose: is and as.

The is operator accepts an object on the left and a type on the right. The is operator returns true if the run-time type of the object on the left is compatible with the type on the right. *Use it to verify that a cast is legal before you attempt the cast.*

You can modify the previous example to avoid the run-time error by using the is operator, as follows:

```
public static void ProcessAmount(BankAccount bankAccount)
```

```
{
  // Deposit a large sum to the account.
  bankAccount.Deposit(10000.00M);
  // If the object is a SavingsAccount . . .
  if (bankAccount is SavingsAccount)
  {
    // ...then collect interest now (cast is guaranteed to work).
    SavingsAccount savingsAccount = (SavingsAccount)bankAccount;
    savingsAccount.AccumulateInterest();
  }
  // Otherwise, don't do the cast - but why is BankAccount not what
  // you expected? This could be an error situation.
}
public static void TestCast()
{
  SavingsAccount sa = new SavingsAccount();
  ProcessAmount(sa);
  BankAccount ba = new BankAccount();
  ProcessAmount(ba);
}
```

The added `if` statement checks the `bankAccount` object to ensure that it's actually of the class `SavingsAccount`. The `is` operator returns `true` when `ProcessAmount()` is called the first time. When passed a `BankAccount` object in the second call, however, the `is` operator returns `false`, avoiding the illegal cast. This version of the program does not generate a run-time error.

On the one hand, I strongly recommend that you protect all casts with the `is` operator to avoid the possibility of a run-time error. On the other hand, you should avoid casts altogether, if possible. But read on.

Avoiding invalid conversions with the as operator

The `as` operator works a bit differently. Instead of returning a `bool` if the cast *would* work, it actually converts the type on the left to the type on the right, but safely returns `null` if the conversion fails — rather than causing a run-time error. You should always use the result of casting with the `as` operator only if it isn't `null`. So using as looks like this:

```
SavingsAccount savingsAccount = bankAccount as SavingsAccount;
if(savingsAccount != null)
{
  // Go ahead and use savingsAccount.
}
// Otherwise, don't use it: generate an error message yourself.
```

Which one should you prefer? Generally, prefer as because it's more efficient. The conversion is already done with the as operator, whereas with is you have two steps: First test with is, and second, do the cast with the cast operator.

Unfortunately, as doesn't work with value-type variables, so you can't use it with types like int, long, double, and so on, nor with char. When you're trying to convert a value-type object, prefer the is operator.

The object Class

Consider the following related classes:

```
public class MyBaseClass {}
public class MySubClass : MyBaseClass {}
```

The relationship between the two classes enables the programmer to make the following run-time test:

```
public class Test
{
  public static void GenericMethod(MyBaseClass mc)
  {
    // If the object truly is a subclass . . .
    MySubClass msc = mc as MyBaseClass;
    if(msc != null)
    {
      // ...then handle as a subclass.
      // . . . continue . . .
    }
  }
}
```

In this case, the method GenericMethod() differentiates between subclasses of MyBaseClass using the as keyword.

How do you differentiate between seemingly unrelated classes using the same as operator? C# extends all classes from the common base class object. That is, any class that does not specifically inherit from another class inherits from the class object. Thus, the following two statements declare classes with the same base class — object — and are equivalent:

```
class MyClass1 : object {}
class MyClass1 {}
```

Sharing the common base class of `object` allows the following generic method:

```
public class Test
{
  public static void GenericMethod(object o)
  {
    MyClass1 mc1 = o as MyClass1;
    if(mc1 != null)
    {
      // Use the converted object mc1.
      // . . .
    }
  }
}
```

`GenericMethod()` can be invoked with any type of object. The as keyword can dig the `MyClass1` pearls from the `object` oysters. (The "generic" that I'm referring to here isn't the kind of generic covered in Bonus Chapter 7 on my Web site at `csharp102.info`.)

Inheritance and the Constructor

The `InheritanceExample` program from earlier in this chapter relies on those awful `Init...()` methods to initialize the `BankAccount` and `SavingsAccount` objects to a valid state. Outfitting these classes with constructors is definitely the right way to go, but it introduces a little complexity. That's why I fell back to using those ugly `Init...()` methods earlier until I could cover the features in this section.

Invoking the default base class constructor

The default base class constructor is invoked any time a subclass is constructed. The constructor for the subclass automatically invokes the constructor for the base class, as the following simple program demonstrates:

```
// InheritingAConstructor - Demonstrate that the base class
//     constructor is invoked automatically.
using System;
namespace InheritingAConstructor
{
  public class Program
  {
    public static void Main(string[] args)
    {
```

```
        Console.WriteLine("Creating a BaseClass object");
        BaseClass bc = new BaseClass();
        Console.WriteLine("\nnow creating a SubClass object");
        SubClass sc = new SubClass();
        // Wait for user to acknowledge.
        Console.WriteLine("Press Enter to terminate...");
        Console.Read();
    }
}
public class BaseClass
{
    public BaseClass()
    {
        Console.WriteLine("Constructing BaseClass");
    }
}
public class SubClass : BaseClass
{
    public SubClass()
    {
        Console.WriteLine("Constructing SubClass");
    }
}
}
```

The constructors for `BaseClass` and `SubClass` do nothing more than
output a message to the command line. Creating the `BaseClass` object
invokes the default `BaseClass` constructor. Creating a `SubClass` object
invokes the `BaseClass` constructor *before invoking its own constructor.*

The output from this program is as follows:

```
Creating a BaseClass object
Constructing BaseClass

Now creating a SubClass object
Constructing BaseClass
Constructing SubClass
Press Enter to terminate...
```

A *hierarchy* of inherited classes is much like the floors of a building. Each
class is built on the classes that it extends, as upper floors build on lower
ones. There's a clear reason for this: Each class is responsible for itself. A
subclass should not be held responsible for initializing the members of the
base class. The `BaseClass` must be given the opportunity to construct its
members before the `SubClass` members are given a chance to access them.
You want the horse well out in front of the cart.

Passing arguments to the base class constructor — mama sing base

The subclass invokes the default constructor of the base class, unless specified otherwise — even from a subclass constructor other than the default. The following, slightly updated example demonstrates this feature:

```
using System;
namespace Example
{
  public class Program
  {
    public static void Main(string[] args)
    {
      Console.WriteLine("Invoking SubClass() default");
      SubClass sc1 = new SubClass();
      Console.WriteLine("\nInvoking SubClass(int)");
      SubClass sc2 = new SubClass(0);
      // Wait for user to acknowledge.
      Console.WriteLine("Press Enter to terminate...");
      Console.Read();
    }
  }
  public class BaseClass
  {
    public BaseClass()
    {
      Console.WriteLine("Constructing BaseClass (default)");
    }
    public BaseClass(int i)
    {
      Console.WriteLine("Constructing BaseClass (int)");
    }
  }
  public class SubClass : BaseClass
  {
    public SubClass()
    {
      Console.WriteLine("Constructing SubClass (default)");
    }
    public SubClass(int i)
    {
      Console.WriteLine("Constructing SubClass (int)");
    }
  }
}
```

Executing this program generates the following results:

```
Invoking SubClass()
Constructing BaseClass (default)
```

```
Constructing SubClass (default)

Invoking SubClass(int)
Constructing BaseClass (default)
Constructing SubClass (int)
Press Enter to terminate...
```

The program first creates a default object. As expected, C# invokes the default SubClass constructor, which first passes control to the default BaseClass constructor. The program then creates an object, passing an integer argument. Again as expected, C# invokes the SubClass(int). This constructor invokes the default BaseClass constructor, just as in the earlier example, because it has no data to pass.

Getting specific with base

A subclass constructor can invoke a specific base class constructor using the keyword base.

This feature is similar to the way that one constructor invokes another within the same class using the this keyword. See Chapter 11 for the inside scoop on constructors and this.

For example, consider the following small program, InvokeBaseConstructor:

```
// InvokeBaseConstructor - Demonstrate how a subclass can
//     invoke the base class constructor of its choice using
//     the base keyword.
using System;
namespace InvokeBaseConstructor
{
  public class BaseClass
  {
    public BaseClass()
    {
      Console.WriteLine("Constructing BaseClass (default)");
    }
    public BaseClass(int i)
    {
      Console.WriteLine("Constructing BaseClass({0})", i);
    }
  }
  public class SubClass : BaseClass
  {
    public SubClass()
```

```
    {
      Console.WriteLine("Constructing SubClass (default)");
    }
    public SubClass(int i1, int i2) : base(i1)
    {
      Console.WriteLine("Constructing SubClass({0}, {1})", i1,  i2);
    }
  }
  public class Program
  {
    public static void Main(string[] args)
    {
      Console.WriteLine("Invoking SubClass()");
      SubClass sc1 = new SubClass();

      Console.WriteLine("\ninvoking SubClass(1, 2)");
      SubClass sc2 = new SubClass(1, 2);

      // Wait for user to acknowledge.
      Console.WriteLine("Press Enter to terminate...");
      Console.Read();
    }
  }
}
```

The output from this program is as follows:

```
Invoking SubClass()
Constructing BaseClass (default)
Constructing SubClass (default)

Invoking SubClass(1, 2)
Constructing BaseClass(1)
Constructing SubClass(1, 2)
Press Enter to terminate...
```

This version begins the same as the previous examples, by creating a default SubClass object using the default constructor of both BaseClass and SubClass.

The second object is created with the expression new SubClass(1, 2). C# invokes the SubClass(int, int) constructor, which uses the base keyword to pass one of the values on to the BaseClass(int) constructor. SubClass passes the first argument to the base class for processing and then uses the second value itself.

The Updated BankAccount Class

The program ConstructorSavingsAccount, found on the Web site, is an
updated version of the SimpleBankAccount program. In this version, however, the SavingsAccount constructor can pass information back up to the
BankAccount constructors. Only Main() and the constructors themselves
are shown here:

```
// ConstructorSavingsAccount - Implement a SavingsAccount as
//     a form of BankAccount; don't use any virtual methods but
//     do implement the constructors properly.
using System;
namespace ConstructorSavingsAccount
{
  // BankAccount - Simulate a bank account, each of which carries an
  //     account ID (which is assigned upon creation) and a balance.
  public class BankAccount
  {
    // Bank accounts start at 1000 and increase sequentially from there.
    public static int _nextAccountNumber = 1000;
    // Maintain the account number and balance for each object.
    public int _accountNumber;
    public decimal _balance;
    // Constructors.
    public BankAccount() : this(0)
    {
    }
    public BankAccount(decimal initialBalance)
    {
      _accountNumber = ++_nextAccountNumber;
      _balance = initialBalance;
    }
    public decimal Balance
    {
      get { return _balance; }
      // Protected setter lets subclass use Balance property to set.
      protected set { _balance = value; }
    }
    // Deposit - Any positive deposit is allowed.
    public void Deposit(decimal amount)
    {
      if (amount > 0)
      {
        Balance += amount;
      }
    }
    // Withdraw - You can withdraw any amount up to the
    //     balance; return the amount withdrawn.
    public decimal Withdraw(decimal withdrawal)
    {
```

```
      if (Balance <= withdrawal)
      {
        withdrawal = Balance;
      }
      Balance -= withdrawal;
      return withdrawal;
    }
    // ToString - Stringify the account.
    public string ToBankAccountString()
    {
      return String.Format("{0} - {1:C}",
        _accountNumber, Balance);
    }
  }
  // SavingsAccount - A bank account that draws interest.
  public class SavingsAccount : BankAccount
  {
    public decimal _interestRate;
    // InitSavingsAccount - Input the rate expressed as a
    //   rate between 0 and 100.
    public SavingsAccount(decimal interestRate) : this(interestRate, 0) { }
    public SavingsAccount(decimal interestRate, decimal initial) : base(initial)
    {
      this._interestRate = interestRate / 100;
    }
    // AccumulateInterest - Invoke once per period.
    public void AccumulateInterest()
    {
      // Use protected setter and public getter via Balance property.
      Balance = Balance + (decimal)(Balance * _interestRate);
    }
    // ToString - Stringify the account.
    public string ToSavingsAccountString()
    {
      return String.Format("{0} ({1}%)",
        ToBankAccountString(), interestRate * 100);
    }
  }
  public class Program
  {
    // DirectDeposit - Deposit my paycheck automatically.
    public static void DirectDeposit(BankAccount ba, decimal pay)
    {
      ba.Deposit(pay);
    }
    public static void Main(string[] args)
    {
      // Create a bank account and display it.
      BankAccount ba = new BankAccount(100M);
      DirectDeposit(ba, 100M);
      Console.WriteLine("Account {0}", ba.ToBankAccountString());
      // Now a savings account.
```

```
        SavingsAccount sa = new SavingsAccount(12.5M);
        DirectDeposit(sa, 100M);
        sa.AccumulateInterest();
        Console.WriteLine("Account {0}", sa.ToSavingsAccountString());
        // Wait for user to acknowledge the results.
        Console.WriteLine("Press Enter to terminate...");
        Console.Read();
      }
    }
  }
```

`BankAccount` defines two constructors: one that accepts an initial account balance and the default constructor, which does not. To avoid duplicating code within the constructor, the default constructor invokes the `BankAccount(initial balance)` constructor using the `this` keyword.

The `SavingsAccount` class provides two constructors, as well. The `SavingsAccount(interest rate)` constructor invokes the `SavingsAccount(interest rate, initial balance)` constructor, passing an initial balance of 0. This most general constructor passes the initial balance to the `BankAccount(initial balance)` constructor using the `base` keyword, as shown graphically in Figure 12-1.

Figure 12-1:
The path taken when constructing a `Savings Account` object using the default constructor.

```
Bank Account (0)
                  ↖ passes balance to base class
                  )
Savings Account (12.5%), 0)
                  ↖ defaults balance to 0
                  )
Savings Account (12.5%)
```

I've modified `Main()` to get rid of those infernal `Init...()` methods, replacing them with constructors instead. The output from this program is the same.

Notice the `Balance` property in `BankAccount`, which has a `public` getter but a `protected` setter. Using `protected` here prevents use from outside of `BankAccount` but permits using the `protected` setter in subclasses, which occurs in `SavingsAccount.AccumulateInterest`, with `Balance` on the left side of the assignment operator. (Properties are introduced in Chapter 11 and the `protected` keyword in Bonus Chapter 1.)

Garbage collection and the C# destructor

C# provides a method that's inverse to the constructor, called the *destructor*. The destructor carries the name of the class with a tilde (~) in front. For example, the ~BaseClass() method is the destructor for BaseClass.

C# invokes the destructor when it is no longer using the object. The default destructor is the only destructor that can be created because the destructor cannot be invoked directly. In addition, the destructor is always virtual. I explain virtual methods in Chapter 13.

When an inheritance ladder of classes is involved, the destructors are invoked in the reverse order of the constructors. That is, the destructor for the subclass is invoked before the destructor for the base class.

The destructor method in C# is much less useful than it is in some other object-oriented languages, such as C++, because C# has *nondeterministic destruction*. Understanding what that means — and why it's important — requires some explanation.

The memory for an object is borrowed from the heap when the program executes the new command, as in new SubClass(). This block of memory remains reserved as long as any valid references to that memory are running around. You may have several variables that reference the same object.

The memory is said to be "unreachable" when the last reference goes out of scope. In other words, no one can access that block of memory after no more references to it exist.

C# doesn't do anything in particular when a memory block first becomes unreachable. A low-priority system task executes in the background, looking for unreachable memory blocks. This so-called "garbage collector" executes when little is happening in your program, to avoid negatively affecting program performance. As the garbage collector finds unreachable memory blocks, it returns them to the heap.

Normally, the garbage collector operates silently in the background. The garbage collector only takes over control of the program for a short period when heap memory begins to run out.

The C# destructor, for example ~BaseClass(), is nondeterministic because it is not invoked until the object is garbage-collected, and that could occur long after the object is no longer being used. In fact, if the program terminates before the object is found and returned to the heap, the destructor is never invoked. *Nondeterministic* means you can't predict when the object will be garbage-collected. It could take quite a while before the object is garbage-collected and its destructor called.

C# programmers seldom use the destructor. C# has other ways to return borrowed system resources when they're no longer needed, using a Dispose() method, a topic that is beyond the scope of this book. (Look up "Dispose method" in Help.)

Chapter 13

Poly-what-ism?

· ·

In This Chapter

▶ Deciding whether to hide or override a base class method — so many choices!

▶ Building abstract classes — are you for real?

▶ Declaring a method and the class that contains it to be abstract

▶ ToString — the class business card

▶ Sealing a class from being subclassed

· ·

*I*nheritance allows one class to "adopt" the members of another. Thus I can create a class SavingsAccount that inherits data members like account id and methods like Deposit() from a base class BankAccount. That's nice, but this definition of inheritance is not sufficient to mimic what's going on out there in the trenches.

Drop back 10 yards to Chapter 12 if you don't remember much about class inheritance.

A microwave oven is a type of oven, not because it looks like an oven, but because it performs the same functions as an oven. A microwave oven may perform additional functions, but at the least, it performs the base oven functions — most importantly, heating up my nachos when I say, "StartCooking." (I rely on my object of class Refrigerator to cool the beer.) I don't particularly care what the oven must do internally to make that happen, any more than I care what type of oven it is, who made it, or whether it was on sale when my wife bought it . . . hey, wait, I do care about that last one.

From our human vantage point, the relationship between a microwave oven and a conventional oven doesn't seem like such a big deal, but consider the problem from the oven's point of view. The steps that a conventional oven performs internally are completely different from those that a microwave oven may take.

The power of inheritance lies in the fact that a subclass doesn't *have* to inherit every single method from the base class just the way it's written. A subclass can inherit the essence of the base class method while implementing the details differently.

Overloading an Inherited Method

As described in Chapter 8, two or more methods can have the same name as long as the number and/or types of the arguments differ.

It's a simple case of method overloading

Giving two methods the same name is called *overloading,* as in "Keeping them straight is overloading my brain."

The arguments of a method become a part of its extended name, as the following example demonstrates:

```
public class MyClass
{
  public static void AMethod()
  {
    // Do something.
  }
  public static void AMethod(int)
  {
    // Do something else.
  }
  public static void AMethod(double d)
  {
    // Do something even different.
  }
  public static void Main(string[] args)
  {
    AMethod();
    AMethod(1);
    AMethod(2.0);
}
```

C# can differentiate the methods by their arguments. Each of the calls within `Main()` accesses a different method.

The return type is not part of the extended name. You can't have two methods that differ only in their return type.

Different class, different method

Not surprisingly, the class to which a method belongs is also a part of its extended name. Consider the following code segment:

```
public class MyClass
{
  public static void AMethod1();
  public void AMethod2();
}
public class UrClass
{
  public static void AMethod1();
  public void AMethod2();
}
public class Program
{
  public static void Main(string[] args)
  {
    UrClass.AMethod1();  // Call static method.
    // Invoke the MyClass.AMethod2() instance method:
    MyClass mcObject = new MyClass();
    mcObject.AMethod2();
  }
}
```

The name of the class is a part of the extended name of the method. The method `MyClass.AMethod1()` has about as much to do with `UrClass.A Method1()` as `YourCar.StartOnAColdMorning()` and `MyCar.StartOn AColdMorning()` — at least yours works.

Peek-a-boo — hiding a base class method

Okay, so a method in one class can overload another method in its own class by having different arguments. As it turns out, a method can also overload a method in its own base class. Overloading a base class method is known as *hiding* the method.

Suppose your bank adopts a policy that makes savings account withdrawals different from other types of withdrawals. Suppose, just for the sake of argument, that withdrawing from a savings account costs $1.50.

Taking the procedural approach, you could implement this policy by setting a flag (variable) in the class to indicate whether the object is a `Savings`

Account or just a simple BankAccount. Then the withdrawal method would have to check the flag to decide whether it needs to charge the $1.50, as shown in the following code:

```
public class BankAccount
{
  private decimal _balance;
  private bool _isSavingsAccount;  // The flag.
  // Indicate the initial balance and whether the account that
  // you're creating is a savings account or not.
  public BankAccount(decimal initialBalance, bool isSavingsAccount)
  {
    _balance = initialBalance;
    _isSavingsAccount = isSavingsAccount;
  }
  public decimal Withdraw(decimal amountToWithdraw)
  {
    // If the account is a savings account . . .
    if (_isSavingsAccount)
    {
      // ...then skim off $1.50
      _balance -= 1.50M;
    }
    // Continue with the usual withdraw code:
    if (amountToWithdraw > _balance)
    {
      amountToWithdraw = _balance;
    }
    _balance -= amountToWithdraw;
    return amountToWithdraw;
  }
}
class MyClass
{
  public void SomeMethod()
  {
    // I wanna create me a savings account:
    BankAccount ba = new BankAccount(0, true);
  }
}
```

Your method must tell the BankAccount whether it's a SavingsAccount in the constructor by passing a flag. The constructor saves that flag and uses it in the Withdraw() method to decide whether to charge the extra $1.50.

The more object-oriented approach hides the method Withdraw() in the base class BankAccount with a new method of the same name, height, and hair color in the SavingsAccount class, as follows:

```csharp
// HidingWithdrawal - Hide the withdraw method in the base
//    class with a method in the subclass of the same name.
using System;
namespace HidingWithdrawal
{
  // BankAccount - A very basic bank account.
  public class BankAccount
  {
    protected decimal _balance;
    public BankAccount(decimal initialBalance)
    {
      _balance = initialBalance;
    }
    public decimal Balance
    {
      get { return _balance; }
    }
    public decimal Withdraw(decimal amount)
    {
      // Good practice to avoid modifying an input parameter.
      // Modify a copy.
      decimal amountToWithdraw = amount;
      if (amountToWithdraw > Balance)
      {
        amountToWithdraw = Balance;
      }
      _balance -= amountToWithdraw;
      return amountToWithdraw;
    }
  }
  // SavingsAccount - A bank account that draws interest.
  public class SavingsAccount : BankAccount
  {
    public decimal _interestRate;
    // SavingsAccount - Input the rate expressed as a
    //    rate between 0 and 100.
    public SavingsAccount(decimal initialBalance, decimal interestRate)
    : base(initialBalance)
    {
      _interestRate = interestRate / 100;
    }
    // AccumulateInterest - Invoke once per period.
    public void AccumulateInterest()
    {
      _balance = Balance + (Balance * _interestRate);
    }
    // Withdraw - You can withdraw any amount up to the
    //    balance; return the amount withdrawn.
```

```
    public decimal Withdraw(decimal withdrawal)
    {
        // Take our $1.50 off the top.
        base.Withdraw(1.5M);
        // Now you can withdraw from what's left.
        return base.Withdraw(withdrawal);
    }
}
public class Program
{
    public static void Main(string[] args)
    {
        BankAccount ba;
        SavingsAccount sa;
        // Create a bank account, withdraw $100, and
        // display the results.
        ba = new BankAccount(200M);
        ba.Withdraw(100M);
        // Try the same trick with a savings account.
        sa = new SavingsAccount(200M, 12);
        sa.Withdraw(100M);
        // Display the resulting balance.
        Console.WriteLine("When invoked directly:");
        Console.WriteLine("BankAccount balance is {0:C}", ba.Balance);
        Console.WriteLine("SavingsAccount balance is {0:C}", sa.Balance);
        // Wait for user to acknowledge the results.
        Console.WriteLine("Press Enter to terminate...");
        Console.Read();
    }
}
```

`Main()` in this case creates a `BankAccount` object with an initial balance of $200 and then withdraws $100. `Main()` repeats the trick with a `Savings Account` object. When `Main()` withdraws money from the base class, `BankAccount.Withdraw()` performs the withdraw function with great aplomb. When `Main()` then withdraws $100 from the savings account, the method `SavingsAccount.Withdraw()` tacks on the extra $1.50.

Notice that the `SavingsAccount.Withdraw()` method uses `BankAccount. Withdraw()` rather than manipulating the balance directly. If possible, let the base class maintain its own data members.

What makes the hiding approach better than adding a simple test?

On the surface, adding a flag to the `BankAccount.Withdraw()` method may seem simpler than all this method-hiding stuff. After all, it's just four little lines of code, two of which are nothing more than braces.

The problems are manifold — I've been waiting all these chapters to use that word. One problem is that the `BankAccount` class has no business worrying about the details of `SavingsAccount`. That would break the "Render unto Caesar" rule. More formally, it's called "breaking the encapsulation of `Savings Account`." Base classes don't normally know about their subclasses. That leads to the real problem: Suppose your bank subsequently decides to add a `CheckingAccount` or a `CDAccount` or a `TBillAccount`. Those are all likely additions, and they all have different withdrawal policies, each requiring its own flag. After three or four different types of accounts, the old `Withdraw()` method starts looking pretty complicated. Each of those types of classes should worry about its own withdrawal policies and leave the poor old `BankAccount.Withdraw()` alone. Classes are responsible for themselves.

What about accidentally hiding a base class method?

Oddly enough, you could hide a base class method accidentally. For example, you may have a `Vehicle.TakeOff()` method that starts the vehicle rolling. Later, someone else extends your `Vehicle` class with an `Airplane` class. Its `TakeOff()` method is entirely different. In airplane lingo, "take off" means more than just "start moving." Clearly, this is a case of mistaken identity — the two methods have no similarity other than their identical name.

Fortunately, C# detects this problem.

C# generates an ominous-looking warning when it compiles the earlier `HidingWithdrawal` example program. The text of the warning message is long, but here's the important part:

```
'...SavingsAccount.Withdraw(decimal)' hides inherited member
 '...BankAccount.Withdraw(decimal)'.
 Use the new keyword if hiding was intended.
```

C# is trying to tell you that you've written a method in a subclass with the same name as a method in the base class. Is that what you really meant to do?

This message is just a warning. You don't even notice it unless you switch over to the Error List window to take a look. But it's very important to sort out and fix all warnings. In almost every case, a warning is telling you about something that could bite you if you don't fix it.

It's a good idea to tell the C# compiler to treat warnings as errors, at least part of the time. To do so, choose Project⇨Properties. In the Build pane of your project's properties page, scroll down to Errors and Warnings. Set the Warning Level to 4, the highest level. This turns the compiler into more of a chatterbox. Also, in the Treat Warnings as Errors section, select All. (If a particular warning gets annoying, you can list it in the Suppress Warnings box to keep it out of your face.) When you treat warnings as errors, you're forced to fix the warnings — just as you would be to fix real compiler errors.

This makes for better code. Even if you don't enable Treat Warnings as Errors, it's helpful to leave the Warning Level at 4 and check the Error List window after each build.

The descriptor new, shown in the following code, tells C# that the hiding of methods is intentional and not the result of some oversight (and makes the warning go away):

```
// No withdraw() pains now.
new public decimal Withdraw(decimal withdrawal)
{
    // . . . no change internally . . .
}
```

This use of the keyword new has nothing to do with the same word new that's used to create an object. (C# even overloads itself!)

Calling back to base

Return to the SavingsAccount.Withdraw() method in the Hiding Withdrawal example shown earlier in this chapter. The call to BankAccount.Withdraw() from within this new method includes the new keyword base.

The following version of the method without the base keyword doesn't work:

```
new public decimal Withdraw(decimal withdrawal)
{
    decimal amountWithdrawn = Withdraw(withdrawal);
    amountWithdrawn += Withdraw(1.5);
    return amountWithdrawn;
}
```

This call has the same problem as the following one:

```
void fn()
{
    fn(); // call yourself
}
```

The call to fn() from within fn() ends up calling itself — *recursing* — over and over. Similarly, a call to Withdraw() from within the method calls itself in a loop, chasing its tail until the program eventually crashes.

Somehow, you need to indicate to C# that the call from within SavingsAccount.Withdraw() is meant to invoke the base class BankAccount.Withdraw() method. One approach is to cast the this reference into an object of class BankAccount before making the call, as follows:

```
// Withdraw - This version accesses the hidden method in the base
//    class by explicitly recasting the "this" object.
new public decimal Withdraw(decimal withdrawal)
{
  // Cast the this reference into an object of class BankAccount.
  BankAccount ba = (BankAccount)this;
  // Invoking Withdraw() using this BankAccount object
  // calls the method BankAccount.Withdraw().
  decimal amountWithdrawn = ba.Withdraw(withdrawal);
  amountWithdrawn += ba.Withdraw(1.5);
  return amountWithdrawn;
}
```

This solution works: The call ba.Withdraw() now invokes the BankAccount method, just as intended. The problem with this approach is the explicit reference to BankAccount. A future change to the program may rearrange the inheritance hierarchy so that SavingsAccount no longer inherits directly from BankAccount. Such a rearrangement breaks this method in a way that future programmers may not easily find. Heck, I would never be able to find a bug like that.

You need a way to tell C# to call the Withdraw() method from "the class immediately above" in the hierarchy without naming it explicitly. That would be the class that SavingsAccount extends. C# provides the keyword base for this purpose.

This is the same keyword base that a constructor uses to pass arguments to its base class constructor.

The C# keyword base, shown in the following code, is the same sort of beast as this but is automatically recast to the base class no matter what that class may be:

```
// Withdraw - You can withdraw any amount up to the
//    balance; return the amount withdrawn.
new public decimal Withdraw(decimal withdrawal)
{
  // Take our $1.50 off the top.
  base.Withdraw(1.5M);
  // Now you can withdraw from what's left.
  return base.Withdraw(withdrawal);
}
```

The call base.Withdraw() now invokes the BankAccount.Withdraw() method, thereby avoiding the recursive "invoking itself" problem. In addition, this solution won't break if the inheritance hierarchy is changed.

Polymorphism

You can overload a method in a base class with a method in the subclass. As simple as this sounds, it introduces considerable capability, and with capability comes danger.

Here's a thought experiment: Should the decision to call `BankAccount.Withdraw()` or `SavingsAccount.Withdraw()` be made at compile time or at run time?

To illustrate the difference, I'll change the previous `HidingWithdrawal` program in a seemingly innocuous way. I call this new version `Hiding WithdrawalPolymorphically`. (I've streamlined the listing by leaving out the stuff that doesn't change.) The new version is as follows:

```
// HidingWithdrawalPolymorphically - Hide the Withdraw() method in the base
//    class with a method in the subclass of the same name.
public class Program
{
  public static void MakeAWithdrawal(BankAccount ba, decimal amount)
  {
    ba.Withdraw(amount);
  }
  public static void Main(string[] args)
  {
    BankAccount ba;
    SavingsAccount sa;

    // Create a bank account, withdraw $100, and
    // display the results.
    ba = new BankAccount(200M);
    MakeAWithdrawal(ba, 100M);

    // Try the same trick with a savings account.
    sa = new SavingsAccount(200M, 12);
    MakeAWithdrawal(sa, 100M);

    // Display the resulting balance.
    Console.WriteLine("When invoked through intermediary:");
    Console.WriteLine("BankAccount balance is {0:C}", ba.Balance);
    Console.WriteLine("SavingsAccount balance is {0:C}", sa.Balance);

    // Wait for user to acknowledge the results.
    Console.WriteLine("Press Enter to terminate...");
    Console.Read();
  }
}
```

The following output from this program may or may not be confusing, depending on what you expected:

```
When invoked through intermediary
BankAccount balance is $100.00
SavingsAccount balance is $100.00
Press Enter to terminate...
```

This time, rather than performing a withdrawal in `Main()`, the program passes the bank account object to the method `MakeAWithdrawal()`.

The first question is fairly straightforward: Why does the MakeAWithdrawal() method even accept a SavingsAccount object when it clearly states that it is looking for a BankAccount? The answer is obvious: "Because a Savings Account IS_A BankAccount." (See Chapter 12.)

The second question is subtle. When passed a BankAccount object, MakeA Withdrawal() invokes BankAccount.Withdraw() — that's clear enough. But when passed a SavingsAccount object, MakeAWithdrawal() calls the same method. Shouldn't it invoke the Withdraw() method in the subclass?

The prosecution intends to show that the call `ba.Withdraw()` should invoke the method `BankAccount.Withdraw()`. Clearly, the `ba` object is a `BankAccount`. To do anything else would merely confuse the state. The defense has witnesses back in `Main()` to prove that although the `ba` object is declared `BankAccount`, it is, in fact, a `SavingsAccount`. The jury is dead-locked. Both arguments are equally valid.

In this case, C# comes down on the side of the prosecution: The safer of the two possibilities is to go with the declared type because it avoids any mis-communication. The object is declared to be a `BankAccount`, and that's that. However, that may not be what you want.

What's wrong with using the declared type every time?

In some cases, you don't want to go with the declared type. "What you want, what you really, really want . . ." is to make the call based on the *real type* — that is, the run-time type — as opposed to the declared type. For example, you want to go with the `SavingsAccount` actually stored in a `BankAccount` variable. This capability to *decide at run time* is called *polymorphism* or *late binding*. Going with the declared type every time is called *early binding* because that sounds like the opposite of late binding.

The ridiculous term *polymorphism* comes from the Greek: *poly* meaning more than one, *morph* meaning action, and *ism* meaning some ridiculous Greek term. But we're stuck with it.

Polymorphism and late binding are not exactly the same — but the difference is subtle. *Polymorphism* refers to the general ability to decide which method to invoke at run time. *Late binding* refers to the specific way a language implements polymorphism.

Polymorphism is the key to the power of object-oriented (OO) programming. It's so important that languages that don't support polymorphism can't advertise themselves as OO languages. (I think it's an FDA regulation: You can't label a language that doesn't support it as OO unless you add a disclaimer from the Surgeon General, or something like that.)

Languages that support classes but not polymorphism are called *object-based languages.* Visual Basic 6.0 (not VB .NET) is an example of such a language.

Without polymorphism, inheritance has little meaning. Let me spring yet another example on you to show you why. Suppose you had written this really boffo program that used some class called, just to pick a name out of the air, `Student`. After months of design, coding, and testing, you release this application to rave reviews from colleagues and critics alike. (There's even talk of starting a new Nobel Prize category for software, but you modestly brush such talk aside.)

Time passes, and your boss asks you to add to this program the capability of handling graduate students, who are similar but not identical to undergraduate students. (The graduate students probably claim that they're not similar at all.) Suppose that the formula for calculating the tuition for a graduate student is completely different from that for an undergrad. Now, your boss doesn't know or care that, deep within the program, there are numerous calls to the member method `CalcTuition()`. (There's a lot that he doesn't know or care about, by the way.) The following shows one of those many calls to `CalcTuition()`:

```
void SomeMethod(Student s)  // Could be grad or undergrad.
{
  // . . . whatever it might do . . .
  s.CalcTuition();
  // . . . continues on . . .
}
```

If C# didn't support late binding, you would need to edit `someMethod()` to check whether the `student` object passed to it is a `GraduateStudent` or a `Student`. The program would call `Student.CalcTuition()` when s is a `Student` and `GraduateStudent.CalcTuition()` when it's a graduate student.

That doesn't seem so bad, except for two things:

- ✔ This is only one method. Suppose that `CalcTuition()` is called from many places.

- ✔ Suppose that `CalcTuition()` is not the only difference between the two classes. The chances are not good that you'll find all the items that need to be changed.

With polymorphism, you can let C# decide which method to call.

Using "is" to access a hidden method polymorphically

How can you make your program polymorphic? C# provides one approach to solving the problem manually, using the keyword `is`. (I introduce `is`, and its cousin, `as`, in Chapter 12.) The expression `ba is SavingsAccount` returns `true` or `false` depending on the run-time class of the object. The declared type may be `BankAccount`, but what type is it really? The following code uses `is` to access the `SavingsAccount` version of `Withdraw()` specifically:

```
public class Program
{
  public static void MakeAWithdrawal(BankAccount ba, decimal amount)
  {
    if(ba is SavingsAccount)
    {
      SavingsAccount sa = (SavingsAccount)ba;
      sa.Withdraw(amount);
    }
    else
    {
      ba.Withdraw(amount);
    }
  }
}
```

Now, when `Main()` passes the method a `SavingsAccount` object, `MakeAWithdrawal()` checks the run-time type of the `ba` object and invokes `SavingsAccount.Withdraw()`.

Just as an aside, the programmer could have performed the cast and the call in the following single line:

```
((SavingsAccount)ba).Withdraw(amount);  // Notice locations of parentheses.
```

I mention this only because you see it a lot in programs written by show-offs. (It's okay but harder to read than using multiple lines. Anything written confusingly or cryptically tends to be more error-prone, too.)

Actually, the "is" approach works but it's a really bad idea. The `is` approach requires `MakeAWithDrawal()` to be aware of all the different types of bank accounts and which of them are represented by different classes. That puts too much responsibility on poor old `MakeAWithdrawal()`. Right now, your application handles only two types of bank accounts, but suppose your boss asks you to implement a new account type, `CheckingAccount`, and this new account has different `Withdraw()` requirements. Your program won't work properly if you don't search out and find every method that checks the run-time type of its argument. D'oh!

Declaring a method virtual and overriding it

As the author of `MakeAWithdrawal()`, you don't want to know about all the different types of accounts. You want to leave it up to the programmers who use `MakeAWithdrawal()` to know about their account types and leave you alone. You want C# to make decisions about which methods to invoke based on the run-time type of the object.

You tell C# to make the run-time decision of the version of `Withdraw()` by marking the base class method with the keyword `virtual` and each subclass version of the method with the keyword `override`.

I've rewritten the previous example program using polymorphism. I have added output statements to the `Withdraw()` methods to prove that the proper methods are indeed being invoked. (I've cut out the duplicated stuff to avoid boring you any more than you already have to put up with.) Here's the `PolymorphicInheritance` program:

```
// PolymorphicInheritance - Hide a method in the
//    base class polymorphically. Shows how to use
//    the virtual and override keywords.
using System;
namespace PolymorphicInheritance
{
  // BankAccount - A very basic bank account.
  public class BankAccount
  {
    protected decimal _balance;
    public BankAccount(decimal initialBalance)
    {
      _balance = initialBalance;
    }
```

```
  public decimal Balance
  {
    get { return _balance; }
  }
  public virtual decimal Withdraw(decimal amount)
  {
    Console.WriteLine("In BankAccount.Withdraw() for ${0}...", amount);
    decimal amountToWithdraw = amount;
    if (amountToWithdraw > Balance)
    {
      amountToWithdraw = Balance;
    }
    _balance -= amountToWithdraw;
    return amountToWithdraw;
  }
}
// SavingsAccount - A bank account that draws interest.
public class SavingsAccount : BankAccount
{
  public decimal _interestRate;
  // SavingsAccount - Input the rate expressed as a
  //    rate between 0 and 100.
  public SavingsAccount(decimal initialBalance, decimal interestRate)
                        : base(initialBalance)
  {
    _interestRate = interestRate / 100;
  }
  // AccumulateInterest - Invoke once per period.
  public void AccumulateInterest()
  {
    _balance = Balance + (Balance * _interestRate);
  }
  // Withdraw - You can withdraw any amount up to the
  //    balance; return the amount withdrawn.
  override public decimal Withdraw(decimal withdrawal)
  {
    Console.WriteLine("In SavingsAccount.Withdraw()...");
    Console.WriteLine("Invoking base-class Withdraw twice...");
    // Take our $1.50 off the top.
    base.Withdraw(1.5M);
    // Now you can withdraw from what's left.
    return base.Withdraw(withdrawal);
  }
}
public class Program
{
  public static void MakeAWithdrawal(BankAccount ba, decimal amount)
  {
    ba.Withdraw(amount);
  }
  public static void Main(string[] args)
  {
```

```
        BankAccount ba;
        SavingsAccount sa;
        // Display the resulting balance.
        Console.WriteLine("Withdrawal: MakeAWithdrawal(ba, ...)");
        ba = new BankAccount(200M);
        MakeAWithdrawal(ba, 100M);
        Console.WriteLine("BankAccount balance is {0:C}", ba.Balance);
        Console.WriteLine("Withdrawal: MakeAWithdrawal(sa, ...)");
        sa = new SavingsAccount(200M, 12);
        MakeAWithdrawal(sa, 100M);
        Console.WriteLine("SavingsAccount balance is {0:C}", sa.Balance);
        // Wait for user to acknowledge the results.
        Console.WriteLine("Press Enter to terminate...");
        Console.Read();
      }
    }
  }
```

The output from executing this program is as follows:

```
Withdrawal: MakeAWithdrawal(ba, ...)
In BankAccount.Withdraw() for $100...
BankAccount balance is $100.00
Withdrawal: MakeAWithdrawal(sa, ...)
In SavingsAccount.Withdraw()...
Invoking base-class Withdraw twice...
In BankAccount.Withdraw() for $1.5...
In BankAccount.Withdraw() for $100...
SavingsAccount balance is $98.50
Press Enter to terminate...
```

The `Withdraw()` method is flagged as `virtual` in the base class `BankAccount`, while the `Withdraw()` method in the subclass is flagged with the keyword `override`. The `MakeAWithdrawal()` method is unchanged and yet the output of the program is different because the call `ba.Withdraw()` is resolved based on `ba`'s run-time type.

To get a good feel for how this works, you really need to step through the program in the Visual Studio 2005 debugger. Just build the program as normal and then repeatedly press F11 to watch the program go through its paces. Watch the `Withdraw()` calls carefully. It's impressive to watch the same call end up in two different methods at two different times.

Be sparing in which methods you make virtual. They have a cost, so use the `virtual` keyword only when you must. It's a trade-off between a class that's highly flexible and overridable (lots of virtual methods) and a class that's not flexible enough (hardly any virtuals).

Getting the most out of polymorphism — the do-to-each trick

Much of the power of polymorphism springs from polymorphic objects sharing a common interface. For example, given a hierarchy of Shape objects — Circles, Squares, Triangles, and such — you can count on all shapes having a Draw() method. Each object's Draw() method will, of course, be implemented quite differently. But the point is that, given a collection of these objects, you can freely use a foreach loop to call Draw() or any other method in the polymorphic interface on the objects. I call this the "do-to-each" trick. (Chapter 16 introduces a variation of do-to-each using the new *lambda expressions*.)

The Class Business Card: ToString()

All classes inherit from a common base class that carries the clever name Object. However, it's worth mentioning here that Object includes a method, ToString(), that converts the contents of the object into a string. The idea here is that each class should override the ToString() method to display itself in a meaningful way. I used the method GetString() in the earlier part of the book because I didn't want to get into inheritance issues until Chapter 12. Now that you've seen inheritance, the virtual keyword, and overriding, we can talk about ToString(). By overriding ToString() for each class, you give each class the ability to display itself in its own way. For example, a useful, appropriate Student.ToString() method may display the student's name and ID.

Most methods — even those built into the C# library — use the ToString() method to display objects. Thus overriding ToString() has the very useful side effect that the object will be displayed in its own unique format, no matter who does the displaying.

Always override ToString().

C# During Its Abstract Period

A duck is a type of bird, I think. So are the cardinal and the hummingbird. In fact, every bird out there is actually some subtype of bird. The flip side of that argument is that no bird exists that *isn't* some subtype of bird. That doesn't sound too profound, but in a way, it is. The software equivalent of that statement is that all `bird` objects are instances of some subclass of `Bird` — there's never an instance of class `Bird`. What's a bird? It's always a robin or a grackle or some other specific species.

Different types of birds share many properties (otherwise they wouldn't be birds), but no two types share every property. If they did, they wouldn't be different types. To pick a particularly gross example, not all birds `Fly()` the same way. Ducks have one style. The cardinal's style is similar but not identical. The hummingbird's style is completely different. Don't even get me started about emus and ostriches or the rubber ducky in my tub.

But if birds don't all fly the same way, and there's no such thing as a `Bird`, then what the heck is `Bird.Fly()`? The subject of the following sections, that's what.

Class factoring

People generate taxonomies of objects by factoring out commonalities. To see how factoring works, consider two classes, `HighSchool` and `University`, as shown in Figure 13-1. This figure uses the Unified Modeling Language (UML), a graphical language that describes a class along with the relationship of that class to others. UML has become universally popular with programmers and is worth learning (to a reasonable extent) in its own right.

A Car IS_A Vehicle but a Car HAS_A Motor.

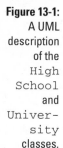
Figure 13-1:
A UML
description
of the
High
School
and
Univer-
sity
classes.

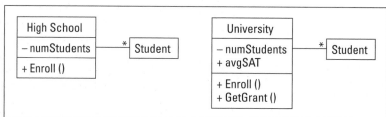

You can see in Figure 13-1 that high schools and universities have several similar properties — actually many more than you may think. Both schools offer a publicly available `Enroll()` method for adding `Student` objects to the school. In addition, both classes offer a private member `numStudents`

that indicates the number of students attending the school. One final common feature is the relationship between students: One school can have any number of students — a student can attend only a single school at one time. Even high schools and most universities offer more than I've described, but one of each type of member is all I need for illustration.

In addition to the features of a high school, the university contains a method `GetGrant()` and a data member `avgSAT`. High schools don't have an SAT entrance requirement, and they don't get federal grants — unless I went to the wrong high school.

TECHNICAL STUFF

UML Lite

The Unified Modeling Language (UML) is an expressive language that's capable of clearly defining a great deal about the relationships of objects within a program. One advantage of UML is that you can ignore the more specific language features without losing the meaning entirely.

The most basic features of UML are as follows:

- ✔ Classes are represented by a box divided vertically into three sections. The name of the class appears in the uppermost section.

- ✔ The data members of the class appear in the middle section, and the methods of the class in the bottom. You can omit either the middle or bottom section if the class has no data members or methods or if you want just a high-level classes-only view.

- ✔ Members with a plus sign (+) in front are public; those with a minus sign (–) are private. For protected and internal visibility, most people use the pound sign (#) — or should I say the "sharp" sign? — and the tilde (~), respectively.

A private member is only accessible from other members of the same class. A public member is accessible to all classes. See Chapter 11.

- ✔ The label {abstract} next to the name indicates an abstract class or method.

UML actually uses a different symbol for an abstract method, but I'll keep it simple. This is UML Lite. You can also just show abstract items in italics.

- ✔ An arrow between two classes represents a relationship between the two classes. A number above the line expresses cardinality — the number of items you can have at each end of the arrow. The asterisk symbol (*) means *any number*. If no number is present, the cardinality is assumed to be 1. Thus, in Figure 13-1, you can see that a single university has any number of students — a one-to-many relationship.

- ✔ A line with a large, open arrowhead, or a triangular arrowhead, expresses the IS_A relationship (inheritance). The arrow points *up* the class hierarchy to the base class. Other types of relationships include the HAS_A relationship (a line with a filled diamond at the owning end).

If you want to explore UML further, check out *UML 2 For Dummies* by Michael Jesse Chonoles and James A. Schardt, from Wiley Publishing.

Figure 13-1 is fine, as far as it goes, but lots of information is duplicated, and duplication in code (and UML diagrams) stinks. You could reduce the duplication by allowing the more complex class `University` to inherit from the simpler `HighSchool` class, as shown in Figure 13-2.

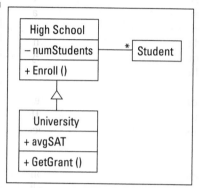

Figure 13-2: Inheriting `High School` simplifies the `University` class, but it introduces problems.

The `HighSchool` class is left unchanged, but the `University` class is easier to describe. We say that "a `University` is a `HighSchool` that also has an `avgSAT` and a `GetGrant()` method." But this solution has a fundamental problem: A university is not a high school with special properties.

You say, "So what? Inheriting works, and it saves effort." True, but my reservations are more than stylistic trivialities. My reservations are at some of the best restaurants in town — at least, that's what all the truckers say. Such misrepresentations are confusing to the programmer, both now and in the future. Someday, a programmer who is unfamiliar with your programming tricks will have to read and understand what your code does. Misleading representations are difficult to reconcile and understand.

In addition, such misrepresentations can lead to problems down the road. Suppose the high school decides to name a "favorite" student at the prom — not that I would know anything about that sort of thing. The clever programmer adds the `NameFavorite()` method to the `HighSchool` class, which the application invokes to name the favorite `Student` object.

But now you have a problem. Most universities don't name a favorite anything, other than price. However, as long as `University` inherits from `HighSchool`, it inherits the `NameFavorite()` method. One extra method may not seem like a big deal. "Just ignore it," you say.

One extra method isn't a big deal, but it's just one more brick in the wall of confusion. Extra methods and properties accumulate over time, until the `University` class is carrying lots of extra baggage. Pity the poor software developer who has to understand which methods are "real" and which are not.

"Inheritances of convenience" lead to another problem. The way it's written, Figure 13-2 implies that a `University` and a `HighSchool` have the same enrollment procedure. As unlikely as that sounds, assume that it's true. The program is developed, packaged up, and shipped off to the unwitting public — of course, I've embedded the requisite number of bugs so they'll want to upgrade to Version 2.0 with all the bug fixes — for a small fee, of course.

Months pass before the school district decides to modify the enrollment procedure. It won't be obvious to anyone that by modifying the high school enrollment procedure, they've also modified the sign-up procedure at the local college.

How can you avoid these problems? Not going to school is one way, but another would be to fix the source of the problem: A university is not a particular type of high school. A relationship exists between the two, but IS_A is not the right one. (HAS_A doesn't work either. A university HAS_A high school? A high school HAS_A university? Come on!) Instead, both high schools and universities are special types of schools. That's what they have most in common.

Figure 13-3 describes a better relationship. The newly defined class `School` contains the common properties of both types of schools, including the relationship they both have with `Student` objects. `School` even contains the common `Enroll()` method, although it's abstract because `HighSchool` and `University` usually don't implement `Enroll()` the same way.

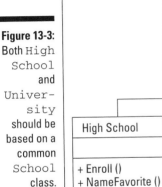

Figure 13-3: Both `High School` and `University` should be based on a common `School` class.

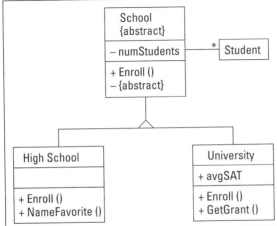

The classes `HighSchool` and `University` now inherit from a common base class. Each contains its unique members: `NameFavorite()` in the case of `HighSchool`, and `GetGrant()` for the `University`. In addition, both classes override the `Enroll()` method with a version that describes how that type of school enrolls students. In effect, I've extracted a superclass, or base class, from two similar classes, which now become subclasses.

The introduction of the `School` class has at least two big advantages:

- ✔ **It corresponds with reality.** A `University` is a `School`, but it is not a `HighSchool`. Matching reality is nice but not conclusive.

- ✔ **It isolates one class from changes or additions to the other.** When my boss comes along later, as will undoubtedly happen, and asks that I introduce the commencement exercise to the university, I can add the `CommencementSpeech()` method to the `University` class without impacting `HighSchool`.

This process of culling out common properties from similar classes is called *factoring*. This is an important feature of object-oriented languages for the reasons described so far, plus one more: reduction in redundancy. Let me repeat, redundancy is bad; there is no place for redundancy. Said another way. . . .

Factoring is legitimate only if the inheritance relationship corresponds to reality. Factoring together a class `Mouse` and `Joystick` because they're both hardware pointing devices is legitimate. Factoring together a class `Mouse` and `Display` because they both make low-level operating-system calls is not.

Factoring can and usually does result in multiple levels of abstraction. For example, a program written for a more developed school hierarchy may have a class structure more like that shown in Figure 13-4.

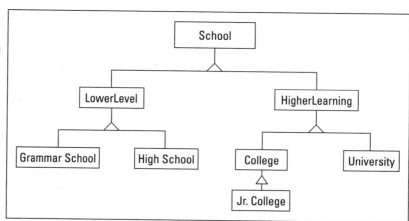

Figure 13-4: Class factoring can (and usually does) result in added layers of inheritance hierarchy.

You can see that I have inserted a pair of new classes between University and School: HigherLearning and LowerLevel. For example, I've subdivided the new class HigherLearning into College and University. This type of multitiered class hierarchy is common and desirable when factoring out relationships. They correspond to reality, and they can teach you sometimes subtle features of your solution.

Note, however, that no Unified Factoring Theory exists for any given set of classes. The relationship in Figure 13-4 seems natural, but suppose that an application cared more about differentiating types of schools that are administered by local politicians from those that aren't. This relationship, shown in Figure 13-5, is a more natural fit for that type of problem.

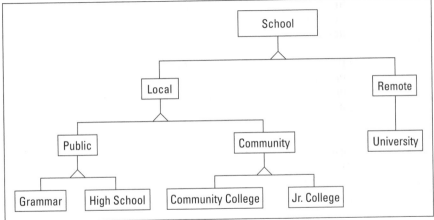

Figure 13-5: There's no "correct" factoring. The proper way to break down the classes is partially a function of the problem being solved.

I'm left with nothing but a concept — the abstract class

As intellectually satisfying as factoring is, it introduces a problem of its own. Return one more time to BankAccount, which was introduced at the beginning of the chapter. Think for a minute about how you may go about defining the different member methods defined in BankAccount.

Most BankAccount member methods are no problem because both account types implement them in the same way. You should implement those common methods in BankAccount. Withdraw() is different, however. The rules for withdrawing from a savings account differ from those for withdrawing from a checking account. You'll have to implement SavingsAccount.Withdraw() differently from CheckingAccount.Withdraw(). But how are you supposed to implement BankAccount.Withdraw()?

Ask the bank manager for help. I imagine the conversation going something like the following:

"What are the rules for making a withdrawal from an account?" you ask, expectantly.

"What type of account? Savings or checking?" comes the reply.

"From an account," you say. "Just an account."

Blank look. (One may say a "blank bank look." . . . Then again, maybe not.)

The problem is that the question doesn't make sense. There's no such thing as "just an account." All accounts (in this example) are either checking accounts or savings accounts. The concept of an account is an *abstract* one that factors out properties common to the two concrete classes. It is incomplete, because it lacks the critical property `Withdraw()`. (After you get further into the details, you may find other properties that a simple account lacks.)

The concept of a `BankAccount` is abstract.

How do you use an abstract class?

Abstract classes are used to describe abstract concepts.

An *abstract class* is a class with one or more abstract methods. (Oh, great! That helps a lot.) Okay, an abstract method is a method marked `abstract`. (We're really moving now.) Let me try again: An abstract method has no implementation — now you're *really* confused.

Consider the following stripped-down demonstration program:

```
// AbstractInheritance - The BankAccount class is actually abstract because
//    there is no single implementation for Withdraw.
namespace AbstractInheritance
{
  using System;
  // AbstractBaseClass - Create an abstract base class with nothing
  //    but an Output() method. You can also say "public abstract".
  abstract public class AbstractBaseClass
  {
    // Output - Abstract method that outputs a string.
    abstract public void Output(string outputString);
  }
  // SubClass1 - One concrete implementation of AbstractBaseClass.
  public class SubClass1 : AbstractBaseClass
  {
    override public void Output(string source) // Or "public override".
    {
```

```
      string s = source.ToUpper();
      Console.WriteLine("Call to SubClass1.Output() from within {0}", s);
   }
}
// SubClass2 - Another concrete implementation of AbstractBaseClass.
public class SubClass2 : AbstractBaseClass
{
   public override void Output(string source)  // Or "override public".
   {
      string s = source.ToLower();
      Console.WriteLine("Call to SubClass2.Output() from within {0}", s);
   }
}
class Program
{
   public static void Test(AbstractBaseClass ba)
   {
      ba.Output("Test");
   }
   public static void Main(string[] strings)
   {
      // You can't create an AbstractBaseClass object because it's
      // abstract - duh. C# generates a compile time error if you
      // uncomment the following line.
      // AbstractBaseClass ba = new AbstractBaseClass();
      // Now repeat the experiment with Subclass1.
      Console.WriteLine("\ncreating a SubClass1 object");
      SubClass1 sc1 = new SubClass1();
      Test(sc1);
      // And finally a Subclass2 object.
      Console.WriteLine("\ncreating a SubClass2 object");
      SubClass2 sc2 = new SubClass2();
      Test(sc2);
      // Wait for user to acknowledge.
      Console.WriteLine("Press Enter to terminate... ");
      Console.Read();
   }
}
}
```

The program first defines the class AbstractBaseClass with a single
abstract Output() method. Because it is declared abstract, Output() has
no implementation — that is, no method body.

Two classes inherit from AbstractBaseClass: SubClass1 and
SubClass2. Both are concrete classes because they override the Output()
method with "real" methods and themselves contain no abstract methods.

A class can be declared abstract whether it has abstract members or not;
however, a class can be concrete only when all the abstract methods in any
base class above it have been overridden with full methods.

The two subclass `Output()` methods differ in a trivial way. Both accept an input string, which they regurgitate to the user. However, one converts the string to all caps before output and the other to all lowercase characters.

The following output from this program demonstrates the polymorphic nature of `AbstractBaseClass`:

```
Creating a SubClass1 object
Call to SubClass1.Output() from within TEST

Creating a SubClass2 object
Call to SubClass2.Output() from within test
Press Enter to terminate...
```

An abstract method is automatically virtual, so you don't add the `virtual` keyword to an abstract method.

Creating an abstract object — not!

Notice something about the `AbstractInheritance` program: It is not legal to create an `AbstractBaseClass` object, but the argument to `Test()` is declared to be an object of the class `AbstractBaseClass` *or one of its subclasses.* It's the "subclasses" clause that's critical here. The `SubClass1` and `SubClass2` objects can be passed because they are both concrete subclasses of `AbstractBaseClass`. The IS_A relationship applies. This is actually a powerful technique, allowing you to write highly general methods.

Sealing a Class

You may decide that you don't want future generations of programmers to be able to extend a particular class. You can lock the class using the keyword `sealed`.

A sealed class cannot be used as the base class for any other class.

Consider the following code snippet:

```
using System;
public class BankAccount
{
  // Withdrawal - You can withdraw any amount up to the
  //     balance; return the amount withdrawn
  virtual public void Withdraw(decimal withdrawal)
  {
    Console.WriteLine("invokes BankAccount.Withdraw()");
  }
```

```
}
public sealed class SavingsAccount : BankAccount
{
  override public void Withdraw(decimal withdrawal)
  {
    Console.WriteLine("invokes SavingsAccount.Withdraw()");
  }
}
public class SpecialSaleAccount : SavingsAccount   // Oops!
{
  override public void Withdraw(decimal withdrawal)
  {
    Console.WriteLine("invokes SpecialSaleAccount.Withdraw()");
  }
}
```

This snippet generates the following compiler error:

```
'SpecialSaleAccount' : cannot inherit from sealed class 'SavingsAccount'
```

The `sealed` keyword enables you to protect your class from the prying methods of some subclass. For example, allowing programmers to extend a class that implements system security would enable someone to create a security back door.

Sealing a class prevents another program, possibly somewhere on the Internet, from using a modified version of your class. The remote program can use the class as is, or not, but it can't inherit bits and pieces of your class while overriding the rest.

Chapter 14

Interfacing with the Interface

In This Chapter

▶ Beyond IS_A and HAS_A: the C# interface

▶ Creating your own interfaces or using those provided by .NET

▶ Unifying separate class hierarchies with interfaces

▶ Hiding part of your class's public interface behind an interface

▶ Managing software change — flexibility via interfaces

A class can *contain* a reference to another class. This is the simple HAS_A relationship. One class can *extend* another class through the marvel of inheritance. That's the IS_A relationship. The C# interface implements another, equally important association: the CAN_BE_USED_AS relationship.

This chapter introduces C# *interfaces* and shows some of the numerous ways they increase the power and flexibility of object-oriented programming.

What Is CAN_BE_USED_AS?

If you want to jot a note, you may scribble it with a pen, stroke it into your personal digital assistant (PDA), or type it on your laptop. You can fairly say that all three objects — pen, PDA, and computer — implement the TakeANote operation. Suppose you use the magic of inheritance to implement this in C# as follows:

```
abstract class ThingsThatRecord          // The base class.
{
    abstract public void TakeANote(string note);
}
public class Pen : ThingsThatRecord      // A subclass.
{
    override public void TakeANote(string note)
    {
```

```
      // ... scribble a note with a pen ...
    }
}
public class PDA : ThingsThatRecord       // Another subclass.
{
    override public void TakeANote(string note)
    {
      // ... stroke a note on the PDA ...
    }
}
public class LapTop : ThingsThatRecord   // A third subclass.
{
    override public void TakeANote(string note)
    {
      // ... tap, tap, tap ...
    }
}
```

If the term *abstract* has you stumped, drop back one pace to Chapter 13, and see the discussion later in this chapter. If this whole concept of inheritance is a mystery, check out Chapter 12.

The following simple method shows the inheritance approach working just fine:

```
void RecordTask(ThingsThatRecord recorder) // Parameter type is base class.
{
  // All classes that extend ThingsThatRecord have a TakeANote method.
  recorder.TakeANote("Shopping list");
  // ... and so on.
}
```

The parameter type is `ThingsThatRecord`, so you can pass any of the subclasses to this method, making the method very general.

That might seem great, but it has two big drawbacks:

✔ **A fundamental problem:** Do `Pen`, `PDA`, and `LapTop` really have an IS_A relationship? Are those three things all the same kind of thing in real life? I don't think so, do you? All we can say is that `ThingsThatRecord` makes a poor base class here.

✔ **A purely technical problem:** You might reasonably derive both `LapTop` and `PDA` as subclasses of `Computer`. But nobody would say a `Pen` IS_A `Computer`. You'd have to characterize a pen as some type of `MechanicalWritingDevice` or `DeviceThatStainsYourShirt`. But a C# class can't inherit from two different base classes at the same time — a C# class can be only one type of thing.

So the `Pen`, `PDA`, and `LapTop` classes have in common only the fact that they CAN_BE_USED_AS recording devices. Inheritance doesn't apply.

What Is an Interface?

An *interface* in C# resembles a class with no data members and nothing but abstract methods, almost like an abstract class — almost:

```
interface IRecordable
{
  void TakeANote(string note);
}
```

The interface begins with the `interface` keyword. It contains nothing but abstract methods. No data members and no implemented methods.

Actually, interfaces can contain a few other things, including properties (covered in Chapter 11), events (covered in Chapter 15), and indexers (see Bonus Chapter 7 on my Web site).

Among the things that a C# interface *can't* exhibit are:

- Access specifiers, such as `public` or `private` (Chapter 11)
- Keywords like `virtual`, `override`, or `abstract` (Chapter 13)
- Data members (Chapter 7)
- Implemented methods — nonabstract methods with bodies

All members of a C# interface are public (you can't even mention access specifiers in defining interface methods), and a C# interface isn't involved in normal inheritance, hence none of those keywords. (An interface itself can be `public`, `protected`, `internal`, or `private`.)

Unlike an abstract class, a C# interface is not a class. It can't be subclassed, and none of the methods it contains can have bodies.

How to implement an interface

To put a C# interface to use, you *implement* the interface with one or more classes. The class heading looks like the following:

```
class Pen : IRecordable  // Looks like inheritance, but isn't.
```

A C# interface specifies items that classes which implement the interface *must* define with specific implementations. Must. For example, any class that implements the `IRecordable` interface must provide an implementation for the `TakeANote` method. The method that implements `TakeANote` doesn't use the `override` keyword. This isn't like overriding a virtual method in classes.

Class `Pen` might look like this:

```
class Pen : IRecordable
{
  public void TakeANote(string note)    // Interface method implementations
  {                                      // MUST be declared public.
    // ... scribble a note with a pen ...
  }
}
```

This fulfills two requirements: noting that the class implements `IRecordable`, and providing a method implementation for `TakeANote()`.

The syntax indicating that a class inherits a base class, say `ThingsThatRecord`, is essentially no different from the syntax indicating that the class implements a C# interface such as `IRecordable`:

```
public class PDA : ThingsThatRecord ...
public class PDA : IRecordable ...
```

Visual Studio can help you implement an interface. Hover the mouse pointer over the interface name in the class heading. A little underline appears under the first character of the interface name. Move the mouse until a menu opens and choose Implement interface *<name>*. Presto! A skeleton framework appears — you fill in the details.

How to name your interface

The .NET naming convention for interfaces precedes the name with the letter *I*. Interface names are typically adjectives, such as `IRecordable`.

So why does C# include interfaces?

The bottom line is that an interface describes a capability, like Swim Safety Training or Class A Driver's License. As a class, I earn my `IRecordable` badge when I implement the `TakeANote` ability.

More than that, an interface is a *contract*. If you agree to implement every method defined in the interface, you get to claim its capability. Not only that, but a client using your class in her program is guaranteed to be able to call those methods. Implementing an interface is a promise — enforced by the compiler. (Enforcing things through the compiler reduces errors.)

Mixing inheritance and interface implementation

Unlike some languages such as C++, C# doesn't allow *multiple inheritance* — a class inheriting from two or more base classes. Think of class `HouseBoat` inheriting from `House` and `Boat`. Just don't think of it in C#.

But although a class can inherit from only one base class, it can *in addition* implement as many interfaces as needed. Treating *recordability* as an interface, a couple of our recording devices look like this:

```
public class Pen : IRecordable          // Base class is Object.
{
  public void TakeANote(string note)
  {
    // Record the note with a pen.
  }
}
public class PDA : ElectronicDevice, IRecordable
{
  public void TakeANote(string note)
  {
    // Record the note with your thumbs or a stylus.
  }
}
```

Class `PDA` inherits from a base class *and* implements an interface.

And here's the payoff

To begin to see the usefulness of an interface like `IRecordable`, consider the following:

```
public class Program
{
  static public void RecordShoppingList(IRecordable recorder)
  {
    // Jot it down, using whatever device was passed in.
    recorder.TakeANote(...);
  }
  public static void Main(string[] args)
  {
    PDA pda = new PDA();
    RecordShoppingList(pda);  // Oops, battery's low ...
    RecordShoppingList(pen);
  }
}
```

What's the `IRecordable` parameter? It's an instance of any class that implements the `IRecordable` interface. `RecordShoppingList()` makes no assumptions about the exact type of recording object. It's not important whether the device is actually a `PDA`, or that it's a type of `ElectronicDevice`, as long as it can take a note.

That's immensely powerful, because it lets the `RecordShoppingList()` method be highly general — and thus possibly reusable in other programs. It's even more general than using a base class such as `ElectronicDevice` for the argument type, because the interface allows you to pass almost arbitrary objects that don't necessarily have anything in common other than implementing the interface. They don't even have to come from the same class hierarchy. This really simplifies designing hierarchies, for one thing.

Overworked Word Alert: Programmers use the term *interface* in more than one way. You've been introduced to the C# keyword `interface` and how it's used. People also talk about a class's *public interface*, meaning the public methods and properties that it exposes to the outside world. I'll try to keep the distinction clear by using "C# interface" most of the time when that's what I mean, and "public interface" when I mean a class's set of public methods.

C# structures ("structs," covered in Bonus Chapter 4 on the Web site) can implement interfaces just as classes can.

Using an Interface

As well as using a C# interface for a parameter type, interfaces are useful:

- ✔ As method return types
- ✔ As the base type of a highly general array or collection
- ✔ As a more general kind of object reference for variable types

You saw the advantage of using a C# interface as a method parameter type in the previous section. How about the others?

As a method return type

I like to farm out the task of creating key objects I need to a *factory method*. Suppose I have a variable like this:

```
IRecordable recorder = null;  // Yes, you can have interface-type variables.
```

Somewhere, maybe in my constructor, I call a factory method to deliver some particular kind of `IRecordable` object:

```
recorder = MyClass.CreateRecorder("Pen");   // A factory method is often static.
```

where `CreateRecorder()` is a method, often on the same class, that returns not a reference to a `Pen`, but an `IRecordable` reference:

```
static IRecordable CreateRecorder(string recorderType)
{
  if(recorderType == "Pen") return new Pen();
  ...
}
```

I'll say more about this factory idea later in the chapter. But note that the return type for `CreateRecorder()` is an interface type.

As the base type of an array or collection

Suppose you have two classes, `Animal` and `Robot`, both abstract classes. How could you set up an array to hold both `thisCat` (an `Animal`) and `thatRobot` (a cute droid)? The only way is to fall back on type `Object`, the ultimate base class in C#, and the only base class common to both `Animal` and `Robot` as well as their subclasses:

```
object[] things = new object[] { thisCat, thatRobot };
```

That's poor for lots of reasons. But suppose you're focused on the objects' movements. You could have each class implement an `IMovable` interface:

```
interface IMovable
{
  void Move(int direction, int speed, int distance);
}
```

and then set up an array of `IMovables` to manipulate your otherwise incompatible objects:

```
IMovable[] movables = { thisCat, thatRobot };
```

The interface gives you a commonality that you can exploit in collections.

As a more general type of object reference

The following variable declaration refers to a very specific, physical, *concrete* object (see the section "Abstract or concrete?" later in this chapter):

```
Cat thisCat = new Cat();
```

But one alternative is to use a C# interface for the reference:

```
IMovable thisMovableCat = (IMovable)new Cat();   // Note the required cast.
```

Now you can put any object into the variable that implements `IMovable`. This has wide, powerful uses in object-oriented programming, as you'll see later in this chapter.

Using C#'s Predefined Interface Types

Because interfaces are so useful, you'll find more interfaces in the .NET class library than gun racks at an NRA convention. I counted dozens in Help before I got tired and quit. Among the dozen or more interfaces in the `System` namespace alone are `IComparable`, `IComparable<T>`, `IDisposable`, and `IFormattable`. The `System.Collections.Generics` namespace includes `IEnumerable<T>`, `IList<T>`, `ICollection<T>`, and `IDictionary<TKey, TValue>`. And there are many more. Those with the `<T>` notation are generic interfaces, which I discuss in general in Bonus Chapter 8 on my Web site. I explain the `<T>` notation in Chapter 5's discussion of collection classes.

The Help files show all of the `ISomething<T>` types with a little tick mark — `IList`1` — but look for "IList<T>" in the Help index.

Two interfaces very commonly used are `IComparable` and `IEnumerable` — largely superseded now by their generic versions `IComparable<T>` (read as "IComparable *of* T") and `IEnumerable<T>`.

I'll show you `IComparable<T>` in this chapter. It's what makes it possible to compare all sorts of objects, such as `Students`, to each other, and what enables the `Sort()` method that all arrays and most collections supply. `IEnumerable<T>` is what makes the powerful `foreach` loop work — most collections implement `IEnumerable<T>`, so you can iterate the collections with `foreach`. You'll meet an additional major use for `IEnumerable<T>` in Chapter 17, as the basis for C# 3.0's new query expressions.

Can I See a Program That CAN_ BE_USED_AS an Example?

The following `SortInterface` program is a special offer. These capabilities brought to you by two different interfaces cannot be matched in any inheritance relationship, anywhere. Interface implementations are standing by.

However, I want to break the `SortInterface` program into sections to demonstrate various principles — pfft! As if I had any principles. I just want to make sure that you can see exactly how the program works.

Creating your own interface at home in your spare time

The following `IDisplayable` interface is satisfied by any class that contains a `Display()` method (and declares that it implements `IDisplayable`, of course). `Display()` returns a string representation of the object that can be displayed using `WriteLine()`.

```
// IDisplayable - Any object that implements the Display() method.
interface IDisplayable
{
  // Return a description of yourself.
  string Display();
}
```

The following `Student` class implements `IDisplayable`:

```
class Student : IDisplayable
{
  public Student(string name, double grade)
  { Name = name; Grade = grade; }
  public string Name { get; private set; }
  public double Grade { get; private set; }
  public string Display()
  {
    string padName = Name.PadRight(9);
    return String.Format("{0}: {1:N0}", padName, Grade);
  }
}
```

`Display()` uses `String`'s `PadRight()` and `Format()` methods, covered in Chapter 6, to return a neatly formatted string.

The following `DisplayArray()` method takes an array of any objects that implement the `IDisplayable` interface. Each of those objects is guaranteed (by the interface) to have its own `Display()` method. (The entire program appears in the section "Putting it all together," later in this chapter.)

```
// DisplayArray - Display an array of objects that implement
//   the IDisplayable interface.
public static void DisplayArray(IDisplayable[] displayables)
{
  foreach(IDisplayable disp in displayables)
  {
```

```
        Console.WriteLine("{0}, disp.Display());
    }
}
```

The following is an example of the output from `DisplayArray()`:

```
Homer    : 0
Marge    : 85
Bart     : 50
Lisa     : 100
Maggie   : 30
```

Implementing the incomparable IComparable<T> interface

C# defines the interface `IComparable<T>` as follows:

```
interface IComparable<T>
{
  // Compare the current T object to the object 'item'; return a
  // 1 if larger, -1 if smaller, and 0 if the same.
  int CompareTo(T item);
}
```

A class implements the `IComparable<T>` interface by implementing a `CompareTo()` method. Notice that `CompareTo()` takes an argument of type T, some type that you supply when you *instantiate the interface* for a particular data type — as in the following example:

```
class SoAndSo : IComparable<SoAndSo>  // Make me comparable.
```

When you implement `IComparable<T>` for your class, its `CompareTo()` method should return 0 if the two items being compared (of your class type) are "equal" in some way that you define. If not, it should return 1 or –1, depending on which object is "greater."

It seems a little Darwinian, but you could say that one `Student` object is "greater than" another `Student` object if his or her grade-point average is higher. (Okay, either a better student or a better apple-polisher — it doesn't really matter.)

Implementing the `CompareTo()` method implies that the objects have a sorting order. If one student is "greater than" another, you must be able to sort the students from "least" to "greatest." In fact, most collection classes (including arrays but not dictionaries) supply a `Sort()` method something like this:

```
void Sort(IComparable<T>[] objects);
```

This method sorts a collection of objects that implement the IComparable <T> interface. It doesn't even matter which class the objects belong to. For example, they could even be Student objects. Collection classes like arrays or List<T> could even sort the following version of Student:

```
// Student - Description of a student with name and grade.
class Student : IComparable<Student>, IDisplayable   // Instantiation.
{
    // Constructor - initialize a new student object.
    public Student(double grade)
    { Grade = grade; }
    public double Grade { get; private set; }
    // Implement the IComparable<T> interface:
    // CompareTo - Compare another object (in this case, Student objects) and
    //    decide which one comes after the other in the sorted array.
    public int CompareTo(Student rightStudent)
    {
        // Compare the current Student (let's call her 'left') against the other
        // student (we'll call her 'right').
        Student leftStudent = this;

        // Now generate a -1, 0 or 1 based upon the Sort criteria (the student's
        // grade). We could use class Double's CompareTo() method instead).
        if (rightStudent.Grade < leftStudent.Grade)
        {
            return -1;
        }
        if (rightStudent.Grade > leftStudent.Grade)
        {
            return 1;
        }
        return 0;
    }
}
```

Sorting an array of Students is reduced to a single call, as follows:

```
void MyMethod(Student[] students) // Where Student implements IComparable<T>.
{
    Array.Sort(students); // Sort array of IComparable<Student>s.
}
```

You provide the comparator (CompareTo()), and Array does all the work. Sounds fair to me.

Putting it all together

This is the moment you've been waiting for: the complete SortInterface program that uses the features that I describe earlier in this chapter:

```
// SortInterface - Demonstrates how the interface concept can be used
//    to provide an enhanced degree of flexibility in factoring
//    and implementing classes.
using System;
namespace SortInterface
{
  // IDisplayable - An object that can convert itself into a displayable
  //    string format. (This duplicates what you can do by overriding
  //    ToString(), but it helps me make a point.)
  interface IDisplayable
  {
    // Display - return a string representation of yourself.
    string Display();
  }
  class Program
  {
    public static void Main(string[] args)
    {
      // Sort students by grade...
      Console.WriteLine("Sorting the list of students");
      // Get an unsorted array of students.
      Student[] students = Student.CreateStudentList();
      // Use the IComparable<T> interface to sort the array.
      Array.Sort(students);
      // Now the IDisplayable interface to display the results.
      DisplayArray(students);

      // Now sort an array of birds by name using the same routines even
      // though the classes Bird and Student have no common base class.
      Console.WriteLine("\nsorting the list of birds");
      Bird[] birds = Bird.CreateBirdList();
      // Notice that it's not necessary to cast the objects explicitly
      // to an array of IDisplayables (and wasn't for Students either) ...
      Array.Sort(birds);
      DisplayArray(birds);
      // Wait for user to acknowledge the results.
      Console.WriteLine("Press Enter to terminate...");
      Console.Read();
    }
    // DisplayArray - Display an array of objects that
    //    implement the IDisplayable interface.
    public static void DisplayArray(IDisplayable[] displayables)
    {
      foreach(IDisplayable displayable in displayables)
      {
        Console.WriteLine("{0}", displayable.Display());
      }
    }
  }
}
// ---------- Students - Sort students by grade -------
// Student - Description of a student with name and grade.
class Student : IComparable<Student>, IDisplayable
{
```

```
// Constructor - initialize a new student object.
public Student(string name, double grade)
{ Name = Name; Grade = grade; }
// CreateStudentList - To save space here, just create
// a fixed list of students.
static string[] names = {"Homer", "Marge", "Bart", "Lisa", "Maggie"};
static double[] grades = {0, 85, 50, 100, 30};
public static Student[] CreateStudentList()
{
  Student[] students = new Student[names.Length];
  for (int i = 0; i < names.Length; i++)
  {
    students[i] = new Student(names[i], grades[i]);
  }
  return students;
}
// Access read-only properties.
public string Name { get; private set; }   // See Chapter 12, on properties.
public double Grade { get; private set; }
// Implement the IComparable interface:
// CompareTo - Compare another object (in this case, Student objects)
//     and decide which one comes after the other in the sorted array.
public int CompareTo(Student rightStudent)
{
  // Compare the current Student (let's call her 'left') against
  // the other student (we'll call her 'right').
  Student leftStudent = this;
  // Now generate a -1, 0 or 1 based upon the Sort criteria (the student's
  // grade). Double's CompareTo() method would work too.
  if (rightStudent.Grade < leftStudent.Grade)
  {
    return -1;
  }
  if (rightStudent.Grade > leftStudent.Grade)
  {
    return 1;
  }
  return 0;
}
// Display - Implement the IDisplayable interface:
public string Display()
{
  string padName = Name.PadRight(9);
  return String.Format("{0}: {1:N0}", padName, Grade);
}
}
// ----------Birds - Sort birds by their names--------
// Bird - Just an array of bird names.
class Bird : IComparable<Bird>, IDisplayable
{
  // Constructor - initialize a new Bird object.
  public Bird(string name) { Name = name; }
  // CreateBirdList - Return a list of birds to the caller;
```

```
//    Use a canned list here to save space.
static string[] birdNames =
   { "Oriole", "Hawk", "Robin", "Cardinal", "Bluejay", "Finch", "Sparrow"};
public static Bird[] CreateBirdList()
{
  Bird[] birds = new Bird[birdNames.Length];
  for(int i = 0; i < birds.Length; i++)
  {
    birds[i] = new Bird(birdNames[i]);
  }
  return birds;
}
public string Name { get; private set; }
// Implement the IComparable interface:
// CompareTo - Compare the birds by name; use the
//    built-in String class compare method.
public int CompareTo(Bird rightBird)
{
  // We'll compare the "current" bird to the "right hand object" bird.
  Bird leftBird = this;
  return String.Compare(leftBird.Name, rightBird.Name);
}
// Display - Implement the IDisplayable interface.
public string Display() { return Name; }
}
}
```

The Student class (it's about in the middle of the program listing) imple-ments the IComparable<T> and IDisplayable interfaces, as described earlier. The CompareTo() method compares the students by grade, which results in the students being sorted by grade. Student's Display() method returns the name and grade of the student.

The other methods of Student include the read-only Name and Grade prop-erties, a simple constructor, and a CreateStudentList() method. This method just returns a fixed list of students for the code to work on.

The Bird class at the bottom of the listing also implements the interfaces IComparable<T> and IDisplayable. It implements CompareTo() by comparing the names of the birds using String.Compare(). So one bird is greater than another if its name is greater. Bird.CompareTo() alphabetizes the list. Bird's Display() method just returns the name of the bird.

Getting back to the Main () event

Now you're set up for the good part back in Main(). The CreateStudentList() method is used to return an unsorted list, which is stored in the array students.

You might think it necessary to cast the array of students into an array of `comparableObjects` so you can pass the students to `Array`'s `Sort()` method:

```
IComparable<Student>[] comparables = (IComparable<Student>[])students;
```

But not so, my friend. `Sort()` sees that the array passed in consists of objects that implement `IComparable<something>` and simply calls `CompareTo()` on each `Student` object to sort them. Great, eh?

The sorted array of `Student` objects is then passed to the locally defined `DisplayArray()` method. `DisplayArray()` uses `foreach` to iterate through an array of objects that implement a `Display()` method (guaranteed by the objects' having implemented `IDisplayable`). In the loop, it calls `Display()` on each object and displays the result to the console using `WriteLine()`.

The program in `Main()` continues by sorting and displaying birds! I think we can agree that birds have nothing to do with students. Yet the same `Sort()` and `DisplayArray()` methods work on `Bird` as on `Student`.

The output from the program appears as follows:

```
Sorting the list of students
Lisa      : 100
Marge     : 85
Bart      : 50
Maggie    : 30
Homer     : 0

Sorting the list of birds
Bluejay
Cardinal
Finch
Hawk
Oriole
Robin
Sparrow
Press Enter to terminate...
```

Unifying Class Hierarchies

Figure 14-1 shows the `Robot` and `Animal` hierarchies. Some, but not all, of the classes in each hierarchy not only inherit from the base classes, `Robot` or `Animal`, but they also implement the `IPet` interface (not all animals are pets, you see) as shown in the following code — I've skipped lots of details here:

```
// Two abstract base classes and one interface.
abstract class Animal
{
  abstract public void Eat(string food);
  abstract public void Sleep(int hours);
  abstract public int NumberOfLegs { get; }
  public void Breathe() { ... } // Nonabstract, implementation not shown.
}
abstract class Robot
{
  public virtual void Speak(string whatToSay) { ... } // Impl not shown.
  abstract public void LiftObject(object o);
  abstract public int NumberOfLegs { get; }
}
interface IPet
{
  void AskForStrokes();
  void DoTricks();
  int NumberOfLegs { get; }  // Properties in interfaces look like this.
  string Name { get; set; }  // get/set must be public in implementations.
}
// Cat - A concrete class that inherits (and partially
//    implements) class Animal, and also implements interface IPet.
class Cat : Animal, IPet
{
  public Cat(string name) { Name = name; }
  // 1. Overrides and implements Animal members (not shown).
  // 2. Provides additional implementation for IPet.
  #region IPet Members
  public void AskForStrokes() ...
  public void DoTricks() ...
  public string Name { get; set; }
  // Inherits NumberOfLegs property from base class, thus meeting
  // IPet's requirement for a NumberOfLegs property.
  #endregion IPet Members
  public override string ToString() { return Name; }
}
class Cobra : Animal
{
  // 1. Inherits or overrides all Animal methods only (not shown).
}
class Robozilla : Robot     // Not IPet.
{
  // 1. Overrides Speak.
  public override void Speak(string whatToSay)
  { Console.WriteLine("DESTROY ALL HUMANS!"); }
  // 2. Implements LiftObject and NumberOfLegs, not all shown.
  public override void LiftObject(object o) ...
  public override int NumberOfLegs { get { return 2; } }
}
class RoboCat : Robot, IPet
{
  public RoboCat(string name) { Name = name; }
```

```
// 1. Overrides some Robot members, not all shown:
#region IPet Members
public void AskForStrokes() ...
public void DoTricks() ...
public string Name { get; set; }
#endregion IPet Members
}
```

(Notice the properties in `IPet`. This is how you specify properties in interfaces. If you need both getter and setter, just add `set;` after `get;`.)

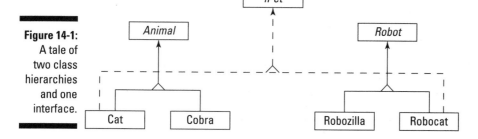

Figure 14-1:
A tale of
two class
hierarchies
and one
interface.

I've shown two concrete classes that inherit from `Animal` and two that inherit from `Robot`. However, you can see that neither class `Cobra` nor class `Robozilla` implements `IPet` — probably for very good reasons. I have no plans to watch TV with my pet cobra beside me on the couch, and a robozilla sounds pretty nasty too. Some of the classes in both hierarchies exhibit what you might call "petness," and some don't.

The `InterfacesBridgingHierarchies` example on the Web site puts these items through their paces.

The point of this section is that *any* class can implement an interface, as long as it provides the right methods and properties. `Robotcat` and `Robodog` can carry out the `AskForStrokes()` and `DoTricks()` actions and have the `NumberOfLegs` property, as can `Cat` and `Dog` in the `Animal` hierarchy. All while other classes in the same hierarchies don't implement `IPet`.

You can add support for an interface to any class — but only if you're free to modify the source code.

Hiding Behind an Interface

Often in these pages I'm discussing code that (a) you write, but (b) someone else (a client) uses in her programs (you may be the client yourself, of course). Sometimes you have a complex or tricky class for which you'd really rather not expose the whole public interface to clients. For various reasons, it includes some dangerous operations that nonetheless have to be public. Ideally, you'd expose some safe subset of your class's public methods and properties but hide the dangerous ones. C# interfaces can do that too.

Here's a different `Robozilla` class, with several methods and properties that amateurs can use safely and enjoyably. But `Robozilla` also has some advanced features that can be, well, scary.

```
public class Robozilla   // Doesn't implement IPet!
{
    public void ClimbStairs();                      // Safe.
    public void PetTheRobodog();                    // Safe? Might break it.
    public void Charge();                           // Maybe not safe.
    public void SearchAndDestroy();                 // Dangerous.
    public void LaunchGlobalThermonuclearWar();     // Catastrophic.
}
```

You'd like to expose only the two safer methods while hiding the last three dangerous ones. Here's how you can do that with a C# interface.

1. First, design a C# interface that exposes only the safe methods:

```
public interface IRobozillaSafe
{
    void ClimbStairs();
    void PetTheRobodog();
}
```

2. Now modify the `Robozilla` class to implement the interface. Since it already has implementations for the required methods, all you need is the : `IRobozillaSafe` notation on the class heading:

```
public class Robozilla : IRobozillaSafe  ...
```

3. Now you can just keep `Robozilla` itself a secret from, say, everybody but Gandhi, Martin Luther King, and Mother Theresa, and give most users the `IRobozillaSafe` interface. Give your clients a way to instantiate a new `Robozilla`, but return them a reference to the interface (here via a static factory method added to class `Robozilla`):

```
// Creates a Robozilla, but returns only an interface reference to it.
public static IRobozillaSafe CreateRobozilla(<parameter list>)
{
    return (IRobozillaSafe)new Robozilla(<parameter list>);
}
```

Clients then use `Robozilla` like this:

```
IRobozillaSafe myZilla = Robozilla.CreateRobozilla(...);
myZilla.ClimbStairs();
myZilla.PetTheRobodog();
```

It's that simple. Through the interface, they can call the Robozilla methods that it specifies. But not any other Robozilla methods.

Programmers (I think I can guess which ones) can defeat my little ploy with a simple cast:

```
Robozilla myKillaZilla = (Robozilla)myZilla;
```

Doing so is usually a bad idea, though. The interface has a purpose. Bill Wagner says, "Programmers who go to that much work to create bugs get what they deserve."

In real life, programmers sometimes use this hand-out-an-interface technique with the complex DataSet class used in ADO .NET to interact with databases. A DataSet can return a set of database tables loaded with records — such as a table of Customers and a table of Orders. (Modern relational databases like Oracle and SQL Server contain *tables* linked by various *relationships*. Each table contains lots of *records*, where each record might be, for example, the name, rank, and serial number of a Customer.)

Unfortunately, if you hand a client a DataSet reference (even through a read-only property's get clause), he can easily muddle things up by reaching into the DataSet and modifying things you don't want modified. One way to prevent such mischief is to return a DataView object, which is read-only. Alternatively, you can create a C# interface to expose a safe subset of the operations available on the DataSet. Then you can subclass DataSet and have the subclass, call it MyDataSet, implement the interface. Finally, give clients a way to obtain an interface reference to a live MyDataSet object and let them have at it in relative safety — through the interface.

It's often best not to return a reference to a collection, either, because that lets anyone alter the collection outside of the class that created it. Remember that the reference you hand out can still point to the original collection inside your class. This is why List<T>, for instance, provides an AsReadOnly() method. This method returns a collection that can't be altered:

```
private List<string> _readWriteNames = ...  // A modifiable data member.
...
ReadonlyCollection<string> readonlyNames = _readWriteNames.AsReadOnly();
return readonlyNames; // Safer to return this than _readWriteNames.
```

Although that's not using an interface, the purpose is the same.

The HidingBehindAnInterface example on the Web site shows the Robozilla code in this section.

Inheriting an Interface

A C# interface can "inherit" the methods of another interface. I use quotes around the word *inherit* because it's not true inheritance, no matter how it may appear. The following interface code lists a *base interface*, much like a base class, in its heading:

```
interface IRobozillaSafe : IPet    // Base interface.
{
    // Methods not shown here ...
}
```

By having `IRobozillaSafe` "inherit" `IPet`, you can let this subset of `Robozilla` implement its own "petness" without trying to impose petness inappropriately on all of `Robozilla`:

```
class PetRobo : Robozilla, IRobozillaSafe // (also an IPet by inheritance).
{
    // Implement Robozilla operations.
    // Implement IRobozillaSafe operations, then ...
    // Implement IPet operations too (required by the inherited IPet interface).
}
...
// Hand out only a safe reference, not one to PetRobo itself.
IPet myPetRobo = (IPet)new PetRobo();
// ... now call IPet methods on the object.
```

The `IRobozillaSafe` interface inherits from `IPet`. Classes that implement `IRobozillaSafe` must therefore also implement `IPet` to make their implementation of `IRobozillaSafe` complete.

This inheritance is not the same thing as class inheritance. For instance, class `PetRobo` above can have a constructor, but there's no equivalent of a base-class constructor for `IRobozillaSafe` or `IPet`. Interfaces don't have constructors. More important, polymorphism doesn't work the same with interfaces. While you can call a method of a subclass through a reference to the base class (class polymorphism), the parallel operation involving interfaces (so-called interface polymorphism) doesn't work: you can't call a method of the derived interface (`IRobozillaSafe`) through a base interface reference (`IPet`).

Although interface inheritance isn't polymorphic in the same way that class inheritance is, you *can* pass an object of a derived interface type (`IRobozillasafe`) through a parameter of its base interface type (`IPet`). This means you can also put `IRobozillasafe` objects into a collection of `IPet` objects. The `PassInterface` example on the Web site demonstrates the ideas in this section.

Using Interfaces to Manage Change in Object-Oriented Programs

Interfaces are the key to object-oriented programs that bend flexibly with the winds of change. Your code will laugh in the face of new requirements.

You've no doubt heard it said that "Change is a constant." When you hand a new program to a bunch of users, they soon start requesting changes. Add this feature, please. Fix that problem, please. Mattell's RoboWarrior has feature X, so why doesn't Robozilla? Many programs have a long shelf-life — thousands of programs, especially old Fortran and Cobol programs, have been in service for 20 or 30 years, or longer. They undergo lots of *maintenance* in that kind of time span. *This makes planning and designing for change one of your highest priorities.*

Here's an example:

In the `Robot` class hierarchy, suppose that all robots can move in one way or another. `Robocats` *saunter*. `Robozillas` *charge* — at least when operated by a power (hungry) user. And `Robosnakes` *slither*. One way to implement these different modes of travel involves inheritance: giving the base class, `Robot`, an abstract `Move()` method. Then each subclass overrides the `Move()` method to implement it differently:

```
abstract public class Robot
{
   abstract public void Move(int direction, int speed);
   // ...
}
public class Robosnake : Robot
{
   public override void Move(int direction, int speed)
   {
      // A real Move() implementation here: slithering.
      ... some real code that computes angles and changes
      snake's location relative to a coordinate system, say ...
   }
}
```

But suppose you often get requests to add new types of movement to existing `Robot` subclasses. "Please make `Robosnake` *undulate* instead of *slithering*," maybe. (Don't ask me what the difference is.) Now you have to open up the `Robosnake` class and modify its `Move()` method directly.

Once the `Move()` method is working correctly for *slithering*, most programmers would prefer not to meddle with it. Implementing slithering is hard, and changing the implementation can introduce brand new bugs. If it ain't broke, don't fix it.

The code just given here illustrates the problem. The `StrategyExample` program on the Web site illustrates the solution, discussed in the next several sections. The solution has the advantage of allowing the old slithering code to flourish for some applications while providing the new undulating movement in newer applications. Everybody's happy.

Flexible dependencies through interfaces

Is there a way to implement `Move()` that won't require you to open the can of worms every time some client wants *wriggling* instead? Interfaces, of course!

Look at the following code that uses HAS_A, a now-familiar relationship between two classes in which one class *contains* the other:

```
public class Robot
{
  // This object is used to implement motion.
  protected Motor _motor = new Motor(); // Refers to Motor by name.
  // ...
}
internal class Motor { ... }
```

The point about this example is that the contained object is of type `Motor`, where `Motor` is a concrete object. (That is, it represents a real thing, not an abstraction.) HAS_A sets up a *dependency* between classes `Robot` and `Motor`: `Robot` *depends on* the concrete class `Motor`. A class with concrete dependencies is *tightly coupled* to them: when you need to replace `Motor` with something else, code that depends directly on `Motor` like this has to change too. Instead, you should insulate your code by relying only on the public interface of dependencies, which you can do with interfaces. You can depend on dependent objects in a, er, *less dependent* way.

Depend on abstractions, not concrete classes. I'll show you how.

Abstract or concrete? When to use an abstract class, when to use an interface

In Chapter 13, I give a little discourse about birds. I say there, "Every bird out there is actually some subtype of `Bird`." In other words, a duck is an instance of a subclass `Duck`. You'll never see an instance of `Bird` itself — `Bird` is an *abstraction*. Instead, you always see *concrete*, physical ducks, sparrows, or hummingbirds. Abstractions are concepts. As living things, ducks are real, concrete objects. And concrete objects are instances of concrete classes. (A concrete class is a class that you can instantiate. It lacks the `abstract` keyword, and it implements all methods.)

You can represent abstractions in two ways in C#: with abstract classes, or with C# interfaces. The two have differences that can affect your choice of which to use.

- ✔ **Use an abstract class** when there's some implementation that you can profitably share with subclasses — the abstract base class can contribute some real code that its subclasses can use by inheritance. For instance, maybe class `Robot` can handle part of the robot's tasks, just not movement.

  An abstract class doesn't have to be completely abstract. While it has to have at least one abstract, unimplemented method or property, some can provide implementations (bodies). Using an abstract class to provide some implementation for its subclasses to inherit prevents duplication of code. That's always a good thing.

- ✔ **Use an interface** when you can't share any implementation or your implementing class already has a base class.

  C# interfaces are purely, totally abstract. A C# interface supplies no implementation of any of its methods. Yet it can also add flexibility not otherwise possible. The abstract class option may not be available because you want to add a capability to a class that already has a base class (that you can't modify). For example, class `Robot` may already have a base class in a library that you didn't write and therefore can't alter. Interfaces are especially great for representing completely abstract capabilities, such as movability or displayability, that you'd like to add to multiple classes that may otherwise have nothing in common — for example, being in the same class hierarchy.

Doing HAS_A with interfaces

I mentioned earlier that you can use interfaces as a more general reference type. The containing class can refer to the contained class not with a reference to a concrete class but with a reference to an abstraction — either an abstract class or a C# interface will do:

```
AbstractDependentClass dependency1 = ...;
ISomeInterface dependency2 = ...;
```

Suppose you have an `IPropulsion` interface:

```
interface IPropulsion
{
  void Movement(int direction, int speed);
}
```

Class `Robot` can contain a data member of type `IPropulsion` instead of the concrete type `Motor`:

```
public class Robot
{
    private IPropulsion _propel;      //<--Notice the interface type here.
    // Somehow, you supply a concrete propulsion object at run-time ...
    // Other stuff..., then:
    public void Move(int speed, int direction)
    {
        // Use whatever concrete propulsion device is installed in _propel.
        _propel.Movement(speed, direction); // Delegate to its methods.
    }
}
```

Robot's `Move()` method delegates the real work to the object referred to through the interface. Be sure you provide some way to install a concrete `Motor`, `Engine`, or other implementer of `IPropulsion` in the data member. Programmers often install that concrete object — "inject the dependency" — by passing it to a constructor:

```
Robot r = new Robosnake(someConcreteMotor);   // Type IPropulsion.
```

or by assigning it via a setter property:

```
r.PropulsionDevice = someConcreteMotor;       // Invokes the set clause.
```

Another approach to dependency injection is to use a *factory method*, which I discussed earlier in the chapter, in the section "As a method return type," and illustrated in the section "Hiding Behind an Interface":

```
IPropulsion _propel = CreatePropulsion();     // A factory method.
```

The Strategy Design Pattern

All of the approaches in the previous section are examples of a software *design pattern* so common that it has a name: the Strategy pattern. Figure 14-2 diagrams the Strategy pattern.

Design patterns are solutions to common software problems that have often proven useful in the past. You can begin finding out more about design patterns in *Design Patterns For Dummies*, by Steve Holzner.

In the Strategy pattern, the `Client` class HAS_A reference to an `IServer` interface. `IServer` is an abstraction that sits at the top of a hierarchy of concrete implementations. (Those terms are defined below.) In our `Robot` case, `Robot` is the client, whose `IPropulsion` data member refers indirectly to some concrete object that implements `IPropulsion` (the server).

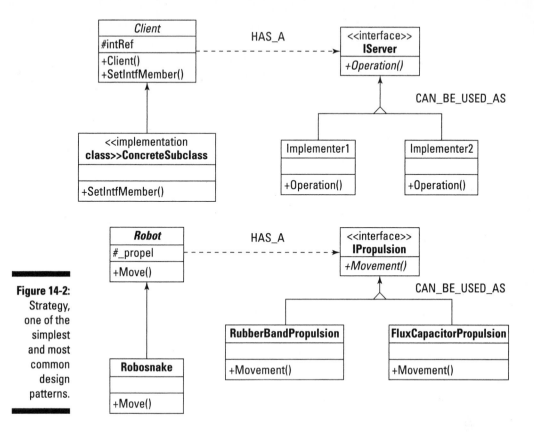

Figure 14-2:
Strategy,
one of the
simplest
and most
common
design
patterns.

The term *client* is an Overworked Word, meaning either the entity for whom you're writing the software, or some piece of software (such as a class) that uses the services of some other piece of software, the server. *Server*, meanwhile, is another Overworked Word, meaning both a computer that serves up Web pages and the like *and* a software class or component that provides some kind of service to other software. For example, a `Motor`.

What makes this pattern so useful?

Because the `Client` depends on an abstraction, not a concrete class, you can freely substitute any concrete class that fills the requirements. This makes for great flexibility.

This pattern is an example of *indirection*. Yes, the robot refers to a concrete motor of some kind, but it does so only indirectly, through an abstraction. Programmers love indirection.

Indirection gives you flexibility through substitutability. Your robot can be powered by a rubber band today, a jet engine tomorrow, and a flux capacitor the day after that. You can then modify a class *without actually editing it.* All you have to do is add yet another little concrete class that implements the interface (or subclasses an abstract base class) and inject the substitute dependency as described earlier, in the section "Doing HAS_A with interfaces."

If a Robosnake is powered by a rubber band:

```
public class RubberBandPropulsion : IPropulsion
{
   public void Movement(int direction, int speed) { ... }
}
```

To change a Robosnake's power plant, write a new class that implements IPropulsion:

```
public class FluxCapacitorPropulsion : IPropulsion
{
   // Implementation elementary, left to the reader.
   public void Movement(int direction, int speed) { ... }
}
```

And initialize your Robosnake instance with the new go juice:

```
FluxCapacitorPropulsion myFluxCapacitor = new FluxCapacitorPropulsion();
Robot robo = new Robosnake(myFluxCapacitor);  // Constructor injection.
```

The robo object now refers to its new flux capacitor power source through an IPropulsion interface. (Note that I also assign the Robosnake instance to a variable of the base class type: Robot. Not a bad idea.)

Initially, you *will* have to modify the Client class (that is, Robosnake) to use an interface in referring to the dependent IPropulsion object and to provide for injecting an IPropulsion object into the client. That's called "taking the first bullet." But thereafter you never have to take a second bullet, and at least one change problem is solved.

You might use Strategy to . . .

- ✔ Implement the swimming behaviors of various Fish subclasses, since different fish swim very differently.
- ✔ Provide alternative algorithms for computing a mathematical function, such as computing a factorial or generating prime numbers.

✔ Implement a variety of savings account policies: `ISavingsPolicy` would define a `Withdraw()` method that the owning `BankAccount` could call to implement its own `Withdraw()` method. You might implement `ISavingsPolicy` with `PreferredSavingsPolicy` and `StandardSavingsPolicy`, among others. Each class would handle withdrawal differently.

In the `StrategyExample` program on the Web site, I stick to slithering and undulating, the original problem. Sorry, couldn't resist the flux capacitor.

You can learn more about indirection and programming to abstractions on my Web site at `csharp102.info`.

Part V
Now Showing in C# 3.0

"Well, whoever stole my passwords was sure clever. Especially since none of my reminders are missing."

In this part . . .

1t's time to solo. So far, your objects have been simple things, like integers and strings and `BankAccounts`. But C# comes equipped right out of the box with several other kinds of objects. In this part, after a warm-up tour of *delegates* and *events* (in C# all along but never before viewed by human eyes — in this book, anyway) you meet the newest kid on the block: C# 3.0. His name is Language Integrated Query, but you can call him LINQ for short, and he's a regular lamb.

Lamb-da, that is, as in *lambda expressions*. Sounds like Chinese arithmetic, but once you get delegates under your belt, a bit of lambda makes perfect sense. Not only that, but you then get to see lambda expressions do back flips inside the new *query expressions*. If you dug loops in Chapter 4 and arrays and collections in Chapter 5, you'll really go for queries. Use them to boss your computer around like nobody's business. In no time at all, you'll be bending and twisting those collections all over the place — in just a line or two of code. Wow! And beyond that, you'll be ready to move on to graduate-level LINQ for databases and Extended Markup Language (XML) — though not in this book.

(And don't forget the extras on my Web site at `csharp 102.info`.)

Chapter 15

Delegating Those Important Events

This chapter finally brings up a corner of C# that has been around since the language's birth, but that I've avoided getting into until this third edition because it's fairly challenging stuff. However, if you can bear with me — and I'll try to go as easy on you as possible — the payoff in Chapters 16 and 17 is well worth it.

E.T. Phone Home — The Callback Problem

If you've seen the Steven Spielberg movie *E.T., the Extraterrestrial* (1982), you watched the cute/ugly little alien stranded on Earth try to build an apparatus out of old toy parts with which he could "phone home." He needed his ship to pick him up.

It's a big jump from E.T. to C#, but code sometimes needs to phone home too. For example, did you ever wonder how the Windows progress bar works? You know, the horizontal "bar" that gradually fills up with green or blue to show progress during a lengthy operation, such as copying some files. (On my machine, of course, Murphy seems to fill it up well before the task really finishes — good old Murphy: "What can go wrong will.") Figure 15-1 shows a green progress bar (though it's not easy being green in a black-and-white book).

The progress bar is based on some lengthy operation pausing periodically to "phone home." In programmerese, it's called a *callback*. Usually, the lengthy operation estimates how long its task should take, then keeps checking frequently how far it has progressed. Periodically, it sends a signal by calling a *callback method* back on the mother ship — the class that kicked off the long operation. The mother ship can update its progress bar.

The trick is that you have to supply this callback method for the long operation to use.

That callback method may be on the same class as the lengthy operation — like phoning your sister on the other side of the house. Or, more often, it's on some other class that knows about the progress bar — like phoning Aunt Maxie in Minnesota. Somehow, at its start, the lengthy operation has been handed a mechanism for phoning home — sort of like giving your kid a cell phone so she can call you at 10:00 p.m.

This chapter is about how your code can set up this callback mechanism and then invoke it to phone home when needed.

Callbacks are used a lot in Windows programming, typically for some piece of code down in your program's guts to notify a higher-level module that the task has finished, to ask for needed data, or to let that module take some useful action, such as writing a log entry or updating a progress bar.

Figure 15-1:
Making
progress
with the
Windows
ProgressBa
r control.

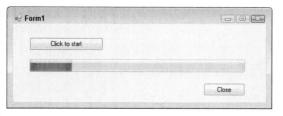

What's a Delegate?

C# provides *delegates* for doing callbacks — and a number of other things. Delegates are C#'s way (.NET's way, really, since any .NET language can use them) for you to *pass around methods as if they were data*.

You're saying, "Here, execute this method when you need it" (*you hand over the method to execute*).

This chapter will help you get a handle on that concept, see its usefulness, and start using it yourself.

You may be an experienced coder who will recognize immediately that delegates are like C/C++ function pointers, only much, much better. But I'm assuming in this section that you aren't and you don't.

Think of a delegate as a vehicle for passing a callback method to some "work-horse" method that needs to call you back, or needs help with that action, as in doing the same action to each element of a collection — since the collection doesn't know about your custom action, you need a way to provide the action for the collection to carry out. Figure 15-2 shows how the parts of this scheme fit together.

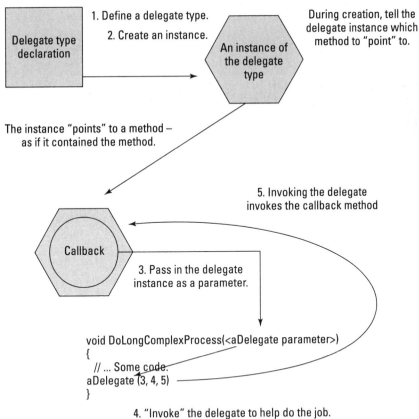

Figure 15-2:
Sending
your
delegate to
the bungee
jump on
your behalf.

1. Define a delegate type.

2. Create an instance.

During creation, tell the delegate instance which method to "point" to.

Delegate type declaration

An instance of the delegate type

The instance "points" to a method – as if it contained the method.

5. Invoking the delegate invokes the callback method

Callback

3. Pass in the delegate instance as a parameter.

```
void DoLongComplexProcess(<aDelegate parameter>)
{
    // ... Some code.
    aDelegate (3, 4, 5)
}
```

4. "Invoke" the delegate to help do the job.

A delegate is a data type, similar to a class. As with a class, you create an instance of the delegate type in order to use the delegate. Figure 15-2 shows the sequence of events in the delegate's life cycle as you:

1. Define the delegate type (much as you would define a class).

   Sometimes C# has already defined a delegate that you can use. Much of the time, though, you'll need to define your own custom delegates.

   Under the surface, a delegate *is* a class, derived from a class called `System.MulticastDelegate`, which knows how to store one or more "pointers" to methods and invoke them for you. But relax — the compiler writes the class part of it for you.

2. Create an instance of the delegate type — like instantiating a class.

   During creation, you hand the new delegate instance the name of a method that you want it to use as a callback or action method.

3. Pass the delegate instance to some workhorse method, *which has a parameter of the delegate type*. That's the doorway through which you insert the delegate instance into the workhorse method.

   It's like smuggling a candy bar into a movie theater — except that here the movie theater expects, even invites, the contraband candy.

4. When the workhorse method is ready — for example, when it's time to update the progress bar — the workhorse "invokes" the delegate, passing it any expected arguments.

5. Invoking the delegate in turn invokes (calls) the callback method that the delegate "points" to. Using the delegate, the workhorse phones home. (Older readers may remember Mr. Ed: "A horse is a horse. . . .")

This fundamental mechanism solves the callback problem — and it has other uses too.

Delegate types can also be generic, allowing you to use the same delegate for different data types, much as you can instantiate a `List<T>` collection for `string` or `int`. Bonus Chapter 8 on my Web site at `csharp102.info` explores C#'s generic features.

Pass Me the Code, Please — Examples

Let's just jump right into a couple of examples — and solve the callback problem discussed at the beginning of this chapter.

I delegated the example to Igor

In this section, I'll take you through two examples of using a callback — that is, a delegate instance phoning home to the object that created it, like E.T. But first, take a look at some common variations on what you can use a callback delegate for:

✔ Notifying the delegate's home base of something: that a lengthy operation has finished, or made some progress, or perhaps run into an error. "Mother, this is E.T. Can you come get me at Elliot's house?"

✔ Calling back to home base to ask for some data needed to complete a task. "Honey, I'm at the store. Should I get white bread or wheat?"

✔ More generally, delegates let you customize a method. The method you're customizing provides a framework, while its caller supplies a delegate to do the work. "Honey, take this grocery list to the store and follow it exactly." The delegate method carries out a task that the customized method needs done (but can't handle by itself). The customized method is responsible for invoking the delegate at the appropriate moment. (I discuss using delegate customization for a problem I call "do-to-each," in Chapter 16.)

First, a very simple example

The `SimpleDelegateExample` program on the Web site demonstrates a pretty simple delegate:

```
// SimpleDelegateExample - Demonstrate a very simple delegate callback.

using System;
namespace SimpleDelegateExample
{
  class Program
  {
    delegate int MyDelType(string name);   // Inside class or inside namespace.

    static void Main(string[] args)
    {
      // Create a delegate instance pointing to the CallBackMethod below.
      // Note that the callback method is static, so we prefix the name
      // with the class name, Program.
      MyDelType del = new MyDelType(Program.CallBackMethod);
      // Call a method that will invoke the delegate.
      UseTheDel(del, "hello");
      // Wait for user to acknowledge results.
      Console.WriteLine("Press Enter to terminate...");
      Console.Read();
    }
```

```
// UseTheDel - A "workhorse" method that takes a MyDelType delegate
//    argument and invokes the delegate. arg is a string I want to pass
//    to the delegate invocation.
private static void UseTheDel(MyDelType del, string arg)
{
   if (del == null) return; // Don't invoke a null delegate!
   // Here's where we invoke the delegate.
   // What's written here? A number representing the length of arg.
   Console.WriteLine("UseTheDel writes {0}", del(arg));
}
// CallBackMethod - A method that conforms to the MyDelType
//    delegate signature (takes a string, returns an int).
//    The delegate will call this method.
public static int CallBackMethod(string stringPassed)
{
   // Leave tracks to show we were here.
   // What's written here? stringPassed.
   Console.WriteLine("CallBackMethod writes: {0}", stringPassed);
   // Return an int.
   return stringPassed.Length;  // Delegate requires an int return.
}
}
}
```

The delegate-related parts of this example are highlighted in boldface.

First, you see the delegate definition. `MyDelType` defines a *signature* — you can pass any method with the delegate; such a method must take a `string` argument and return an `int`. Second, the `CallBackMethod()`, defined at the bottom of the listing, matches that signature. Third, `Main()` creates an instance of the delegate, called `del`, and then passes the delegate instance to a "workhorse" method, `UseTheDel()`, along with some string data, `"hello"`, that the delegate requires.

With that setup, here's the sequence of events:

1. `UseTheDel()` takes two arguments, a `MyDelType` delegate, and a `string` that it calls `arg`. So when `Main()` calls `UseTheDel`, it passes my delegate instance to be used inside the method. When I created the delegate instance, `del`, in `Main()`, I passed the *name* of the `CallBackMethod()` as the method to be called. Since `CallBackMethod()` is static, I had to prefix the name with the class name, `Program`. More about this later.

2. Inside `UseTheDel()`, the method makes sure the delegate isn't `null`, then starts a `WriteLine()` call. Within that call, before it finishes, the method invokes the delegate by calling `del(arg)`. `arg` is just something we can pass to the delegate. This causes our `CallBackMethod()` to be called.

3. Inside `CallBackMethod()`, the method writes its own message, includ- ing the string that was passed when `UseTheDel()` invoked the delegate. Then `CallBackMethod()` returns the length of the string it was passed, and that length is written out as the last part of the `WriteLine()` in `UseTheDel()`.

The output looks like the following:

```
CallBackMethod writes: hello
UseTheDel writes 5
Press Enter to terminate...
```

`UseTheDel()` phones home, and `CallBackMethod()` answers the call.

How About a More Real-World Example?

For something more realistic, I'll write a little app that puts up a progress bar and updates it each time a lengthy method invokes a delegate.

Getting an overview of the bigger example

The `SimpleProgress` example on the Web site demonstrates the Windows Forms `ProgressBar` control that I discussed at the top of this chapter. (By the way, this is the only example of Windows *graphical* programming in this book — even if it's pretty simple-minded — so I'll step through it carefully. I urge you to do the steps as I provide them.)

The example displays a small dialog box-style window with two buttons and a progress bar, as shown back in Figure 15-1. When you load the example solu- tion into Visual Studio and build it, then run it, then click the upper button, marked "Click to Start," the progress bar runs for a few seconds. You see it gradually fill up, one-tenth of its length at a time. When it's completely full, you can click the Close button to end the program, or click Click to Start again.

Putting the app together

To create the example app on your own, rather than just loading it from the Web site example — and experience a bit of Windows graphical programming — take these steps, working first in *design mode*, where you're just laying out the appearance of your app.

First, create the project and position the necessary controls on your "window":

1. Choose File⇨New Project and select Windows on the left, under C#, but this time, select Windows Forms Application on the right instead of the usual Console Application. Name your project `SimpleProgress`.

2. The first thing you see is the *form*: a window that you'll lay out yourself with several *controls*. Choose View⇨Toolbox, and from the Toolbox window's Common Controls group, drag a `ProgressBar` control onto the form and drop it. Then drag two `Button`s onto the form.

3. Position the buttons and the `ProgressBar` so they look somewhat like Figure 15-1. Note the handy guide lines that help with positioning.

Next, set properties for these controls: Choose View⇨Properties, select a control on the form, and set the control's properties, as follows:

1. For the progress bar — called `progressBar1` in the code — make sure that the `Minimum` property is 0, the `Maximum` property is 100, the `Step` property is 10, and the `Value` property is 0.

2. For the upper button, change the `Text` property to `"Click to Start"` and drag the sizing handles on the button image until it looks right and shows all of its text.

3. For the lower button, change the `Text` property to `"Close"` and adjust the button's size to your liking.

For this simple example, you're putting all the code in the *form* class. (The form is your window; its class — here called `Form1` — is responsible for all things graphical.) Generally, it's better to put all "business" code — the code that does your calculations, data access, and other important work — in other classes. Reserve the form class for code that's intimately involved with displaying things on the form and responding to its controls. I break that rule here — but the delegate works no matter where its callback method is.

Now, still in design mode, add a *handler method* for each button:

1. On the form, double-click your new Close button. This generates a method in the "code behind the form" (or simply "the code-behind") — the code that makes the form work. It looks like this — you add the boldfaced code:

```
private void button2_Click(object sender, EventArgs e)
{
    this.Close();  // 'this' refers to the Form1 class.
}
```

To toggle back and forth between the form's code and its image, choose View⇨Code or View⇨Designer.

2. Double-click your new Click to Start button to generate its handler method, which looks like the following in the code-behind:

```
private void button1_Click(object sender, EventArgs e)
{
```

```
UpdateProgressCallback callback = UpdateProgressCallback(this.DoUpdate);
// Do something that needs periodic progress reports.
// This passes a delegate instance that knows how to update the bar.
DoSomethingLengthy(callback);
// Clear the bar so it can be used again.
progressBar1.Value = 0;
}
```

3. Add the following callback method to the form class:

```
private void DoUpdate()
{
  progressBar1.PerformStep(); // Tells progress bar to update itself.
}
```

4. Finally, you can move from design mode to execution mode by taking the program for a spin. Run it and kick its tires.

I'll take you through the remaining code, all of it on the form class, in the next section. Later I'll show you other variations on the delegate passed.

Looking at the code

The remaining bits of code tucked into the `Form1` class consist of the parts of the delegate life cycle covered earlier. I'll show the class, then show where the parts are. The boldfaced lines are new code that you add beyond the items you added above:

```
using System;

using System.Windows.Forms;
namespace SimpleProgress
{
  public partial class Form1 : Form
  {
    // Declare the delegate. This one is void.
    delegate void UpdateProgressCallback();

    public Form1()
    {
      InitializeComponent();
    }
    // DoSomethingLengthy - Our work-horse method that takes a delegate.
    private void DoSomethingLengthy(UpdateProgressCallback updateProgress)
    {
      int duration = 2000;
      int updateInterval = duration / 10;
      for (int i = 0; i < duration; i++)
      {
        Console.WriteLine("Something or other");
```

```
        // Update every tenth of the duration.
        if ((i % updateInterval) == 0 && updateProgress != null)
        {
            updateProgress();  // Invoke the delegate.
        }
    }
}
// DoUpdate - Our callback method.
private void DoUpdate()
{
    progressBar1.PerformStep();
}
private void button1_Click(object sender, EventArgs e)
{
    // Instantiate the delegate, telling it what method to call.
    UpdateProgressCallback callback = new
            UpdateProgressCallback(this.DoUpdate);
    // Do something that needs periodic progress reports.
    // This passes a delegate instance that knows how to update the bar.
    DoSomethingLengthy(callback);
    // Clear the bar so it can be used again.
    progressBar1.Value = 0;
}
private void button2_Click(object sender, EventArgs e)
{
    this.Close();
}
    }
}
```

The class declaration is interesting as a brief aside:

```
public partial class Form1 : Form
```

The `partial` keyword indicates that this is only part of the full class. The rest can be found in the `Form1.Designer.cs` file listed in Solution Explorer (take a look at it). Later in the chapter, I'll revisit that file to show you a couple of things about "events." Partial classes were introduced in C# 2.0. They let you split a class between two or more files. The compiler generates the `Form1.Designer.cs` file, so don't modify its code directly. You can modify it indirectly, however, by changing things on the form. `Form1.cs` is *your* part.

Tracking the delegate life cycle

Now let's look at the example through the parts of the delegate life cycle:

1. You define the `UpdateProgressCallback` delegate near the top of the class:

   ```
   delegate void UpdateProgressCallback();
   ```

Methods this delegate can "point" to will be `void`, with no parameters. After the `delegate` keyword, the rest defines the *signature* of any method that the delegate can point to: its return type and the number, order, and types of its parameters. Delegates don't have to be `void` — you can write delegates that return any type and take any arguments.

Defining a delegate defines a *type*, just as `class Student {...}` does. You can declare your delegate `public`, `internal`, `protected`, or even `private`, as needed.

It's considered good form to append the name `Callback` to the name of a delegate type that defines a callback method, though C# could care less.

2. You instantiate the delegate and then pass the instance to the `DoSomethingLengthy()` method in the `button1_Click()` method:

```
UpdateProgressCallback callback =
  new UpdateProgressCallback(this.DoUpdate); // Instantiate the delegate.
DoSomethingLengthy(callback); // Pass the delegate instance to a method.
```

This delegate "points" to a method on `this` class (and `this` is optional). To point to a method on another class, you need an instance of that class (if the method is an instance method), and you pass the method like this:

```
SomeClass sc = new SomeClass();
UpdateProgressCallback callback =
  new UpdateProgressCallback(sc.DoUpdate);
```

But if the method is a `static` method (located anywhere), pass it like this:

```
UpdateProgressCallback callback =
  new UpdateProgressCallback(SomeClass.DoUpdate);
```

What you're passing in the instantiation is just the method's *name*, no parameters. What you pass to `DoSomethingLengthy()` is the delegate instance, `callback` (which points to the method).

3. Your `DoSomethingLengthy()` method does some "lengthy processing" and periodically pauses to call back to the form so it can update its progress bar.

Invoking the delegate inside `DoSomethingLengthy()` looks like calling a method, complete with parameters, if any:

```
updateProgress();   // Invoke the delegate instance passed in.
```

`DoSomethingLengthy()` looks like this:

```
private void DoSomethingLengthy(UpdateProgressCallback updateProgress)
{
  int duration = 2000;
  int updateInterval = duration / 10; // Every 200 milliseconds.
  for (int i = 0; i < duration; i++)
  {
```

```
        Console.WriteLine("Something or other");
        // Update the form periodically.
        if ((i % updateInterval) == 0 && updateProgress != null)
        {
          updateProgress();  // Invoke the delegate.
        }
      }
    }
```

Actually, our "lengthy process" doesn't do much. It sets the `duration` variable to 2000 loop iterations — a few seconds at run time, more than enough for this demo. Next, the method computes an "update interval" of 200 iterations by dividing the overall duration into tenths. Then the `for` loop ticks off those 2000 iterations. For each one, it checks whether it's time to update the user interface (the "UI"). Most times through the loop, no update occurs. But whenever the `if` condition is true, the method invokes the `UpdateProgressCallback` instance that was passed to its `updateProgress` parameter. That modulo expression, `i % updateInterval`, only comes out with a 0 remainder, thus satisfying the `if` condition, once every 200 iterations.

Always check a newly instantiated delegate for `null` before invoking it.

4. When `DoSomethingLengthy()` invokes the delegate, the delegate in turn invokes the method that you pointed it at, in this case the `DoUpdate()` method on the `Form1` class.

5. When called via the delegate, `DoUpdate()` carries out the update by calling a method on the `ProgressBar` class called `PerformStep()`:

```
private void DoUpdate()
{
  progressBar1.PerformStep();
}
```

`PerformStep()`, in turn, fills another 10 percent increment of the bar with green, the amount dictated by its `Step` property, set to 10 at the outset. Watch the last step closely — it's just a flicker.

6. Finally, control returns to `DoSomethingLengthy()`, which continues looping. When the loop runs its course, `DoSomethingLengthy()` exits, returning control to the `button1_Click()` method. That method then clears the `ProgressBar` by setting its `Value` property to 0. And the app settles down to wait for another click on one of its buttons (or its Close box).

And there you have it. Using the delegate to implement a callback, the program keeps its progress bar up to date. See the list of uses for delegates in the section "I Delegated the Example to Igor." For more delegate examples, see the `DelegateExamples` program on the Web site.

Write a *custom* delegate when you need to define a type for delegate-type parameters so you can implement a callback. Use *predefined* delegates for things like events and the collection classes' Find() and ForEach() methods.

Shh! Keep It Quiet — Anonymous Methods

Now that you have the gist of using delegates, here's a quick look at Microsoft's *first* cut at simplifying delegates in C# 2.0 a couple of years ago.

To cut out some of the delegate rigmarole, you can use an *anonymous method*. (You meet anonymous methods in a different form in Chapter 16, as *lambda expressions*. Anonymous methods are just written in more traditional notation. Although the syntax and a few details are different, the effect is essentially the same whether you use a "raw" delegate, an anonymous method, or a lambda expression.)

An anonymous method creates the delegate instance and the method it "points" to at the same time — right in place, on the fly, *tout de suite*. Here's the guts of the DoSomethingLengthy() method again, this time rewritten to use an anonymous method (boldfaced):

```
private void DoSomethingLengthy()  // No arguments needed this time.
{
  ...
  for (int i = 0; i < duration; i++)
  {
    if ((i % updateInterval) == 0)
    {
      UpdateProgressCallback anon = delegate() // Create delegate instance.
      {
        progressBar1.PerformStep();            // Method 'pointed' to.
      };
      if(anon != null) anon();                 // Invoke the delegate.
    }
  }
}
```

The code looks like the delegate instantiations you've seen, except that after the = sign, you get the delegate keyword, any parameters to the anonymous method in parentheses (or empty parentheses if none), and the method body. The code that used to be in a separate DoUpdate() method — the method that the delegate "points" to — has moved inside the anonymous method. No more pointing. And this method is utterly nameless.

You still need the UpdateProgressCallback delegate type definition, and you're still invoking a delegate instance, called anon in this example.

Needless to say, this doesn't cover everything there is to know about anonymous methods, but it's a start. Look up "anonymous method" in Help, and see more anonymous method examples in the `DelegateExamples` program on the Web site. **Parting Advice:** Keep your anonymous methods short.

Stuff Happens — C# Events

One more application of delegates deserves discussion here: C# *events*, which are implemented with delegates. Events are a variation on callbacks, but they provide a simpler mechanism than callbacks for alerting "interested observers" when some important event occurs. They're especially useful when more than one anxious relative is waiting for a callback. Events are widely used in C#, especially for connecting up the objects in the user interface to the code that makes them work. The buttons in the `SimpleProgress` example presented earlier illustrate this use.

The Observer design pattern

It's extremely common in programming for various objects in the running program — those anxious relatives I mentioned — to be "interested in" events that occur on other objects. For example, when the user clicks a button, the form that contains the button "wants" to know about it. Events provide the standard mechanism in C# and .NET for notifying any interested parties of important actions.

The event pattern is so common that it has a name: the Observer design pattern. It's one of many common *design patterns* that people have published for anyone to use in their own code. To begin learning about other design patterns, you can consult *Design Patterns For Dummies*, by Steve Holzner.

The Observer pattern consists of an Observable object — the object with interesting events (sometimes called the Subject, though that confuses me) — and any number of Observer objects: those interested in a particular event. The observers register themselves with the Observable in some way and, when events of interest occur, the Observable notifies all registered observers. You can implement this pattern in numerous ways without events (such as callbacks and interfaces), but the C# way is to use events.

An alternative name for "observers" that you may encounter is "listeners." Listeners "listen" for events. And that's not the last of the alternatives.

What's an event? Publish and Subscribe

One analogy for events is your local newspaper. You and many other people contact the paper to subscribe, and then the paper delivers current newspapers to you, typically soaked in a rain puddle. The newspaper company is the Publisher, and its customers are Subscribers, so this variation of Observer is often called "Publish/Subscribe." That's the analogy I'll stick to in this chapter, but keep in mind that the Observer pattern *is* the Publish/Subscribe pattern with different terminology. Observers are subscribers and the Observable object that they observe is a publisher.

In C#, when you have a class on which interesting events arise, you advertise the availability of notifications to any classes that may have an interest in knowing about such events by providing an *event object* (usually public).

The term "event" has two meanings in C#. You can think of "event" as meaning both "some interesting occurrence" and a specific kind of C# object. The former is the real-world concept, and the latter is the way it's set up in C#, using the `event` keyword.

How a publisher advertises its events

To advertise for subscribers, a class declares a delegate and a corresponding event, something like this:

```
public class PublisherOfInterestingEvents
{
  // A delegate type on which to base the event.
  // Should be declared 'internal' if all subscribers are in same assembly.
  public delegate void NewEditionEventHandler(object sender,
                                             NewEditionEventArgs e);

  // The event:
  public event NewEditionEventHandler NewEdition;
  // ... other code.
}
```

The delegate and event definitions announce to the world: "Subscribers welcome!" You can think of the `NewEdition` event as similar to a variable of the `NewEditionEventHandler` delegate type. (So far, no events have been sent. This is just the infrastructure for them.)

It's considered good practice to append `EventHandler` to the name of a delegate type that is the basis for events.

A common example, which you can see in the `SimpleProgress` example code, discussed earlier in the chapter, is a `Button` advertising its various events, including a `Click` event. In C#, class `Button` exposes this event as:

```
event _dispCommandBarControlEvents_ClickEventHandler Click;
```

where the second, loooong item is a delegate defined somewhere in .NET.

Because events are used so commonly, .NET defines two event-related delegate types for you, called `EventHandler` and `EventHandler<TEventArgs>`. (The second form is *generic* — Chapter 5 explains the strange < > notation, and see Bonus Chapter 8 on my Web site.) You could change `NewEditionEventHandler` in the previous code to `EventHandler` or to the generic `EventHandler<TEventArgs>`, and you don't need your own delegate type. Through the rest of this chapter, I'll pretend that I used the built-in `EventHandler<TEventArgs>` delegate type above, not `EventHandler` or my custom type, `NewEditionEventHandler`. You should prefer this form too:

```
event EventHandler<NewEditonEventArgs> NewEdition;
```

The `NewspaperEvents` example on the Web site demonstrates correctly setting up your event and handling it in various subscribers. (A second example program, `NewspaperEventsNongeneric`, avoids the generic stuff if you get code feet. If so, you can mentally omit the `<eventhandlerargs>` stuff in the discussion that follows.)

How do subscribers subscribe to an event?

To receive a particular event, subscribers sign up something like this:

```
publisher.EventName +=
  new EventHandler<some EventArgs type here >(some method name here);
```

where `publisher` is an instance of the publisher class, `EventName` is the event name, and `EventHandler<TEventArgs>` is the delegate underneath the event. More specifically, the code just above might be:

```
myPublisher.NewEdition += new EventHandler<NewEditionEventArgs>(MyPubHandler);
```

Since an event object is a delegate under its little hood, the += syntax is adding a method to the list of methods the delegate will call when you invoke it.

Any number of objects can subscribe this way (and the delegate will hold a list of all of the subscribed "handler" methods) — even the object on which the event was defined can subscribe, if you like. (And yes, this shows that a delegate can "point" to more than one method.)

In the `SimpleProgress` program, look in the `Form1.Designer.cs` file for how the form class registers itself as a subscriber to the buttons' `Click` events.

How do I publish an event?

When the publisher decides that something worthy of publishing to all subscribers has occurred, it *raises* (sends) the event. This is analogous to a real newspaper putting out the Sunday edition.

To publish the event, the publisher would have code like this in one of its methods (but see the section "A recommended way to raise your events"):

```
NewEditionEventArgs e = new NewEditionEventArgs(<args to constructor here>);
NewEdition(this, e);  // Raise the event - 'this' is the publisher object.
```

Or for the `Button` example, though this is hidden in class `Button`:

```
EventArgs e = new EventArgs();  // See next section for more on this.
Click(this, e);                 // Raise the event.
```

In each of these examples, you set up the necessary arguments — which differ from event to event; some events need to pass a lot of info along. Then you raise the event by "calling" its name (like invoking a delegate!):

```
eventName(<argumentlist>); // Raising an event. (Distributing the newspaper.)
NewEdition(this, e);
```

Events can be based on different delegates with different signatures, that have different parameters, as the `NewEditionEventHandler` example showed earlier, but providing the `sender` and e parameters is conventional for events. The built-in `EventHandler` and `EventHandler<TEventArgs>` delegate types define them for you.

Passing along a reference to the event's sender (the object that raises the event) is useful if the event handling method needs to get more information from it. Thus a particular `Button` object, `button1`, could pass a reference to the `Form` class the button is a part of. The button's `Click` event handler resides in a `Form` class, so the sender is the form: you'd pass `this`.

Where do you "raise" an event? You can raise it in any method on the publishing class. *When?* Raise it whenever appropriate. I'll have a bit more to say about raising events after the next brief section.

How do I pass extra information to an event handler?

The e parameter to an event handler method is a custom subclass of the System.EventArgs class. You can write your own NewEditionEventArgs class to carry whatever information you need to convey:

```
public class NewEditionEventArgs : EventArgs
{
  public NewEditionEventArgs(DateTime date, string majorHeadline)
  { PubDate = date; Head = majorHeadline; }
  public DateTime PubDate { get; private set; }  // Compiler creates details.
  public string Head { get; private set; }  // See Chapter 12 on Properties.
}
```

You should implement this class's members as properties, as shown in the code above. The constructor uses the private setter clauses on the properties.

Often your event won't require any extra arguments, and you can just fall back on the EventArgs base class, as shown in the next section.

If you don't need a special EventArgs-derived object for your event, just pass:

```
NewEdition(this, EventArgs.Empty);  // Raise the event.
```

A recommended way to raise your events

The section "How do I publish an event?" shows the bare bones of raising an event. However, I'm going to recommend that you always define a special "event raiser" method, like the following:

```
protected virtual void OnNewEdition(NewEditionEventArgs e)
{
  EventHandler<NewEditionEventArgs> temp = NewEdition;
  if(temp != null)
  {
    temp(this, e);
  }
}
```

Providing this method insures that you always remember to do two steps:

1. Store the event into a temporary variable.

This makes your event more usable in situations where multiple "threads" try to use it at the same time — threads divide your program up into a foreground task and one or more background tasks, which run simultaneously (concurrently). I don't cover writing multithreaded programs in this book; just follow this guideline.

2. Check the event for `null` before you try to raise it. If it's `null`, trying to raise it causes an error. Besides, `null` also means that no other objects have shown an interest in your event (none are subscribed), so why bother raising it? *Always* check the event for `null`, regardless of whether you write this On*SomeEvent* method.

Making the method `protected` and `virtual` allows subclasses to override it. That's optional.

Once you have that method, which always takes the same form (making it easy to write quickly) you call the method when you need to raise the event:

```
void SomeMethod()
{
  // Do stuff here ... then:
  NewEditionEventArgs e =
    new NewEditionEventArgs(DateTime.Today, "Peace Breaks Out!");
  OnNewEdition(e);
}
```

How do observers "handle" an event?

The subscribing object specifies the name of a *handler method* when it subscribes — it's the argument to the constructor (boldfaced):

```
button1.Click += new EventHandler<EventArgs>(button1_Click);
```

This is like saying, "Send my paper to this address, please." Here's a handler for our `NewEdition` event:

```
myPublisher.NewEdition += new EventHandler<NewEditionEventArgs>(NewEdHandler);
...
void NewEdHandler(object sender, NewEditionEventArgs e)
{
  // Do something in response to the event.
}
```

For example, a `BankAccount` class could raise a custom `TransactionAlert` event when anything occurs in a `BankAccount` object, such as a deposit, withdrawal, transfer, or even an error. A `Logger` observer object could subscribe and log these events to a file or a database as an audit trail.

When to delegate, when to event, when to go on the lambda

Events. Use events when there may be multiple subscribers or when communicating with client software that uses your classes.

Delegates. Use delegates or anonymous methods when you need a callback or need to customize an operation.

Lambdas. Chapter 16 describes C# 3.0's new *lambda expressions.* In essence, a lambda expression is just a short way to specify the method you're passing to a delegate. You can use lambdas instead of anonymous methods.

When you create a button handler in Visual Studio (by double-clicking the button on your form), Visual Studio generates the subscription code in the `Form1.Designer.cs` file. You shouldn't edit the subscription, but you can delete it and replace it with the same code written in your half of the partial form class. Thereafter the form designer knows nothing about it.

In your subscriber's handler method, you do whatever is supposed to happen when your class learns of this kind of event. To help you write that code, you can cast the `sender` parameter to the type you know it to be:

```
Button theButton = (Button)sender;
```

and then call methods and properties of that object as needed. Because you have a reference to the sending object, you can ask the subscriber questions and carry out operations on it if you need to — like the paper kid knocking on your door to collect the monthly subscription fees. And you can extract information from the e parameter by getting at its properties in the same way:

```
Console.WriteLine(e.HatSize);
```

You won't always need to use the parameters, but they can be handy.

Chapter 16

Mary Had a Little Lambda Expression

In This Chapter

▶ Posing the do-to-each problem

▶ Using the new lambda expressions in C# 3.0

▶ Solving the do-to-each problem

Yes, she did, and it wasn't, "baaa, baaa." C# 3.0 introduces a number of new features, as covered here and there throughout the book. To better prepare for the material in Chapter 17, we need some additional foundation.

The key new feature in this chapter is *lambda expressions*. They're at the heart of the query expressions explained in Chapter 17 — and query expressions are the payoff for nearly all of the new features in C# 3.0.

Collections and the Do-to-Each Problem

A problem that often shows up when you're working with C# collections is something that I call the *do-to-each* problem. (I cover collections in Chapter 5.)

The idea in do-to-each is that you'd like to ask each item in a collection to, for instance, print its name or write an original Haiku poem. Or you'd like to gather information from each item, such as how many of them have blue eyes.

The key phrase here is "ask each item to [do something]."

Sometimes a `foreach` loop is all you need. But that means *you* get to do the hard work yourself, in the loop. Simply telling each object to do the work for you is much more object-oriented. In other words, you'd like to *delegate* the job to the objects themselves. But often the objects can't do your bidding unless you give them some help — that's where this chapter comes in. I'll help you get a handle on lambda expressions, see their usefulness, and start using them yourself.

New Feature: Using Lambda Expressions

I know — the name was Greek to me too, when I first saw it. But it's the easy way to do-to-each — and a lot more.

Yes, "lambda" is the Greek letter λ. The concept comes from mathematical logic and computer science, where it's deep stuff, as you might guess. But we don't care about that here. We'll make it simple. The details are coming, but here's a simple example:

```
n => n > 4
```

That doesn't look so bad, now does it?

The C# way to do-to-each

All C# arrays and `List<T>` collections have several methods that help you solve the do-to-each problem. The two most commonly used are these:

- `Find()` visits each element in the collection, testing the element against a Boolean condition *that you provide*.

- `ForEach()` visits each element in the collection to carry out some custom action *that you provide*.

Now, the question may occur to you: "That *I* provide? How?" Lambdas.

I often call lambda expressions just "lambdas" for short.

In other words, lambda expressions are a way to pass a bit of custom code as an argument to a method such as `Find()` or `ForEach()`. They let you partner with a method to customize it: The method provides the general part of an algorithm — such as iterating a collection — and you provide the code to carry out some custom processing within that algorithm.

If passing bits of code around sounds like a delegate, it is. (If "delegate" isn't making bells go off in your head, circle back to Chapter 15.) In fact, lambdas were invented to simplify working with delegates even further. Think of a lambda as a stripped-down anonymous method if it helps. (Or don't, if it doesn't.)

The `Find()` and `ForEach()` methods on arrays and `List<T>` collections each take a particular kind of delegate. All you really need to know is how many parameters, of what types, each delegate takes, and what its return type is, if any. Then you can write a lambda expression to pass to `Find()` or `ForEach()`.

The `Find()` method on arrays and collections must look more or less like this:

```
static T Find(<yourcustomcode>)
{
  foreach(T item in <thiscollection>)
  {
    if(<yourcustomcode> matches item)
    {
      return item;  // Search stops if item is found.
    }
  }
}
```

`Find()` does the iterating (all of the non-boldfaced code above) and *invokes* the custom code specified by your lambda expression (or delegate).

What about collections other than arrays and `List<T>` — stacks, queues, dictionaries, hash sets, and so on? Because they lack `Find()` and `ForEach()`, your best strategy is to put them into a `List<T>` where you can use those methods. (Chapter 5 explains how to transform one collection into another.) Or simply use a query expression, as described in Chapter 17.

Grist for the mill: Data for the examples

The examples in this chapter are based on the following collections:

```
int[] theInts = { 1, 8, 4, 5, 3, 9 };
List<string> words = new List<string> { "one", "two", "three", "four" };
```

I'll summarize the rules for lambdas after some examples. See the section "Details of lambda syntax."

Looking for answers: Some Find() examples

I'll number the examples in this chapter to make them easier to locate in the example program, `LambdaExamples`, on the Web site.

Example 1. Given the array of integers above, the following call to `Find()` passes a lambda expression as the custom code to use in the `Find()` algorithm:

```
int result = Array.Find(theInts, n => n > 4);  // result is 8.
```

The lambda expression is the boldfaced stuff in the second argument to
`Find()`:`n => n > 4`. The first argument, `theInts`, is the array to search.

Without this very compact lambda, you might have written this longer code:

```
foreach(int n in theInts)
{
  if(n > 4) return n;
}
return -1; // Not found.
```

In Example 1, `Find()` does essentially what that loop does.

Let's break the lambda down to its parts, as shown in Figure 16-1. The lambda
has two segments, separated by the new *lambda operator*, `=>`. As `Find()`
iterates the array:

1. The first segment, n, gets set to each array element in turn.

2. The current value of n is used in the second segment, the Boolean
   expression `n > 4`, just as you'd use it as the condition in an `if`
   statement or `while` loop.

The variable n is a parameter *to the lambda*, and the compiler infers its type
from the expression to the right of the lambda operator.

You can read the lambda operator, `=>`, as "goes to": n goes to `n > 4`.

Don't confuse the lambda operator (`=>`) with greater-or-equal (`>=`).

The first element in `theInts` is 1 — that's the first value of n — which
doesn't match the condition `n > 4`. But the second element, 8, does, so
`Find()` returns 8 — the first match found. (For the definition of `theInts`,
see the section "Grist for the mill: Data for the examples.")

For now, it's enough to say that `Find()` (for arrays) requires two arguments:
the array to search, and a lambda expression with a single parameter and a
Boolean condition.

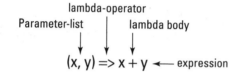

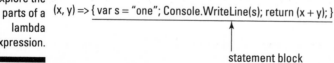

Example 2. The following `Find()` call looks for the first even number in the array:

```
int foundItem = Array.Find(theInts, n => (n % 2) == 0);
```

And again the result is 8, the first even number. The lambda expression is this part: `n => (n % 2) == 0`.

Again, n represents the current element of the array `theInts`. The expression computes the *modulo* of n (the remainder after dividing n by 2, as discussed in Chapter 3). If that equals 0, the expression is true, and n is even. `Find()` visits each element, n, of the collection, testing it against the expression. If a particular element tests true, `Find()` returns that element and stops the search.

Of course, it may seem weird that the second argument to `Find()` takes a parameter of its own, n. Just keep in mind that the lambda is really a method (so of course it can take parameters).

In reality, the `Find()` method on all arrays is defined something like this:

```
public static T Find<T>(T[] array, Predicate<T> match);
```

(`Find()` is a bit different for `List<T>` collections because it's nonstatic there.)

The `<T>` syntax is familiar from collections like `List<T>`, where T defines the type for which the list is being instantiated. `Find<T>()` is actually a *generic method*, which I explain in detail in Bonus Chapter 7 on my Web site at `csharp102.info`, and more briefly in Chapter 17. I'm just saying that `Find()` works on the base type of whatever collection you're calling `Find()` on. In example 1, the array of `int`s that you're searching with `Find()` has the base type of `int`, so you're calling `Find<int>()`.

When you call `Find()`, you don't specify what T is. The compiler infers the type on your behalf, just as when you use the `var` keyword. (See Chapter 2 to find out about `var`.)

Now for the mysterious second parameter to `Find()`. `Predicate<T>`, to put it briefly, defines a delegate that takes a parameter of type T and returns a `bool`. The lambda expressions you've seen so far — `n => n > 4` and `n => (n % 2) == 0` — match that signature: they take an `int` argument and return true or false, so they are equivalent to a method that looks like this:

```
bool SomeMethod(T item);
```

Example 3. The next "predicate lambda expression" queries each word in a `List<string>` of words to see if it starts with the letter *t* or *T*:

```
word => word.ToLower().StartsWith("t")
```

Here `word` is a parameter (the current element in a collection as it is iterated), and the expression after the lambda operator `=>` returns the first word that matches the lambda's requirement.

```
string firstTWord = words.Find(word => word.ToLower().StartsWith("t"));
```

(Note, first, that for `List<T>` collections, `Find()` is an instance method — nonstatic, so you call it differently than you do the array version.)

The result of calling `Find()` on the `words` list I introduced earlier is the word "two," which I store in `firstTWord`. Note that I converted the input word to lowercase before applying the Boolean test, to avoid case problems in the comparison. That kind of manipulation is perfectly legal in lambda expressions.

Examples 4, 5, and 6. Here are a few more examples, which I explain further in the `LambdaExamples` program comments on the Web site:

```
n => true                // 4. What's the first number in the collection?
word => word.Length > 4  // 5. What's the first word longer than 4 characters?
word => word.Contains("r") // 6. What's the first word that contains an 'r'?
```

For Example 4, the lambda means, "Match any n," so the first n matches.

If you find these expressions hard to read, try putting parentheses around the expression to the right of the `=>` operator:

```
n => ((n % 2) == 0) // n 'goes to' the expression in outer parentheses.
```

Extra Examples 1–5. I've only shown you the `Find()` method, but other methods, such as `Exists()`, `RemoveAll()`, and `TrueForAll()` can be pretty powerful. Check them out in the `List<T>` Help, and see Extra Examples 1 through 5 in the `LambdaExamples` program on the Web site.

Taking action: Some ForEach () examples

An *action* differs from the Boolean lambda expressions used for `Find()`. It *does something*, often something that alters the value it's operating on.

The `ForEach()` method used to carry out an action on each element of an array is static and looks something like the boldfaced line below; the second line shows an example of using it:

```
public static void ForEach<T>(T[] array, Action<T> action);
Array.ForEach(theInts, <someactionhere>);  // An example call.
```

and for `List<T>` is an instance method that looks like the boldfaced line below, with an example call below that:

```
public void ForEach<T> (Action<T> action);
words.ForEach(<someactionhere>);          // An example call.
```

Notice that the form of the call is different for arrays and List<T> collections, as it was for Find().

ForEach() is the only action method on collections. For the action parameter, you'll pass a delegate instance — or just a lambda!

Action<T> is another delegate, which requires one parameter, of type T, and has a void return type. Thus any method that looks like this can be attached to the Action<T> delegate:

```
void SomeMethod(T item);
```

Fortunately, both delegates described in this chapter — Predicate<T> and Action<T> — are defined by .NET, in the System namespace, so you can just use them.

Example 7. Your first action lambda calls a method to write out the result of a calculation involving the lambda's parameter n. The value printed is the square of n. To make the results viewable, I've put the calculation (boldfaced) inside a call to Console.Write(), which is also part of the action lambda:

```
n => Console.Write("{0}", n * n)   // n goes to whole expression on right.
```

You call ForEach() on a array of integers, for example:

```
Array.ForEach(theInts, n => Console.Write("{0}, ", n * n));
```

ForEach() visits each element in the list and passes the current element, n, to the lambda, which executes its action, here the Console.Write() statement that wraps the boldfaced squaring calculation. (The Write() call is just there in the example to provide some visible output — you don't always need a Write() or WriteLine().) The result is a printed list of the squares of the array's elements, all on the same line (with a trailing comma), like this:

```
1, 64, 16, 25, 9, 81,
```

Note that the action delegate, like the Find() predicate, takes only one parameter.

This ForEach() method is not the same as the foreach loop keyword, although both iterate a collection. It's as if ForEach() is a way to put the foreach loop inside the list and let the list use it, instead of this standard loop approach:

```
foreach(int n in theInts)
{
    Console.Write("{0}", n * n);
}
```

Example 8. The next action lambda calls a custom method, `NumberAfter-MeIs()`, that prints a number one greater than its parameter value. The expression prints out the number following each n (that is, `n + 1`):

```
n => { NumberAfterMeIs(n); }   // n goes to a method-call statement in { }.
```

where `NumberAfterMeIs()` is a method that contains a `Write()` or `WriteLine()` statement that writes `n + 1`.

Action lambdas can call methods and do other action-type things, *except* return a value, since `Action<T>` defines a `void` method signature.

Example 9. The final action lambda example that I'll discuss in detail is more complex. It contains two C# statements, each ending with a semicolon as usual. The first statement declares a local variable called s (local to the lambda — lambdas are methods); s is the lambda's input parameter n converted to `String`. The second statement writes s to the console. This is pretty contrived, but the point is that you can declare local variables and have multiple statements in a lambda expression.

```
n => { var s = n.ToString(); Console.WriteLine(s); }
```

I happened to use `var` as the type of s, but you could use `string` instead.

Because the lambda consists of two statements, I have to enclose it in curly braces, as I also did in Example 8 with `NumberAfterMeIs()`. However, the braces aren't mandatory in the `NumberAfterMeIs()` example — a single statement — as they are in the two-statement lambda.

When writing complicated statements that have lots of pairs of parentheses and braces, always write both items of the pair, then fill in the stuff between.

Examples 10 and 11. Here are a few more examples of lambdas you could use in a `ForEach()` call:

```
// 10. Write out each word with "flip" appended to its end.
words.ForEach(word => Console.WriteLine(String.Concat(word, "flip")));
// 11. Put each word's length into another list.
List<int> wordLengths = new List<int>();
words.ForEach(word => wordLengths.Add(word.Length));
```

Where the first example just writes out its results, the second one relies on the existence of a `List<int>` variable in the calling method *outside the lambda*, which it uses to store each word length. I'll have more to say about using local variables in the section "Details of lambda syntax."

Extra Example 6 on the Web site is a multi-statement lambda that uses `ForEach()` to write a list of the strings in the `words` list along with their lengths.

A lambda based on a custom delegate

Okay, the plot thickens a bit. (I can hear you muttering, "As if it wasn't thick enough already.")

Example 12. Instead of another lambda based on the `Predicate<T>` or `Action<T>` types, the final examples in this section are based on a different delegate type, one that I wrote myself. This delegate takes two integer parameters, returns an integer, and looks like this:

```
delegate int HandleTwo(int n, int m);  // See Chapter 15 on delegates.
```

And the lambda I'll use looks like this:

```
(n, m) => n * m
```

In this case, there are two parameters to the lambda (as to the delegate), enclosed in parentheses. How does this lambda "return an `int`," as required by the delegate signature? I'll get to that in a moment. Now, suppose you have a workhorse method called `Multiply()` that takes two `int` parameters and a `HandleTwo` delegate parameter:

```
// Multiply two numbers by passing them to a delegate, proc, using a lambda.
// Multiply lets you customize it by passing different lambdas as the proc.
int Multiply(int x, int y, HandleTwo proc)
{
  if(proc != null)       // Always make sure the proc has a value.
  {
    return proc(x, y);   // Invoke proc with the parameters.
  }
  return -1;
}
```

You can call `Multiply()` like this, using the lambda for the delegate parameter:

```
int result = Multiply(2, 3, (n, m) => n * m);  // result is 6.
```

This works because the lambda matches the types and number of parameters to the `HandleTwo` delegate. Weird looking, I know, but this is how you often use delegates — and lambdas. And this is much like how `Find()` and `ForEach()` work. So `result` ends up with the value 6. In this example, you see the delegate being invoked inside the `Multiply()` method. Instead of do-to-each, this is just "do."

As for how the lambda returns an `int` value, note that an `int` times an `int` is an `int` and recall that (a) *expressions* aren't statements, and (b) expressions always return a value, as in the assignment `int x = 1 + 2;`, where the expression `1 + 2` returns the value 3, which is assigned to `x`. (Some *statements*, such as `return`, can also return a value.)

Example 13. To get really weird, I'll use `Multiply()` in a sneaky, underhanded way to *add* the two numbers — don't try this at home:

```
int result = Multiply(2, 3, (n, m) => n + m);  // result is 5.
```

Using a `Multiply()` method for addition is legal here, but is it ethical? Well, it's not *advisable* because it's confusing. But maybe you can see the potential here for writing some very general-purpose methods using delegates and lambdas. Rename `Multiply()` to, say, `DoBinaryOperation()`, and you've got a general method. Kind of overkill in this example, but it has many applications.

Summary of the examples

To summarize the past three sections, I've shown you several examples of passing a lambda to a workhorse method.

For the first set of examples, the method took a `Predicate<T>` delegate as a parameter and was designed to apply a Boolean condition to each element of a collection. For the second set, the workhorse method took an `Action<T>` parameter instead — and was designed to carry out an action on each element of a collection. And the final example called a workhorse that took my own custom `HandleTwo` delegate as a parameter and was designed to carry out a single action via the delegate. No collection involved. In each of the examples, I passed a lambda expression to the delegate-type parameter.

Although this is only a taste of what's possible, you should have enough now to experiment with writing your own lambda expressions for either of the two types of do-to-each solutions for collections: predicate (Boolean) or action. The syntax details in the next section and the numerous examples on the Web site will help, too. And in Chapter 17, you'll see lots of lambdas used in a similar context: writing query expressions in C#. You'll be counting lambdas in your sleep.

Details of lambda syntax

A *lambda expression* consists of a parameter list, possibly empty, and a lambda body, either a single expression or a block of statements.

Lambda parameters

Lambda parameter lists can include zero or more parameters (but no `ref` or `out` parameters):

- Zero parameters — empty parentheses are required:

```
() => <body>
```

- One parameter — parentheses are optional:

```
(name) => <body>  // Or ...
name => <body>
```

- Multiple parameters — parentheses are required:

```
(i, j, k) => <body>
```

Parameters to lambdas can specify their types, or just let C# infer them:

```
string name => name == "Rex"  // Or ...
name => name == "Rex"          // Compiler infers that name is a string.
cust => cust.Name.StartsWith("C");
```

In the third line, the compiler can probably infer that `cust` is a `Customer` object from the surrounding context, including what gets passed as the lambda argument.

If you opt to let C# infer types, *don't* precede the parameter with `var`. (But you can use `var` inside the lambda body, as in Example 9 earlier.) It's possible that the compiler won't be able to infer the types, in which case you'll have to supply them explicitly, as shown in the first line above (although it's unnecessary in that line).

The return type and the number of parameters, and their types, order, and modifying keywords, must conform to those features of a delegate declared somewhere, either by you or predefined by C#. This is called the delegate's *signature*. (See Chapter 15 for the dope on delegates.)

Lambda body: Expressions and blocks

The body of a lambda expression can be either an *expression* or a *block*.

- An *expression lambda* has a single expression without surrounding curly braces as in most of the examples you've seen so far. Any legal C# expression works on the right side. An expression always evaluates to a value. (Chapter 3 discusses expressions and statements.)

- In a *statement lambda*, the block on the right side consists of a pair of curly braces { } which can contain one or more C# *statements*, each ending with a semicolon as usual. (Typically, you'll use no more than three or four statements — try to keep your lambdas small.)

You can call methods in both expression lambdas and statement lambdas:

```
// Expression lambda form:
numbers.ForEach(n =>  Console.WriteLine(NumberAfterMeIs(n).ToString()) );
// Statement lambda (block) form:
numbers.ForEach(n => { string s = n.ToString(); Console.WriteLine(s); } );
```

The block defines a local scope for its variables, as covered in Chapter 4.

Local variables

You can declare local variables in blocks (but not expressions), as with the declaration of the string s just shown.

Lambdas also have access to any local variables defined in the calling method outside the lambda (called *outer* variables). In the following, x can be used inside the lambda:

```
int x = 4; // An outer variable, defined outside the lambda.
int result = numbers.Find(n => n < x);   // Uses x inside the lambda.
```

Outer variables — also referred to as *captured* variables — may stick around until the underlying delegate gets garbage-collected.

Variables local to the lambda, including its parameters, aren't accessible outside of the lambda, as with n in this code:

```
int result = numbers.Find(n => n + 1);
int y = n;                               // n is not defined here.
```

"Jump" statements

A block can include a return statement if the delegate on which you've based the lambda has a return type (which isn't the case with Action<T>, whose return type is void). The return statement needs to be inside a statement block with curly braces.

The break, continue, and goto statements work only if they're inside a loop or switch statement within the lambda. In other words, the target of the jump — where it jumps to — must be inside the lambda block. You also can't jump into a lambda from outside.

For more details, look up "lambda expressions" in Help.

In Chapter 17, you'll really put lambda expressions — and most of the other new C# features — to work in query expressions.

Using Lambda Expressions for Any Delegate

C# 2.0's anonymous methods, covered in Chapter 15, were an improvement over using "raw" delegates, but C# 3.0's lambdas are often even better. Almost anywhere you can use a raw delegate or an anonymous method, you can use a lambda expression instead. This greatly simplifies the process of writing delegate calls.

When a method you're calling takes a delegate argument, you can pass any of the three ways to write a delegate, including a lambda:

```
delegate int MyDelegate(string name);  // Here's the delegate definition.
...
void MyMethod(MyDelegate del) ...       // As with the Multiply() method.
...
// Call MyMethod, passing in a lambda expression for the delegate argument:
MyMethod((aString) => { return aString.Length });
```

That call takes a `string` argument, as dictated by the delegate, and returns an `int` value, in this case the length of the string passed in. When `MyMethod()` invokes the delegate, passing it some string, the delegate call will return that string's length.

Chapter 17

LINQing Up with Query Expressions

*N*ow it's time to blend all the new features described in earlier chapters — and a few more — into the larger structure that is their reason for being. In this chapter, I show you an exciting new way to work with your objects and collections — in fact, with any source of data.

The capabilities you're about to meet are courtesy of the new Language Integrated Query (LINQ) functionality embedded in the .NET Framework, version 3.5. LINQ is ready for C#, Visual Basic .NET, or some other .NET language to build on; C# and VB already have.

LINQ is going to change the way you write C# code and the look of the code you see in programming examples on the Web, in books like this one, and elsewhere.

C# builds on LINQ through a set of new language keywords and the new C# 3.0 features you've already met throughout the book.

You can get a quicker grasp of LINQ if I do a fast recap of the features already covered here and there, so that's coming up. Then we can get on with LINQ.

Reviewing the C# 3.0 Features

Table 17-1 names each feature that I've already introduced in earlier chapters, briefly describes it, and points to the chapter where you'll find more details on it. All of these features have uses in LINQ queries.

Table 17-1	New C# 3.0 Feature Summary	
Feature	*Description*	*Chapter*
The `var` keyword	Lets the compiler take on the chore of *inferring* a variable's type by examining the variable's initializer.	2
Type inference for arrays	Lets the compiler infer array types, as with the `var` keyword.	5
Collection initializers	Provides a compact syntax for initializing collections such as `List<string>`.	5
Extension methods	Lets you add convenience methods to an existing class.	9
Object initializers	Allows compact initialization of class objects.	12
Lambda expressions	Lets you pass around chunks of code as objects.	16

This chapter covers the following two new features:

- **Anonymous types**. You can create instances of nameless objects — invented on the fly as you need them and then discarded like Aunt Phyllis's Christmas fruitcake.

- **Query expressions**. You've probably heard of a database language called Structured Query Language (SQL). Now you can write SQL-style "queries" about almost any sort of data, not just databases — including Extended Markup Language (XML) and C# collections. The query syntax is built right into C#. Most of this chapter is about showing you how to query. Any questions?

What's a Query, and Why Should I Care?

In database programming, a *query* is a request for information. With C#, however, you can query much more than just databases.

Generations of database programmers have accessed data stored in relational databases such as Oracle or SQL Server by issuing commands in the form of queries written in Structured Query Language (SQL). Although this chapter doesn't cover database programming with LINQ — or any other form of database programming — a basic understanding of the queries performed to pull data out of a database will be a spoonful of sugar here. That's because queries are the essence of LINQ, regardless of which data source you query.

Figure 17-1 shows what a typical simple SQL query looks like and how it relates to a table in a database, while Figure 17-2 gives a schematic view of a database table and its parts.

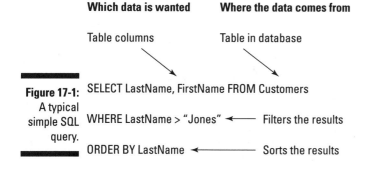

Which data is wanted   Where the data comes from

Table columns   Table in database

Figure 17-1: A typical simple SQL query.

SELECT LastName, FirstName FROM Customers

WHERE LastName > "Jones" ←—— Filters the results

ORDER BY LastName ←—————— Sorts the results

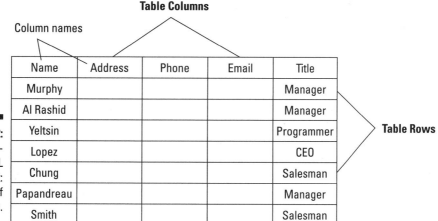

Table Columns

Column names

Name	Address	Phone	Email	Title
Murphy				Manager
Al Rashid				Manager
Yeltsin				Programmer
Lopez				CEO
Chung				Salesman
Papandreau				Manager
Smith				Salesman

Table Rows

Figure 17-2: Understanding the SQL statement: The parts of a table.

Employees ——— Table name

Formerly, database programmers had to encode the SQL query as a string, which the .NET database classes could send to the database. That was error-prone, though; the compiler couldn't check the query's syntax or check whether the requested tables and columns even existed in the database. Not only that, you had no Visual Studio Intellisense to guide you in writing a sensible query, and the resulting code could be hard to debug.

If you'd like to learn more about SQL, check out *SQL For Dummies* by Allen G. Taylor. Richard Mansfield's *Visual Basic .NET Database Programming For Dummies* gets into all of that database stuff. *XML For Dummies*, by Lucinda Dykes and Ed Tittel, gets you started with XML.

At a more general level, the idea of a query is to select and retrieve items from a collection of things (rows in a table, integers in an array). Besides selecting the items, a query can request that it be sorted, grouped, and otherwise organized and presented — even in some transformed shape. (You'll see what that means when I take you through some LINQ queries.)

Why is "language-integrated" query important?

Data comes in a variety of forms, from a variety of sources. In the past, you had to write completely different kinds of code, in multiple languages, to work with those forms. Now LINQ lets you write very similar code for all forms of data — all in C# or VB. That's big.

The general form of a C# query

The general model for querying any kind of data with the new C# query expressions goes like this:

1. **Get the data.** Get the data into a collection somehow. This part varies with the data source. Sometimes you go more directly to the source.

2. **Set up the query.** Use query syntax to specify how you want the data filtered, sorted, grouped, summed, averaged, and selected — the list of things you can do is much longer, something like 50 different *operators*, some of them represented by new C# keywords, some just by methods.

3. **Evaluate the query.** Trigger evaluation of the query, usually with a `foreach` loop. By default, LINQ queries use *deferred execution*, meaning that just writing the query syntax isn't the whole story. You still have to kick off the evaluation, usually by iterating the query results in a `foreach` loop. LINQ obtains query results as the loop executes.

Other LINQ functions

If you're an experienced .NET database programmer, you may be interested in exploring these LINQ capabilities:

✔ **DLINQ — querying databases.** You use DLINQ to query relational databases like Microsoft SQL Server.

Microsoft now calls DLINQ LINQ to ADO.NET or LINQ to SQL, but let's face it: Most coders will use the earlier code name DLINQ.

You can access data directly in the database through a LINQ to SQL data provider that manages communication with the database. Using the LINQ to DataSets provider, you can also work with data already pulled out of the database (into a `DataSet` object). LINQ also works with the new and improved ADO.NET, Microsoft's database technology. Look up "LINQ to Entities" in Help.

✔ **XLINQ — querying Extensible Markup Language (XML).** You use XLINQ, now called LINQ to XML, to query data stored not in databases but in files encoded as XML. You get XPath/XQuery capabilities in C#, and it's more natural than working with the W3C Document Object Model (Google it for details). The XML can come from files, from streams of XML text downloaded from a Web service, hard-coded as a string in your code, and so on.

✔ **PLINQ — LINQ queries that take advantage of a computer with multiple processors** (or a single processor with multiple "cores").

PLINQ, or "Parallel LINQ," is still a bit over the horizon, not yet available, but it will speed queries and help you keep up with the capabilities of better and better hardware. Search Microsoft's Web site for "PLINQ."

LINQ from low Earth orbit

Initially, LINQ actually has three major flavors, depending on the sources of the data you query. You can query any kind of data for which a *data provider* exists. Currently, that's *C# collections, relational databases,* and *XML.*

This chapter covers the *LINQ to Objects* feature. With LINQ to Objects, you can query

> ✔ C# arrays and collections (and they don't necessarily have anything to do with databases or XML)
>
> ✔ Ordinary classes, such as `String` or `Int32`

In this chapter, I show examples of querying against collections and against single objects.

LINQ has other capabilities, but they're beyond the scope of this book. The sidebar "Other LINQ functions" is a summary.

With LINQ to Objects you can pretty much slice, dice, fricassee, and sauté collections of data any way you need to. (You can also think of an object — an instance of a class — *as a collection* of methods, properties, data members, and so on.) That's the rest of this chapter.

With LINQ to Objects under your belt, you'll be well prepared to tackle DLINQ and XLINQ when you're ready. But I'll have to leave those to other books.

Querying in C# 3.0

Take a look at the following *query expression* in C#. What does it query? Not a database, no, just a simple old C# array. You can see the array's definition in the first line. But what's the rest of that stuff (in boldface)?

```
// Example 0.
int[] numbers = {5, 7, 1, 4, 9, 3, 0, 2, 6, 8};
var smallnumbers = from n in numbers
                    where n <= 3
                    orderby n
                    select n;
foreach(var n in smallnumbers)
{ Console.WriteLine("\t{0}", n); }
```

I've numbered the examples in this chapter (here the number's in the first line of code; for the later ones it's in the heading) to help you pinpoint the code for each example in the QueryExamples1 program on the Web site. Like a good C# dude, I've started the numbering from 0, in the example just given.

The output of this query is the "small" numbers from the following array:

```
0
1
2
3
```

You've met the var keyword before, in Chapter 2. So the preceding example has a variable called smallnumbers, whose data type is specified as var. That variable will contain the finished query results. Under the hood, it's really a "sequence" of ints, which the compiler deduces from the rest of the query statement.

But these lines are something new:

```
from n in numbers    // Turn the array into a "queryable sequence."
where n <= 3         // Filter out unwanted items.
orderby n            // Sort the items remaining.
select n;            // Make a final selection to return.
```

Some of the keywords here will seem familiar from the SQL example in Figure 17-1 earlier in the chapter: `from`, `where`, `orderby`, and `select`. Only a few differences separate the two: The keywords in the C# example are more or less backwards from those in the SQL query, and C# makes SQL's `ORDER BY` just `orderby`. Notice that the new C# keywords are all in lowercase letters — and recall that C# is case-sensitive.

But the C# query isn't a database query; it just queries an ordinary array. The query bases its work on the contents of the `numbers` array. That's the `from` keyword, which is called a *generator* because it generates a sequence of items for the other keywords to work on. A *sequence* is a special breed of cat.

The three most important query operators

As I said earlier, C# has some 50 operators that let you do a great many things with your queries.

Seven operators are represented by keywords: `where`, `select`, `group`, `into`, `orderby`, `join`, and `let`. The remaining operators are available as methods only. For the time being, I focus on the keywords first and cover the method-only items later in the chapter. The `from` keyword doesn't query — it just generates a sequence that you can query against.

But three keywords carry most of the freight:

- ✔ `where`
- ✔ `orderby`
- ✔ `select`

To kick off each query, the `from` keyword generates an *iterable sequence* that the rest of the query uses to scan through the array's items. Each keyword in turn also returns an iterable sequence. It's that final sequence that you use in a `foreach` loop. Iterable sequences are home to the methods underlying the query operators and keywords. In essence, an iterable sequence boils down to an `IEnumerable<T>` interface reference. Chapter 14 covers interfaces.

Then, in the next lines, you see the three primary keywords at work:

1. **Filtering with** `where`. With `where`, the query filters the array's contents, making a sequence of only the elements that match the Boolean *filter expression*, `n <= 3`. It tests each item against the filter.

    Think of filtering as picking out the peas on your plate so you can enjoy the rest of what's there. The fancy name for filtering is *restriction*.

2. **Sorting with** `orderby`. The query passes the filtered results to the `orderby` clause, which sorts the values in ascending numerical order, the default. You can also sort in descending order with `orderby descending`:

```
orderby n descending
```

For strings, an ascending sort is in alphabetical order; for numbers, it's from smallest to largest. For more complicated objects, the order depends on what about the objects is sortable (for example, in Chapter 14 you made a list of `Student` objects sortable by grade point). Descending order is the opposite: reverse alphabetical order, largest number to smallest, and so on. You can also easily reverse the order of the items.

3. **Selecting with** `select`. In the last line, the query picks out the values it wants — in this case, all the filtered, sorted items. The `select` keyword can do more, however, as you'll see. In particular, it can carry out *projections* on the input it gets, to alter the output (sometimes unrecognizably).

A projection transforms its input sequence from one thing to something else. You can call it a *transformation* if you like.

Think of projection as taking the stuff returned by the rest of the query (chicken nuggets, say) and transforming them into something else to return (healthy fruit and nuts, yum).

Other things you can do to slice and dice your collections include these:

- ✔ **Grouping.** You can group your query results in various ways. For example, you might group customers by region or by order size all customers in the New England states, those on the eastern seaboard, and so on.

- ✔ **Counting**, **summing**, or **averaging.** Carry out "aggregations" on the items in the collection.

- ✔ **Doing mathematical set operations.** For two collections, you can obtain the union or intersection, eliminate duplicate items, and so on.

- ✔ **Grabbing or skipping this or that.** Take the first or last n items, say.

- ✔ **Converting your selected sequence to a collection.** An array, a `List<T>`, or a `Dictionary<T,U>`, for some types `T` and `U`.

In short, you now have a completely different — and very powerful — way to select, sort, filter, and otherwise manipulate data in C#'s arrays and collections.

Before C# 3.0, you might carry out an operation similar to the preceding query like this, using older C# mechanisms:

```
List<int> results = new List<int>();
for (int i = 0; i < numbers.Length; i++)
{
  if(numbers[i] <= 3)
    results.Add(numbers[i]);
}
results.Sort();
```

This looks comfortingly familiar to non-database coders. But it requires a list declaration, a loop, some comparisons, and then a final sort. Half a dozen statements — and they're the sort of thing you might write over and over, *ad nauseam*. But the more complex the operations you need to perform, the more code it takes. Reducing that drudgery is where queries can really shine. Instead of spelling out every little action to take, as in the preceding old-style code, a query says *what* you want, not *how* to do it.

In contrast with the traditional-style code, the SQL-style query expression is really just one C# statement. Once you get used to writing such queries, and familiar with the most personally useful of the 50-or-so operators, you can do much more sophisticated operations more concisely.

Fifty-odd query operators? Relax. You can stick to just a subset if you want, and gradually increase your repertoire. And not *all* of them are odd.

What is deferred query execution?

The query doesn't actually execute until you iterate the resulting sequence, usually with a `foreach` loop.

Each pass through the `foreach` loop evaluates the next item in the query's results — a just-in-time approach. Running the whole `foreach` loop evaluates the query completely.

Step through a query expression in the debugger to see how it works.

What does "evaluate" mean? It means, for example, that the query doesn't really access the database (if you're querying one) until you get into that `foreach` loop. Until then, the query is just sitting there dolled up for the ball, but without a guy wearing a boutonniere in sight. Finally, Prince Charming shows up with a `foreach` and a corsage, and it's off to the spiked punch bowl.

Under the hood, each query operator is based on a `yield return` statement, which is why the execution is deferred. I cover *iterators* and `yield return` in Bonus Chapter 8 on my Web site at `csharp102.info`; I'll say more about how query operators are implemented later in this chapter.

Evaluating a query immediately

TIP

It's possible to evaluate the query *pronto*, as in immediately, by converting it into an array or a list with the query language's ToArray(), ToList(), and ToDictionary() methods and others. No waiting for Mr. Right. We're talking Mr. Right Now. Sometimes that's what you need. Otherwise deferring evaluation until the last minute is the best default strategy.

Here's what that evaluate-it-right-now code might look like:

```
var results = from p in products
              where p.Name == "Widget"
              select p;
var list = results.ToList<Product>(); // Grab everything now!
. . .
foreach (var product in list)        // Iterate results at your leisure.
{
   Console.WriteLine(product.Name);
}
```

After the query, I call ToList<Product>() on the query results, which converts the results to a List<Product>. ToList() is a generic method ready to handle Products and only Products. (I explain generic methods in the section "End of detour — All aboard!" later in the chapter and in more detail in Bonus Chapter 7 on my Web site at csharp102.info.)

What Can I Do with a Query?

Queries are great for answering questions/fulfilling requests such as these:

- ✔ I want just the .TXT files in directory D.
- ✔ Which customers live in Colorado?
- ✔ Which products are currently out of stock?
- ✔ What's the total cost of order *n* for customer C?
- ✔ How about the average cost of the order's items?
- ✔ Order these strings by their lengths — longest first, and then alphabetically within length groups.
- ✔ Who are the three worst-performing salesmen?
- ✔ Give me just the first character of each of these strings.
- ✔ Give me a list of all students with a grade-point average over 3.0, alphabetized by grade point, and show me name and GPA only.

The rest of this chapter takes you through the basic query operations (with examples that handle questions like the preceding ones) — namely, these:

- ✔ Filtering
- ✔ Selecting and Grouping
- ✔ Ordering (sorting)
- ✔ Querying with the underlying methods instead of keywords
- ✔ Counting, summing, averaging

For each topic, I give you several examples. Along the way, I introduce at least one more new C# query feature: *anonymous types*.

You can look at the code for this chapter's examples in `QueryExamples1` and `QueryExamples2` on the Web site. For more examples, Google for "101 LINQ samples."

Filtering Out the Espresso Grounds

I love the smell of espresso in the morning, but I don't like coffee full of gritty little coffee grounds. I want mine filtered, please. The `where` keyword lets you filter a target collection for all sorts of criteria. It's all in how you write the filter expression.

A *filter expression* is just an ordinary Boolean condition like the ones you've been writing for `if` statements and `while` loops. By the way, under the hood these expressions are lambda expressions (like those covered in Chapter 16). But in query syntax, you write them as ordinary conditions.

Note: Example 0 is the first query example I showed you earlier, in the "Querying in C# 3.0" section.

Example 1: Which customers live in Colorado?

Given a list of customers, perhaps drawn from a database or an XML file earlier in the code (which I don't show here), pick out just those customers based in Colorado — in other words, filter the query by state, like this:

```
var customers = new List<Customer> {   // Get some customers.
      new Customer { Name = "Chandler", State = "OR", Phone = "555-555-5555"
            },
      new Customer { Name = "Monica", State = "CO", Phone = "555-666-6666" },
```

```
        new Customer { Name = "Joey", State = "CO", Phone = "555-777-7777" },
        new Customer { Name = "Ross", State = "NY", Phone = "555-000-0000" },
        new Customer { Name = "Phoebe", State = "NY", Phone = "555-111-1111" },
        new Customer { Name = "Rachel", State = "NJ", Phone = "555-222-2222" }
};
// Filter out any customers not from Colorado ("CO").
var coloradoCustomers = from c in customers
                        where c.State == "CO"
                        select c;
foreach(var cust in coloradoCustomers)
{
  Console.WriteLine("{0} - {1}", cust.Name, cust.State);
}
```

Here's the play-by-play: First, I used the new object-initialization syntax from Chapter 11 to add some new `Customer` objects to a list. Then I queried the list with a filter that compares each customer's `State` property with the abbreviation string `"CO"`. The result, stored in `coloradoCustomers`, is a list of the selected customers. When you print the customer information in a `foreach` loop, you get the following unordered output:

```
Monica - CO
Joey - CO
```

Notice that this query was against a `List<Customer>` collection, not an array. Because both `List<Customer>` and `Array` get their query operators by implementing the `IEnumerable<T>` interface, you can query both. I'll say more about that `IEnumerable<T>` stuff with respect to queries later in the chapter. (You encountered `IEnumerable<T>` back in Chapter 14.)

Similar queries that are mostly about filtering might include these:

- Filtering a list of files for those with a specific extension, such as `.TXT`:

  ```
  var txtFiles = from f in files where f.Extension.ToLower() == ".txt" select f;
  ```

- Finding out which products in inventory are currently out of stock:

  ```
  var productsOutOfStock = from p in products where p.OnHand < 1 select p;
  ```

- Listing all students with a grade point average over 3.0:

  ```
  var topStudents = from s in students where s.GPA > 3.0 select s;
  ```

  You might also rank them by grade point, alphabetized for each grade-point level. And suppose you want to show name and GPA only. You can do all of those things with the query operators covered in this chapter.

See the preceding examples in the `QueryExamples2` program on the Web site.

So far, most of the queries have based their filters on properties of the objects they're filtering: `Extension`, `State`, `OnHand`. That's not entirely necessary, as shown by example 0 in the section "Querying in C# 3.0" The filter can be on just the value of the object: `where n <= 3`. It can also be a compound Boolean condition: `where s.GPA > 3.0 && s.GPA < 2.0`.

A `where` clause isn't mandatory in your query. If you don't need filtering, you can skip it. You'll see examples later that use just `from` and `select`, in which the query result selects all objects from the input, but may modify them or pluck out just a few of their properties.

The order of your query clauses does matters. First you need `from` (always, if you're using the keyword approach, but not if you use the method approach discussed later in the chapter). Next, do your filtering (`where`), sorting (`orderby`), and grouping (`group by`). The order among those can vary, depending on what you want to accomplish. Finally, you need `select`, although in some queries you can finish up with `group by` and no `select`.

Selecting and Grouping What You Want

The examples in the previous section emphasize filtering. Those in this section emphasize using `select` and `group by` to affect exactly what gets returned from the query and how it might be transformed.

You don't *have* to transform the selections. Examples 0 – 2 don't. They simply select every item remaining after filtering:

```
select c;   // Where c is the current customer being selected.
```

As you've seen in the early examples in the chapter, you can use the `select` keyword to return a subset (filtered or not) of the original input items. For example, the input is integers, and the output is a subset of those same integers. Or the input is `Products` and the output is `Products`.

But as I hinted earlier, `select` (and its relative, `group by`) can also perform *projections* on the input data: transforming the input into something else, possibly even a different type of object all together. The new anonymous types come in handy here. I'll explain those when we get there.

Example 2: Give me a sequence of integers two higher than the inputs

Here's a query with a simple projection performed by `select`:

```
var outputs = from i in numbers select i + 2;   // OK to put it all on one line.
int k = 0;
foreach(int n in outputs)
{
  Console.WriteLine("\t{0} --> {1}", inputs[k], n);
  k++;
}
```

The output is:

```
0 --> 2
1 --> 3
// ... a few lines skipped; you see the pattern.
9 --> 11
```

This query does no filtering, so it doesn't eliminate any of the input numbers. Instead, it uses `select` to perform a very simple projection that transforms each `int` into one that's two greater than itself, so that `i` becomes `i + 2`.

Example 3: I want just the name and phone number for each customer

Given a list of customers, select all of them. But do a transformation that captures just the names and phone numbers, skipping everything else about them. This is a more complex projection, as it uses *anonymous types*.

This example uses the `customers` list from Example 2:

```
var namesAndNumbers = from c in customers
                      orderby c.Name
                      select new { Name = c.Name, PhoneNumber = c.Phone };
foreach(var cust in namesAndNumbers)
{
  Console.WriteLine("\t{0} - {1}", cust.Name.PadRight(10),
        cust.PhoneNumber);
}
```

The output is

```
Chandler  - 555-555-5555
Joey      - 555-777-7777
Monica    - 555-666-6666
Phoebe    - 555-111-1111
Rachel    - 555-222-2222
Ross      - 555-000-0000
```

I introduced the `PadRight()` method of class `String` in Chapter 6.

What's key here is the `select` statement. What's that boldfaced thing following `select`? It's an anonymous type. See the next section for the lowdown.

Using anonymous types

The `select` clause in Example 3 creates an *anonymous object* for the desired chunks of information, one object per customer:

```
select new { Name = c.Name, PhoneNumber = c.Phone };
```

Several questions may be nagging at you here:

- ✔ Why doesn't a class name follow the `new` keyword? These are anonymous — nameless — objects you're creating.

- ✔ Where is the class for these objects defined? Right on the spot, using the new object-initialization syntax discussed in Chapter 11. The `select` clause just creates a no-name object for each customer it selects.

- ✔ Where are the methods and properties of these anonymous classes defined? Also right on the spot. Each object has a `Name` property and a `PhoneNumber` property. And that's all it has — no other properties, no methods, nada, nothing, nil. You specify the properties just by naming and initializing them, right there in the `new` call.

- ✔ Uh, why doesn't the name of the anonymous class's `PhoneNumber` property match the name of the `Phone` property on the `Customer` class? I chose a more descriptive name for it in the anonymous objects. Notice that each new property on the anonymous objects *must* be initialized on the spot. In this case, I did so by plucking out the appropriate properties of the current `Customer` object being selected and assigning them to properties on the anonymous object.

- ✔ How many such anonymous objects are created here? One per `Customer` in the original list. That is, six.

- ✔ Are the two classes shown — for `Customer Chandler` and for `Customer Phoebe` — the same class? Yes. The compiler observes that each one has the same properties, and creates just one anonymous class definition, shared among all anonymous classes that fit that model.

In case you're wondering, what's going on here is a bit of C# compiler abracadabra. When the compiler sees the preceding anonymous class syntax, it creates a class somewhere in hyperspace. This class, which you never see (unless you really go digging with the `Ildasm.exe` tool or Lutz Roeder's nifty tool called Reflector), is outside of your code's universe. You can't refer to it at all in code. You never need to.

In very sketchy form, here's what that class looks like:

```
public sealed class ___Anonymous1    // Or some such name.
{
  public string Name { ... }
  public string PhoneNumber { ... }
}
```

It has a few other ingredients beyond what I've shown, such as a default constructor, overrides of class `Object`'s `Equals()`, `GetHashCode()`, and `ToString()` methods, and instance variables representing the underlying state of the properties. But you don't have to care, because you just work with the anonymous type syntax shown in the preceding example.

The `var` keyword on the `namesAndNumbers` declaration is essential in this example. You can't possibly declare a specific type in this situation — but this is what `var` was made for. Let the compiler figure it out!

Anonymous types are useful in quite a few situations — and crucial in this and a few other situations. And, boy, are they convenient. You don't have to stop and write a dumb little data class each time you want to do this kind of projection in a `select` clause. (You can use anonymous types elsewhere too.)

The objects you create in a projection don't have to be anonymous unless you're cherry picking pieces of the input objects as in Example 3 rather than taking the whole objects.

If you're querying `Apples` and want to replace the `Apples` with `Oranges` in your select clause, you can just instantiate new `Oranges` using similar object initialization syntax — for each apple, make an orange:

```
var someOranges = from apple in theApples
          select new Orange { ... initialization of properties ... };
```

Maybe you want to instantiate the `Oranges` with some bits of data taken from the `Apples`, but that's not required:

```
var someOranges = from apple in theApples select new Orange();
```

Example 4: Transforming numbers into their names

The following problem comes up surprisingly often in programming: You have a collection of numbers, but what you really need is their names in English — or (say) Japanese. (Or some variation of the same pattern.) But numbers don't know their names. An *extension method* on class `Int32`, say, would have to be very complicated to give you the name of every possible number. (Extension methods are covered in Chapter 9.)

The traditional technique uses a lookup table: two parallel arrays; one array with the numbers, the other with their names. You can retrieve a number's name by specifying the number itself as the index into the `names` array:

```
string[] names = new [] { "zero", "one", ... }; // This could go on and on.
int[] numbers = new [] { 5, 3, 14 };
Console.WriteLine("{0} is the loneliest number, the number 1", names[1]);
```

Not too hard, but you could also write a solution that manages the table lookup with a projection query to do some real work:

```
string[] names = new [] { "zero", "one", "two", "three", "four", "five",
                          "six", "seven", "eight", "nine" };
int[] numbers = new [] { 5, 7, 1, 4, 9, 3, 0, 2, 6, 8 };
var namesOfNumbers = from n in numbers
                     select names[n];   // Here's the projection.
foreach(var name in namesOfNumbers)
{
  Console.WriteLine("\t{0}", name );
}
```

The output looks like this (with a few items left out to save space):

```
five
seven
...
six
eight
```

While that's not more compact in this example, it is a little clearer, I think. In any case, it shows how you can transform a list of numbers into a corresponding list of strings using a `select` projection. Projection is a very useful tool. Now for groups.

Example 5: Grouping names by their first character

The `group by` keyword pair is an alternative to `select` — you don't necessarily use the two together, though you can. The idea of grouping is to collect the items in your input collection into several baskets, or "groups," based on some property of the items, called the "key." The property used can be a C# property or some other characteristic. You may need employees grouped by time with the company, customers grouped by regions, or files grouped by size ranges.

For example, suppose you want to list a collection of names grouped by their first character. If your words are "aardvark," "ape," "koala," and "yak," for instance, you could get output something like this:

```
A:
aardvark
ape
K:
koala
Y:
yak
```

This groups all of the *a*s together, all of the *k*s together, and all of the *y*s together.

Example 5 shows how to write such a query using `group by`:

```
// Example 5.
var letterGroups = from n in names group n by n[0];  // n[0] is the 'key'.
// Execute the query by iterating the groups.
foreach (var currentLetterGroup in letterGroups)
{
  Console.WriteLine("\tWords that begin with '{0}'":", currentLetterGroup.Key);
  // Within this group, iterate its items, doing something useful with each.
  foreach (var name in currentLetterGroup)
  {
    Console.WriteLine("\t{0}", name);
  }
  Console.WriteLine();
}
```

This query is based on the same list of names as Example 4 — a list of the English names of the first ten integers: "zero," "one," and so on.

The query examines each name in the list to extract its first letter, `n[0]`. The result variable `letterGroups` contains objects that implement the `IGrouping<T>` interface. Each of these `Grouping` objects contains a *key* (the value that the group is based on, such as a letter of the alphabet or a product category) and a list: the items that fit into that group (such as the words beginning with `a`). You access a `Grouping` object's key through its `Key` property and the group's members by iterating the group with `foreach`. Figure 17-3 illustrates this curious creature.

Notice, by the way, that this query has no select statement. The group by keywords can take its place. (Every item goes into one of the groups.)

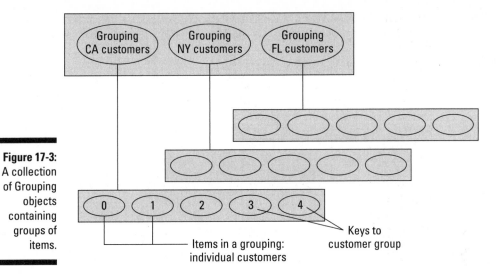

Figure 17-3:
A collection
of Grouping
objects
containing
groups of
items.

Items in a grouping:
individual customers

Keys to
customer group

While the query is simple, extracting the groups requires a pair of `foreach` loops, one nested inside the other. This is a standard pattern for retrieving items from the groups:

```
foreach(var currentGroup in groups)
{
  foreach(var currentItem in currentGroup)
  {
  }
}
```

In Example 5, the outer loop steps through the `Grouping` objects in the query results and writes the letter that characterizes all the words in each group. Thus the `Grouping` for the letter *z* writes out `'z'` at this stage.

The inner loop then digs inside the current `Grouping` object (for `'z'`) to iterate the members of the group — the `'z'` basket, if you will: All the input words beginning with *z*, stored in the `Grouping` object. This loop writes those words out. (Notice that the results are in their original order in the collection, not alphabetized.)

The output looks like this:

```
Words that begin with 'z':
zero
```

```
Words that begin with 'o':
one

Words that begin with 't':
two
three

Words that begin with 'f':
four
five

Words that begin with 's':
six
seven

Words that begin with 'e':
eight

Words that begin with 'n':
nine
```

Example 6: Screening out some groups

Now suppose you want the same listing, but without any words that start with either 't' or 'n' — the same list minus "two," "three," and "nine." Here's the query for Example 6:

```
var nameGroups = from n in names
                 group n by n[0] into tempGrp
                 where tempGrp.Key != 't' && tempGrp.Key != 'n'
                 select tempGrp;
foreach (var nameGroup in nameGroups)
{
  Console.WriteLine("\tWords that begin with '{0}':", nameGroup.Key);
  foreach (var name in nameGroup)
  {
    Console.WriteLine("\t{0}", name);
  }
  Console.WriteLine();
}
```

This query shows several changes from the earlier versions:

✔ The group by clause now adds an into clause. This dumps the group by results into an intermediate variable tempGrp denoting a *group*, and it's this intermediate variable that I select, *after suitable filtering*.

The into clause sets up a *subquery*, whose filter works on groups rather than strings.

✔ I've added a `where` clause after the `group` by clause, to filter the *groups*. The filter weeds out any groups based on the letters *t* or *n*.

✔ At the end of the query, I select the intermediate variable from the `into` clause (`tempGrp`). So I end up with a sequence of groups, not a sequence of strings. A *group* has a `Key` property and can iterate its elements.

✔ Notice how I formatted the query to help convey the fact of the subquery: I indented the subquery clauses.

The output looks like the following:

```
Words that begin with 'z':
zero

Words that begin with 'o':
one

Words that begin with 'f':
four
five

Words that begin with 's':
six
seven

Words that begin with 'e':
eight
```

The "outer" query groups all items in the names array into groups based on first letter. The `into` clause dumps those groups into a temporary container, which the subquery filters to weed out certain groups. It's like grouping a stack of money into denominations before you pick up just the big bills. There are 2 twenties, 3 tens, 4 fives, and 7 ones — four groups — from which you select certain groups: say, just the twenties and tens.

You only need `into` if you want to select groups instead of items and then do something with the groups. Where `groupby` is operating on the string or customer, `into` lets you focus instead on the group, for filtering, ordering, or other processing *of the groups*, using each group's properties, such as a `Key`.

So grouping is like sorting items into unordered categories, and `into` lets you then query on the categories instead of the original individual items.

Example 7: Grouping products by category

Suppose your company's products are represented by `Product` objects with various properties. You want a listing that groups the products by some category, such as `Name`: you want all `Widgets`, all `Sprockets`, and all `Cogs`:

```
// First add a few more products to the list for a better grouping demo.
products.AddRange(new List<Product>() {
  new Product { Name = "Widget", OnHand = 0, UnitCost = 4.53M },
  new Product { Name = "Widget", OnHand = 0, UnitCost = 4.53M },
  new Product { Name = "Widget", OnHand = 0, UnitCost = 4.53M },
  new Product { Name = "Widget", OnHand = 0, UnitCost = 4.53M },
  new Product { Name = "Widget", OnHand = 0, UnitCost = 4.53M },
  new Product { Name = "Sprocket", OnHand = 56, UnitCost = 12.50M },
  new Product { Name = "Sprocket", OnHand = 56, UnitCost = 12.50M },
  new Product { Name = "Cog", OnHand = 300, UnitCost = 1.15M }
});
var categories = from p in products
                 group p by p.Name into tempGrp
                   select new { Name = tempGrp.Key, Products = tempGrp };
foreach (var productGroup in categories)
{
  Console.WriteLine("\tCategory '{0}':", productGroup.Name);
  foreach (var prod in productGroup.Products)
  {
    Console.WriteLine("\t\t{0}", prod.Name);
  }
}
```

You get this output:

```
Category 'Widget':
   Widget
   Widget
   ...
Category 'Sprocket':
   Sprocket
   Sprocket
   ...
...
```

See the discussion of the `into` keyword in Example 6. Note the following misuses of `into`:

The following fails to use `into` correctly:

```
group p by p.Name into tempGrp
select tempGrp;
```

While you can select the `tempGrp` here, there's no point to it. You aren't modifying the group, and you aren't naming it in order to borrow some of its properties. You get the same results with just one line of code:

```
group p by p.Name;  // No need for select or for a temp group.
```

The following is also incorrect usage:

```
group p by p.Category into tempGrp;
```

You don't need an `into` clause here because you aren't doing any processing related to the current group.

Of course, not being an old hand at database code, I ran into more confusion with `into` than with any other keyword. (The C# documentation has more such examples.)

Grouping can also get even more complex and intense, but I have to draw the line here.

Sorting the Stuff You Select

The output listings in the previous section are fine, but it's more typical to *sort* the output: by default, it's alphabetical order for strings, or ascending order for numbers. C#'s queries use the `orderby` keyword for sorting.

Example 8: Ordering the groups from Examples 5 and 6

Start with the same word grouping task from Examples 5 and 6. The goal this time is to alphabetize the overall groups by that single first letter. (We get to the contents of the groups shortly.)

If you put an `orderby` clause in front of Example 5's `group by` clause, you can alphabetize the groups by letter:

```
var wordGroups = from n in names
            orderby n[0]
            group n by n[0];
foreach(var letterGroup in wordGroups)
{
  Console.WriteLine("\tWords that begin with '{0}':", letterGroup.Key);
  foreach(var word in letterGroup)
  {
    Console.WriteLine("\t\t{0}", word);
  }
}
```

The output starts off with the letter e, whose group contains one member: eight. The letter z, for zero, brings up the tail of the list. But the words inside the sublists aren't alphabetized. The sort applies only to the top level — the groups.

Example 9: Ordering within the groups

So the customer says, "Uh, could you alphabetize the items in each group?" Sure. Use a second-level sort:

```
Console.WriteLine("\nExample 9. Ordering the groups from example 8:");
var wordGroups = from n in names
                orderby n[0], n[1]   // Sort the names by their first letter,
                                     // then their second.
                group n by n[0];     // Group them by their first letter.
foreach (var letterGroup in wordGroups)
{
  Console.WriteLine("\t\tWords that begin with '{0}':"", letterGroup.Key);
  foreach (var word in letterGroup)
  {
    Console.WriteLine("\t\t\t{0}", word);
  }
}
```

The two-level sort ensures that the groups are sorted and the words within each group are sorted as well.

C# sorts can use not only the orderby keyword, but one or more secondary *sort keys*, for multilevel sorts. The syntax for a two-level sort looks like the following:

```
orderby n.Length, n  // First by word length, then alphabetically.
```

C#'s query operators include both OrderBy and ThenBy (as well as OrderByDescending and ThenByDescending). But only Orderby is represented in the query *keywords*. In other words, you won't find a thenby keyword. (I'll have more to say about the alternative representation of query operators as methods later in the chapter. The names in mixed case here are actually method names, some of which correspond to keywords.)

Example 10: Another two-level sort

Suppose you want to order the names in our names-of-numbers array primarily by word length and, secondarily, alphabetically within length groups:

```
var sortedNames = from n in names orderby n.Length, n select n;
foreach (var name in sortedNames)
{
  Console.WriteLine("\t{0}", name);
}
```

You can add as many levels as you need, just by stringing the sort keys together with commas. (You can append the `descending` keyword to any or all of the levels.)

The output looks like this, short words first:

```
one
six
two
five
four
nine
zero
eight
seven
three
```

First, you get the three-letter words in alphabetical order. Then come the four-letter words in alphabetical order. (Whew! None of the four-letter words is anything bad.) Finally, you have the five-letter words in alphabetical order.

Example 11: Ordering in descending order

For completeness, I'll give an example of a descending sort. You want the sort in Example 10 done by descending word lengths, but within the lengths still alphabetically:

```
var namesInDescendingLengthGroups =
    from n in names
    orderby n.Length descending, n
    select n;
foreach (var name in namesInDescendingLengthGroups)
{
  Console.WriteLine("\t{0}", name);
}
```

The only difference from Example 10 is the `descending` keyword after the first sort key. To make both keys descending, add the keyword after the second key as well. The output is like that of Example 10, except that the longer words come first.

Is There Any Method to Querying?

Before I continue with examples, I need to pause and discuss using the method approach, an alternative to using keywords. In many cases, no keyword is available, so the methods for query operators are all you have.

Of course, there's something lurking beneath the C# query keywords. (Isn't there always?) In this case, for every keyword — and for lots of additional query operators that aren't represented by a keyword — an implementing C# method is available for use instead of the keywords.

Table 17-2 lists the most frequently used keywords and their method counterparts.

Table 17-2	Query Keywords and Their Method Counterparts
Keyword	**Method**
from	No counterpart; just call the other methods as members of any collection object to *generate* an iterable sequence for the query to use.
where	public static IEnumerable<T> **Where**<T>(...)
select	public static IEnumerable<T> **Select**<T>(...)
group	public static IEnumerable<T> **GroupBy**<T>(...)
orderby	public static IEnumerable<T> **OrderBy**<T>(...)

Notice that the methods are all declared `static`, all return the same type, the generic interface type `IEnumerable<T>`, and all are written as generic methods (the `<T>` notation after the method name). (I'll get into what all that means shortly.)

All of the query methods are extension methods, so there's one more similarity, not shown in the table: The first parameter to each method is of type `IEnumerable<T>` and is preceded by the `this` keyword. You don't pass that parameter when you call a query method, though. It's the "trick" in implementing extension methods (which I discuss in Chapter 9).

The second parameter to these methods is of type `Func<T, U>`, which is a delegate type that takes one parameter and has a return type. You don't need to know much about the `Func<T, U>` delegate, because in queries using the methods you pass a lambda expression to this delegate parameter. In queries written in query syntax rather than with methods, you specify an expression that the compiler turns into a lambda. (You can review delegates in Chapter 15 and lambda expressions in Chapter 16.)

Example 12: Writing queries with methods rather than with keywords

The best way to show how the methods are used to form query expressions is to show you an example. The following duplicates Example 0, from the section "Querying in C# 3.0," but with methods instead of keywords:

```
int[] numbers = new [] {5, 7, 1, 4, 9, 3, 0, 2, 6, 8};
var tinyNumbers = numbers.Where(n => n <= 3)
                    .OrderBy(n => n)
                    .Select(n => n);
foreach(var n in tinyNumbers)
  { Console.WriteLine("\t\t{0}", n); }
```

In this case, the query expression itself can also be written in a single line as

```
numbers.Where(n => n <= 3).OrderBy(n => n).Select(n => n);
```

In the `Where()` call, the parameter is

```
n => n <= 3    // You can read this as "n goes to n <= 3";
```

The first n is the parameter to the lambda expression. Then comes the lambda operator =>. And finally you get the expression itself, which just uses the less-than-or-equal operator (<=) to compare n to the value 5. (The <= comparison operator coming so soon after the lambda operator => puzzled me at first too. But I puzzle easily, as my wife and my cat fondly point out.)

For the `OrderBy()` and `Select()` calls, I passed the same lambda expression:

```
n => n
```

where the first n is again the parameter being passed into the lambda, and the lambda expression itself is just n. This means, for `OrderBy()`, to just order by n, and, for `Select()`, to select all the items.

Notice that when you use the methods to write a query expression, you always pass lambda expressions (or some other delegate form). But when you use the syntax for keywords instead of for methods, you pass just the simple expression: just the part *after* the lambda operator =>.

Now to really see what's behind those method calls.

About train cars: A detour for newbies

What's going on in Example 12 in the previous section? Railroad cars, that's what! This section is for programming newbies. Old hands may skip it.

First, I'm calling the `numbers` array's `Where()` method. That returns an `IEnumerable<T>` result, and I next call `OrderBy()` *on that interface reference*. The same thing happens with the `Select()` call: I call `Select()` on the return value of `OrderBy()`. That return value is also of type `IEnumerable<T>`.

So the whole thing is just a bunch of method calls strung together with "dot" notation. This works because each of the methods returns the same thing: an `IEnumerable<T>` reference.

All those methods are defined on the `Enumerable` class, but they really belong to `IEnumerable<T>`, and thus to every array and collection that implements the `IEnumerable<T>` interface — which is to say, all C# arrays and collections — except for the old-style nongeneric collections, which implement `IEnumerable`, the nongeneric form of the interface. (So can you query nongeneric collections? Yes, but I won't cover that.)

To give you a simpler look at the basic process of calling method after method in a kind of "train-car" string of calls, consider two methods on class `Thing`, called `Do()` and `Go()`, each of which returns an instance of class `Thing` (their own class — sort of like the snake eating its own tail). You get traincar-traincar-traincar, all coupled together.

```
public class Thing
{
  public Thing Do() {...}
  public Thing Go() {...}
}
...
public void MyMethod()
{
  // Written without the "train-car" effect of stringing calls together:
  Thing thing1 = someThing.Do(); // In effect ...
  Thing thing2 = thing1.Go();    // ... Thing2 is the result of both calls,
  // Written with the "train-car."
  Thing thing3 = someThing.Do().Go();
}
```

The "train-car" effect referred to in the example reminds me of the old poem, "This is the house that Jack built":

```
This is the house that Jack built.
This is the malt that lay in the house that Jack built.
This is the rat that ate the malt that lay in the house that Jack built.
...
And on and on and on ...
```

The whole trick works because each new sentence builds on the one before it. In the `Thing` example, the train starts with a `Thing` object, and all of the methods in the chain are on class `Thing`. Furthermore, each method returns a `Thing`. For LINQ, the methods are on type `IEnumerable<T>` — and each method returns an `IEnumerable<T>` sequence of values.

Normally I discourage stringing together train-car method calls. Train-cars often lead to train wrecks of confusing code. But queries are an exception.

End of detour — All aboard!

In the new class `Enumerable`, which lives in the `System.Linq` namespace, those query methods are written as *extension methods* on type `IEnumerable<T>`. Thus, through the magic of C# 3.0 extension methods, the query methods become methods on the `IEnumerable<T>` interface just the way I added several new methods to class `String` in Chapter 9. And because all C# arrays and generic collections implement `IEnumerable<T>`, you can "magically" call the query methods on any array or collection. It's a trifle complicated, but it doesn't rely on a single thing you haven't seen in this book: Interfaces, arrays, generic collections, delegates, lambda expressions, and extension methods are all hanging around in here.

I cover arrays and generic collections in Chapter 5, extension methods in Chapter 9, interfaces and the `IEnumerable<T>` interface in Chapter 14, delegates in Chapter 15, and lambdas in Chapter 16.

Generic methods

One more thing: All of the query methods are implemented in LINQ as *generic methods*, written like this:

```
IEnumerable<T> Where<T>(...parameter list...);
```

Just as you *parameterize* a `List<T>` collection class with the type of objects it will hold, as in `List<string>`, you can parameterize a generic method. When you call the method, you specify a type. Wherever the same symbol, `T`, appears inside the method, including its body, parameter list, and return type, `T` is replaced by the specified type. For example,

```
IEnumerable<string> result = aCollection.Where<string>(...);
```

However, in LINQ, C# takes care of filling in `T` with the base type of the collection whose `Where()` method you're calling. If the collection contains `strings`, the compiler parameterizes its `Where()` method with `string`. So you don't write query method calls with that parameter. You simply write

```
var result = aCollection.Where(...);
```

I discuss generic methods (and classes, interfaces, and delegates) further in Bonus Chapter 7 on my Web site at `csharp102.info`.

What's inside Where()?

As I mentioned earlier, inside each query method, such as `Where()`, you'd find a `yield return` statement. For example, `Where()` is *probably* implemented something like this code taken from an overview document called "The LINQ Project," which is on the LINQ Web site at `msdn2.microsoft.com/en-us/library/aa479865.aspx`:

```
namespace System.Linq {
  using System;
  using System.Collections.Generic;
  public static class Enumerable {         // Host class for Where().
    public static IEnumerable<T> Where<T>(  // Where() method.
           this IEnumerable<T> source,      // For extension method.
                Func<T, bool> predicate) {  // Delegate for filter expression.
      foreach (T item in source)
        if (predicate(item))                // Invoke the predicate delegate.
          yield return item;                // Return 1 item per Where() call.
      }
    }
  }
```

The preceding `Where()` method is placed in the `System.Linq` namespace. `Where()` is implemented as a static extension method on the static class `Enumerable`. The first parameter, `source`, is of type `IEnumerable<T>` and is preceded by the `this` keyword — thus making `Where()` an extension method on the `IEnumerable<T>` type. The second parameter, `predicate`, is of type `Func<T, bool>`, similar to the predicates for lambda expressions in Chapter 16.

`Func<T, bool>` is a delegate type. Because of its second type parameter, `Func<T, bool>` contains a method or, more likely, a lambda expression designed to do a Boolean comparison — that is, it returns `bool`. This delegate is invoked inside the `Where()` method: `if(predicate(item)) . . .` You'll encounter other similar `Func()` delegates with more parameters; the final parameter is always the return type *of the lambda*. `Where()` has its own return type.

Where() iterates the source list and invokes the predicate delegate to compare the current item in the source list with a value provided through the lambda expression or delegate. If the result of the predicate call is true, the foreach loop uses yield return to return an object of type T. It returns another object on each iteration of the loop. I discuss *iterator blocks* like this loop in Bonus Chapter 8 on my Web site at csharp102.info You can review predicate delegates in Chapter 16.

To round out this discussion of query methods, here is another example, which duplicates Example 3 using query methods.

Example 13: Give me all customers, but just their names and numbers

This example reproduces Example 3, using method notation.

```
var customerContacts = customers.OrderBy(c => c.Name)
    .Select(c => new { Name = c.Name, PhoneNumber = c.Phone });
foreach (var c in customerContacts)
{
    Console.WriteLine("\t\t{0} - {1}", c.Name.PadRight(10), c.PhoneNumber);
}
```

Notice how I translate orderby's ordering expression and select's selection expression into lambda expressions. Also note that there's no from clause.

The next section contains several additional examples of the method approach.

Counting, Summing, Averaging, and Stuff Like That

One of the handier uses of LINQ queries in C# is counting things in collections — or summing them up, or averaging them, or finding the minimum or maximum item in the collection. (Some of those operations are limited to numeric collections, of course — or to operations where you're working with string lengths, file sizes, and the like.) This section gives you a tour.

Collectively, these queries are called aggregation queries because they aggregate, or gather, various quantities.

All of these operations require using the method approach to queries. They have no query keyword counterparts.

Example 14: Counting product types in our inventory

Given a list of products, you want to know how many different *types* of products you carry in inventory.

```
var productTypes =
  products.Select(p => new { Name = p.Name }).Distinct().Count();
```

This query counts the number of distinct product types by making three calls:

1. Calling `Select()` on the products list.

   I passed a lambda expression to `Select()` that creates a new anonymous object for each product containing just the product name. The selection gives one new object for each product *unit* in stock — not for each product *type*. So there will be duplicates: four widgets, nine whatchamacallits, three hundred doo-dads, and so on.

2. Calling the `Distinct()` method on the results of `Select()`.

   This culls out the duplicate items from the results of `Select()`, resulting in just one object per product *type*.

3. Calling the `Count()` method on the results of `Distinct()`.

   `Count()` returns the number of product types. `Distinct()` and `Count()` do immediate query execution, not deferred execution.

Here's a simpler example to consider (not shown in the code example on the Web site):

```
var list = new [] { 0, 1, 2, 3, 4, 5, 6, 7, 8, 9 };  // Ten items.
var count = list.Count();  // 10, same as from list.Length.
```

Example 15: Adding up the numbers array

To sum the numbers, you can run this query:

```
int[] numbers = new [] { 5, 7, 1, 4, 9, 3, 0, 2, 6, 8 };
var sum = numbers.Sum();  //Immediate query execution.
Console.WriteLine("\tSum of the numbers is {0}", sum);
```

The result is 45.

Example 16: Summing the cost of order O

Given an order O for customer C, what is the total cost of the order? This example uses an order for five products.

```
// Given order O, which contains five products ...
Order o = ... // An Order object.
// First, we need a list of all the product unit costs.
var productCosts = from p in o.Products // List of products in the order.
            select p.UnitCost;
// Next, we can call Sum on productCosts directly, no keyword here.
var total = productCosts.Sum();
Console.WriteLine("\tOrder o has a total summed cost of {0}", total);
```

The QueryExamples1 sample on the Web site finishes up this example by verifying the total returned by Sum() by iterating the product list and summing the costs manually. Not surprisingly, both results agree.

This is very little code — just these two steps:

1. A query on the order's product list, selecting all of the unit costs.

2. A call to Sum() on the results of the query.

You could write it even more briefly, like this:

```
var total = (from p in o.Products select p.UnitCost).Sum();
```

Example 17: Computing nine factorial (9!)

For any math geeks out there, let's compute the factorial of 9 using a query.

The factorial of 9 = 9 * 8 * 7 * 6 * 5 * 4 * 3 * 2 * 1 = 362880.

The query in this example uses a general-purpose aggregation method called Aggregate(). Aggregate() takes one or two parameters (I show the one-parameter version in a minute here). The two-parameter version takes a "seed," which gives a value to start from and then serves to accumulate a running total or other answer as the calculation proceeds. Either version takes a delegate, anonymous method, or lambda expression that does the calculation. Unlike Sum(), Aggregate() can perform any operation, not just addition.

The Aggregate() method has replaced a method called Fold() in early versions of LINQ. If you use Fold(), you get a compiler warning that Fold() has been *deprecated*, meaning it's defunct and you should use Aggregate() instead.

The operation to perform for each number in the input list is multiplication:

```
running-total * next-factor-in-list
```

Instead of passing the seed, or running total, as the first parameter to `Aggregate()`, you can pass it as the first parameter to the lambda expression. Here's just the lambda expression:

```
(runningTotal, nextFactor) => runningTotal * nextFactor
```

Here's the query — pretty simple after all that build-up, eh?

```
var factors = Enumerable.Range(1, 9).Reverse();   // Get numbers to multiply.
int factorial =
   factors.Aggregate((runningTotal, nextFactor) => runningTotal * nextFactor);
Console.WriteLine("9 factorial (9!) is: {0}", factorial);
```

In this query, you're causing five things to occur:

1. Creating a list of the factors of 9! — 9, 8, 7, ..., 2, 1 — using the `Range()` operator to generate a sequence of integers 1 .. 9, then using the `Reverse()` operator to put the factors in their usual order: 9 .. 1 — not that the order matters, but it demonstrates `Reverse()`.

2. Calling `Aggregate()` on the `factors` sequence, passing in a lambda expression. The `runningTotal` parameter to `Aggregate()`'s lambda is automatically set to 0 initially. It's the seed that will grow into an aggregated total.

3. For each element in the factors sequence (`nextFactor`), you multiply the current `runningTotal` by `nextFactor`.

4. For the next element, you're passing along that running total value.

5. Finally, `Aggregate()` returns the running total, assigning it to `factorial`.

You can duplicate the effect of a `for` loop running from 1 to 10 with the following line of code:

```
Enumerable.Range(1,10).ToList<int>().ForEach(somelambda);
```

Here you're using the `ForEach()` method common to `List<T>` collections and arrays. The `QueryExamples2` file on the Web site includes this code. Chapter 16 gives lots of examples of the `ForEach()` method.

Treating an Object Like a Collection

Using a technique called *reflection*, you can write code to examine the constituents of a class — its methods, properties, and other members, the interfaces it implements, its base classes, and a great deal more. Thus, with a simple statement, you can obtain an array of `MethodInfo` objects, for example. When you have that array, you can apply LINQ query expressions to it.

As a bonus, I've written an example showing how to do this. You can find it in Bonus Chapter 5 on the Web site.

Part VI
The Part of Tens

The 5th Wave   By Rich Tennant

"This program's really helped me learn a new language. It's so buggy I'm constantly talking with overseas service reps."

In this part . . .

What *For Dummies* book would be complete without a Part of Tens? C# is great at finding errors in your programs when you try to build them — you've probably noticed that. However, the error messages it generates can be cryptic — you've probably noted that as well. Chapter 18 reviews the ten most common build-time error messages and what they most likely mean. Knowledge is power, so Chapter 18 also suggests fixes for the problems that are being reported.

Chapter 18

Ten Common Build Errors (And How to Fix Them)

C# makes the ol' college try at finding errors in your C# code. In fact, C# homes in on syntax errors like a tornado heading for a double-wide. Other than really stupid mistakes (like trying to compile your shopping list), what it finds are the same complaints that seem to pop up over and over.

This chapter describes ten common build-time error messages. A few warnings are in order, however. First, C# can get awfully long-winded. I have whittled down some of the error messages so the message can fit on one page, let alone one or two lines. In addition, an error message has places to insert the name of an errant data member or an obnoxious class. In place of these specific names, I have inserted `variableName`, `memberName`, or `className`.

Finally, C# doesn't simply spit out the name of the class. It prefers to tack on the full namespace name — just in case the entire error message would have been visible without scrolling over to your neighbor's house.

The name 'memberName' does not exist in the class or namespace 'className'

This error message could mean that you forgot to declare a variable, as in the following example:

```
for(index = 0; index < 10; index++)
{
  // . . . whatever . . .
}
```

The variable `index` is not defined anywhere. (See Chapter 2 for instructions on declaring variables.) This example should have been written as follows:

```
for(int index = 0; index < 10; index++)
{
  // . . . whatever . . .
}
```

The same applies to data members of a class. (See Chapter 7.)

A more likely possibility is that you misspelled a variable name. The following is a good example:

```
class Student
{
  public string studentName;
  public int ID;
}
class MyClass
{
  static public void MyMethod(Student s)
  {
    Console.WriteLine("Student name = {0}", s.studentName);
    Console.WriteLine("Student Id = {0}", s.Id);
  }
}
```

The problem here is that `MyMethod()` references a data member `Id` rather than the actual data member `ID`. Although you see the similarity, C#, which is case sensitive, does not. The programmer wrote `Id`, but no `Id` exists, and that's all there is to it. The fact that `ID` is lurking around the corner, alphabetically speaking, is irrelevant. (The message here is a bit different: `'class.memberName' does not contain a definition for 'variableName'`. See Chapter 2 for details.)

Less popular but still way up on the Top 10 playlist is the possibility that the variable was declared in a different scope, as follows:

```
class MyClass
{
  static public void AverageInput()
  {
    int sum = 0;
    int count = 0;
    while(true)
    {
      string s = Console.ReadLine();
      int n = Int32.Parse(s);
      // Quit when the user enters a negative number.
      if (n < 0)
      {
        break;
      }
      // Accumulate the value entered.
      sum += n;
      count++;
    }
    Console.WriteLine("The total is {0}", sum);
    Console.WriteLine("The average is {0}", sum / count);
    // This generates a build time error message.
    Console.WriteLine("The terminating value was {0}", s);
  }
}
```

The last line in this method is incorrect. The problem is that a variable is limited to the scope in which it is defined. The variable s is not defined outside of the while() loop. (See Chapter 4.)

Cannot implicitly convert type 'x' into 'y'

This error usually indicates that you're trying to use two different variable types in the same expression — as in this example:

```
int age = 10;
// Generates an error message.
int factoredAge = 2.0 * age;
```

The problem here is that 2.0 is a variable of type double. The int age multiplied by the double 2.0 results in a double value. C# does not automatically store a double into the int variable factoredAge because information may be lost — most notably, any fractional value that the double may possess.

Some conversions are not obvious, as in the following example:

```
class MyClass
{
  static public float FloatTimes2(float f)
  {
    // This generates a build time error.
    float result = 2.0 * f;
    return result;
  }
}
```

You may think that doubling a `float` would be okay, but that's sort of the problem. `2.0` is not a `float` — it defaults to type `double`. A `double` times a `float` is a `double`. C# does not store a `double` value back into a `float` variable due to — you guessed it — possible loss of data; in this case, it is several digits of accuracy. (See Chapters 2 and 3.)

Implicit conversions can further confuse the casual reader (that's me on a good day). The following version of `FloatTimes2()` works just fine:

```
class MyClass
{
  static public float FloatTimes2(float f)
  {
    // This works fine.
    float result = 2 * f;
    return result;
  }
}
```

The constant `2` is of type `int`. An `int` times a `float` is a `float`, which can be stored in the `float` variable `result`.

The implicit-conversion error message can also arise when performing operations on "unnatural" types. For example, you cannot add two `char` variables, but C# can convert `char` variables into `int` values for you when necessary to get the job done. This leads to the following:

```
class MyClass
{
  static public void SomeMethod()
  {
    char c1 = 'a';
    char c2 = 'b';
    // I don't know what this even means, but it's illegal anyway - not for the
    // reason you think.
    char c3 = c1 + c2;
  }
}
```

Adding two characters together makes no sense, but C# tries anyway. Because addition isn't defined for type char, it converts c1 and c2 into int values and then performs the addition. (char is technically listed as an integral type.) Unfortunately, the resulting int value cannot be converted back into a char without some help from an explicit cast to char. (See Chapters 2 and 3.)

Most, but not all, conversions are okay with an explicit cast. Thus, the following method works without complaint:

```
class MyClass
{
    static public float FloatTimes2(float f)
    {
        // This works OK with the explicit cast.
        float result = (float)(2.0 * f);
        return result;
    }
}
```

The result of 2.0 * f is still of type double, but the programmer has indicated that she specifically wants the result down-converted to a float, even in the unlikely event that it results in the loss of data. (See Chapters 2 and 3.)

A second approach would be to make sure that all constants are of the same type, as follows:

```
class MyClass
{
    static public float FloatTimes2(float f)
    {
        // This works OK because 2.0F is a float constant
        float result = 2.0F * f;
        return result;
    }
}
```

This version of the method uses a constant 2.0 of type float rather than the default double. A float times a float is a float. (Signify a float by appending 'F' or 'f' to a literal number like 2.0.)

'className.memberName' is inaccessible due to its protection level

This error indicates that a method is trying to access a member to which it does not have access. For example, a method in one class may be trying to access a private member in another class (see Chapter 11), as shown in the following code:

```
public class MyClass
{
  public void SomeMethod()
  {
    YourClass uc = new YourClass();
    // This doesn't work properly because MyClass can't access
    // the private member.
    uc._privateMember = 1;
  }
}
public class YourClass
{
  private int _privateMember = 0;
}
```

Usually the error is not so blatant. Often, you've simply left the descriptor off of either the member object or the class itself. By default, a member of a class is private while a class is internal by default. Thus, _privateMember is still private in the following example:

```
class MyClass      // Undeclared class access level defaults to internal.
{
  public void SomeMethod()
  {
    YourClass uc = new YourClass();
    // This doesn't work properly because MyClass can't access the
    // private member.
    uc._privateMember = 1;
  }
}
public class YourClass
{
  int _privateMember = 0;      // This member is still private.
}
```

In addition, even though SomeMethod() is declared public, it still can't be accessed from classes in other modules because MyClass itself is internal. A method's accessibility is no better than its class's accessibility.

The moral of the story is this: "Always specify the protection level of your classes and their members." You can add: "Don't declare public members in a class that itself is internal — it doesn't do any good and it's just confusing."

Use of unassigned local variable 'n'

Just as it says, this message indicates that you declared a variable but didn't give it an initial value. This is usually an oversight, but it can occur when you really meant to pass a variable as an out argument to a method, as shown in the following example:

```
public class MyClass
{
  public void SomeMethod()
  {
    int n;  // Not initialized with a value.
    // This is OK because C# only returns a value in n; it does not
    // pass a value into the method.
    SomeOtherMethod(out n);
  }
  public void SomeOtherMethod(out int n)
  {
    n = 1;  // Value is assigned here.
  }
}
```

In this case, n is not assigned a value inside of SomeMethod(), but it is in SomeOtherMethod(). In fact, SomeOtherMethod() ignores the value of an out argument as if it didn't exist — which it doesn't in this case. (Chapter 2 covers variables. Chapter 8 explains out.)

Unable to copy the file 'programName.exe' to 'programName.exe'. The process cannot . . .

Usually, this message repeats multiple times. In almost every case, it means you forgot to terminate the program before you rebuilt it. In other words, you did the following:

1. You successfully built your program. (I assume that it's a console application, although it can happen to any C# output.)

2. When you ran the program by choosing Debug➪Start Without Debugging, you got to the message Press Enter to terminate, but in your haste, you didn't press Enter. So, your program is still executing. Instead, you switched back to Visual Studio to edit the file.

   Note: If you run the program by choosing Debug➪Start Debugging and forget to terminate, you're simply asked whether you want to stop debugging.

3. You tried to build the program again with the new updates. At this point, you get this error message in the Error List window.

An executable (.EXE) file is locked by Windows until the program actually quits. Visual Studio cannot overwrite the old .EXE file with the new version until the program terminates.

To get rid of the error, switch to the application and terminate it. In the case of a console application, just press Enter to terminate the program. You can also terminate the program from within Visual Studio by choosing Debug⇨ Stop Debugging. After the older program has terminated, rebuild the application.

If you can't get rid of the error by terminating the program, the directory may be messed up. Close the solution, exit Visual Studio, reboot, and then reopen the solution. If that doesn't work, I'm sorry — punt.

'subclassName.methodName' hides inherited member 'baseclassName. methodName'. Use the new keyword if hiding was intended

With this message, C# is telling you that your subclass overloads a method in a base class without overriding it. (See Chapter 13 for details.) Consider the following example:

```
public class BaseClass
{
  public void Method()  // Here's the base-class version.
  {
  }
}
public class SubClass : BaseClass
{
  public void Method()  // Here's the overload.
  {
  }
}
public class MyClass
{
  public void Test()
  {
    SubClass sb = new SubClass();
    sb.Method();
  }
}
```

The method Test() cannot get at the method BaseClass.Method() from the subclass object sb because it is hidden by SubClass.Method(). You intended to do one of the following:

✔ You intended to hide the base class method. In that case, add the `new` keyword to the `SubClass` definition, as in the following example:

```
public class SubClass : BaseClass
{
  new public void Method()
  {
  }
}
```

✔ You meant to inherit the base class polymorphically, in which case you should have declared the two classes as follows:

```
public class BaseClass
{
  public virtual void Method()
  {
  }
}

public class SubClass : BaseClass
{
  public override void Method()
  {
  }
}
```

This is not an error — just a warning in the Error List window.

'subclassName' : cannot inherit from sealed class 'baseclassName'

This message indicates that someone has sealed the class (see Chapter 13), so you can't inherit from it or change any of its properties. Typically, only library classes are sealed. You can't get around your inability to inherit from the sealed class, but try using the class via a HAS_A relationship. (See Chapter 12.)

'className' does not implement interface member 'methodName'

Implementing an interface represents a promise to provide a definition for all the methods of that interface. This message says that you broke that promise by not implementing the named method. The following possible reasons exist:

> ✔ Your dog ate your homework. Basically, you just forgot or were unaware of the method. Be more careful next time.
>
> ✔ You misspelled the method or gave the wrong parameters.

Consider the following example:

```
interface IMyInterface
{
  void SomeMethod(float f);
}
public class MyClass : IMyInterface
{
  public void SomeMethod(double d)
  {
  }
}
```

The class `MyClass` does not implement the interface method `SomeMethod(float)`. The method `SomeMethod(double)` doesn't count because the parameters don't match.

Go back to the drawing board and continue implementing methods until the interface has been completely fulfilled. (See Chapter 14, which shows how Visual Studio makes implementing an interface a slam dunk.)

Not fully implementing an interface is essentially the same thing as trying to create a concrete class from an abstract one without overriding all the abstract methods.

'methodName' : not all code paths return a value

With this message, C# is telling you that your method was declared nonvoid and one or more paths don't return anything. This can happen in either of the following two ways:

> ✔ You embedded a return call in an `if` statement or loop without specifying a value to return.
>
> ✔ More likely, you calculated a value and never returned it.

Both of these possibilities are demonstrated in the following class:

```
public class MyClass
{
  public string ConvertToString(int n)
  {
    // Convert the int n into a string s.
    string s = n.ToString();
    // Need a return here.
  }
  public string ConvertPositiveNumbers(int n)
  {
    // Only positive numbers are valid for conversion.
    if (n > 0)
    {
      string s = n.ToString();
      return s;   // Embedded return okay, but need one outside the if too.
    }
    Console.WriteLine("the argument {0} is invalid", n);
    // Need another return here.
  }
}
```

ConvertToString() calculates a string to return but never returns it.
Just add a return s; at the bottom of the method.

ConvertPositiveNumbers() returns the string version of the int argument n when n is positive. In addition, it correctly generates an error message
when n is not positive. But even if n is not positive, the method still has
to return something. Return either a null or an empty string "" in these
cases — which one works best depends on the application. (See Chapter 8.)

} expected

This error indicates that C# was expecting a closing brace when the program
listing just stopped. Somewhere along the way, you forgot to close a class
definition, a method, a loop, or an if block. Go back through the listing,
matching the open and closed braces, until you find the culprit.

This error message is often the last in a series of often-nonsensical error
messages. Don't worry about addressing the other error messages until
you've fixed this one. Also, Visual Studio helps you match parentheses and
braces. Select one brace, and Visual Studio highlights the match.

Index

• B •

• C •

• *M* •

BUSINESS, CAREERS & PERSONAL FINANCE

0-7645-9847-3

0-7645-2431-3

Also available:
- Business Plans Kit For Dummies
  0-7645-9794-9
- Economics For Dummies
  0-7645-5726-2
- Grant Writing For Dummies
  0-7645-8416-2
- Home Buying For Dummies
  0-7645-5331-3
- Managing For Dummies
  0-7645-1771-6
- Marketing For Dummies
  0-7645-5600-2

- Personal Finance For Dummies
  0-7645-2590-5*
- Resumes For Dummies
  0-7645-5471-9
- Selling For Dummies
  0-7645-5363-1
- Six Sigma For Dummies
  0-7645-6798-5
- Small Business Kit For Dummies
  0-7645-5984-2
- Starting an eBay Business For Dummies
  0-7645-6924-4
- Your Dream Career For Dummies
  0-7645-9795-7

HOME & BUSINESS COMPUTER BASICS

0-470-05432-8

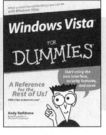

0-471-75421-8

Also available:
- Cleaning Windows Vista For Dummies
  0-471-78293-9
- Excel 2007 For Dummies
  0-470-03737-7
- Mac OS X Tiger For Dummies
  0-7645-7675-5
- MacBook For Dummies
  0-470-04859-X
- Macs For Dummies
  0-470-04849-2
- Office 2007 For Dummies
  0-470-00923-3

- Outlook 2007 For Dummies
  0-470-03830-6
- PCs For Dummies
  0-7645-8958-X
- Salesforce.com For Dummies
  0-470-04893-X
- Upgrading & Fixing Laptops For Dummies
  0-7645-8959-8
- Word 2007 For Dummies
  0-470-03658-3
- Quicken 2007 For Dummies
  0-470-04600-7

FOOD, HOME, GARDEN, HOBBIES, MUSIC & PETS

0-7645-8404-9

0-7645-9904-6

Also available:
- Candy Making For Dummies
  0-7645-9734-5
- Card Games For Dummies
  0-7645-9910-0
- Crocheting For Dummies
  0-7645-4151-X
- Dog Training For Dummies
  0-7645-8418-9
- Healthy Carb Cookbook For Dummies
  0-7645-8476-6
- Home Maintenance For Dummies
  0-7645-5215-5

- Horses For Dummies
  0-7645-9797-3
- Jewelry Making & Beading For Dummies
  0-7645-2571-9
- Orchids For Dummies
  0-7645-6759-4
- Puppies For Dummies
  0-7645-5255-4
- Rock Guitar For Dummies
  0-7645-5356-9
- Sewing For Dummies
  0-7645-6847-7
- Singing For Dummies
  0-7645-2475-5

INTERNET & DIGITAL MEDIA

0-470-04529-9

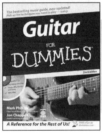

0-470-04894-8

Also available:
- Blogging For Dummies
  0-471-77084-1
- Digital Photography For Dummies
  0-7645-9802-3
- Digital Photography All-in-One Desk Reference For Dummies
  0-470-03743-1
- Digital SLR Cameras and Photography For Dummies
  0-7645-9803-1
- eBay Business All-in-One Desk Reference For Dummies
  0-7645-8438-3
- HDTV For Dummies
  0-470-09673-X

- Home Entertainment PCs For Dummies
  0-470-05523-5
- MySpace For Dummies
  0-470-09529-6
- Search Engine Optimization For Dummies
  0-471-97998-8
- Skype For Dummies
  0-470-04891-3
- The Internet For Dummies
  0-7645-8996-2
- Wiring Your Digital Home For Dummies
  0-471-91830-X

* Separate Canadian edition also available
† Separate U.K. edition also available

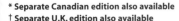

Available wherever books are sold. For more information or to order direct: U.S. customers visit www.dummies.com or call 1-877-762-2974.
U.K. customers visit www.wileyeurope.com or call 0800 243407. Canadian customers visit www.wiley.ca or call 1-800-567-4797.

SPORTS, FITNESS, PARENTING, RELIGION & SPIRITUALITY

0-471-76871-5

0-7645-7841-3

Also available:
- Catholicism For Dummies
  0-7645-5391-7
- Exercise Balls For Dummies
  0-7645-5623-1
- Fitness For Dummies
  0-7645-7851-0
- Football For Dummies
  0-7645-3936-1
- Judaism For Dummies
  0-7645-5299-6
- Potty Training For Dummies
  0-7645-5417-4
- Buddhism For Dummies
  0-7645-5359-3

- Pregnancy For Dummies
  0-7645-4483-7 †
- Ten Minute Tone-Ups For Dummies
  0-7645-7207-5
- NASCAR For Dummies
  0-7645-7681-X
- Religion For Dummies
  0-7645-5264-3
- Soccer For Dummies
  0-7645-5229-5
- Women in the Bible For Dummies
  0-7645-8475-8

TRAVEL

0-7645-7749-2

0-7645-6945-7

Also available:
- Alaska For Dummies
  0-7645-7746-8
- Cruise Vacations For Dummies
  0-7645-6941-4
- England For Dummies
  0-7645-4276-1
- Europe For Dummies
  0-7645-7529-5
- Germany For Dummies
  0-7645-7823-5
- Hawaii For Dummies
  0-7645-7402-7

- Italy For Dummies
  0-7645-7386-1
- Las Vegas For Dummies
  0-7645-7382-9
- London For Dummies
  0-7645-4277-X
- Paris For Dummies
  0-7645-7630-5
- RV Vacations For Dummies
  0-7645-4442-X
- Walt Disney World & Orlando
  For Dummies
  0-7645-9660-8

GRAPHICS, DESIGN & WEB DEVELOPMENT

0-7645-8815-X

0-7645-9571-7

Also available:
- 3D Game Animation For Dummies
  0-7645-8789-7
- AutoCAD 2006 For Dummies
  0-7645-8925-3
- Building a Web Site For Dummies
  0-7645-7144-3
- Creating Web Pages For Dummies
  0-470-08030-2
- Creating Web Pages All-in-One Desk
  Reference For Dummies
  0-7645-4345-8
- Dreamweaver 8 For Dummies
  0-7645-9649-7

- InDesign CS2 For Dummies
  0-7645-9572-5
- Macromedia Flash 8 For Dummies
  0-7645-9691-8
- Photoshop CS2 and Digital
  Photography For Dummies
  0-7645-9580-6
- Photoshop Elements 4 For Dummies
  0-471-77483-9
- Syndicating Web Sites with RSS Feeds
  For Dummies
  0-7645-8848-6
- Yahoo! SiteBuilder For Dummies
  0-7645-9800-7

NETWORKING, SECURITY, PROGRAMMING & DATABASES

0-7645-7728-X

0-471-74940-0

Also available:
- Access 2007 For Dummies
  0-470-04612-0
- ASP.NET 2 For Dummies
  0-7645-7907-X
- C# 2005 For Dummies
  0-7645-9704-3
- Hacking For Dummies
  0-470-05235-X
- Hacking Wireless Networks
  For Dummies
  0-7645-9730-2
- Java For Dummies
  0-470-08716-1

- Microsoft SQL Server 2005 For Dummies
  0-7645-7755-7
- Networking All-in-One Desk Reference
  For Dummies
  0-7645-9939-9
- Preventing Identity Theft For Dummies
  0-7645-7336-5
- Telecom For Dummies
  0-471-77085-X
- Visual Studio 2005 All-in-One Desk
  Reference For Dummies
  0-7645-9775-2
- XML For Dummies
  0-7645-8845-1